PRETEXTS FOR WRITING

NEW STUDIES IN THE AGE OF GOETHE

New Studies in the Age of Goethe, sponsored by the Goethe Society of North America, aims to publish innovative research that contextualizes the "Age of Goethe," whether within the fields of literature, history (including art history and history of science), philosophy, art, music, or politics. Though the series editors welcome all approaches and perspectives, they are especially interested in interdisciplinary projects, creative approaches to archival or original source materials, theoretically informed scholarship, work that introduces previously undiscovered materials, and projects that re-examine traditional epochal boundaries or open new channels of interpretations.

TITLES IN THE SERIES

Ellwood Wiggins, *Odysseys of Recognition: Performing Intersubjectivity in Homer, Aristotle, Shakespeare, Goethe, and Kleist*

Seán M. Williams, *Pretexts for Writing: German Romantic Prefaces, Literature, and Philosophy*

Vance Byrd, *A Pedagogy of Observation: Nineteenth-Century Panoramas, German Literature, and Reading Culture*

Christine Lehleiter, *Romanticism, Origins, and the History of Heredity*

Benjamin Bennett, *Aesthetics as Secular Millenialism: Its Trail from Baumgarten and Kant to Walt Disney and Hitler*

Mary Helen Dupree, *The Mask and the Quill: Actress-Writers in Germany from Enlightenment to Romanticism*

Peter J. Schwartz, *After Jena: Goethe's* Elective Affinities *and the End of the Old Regime*

Brian Tucker, *Reading Riddles: Rhetorics of Obscurity from Romanticism to Freud*

PRETEXTS FOR WRITING

German Romantic Prefaces, Literature, and Philosophy

Seán M. Williams

Bucknell University | BUCKNELL UNIVERSITY PRESS

Lewisburg, Pennsylvania

Library of Congress Cataloging-in-Publication Data

Names: Williams, Seán M. (Seán Martin), 1985– author.
Title: Pretexts for writing : German Romantic prefaces, literature, and philosophy / Sean M. Williams.
Description: Lewisburg : Bucknell University Press, 2019. | Series: New studies in the age of Goethe
Identifiers: LCCN 2018030779 | ISBN 9781684480531 (hardback) | ISBN 9781684480524 (paperback)
Subjects: LCSH: German literature—18th century—History and criticism. | Prefaces—History and criticism. | Goethe, Johann Wolfgang von, 1749–1832—Criticism and interpretation. | Jean Paul, 1763–1825—Criticism and interpretation. | Hegel, Georg Wilhelm Friedrich, 1770–1831—Criticism and interpretation. | BISAC: LITERARY CRITICISM / European / German. | LITERARY CRITICISM / Gothic & Romance. | PHILOSOPHY / Aesthetics.
Classification: LCC PT311 .W547 2019 | DDC 830.9/006—dc23
LC record available at https://lccn.loc.gov/2018030779

A British Cataloging-in-Publication record for this book is available from the British Library.

♾ The paper used in this publication meets the requirements of the American National Standard for Information Sciences—Permanence of Paper for Printed Library Materials, ANSI Z39.48-1992.

www.bucknell.edu/UniversityPress

Distributed worldwide by Rutgers University Press

Manufactured in the United States of America

CONTENTS

ABBREVIATIONS

FA	Goethe, *Sämtliche Werke*. General editor Friedmar Apel et al. 40 vols. Frankfurt am Main: Deutscher Klassiker Verlag, 1987–2013. Cited by volume and page number.
HGW	Hegel, *Gesammelte Werke*. General editor Walter Jaeschke. 31 vols. Hamburg: Felix Meiner, 1968–. Cited by volume and page number.
HW	Hegel, *Werke in zwanzig Bändern*. 2nd ed. Edited by Eva Moldenhauer and Karl Markus Michel. 21 vols.: vol. 13, *Vorlesungen über die Ästhetik I* (Ä 1); vol. 14, *Vorlesungen über die Ästhetik II* (Ä 2); vol. 15, *Vorlesungen über die Ästhetik III* (Ä 3). Frankfurt am Main: Suhrkamp, 1986. Cited by Ä 1, Ä 2, or Ä 3, and page number.
SW	Jean Paul, *Sämtliche Werke*. Edited by Eduard Berend et al. Vols. 1.1–1.17, 2.10.1, and 3.3. Weimar: Böhlau, 1927–. Cited by volume and page number.
WA	Goethe, *Goethes' Werke*. Edited on behalf of Sophie von Sachsen. 143 vols. Weimar: Böhlau, 1919. Cited by volume and page number.

A NOTE ON TRANSLATIONS

All translations from German are my own.

PRETEXTS FOR WRITING

Introduction

What Prefaces Are Not: Pedantic Notes

ALL READERS HAVE encountered prefaces. But many will readily admit that they flick over the preliminary pages of a book, in order to access the work proper more quickly. Indeed, Jean Paul jokes about this phenomenon in his debut novel, *Die Unsichtbare Loge* [The Invisible Lodge]. First published in 1793, it gained a writer's preface with each new edition, totaling three by its posthumous republication in 1826 (the third preface is dated October 1825, the month before Jean Paul died). Despite the author's continual attention to prefatorial form, however, the final footnote to his first chapter quips that the reader will have likely turned over the page without reading the original preface. For this reason, Jean Paul repeats a point made in this preface in the "Note, die nicht zu überschlagen ist"[1] [note that is not to be skipped over].[2] The inconspicuous, if apparently indispensable footnote and the obvious, though allegedly avoidable preface have a complementary function: together, they advance an idiosyncratic image of authorship. They reveal that "das Einbein" [the monoped], a one-legged figure to whom the preface writer proposes to talk and who reappears throughout the work, turns out to be an alter ego, or double, of the preface's and work's writer himself: a persona who is apparently identical to the person whose name is listed on the author's baptism certificate—which in fact states Johann Paul Richter, because Jean Paul was a pen name adopted as homage to Jean-Jacques Rousseau.

The historical symbolism of "das Einbein"—this bizarre, semifictive character of the preface, who is then absorbed into the main text and its notes—stems from medieval marginalia and classical invocation of a muse. On the one hand, Jean Paul's single leg connotes the monoped, a mythical human creature who, according Greek and early medieval lore, resided in the Orient: initially in India, before later Occidental imagination relocated him to the South of Africa. The sciapod, as he was also called, was a staple of books and their woodcuts throughout late medieval Europe, such as in versions of the fictional work *The Travels of Sir John Mandeville*.[3] Jean Paul's preface is a mock travelogue, recounting the excursion during which the prefatory text was composed: on a horse-drawn journey through the Upper Franconian mountain range of the Fichtelgebirge. It turns out that his persona does not so much have one leg as a shorter left leg than the right one—such that he stumbles—and so he is "gleich den ostindischen Hummern" (SW, 1.2: 18) [like East Indian lobsters], which have one pincer longer than the other. This reference to East India evokes the distant lands in which monocoli (one-footed, monster-like men) were thought to have resided. The suggestion of stumbling connects the character, according to Stephen Fennell, to a devilish, limping figure of the German late Middle Ages ("der Hinkefuß"); Magnus Wieland likens him to the French early modern equivalent ("le Diable boiteux").[4] Jean Paul describes his left stump as a flat, two-dimensional space rather than a three-dimensional one, "mehr ein Quadrat- als Kubikfuß" (SW, 1.2: 18) [more a square than a cubic foot], which also suggests the association "Quadratbein," or the quadrate bone that forms part of the skull in tetrapods (of which a monoped, ironically, is one). Most significant for our purposes, however, is that the literary manifestation of the monoped as a strange man from the East had been illustrated in the margins of medieval manuscripts, especially appearing on the edges of European maps of the world (*mappae mundi*)—for, after all, he hailed from a far-flung land.[5] He was thus a character on the periphery: both in geographical terms and on the page. Jean Paul rehabilitates the depiction of this figure at the outset, and in the middle, of *Die Unsichtbare Loge*. His "Einbein" recurs throughout the book in amusing twists on earlier imagery: analogous to the scholar who comically clings to his learning, for example, the prefatorial lobster becomes "die einbeinige Muschel" (SW, 1.2: 361) [the one-legged mussel] on the rocks.

On the other hand, Stephen Fennell observes that Jean Paul's idea of a single leg is not only corporeal, but metonymic of the writer's quill and—through its additional association with a pipe in the opening chapter (SW, 1.2: 38)—the classical concept of the reed (*harundo*), out of which musical instruments and writing implements were once made.[6] Thus "das Einbein" is a reference that is as classical as it is medieval. Virgil had appropriated the reed pipe as a symbol through which to call the muse for ancient pastoral poetry in the *Eclogues*, which were composed in opposition to epic tales.[7] Ovid's epic works invoked inspiration through the strings of a lyre rather than a reed. Martin Opitz placed a preface writer, or "Vorreder," before *Dafne* (1627), subtitled a tribute to Ovid, and his lyric persona claims: "Ich bin der Mann, der ich so rhümlich sang / In meine Harff' vnd die beruffnen seiten"[8] [I am the man who sang so laudably / Into my harp and the pages invoked]. Jean Paul satirically refers to "das Einbein" as an anti-epic name for his preface writer ("Vorredner") (SW, 1.2: 18), and so his work aligns itself with a counterepic tradition.

Through such references, it becomes evident that Jean Paul's prose writes itself into the history of the book. His prefatory and poetological character has an historical and European precedent. We shall pay more detailed attention to the history of the preface as a specific textual form around 1800 in the next section. But why focus on the *preface* in particular? Since Jean Paul stresses in his footnote, "daß ich nicht mehr habe als *ein* Bein" (SW, 1.2; 37) [that I have no more than *one* leg]; and since the fictional—albeit also purportedly empirical—authorial character introduced in the preface returns for the reader in the subsequent novel, we are reminded to interpret the whole of Jean Paul's work as a product of one pen, body, mind—or skull. Accordingly, the 1793 preface is as much a creative and theoretical part of Jean Paul's life and oeuvre as any other. The preface, then, may be significant as literature, but by itself it might now not appear to matter much. As Walther Rehm puts it, Jean Paul's notes *complement* his prefaces;[9] and both can be supplemented by, or exchanged for, the work of fiction as a whole. And so to read a preface of Jean Paul's is to grapple with more than just the preliminary pages to his books. Placing prefaces alongside footnotes and, indeed, chapters was common among contemporary writers, and in fact is still so among literary critics today. As a consequence, this introduction goes on to consider prefaces theoretically, as *paratexts*, after it has read them historically.

But as useful as such a concept of the paratext is, it enforces a generality of perspective onto types of texts that obscures the particularity—and peculiarity—of *prefacing* by literary and philosophical writers around 1800, and since. This was a time of profound change in print culture, and the period's prefaces have had lasting implications for post-Structuralist literature and continental philosophy. And so this study also considers Kierkegaard, Heidegger, and Derrida (among others), problematizing what it means to write at all, and then to summarize that activity for the reader before a work. There are many conceptual and scholarly ways into such a problem.

However, this book emphasizes the very resistance to framing the issue with scholarly theories first—that is, to employing external, accepted, given, and guiding concepts for a supposedly fixed subject of inquiry—by attending to particular instances of conflicted textuality that prompt close, inductive reading.

To preface is to reflect fundamentally on a work itself, in the abstract—at a point of remove to which Romantic writers were resistant, insofar as in any conventional understanding such distance would bring external, accepted doctrines to bear on the reading of their original works. And yet prefaces were paradoxically essential for authors such as Goethe, Jean Paul, and Hegel, in order for them to posit some sort of intellectual "objectivity"—a claim to systematicity or scientific insight, without subordination to disciplinary science (or academia) as some pre-established, agreed entity—and, more practically, in order to be read at all. As such, the form of the preface changed significantly over the course of the eighteenth century, and above all around 1800; and so its position altered within the book, too. In the middle of the second volume of *Grönländische Prozesse* [The Greenland Trials] (1784), Jean Paul states: "Du liest, lieber Leser, nicht gern eine Vorrede; wie viel weniger zwo Vorreden. Allein viellecht eben, weil du meine erste überschlagen, wirst du mir verzeihen, das in der andern lesen zu müssen, was ich in der überschlagenen zu sagen vergessen" (SW, 1.1: 165) [You do not like reading, dear reader, one preface—much less two prefaces. But perhaps precisely because you skipped over my first preface you will forgive me for having to read in the other one what I forgot to say in the first—the one you skipped over]. Commentary on a text, in the middle of that text, is called "prefatory" around 1800 because the term "preface" still evoked explication as much as writers now sought to resist explicit explanation of their works. Jean Paul and fellow contemporary, intellectually ambitious writers—here termed *Romantic*—sought to overcome prefatorial tradition rather than banish it entirely, which opened up plentiful opportunity for play with textual conventions.

If the invocation of Jean Paul as a "Romantic" writer jars with readers, René Wellek has suggested that Friedrich Schlegel's and Jean Paul's "basic views of poetry are identical," and that "Jean Paul's concept of humor is very near that of romantic irony as elaborated by Friedrich Schlegel."[10] The difference, as chapter 2 of the present book reveals, is that Jean Paul materializes Schlegelian irony, and objectifies it in an ironic, Romantic move. Indeed, the subsequent chapters subscribe to Wellek's broad view of Romanticism in European writing generally across English, French, and German literatures, though narrower periodizations for the German literary scene can be useful in other circumstances. Their utility depends on the text types and topics we might want to scrutinize.[11]

Formal "rules" and advice on prefacing date back to antiquity, to the handbooks of classical rhetoric. Given this tradition, which was influential on, but radically adapted in the eighteenth century, it makes sense to read the preface as a discrete, traditional form that may be subsumed into the modern "paratext" of print culture, yet retains its specificity in modernity nevertheless. The historical shift in the textual appropriation of rhetorical thought is sketched in the course of this introductory chapter, before we take another theoretical turn: Romantic German prefacing around 1800 introduces us to the conceptual complexity and creativity of literature and philosophy generally at that time.

What follows in this book's three main chapters are close readings of a trio of canonical German authors—Goethe, Jean Paul, and Hegel—intended as an investigation into the preface around 1800, which together soon turn into a study of what it has meant to write a book: both in that period and, more tentatively, in a countercultural, avant-garde, Romantic way ever since. Prefaces are read on their own terms: historically, sympathetically (through the lens of the author's own theory), rhetorically, and formally—irrespective of our present-day disciplinary division between literature and philosophy; and without the analytical "tools" offered by the literature on paratexts. The case for this approach is made in the present introduction. The "research findings" of this monograph might not be easily or satisfactorily summarized in some future scholarly footnote, but such an accomplishment would be a rather unromantic endeavor, anyway. Perhaps less an exposition and more an exploration of Romanticism—broadly construed—is the point of this book. Such a claim is antagonistic, admittedly, since it limits a reader's ability to leaf through a work, and insists the chapters are read in their entirety. To start with a refusal to summarize succinctly is itself a very Romantic argumentative maneuver, and one this book seeks to interrogate by way of examples—and to some extent instantiate as an example.

HISTORICAL CONTEXT AND PRECEDENT

Critical surveys agree that the eighteenth century was the German preface's Golden Age.[12] This book considers prefaces written by authors to their own works. These were not a formal innovation around 1800, but they became predominant over prefaces by third parties on a writer's behalf over the course of the century. Friedrich von Hagedorn jokes in his epigram "Die Schriftsteller" [Writers], originally published mid-century: "Daß ein beredter Held im schärfsten Vorbericht, / Für unsers Namens Ruhm mit allen Tropen ficht"[13] [That an eloquent hero in the sharpest preface / Fights with all tropes for fame in our name]. In 1793, Christoph Martin Wieland did not want to preface his *Sämmtliche Werke* [Collected Works] himself, and requested that his publisher Georg Joachim Göschen ask Schiller or Carl Leonhard Reinhold to compose the opening text. But Göschen objected, declaring such a practice outmoded by this time.[14] Twenty years later, E.T.A. Hoffmann only reluctantly agreed to his publisher, Karl Friedrich Kunz, asking Jean Paul to preface *Fantasiestücke in Callot's Manier* [Fantasy Pieces in Callot's Manner] (1814–1815): he conceded that, as a new author, it might be advantageous from a marketing point of view.[15] Thus in German writing around 1800, it was self-authored prefaces that were in greatest supply. By contrast, prefaces written by publishers themselves declined from their own heyday in the sixteenth and seventeenth centuries,[16] even if publishers' self-fashioning within society increased relative to their ever more substantial wealth.[17] Those third parties who marketed books now placed adverts in periodicals and catalogs, which enjoyed ever widening exposure—although these, too, were increasingly written by authors themselves.[18]

Although self-authored prefaces constituted a newly predominant type, there was much terminological variation across them. It is popular among present-day academics to subcategorize, typologize the form, but the German terms for the "preface" around 1800 are slippery. In reviewing dictionary definitions and through a historical survey, Steven Tötösy de Zepetnek proposes that an eighteenth-century "Einleitung" or "introduction" is more typical of instructional, nonliterary texts.[19] But Wieland titled prefatorial poetry an "Einleitung" in the second half of the century, introducing his *Erzählungen* [Stories] in 1752—which were later prefaced in prose (via a "Vorbericht") and preceded by an addendum ("Zusatz"). By Annette Retsch's count, an eighteenth-century literary preface termed a "Vorbericht" was between one and five sides, whereas its sister form the "Vorrede" was longer, usually up to twenty pages.[20] However, Retsch's sample size is both small and unconvincing. Klopstock wrote an "Einleitung" to his *Geistliche Lieder* [Spiritual Songs] in 1758, a "Vorbericht" to *Veränderte Lieder* [Amended Songs] the same year, and a "Vorrede" to his next volume of *Geistliche Lieder* in 1769—all without discernible differences in content or the extent to which they are essayistic or apologetic. (Notably Gérard Genette understands an "*introduction*, *note*, and *notice*" as a "more modest" prefatory form.)[21] Moreover, Klopstock's "Vorrede" is three and a half pages long, while the "Vorbericht" is ten—the inversion of Retsch's definition.[22] Among philosophical texts, this distinction is similarly seldom upheld: Johann Friedrich Flatt published a "Vorrede" of under two sides in 1792; but Carl Philipp Conz published a "Vorbericht" of the same, brief length, with the same publisher two years later.[23] Indeed, perhaps "Vorrede" and "Vorbericht" were interchangeable: Wieland refers to his "Vorrede" to *Peregrinus Proteus* in 1791 as "diese[r] kleine Vorbericht"[24] [this small preface] in the preface itself, either because there was no difference in the terminology of the two words, or in order to emphasize the exceptionality of his example that, it turns out, was not remarkably unusual. At other times there was no prefatorial title above a preliminary paragraph at all, or it was deleted in a work's subsequent editions. In addition, there were alternative, competing terms such as the older "Vor-Ansprache," the more Romantic "Vorerinnerung" (literally: "Prior Reminiscence"), or "Vorwort"—and the last has been the unmarked German term for the preface since the nineteenth century. Francis Paul Greene argues that E.T.A. Hoffmann objected to the "Vorrede" as a form (as alluded to above), but neither to the academic "Prolegomenon," nor necessarily to the "Vorwort." Greene then attempts, implausibly, to draw boundaries between the literary manifestations of "Vorrede" and "Vorwort," yet he also admits that "the two words can be and were, at the time, used almost synonymously."[25] Thus the end of the eighteenth and the beginning of the nineteenth centuries was an era of unusual lexical instability in self-authored prefaces, and it defies scholarly sense to try and delineate the self-authored prefatory forms any further.

As the eighteenth century was the period in which German authors now seized the platform of the preface in order to defend their works themselves, the prefatory mode underwent substantial change. Historical scholarship on German *literary* prefaces has suggested that the form can be traced through three major phases in the long eighteenth century. The protean textual form of the preface is less a flower that blossomed, wilted, and then flowered again over the course of the eighteenth century, but more resembles a caterpillar that retreated into itself, as if forming a cocoon, and which later turned, rather romantically, into a butterfly. The development of the *philosophical* preface is somewhat different, as described below in the final section of this introduction. The three main chapters of the present book are concerned with the third, broadly Romantic stage of literary and what will become philosophical prefacing, even if Goethe, Jean Paul, and Hegel are not obviously "Romantic" authors according to conservative German periodization.

The first historical phase of German prefacing extends from early printing into the middle of the eighteenth century, whereby the preface was the primary site of textual theory or "poetics" (which Bruno Markwardt calls "Vorredenpoetik"),[26] as well as a pragmatic act by the writer to win the goodwill of his audience, attracting and retaining readers.[27] Above all, these generalizations hold true for novels: the preface was the main space of reflection on early modernity's novel form, the "Roman."[28] Exceptions are rare.[29] While Hermann Riefstahl states in his survey of prefaces to court poetry that before 1680 and after 1750 there are no examples of explanatory prefaces,[30] Stefanie Stockhorst reasons that earlier absence of a preface was usually limited to occasional lyric, where the cause of composition is self-evident, or at least pragmatic.[31] The very presence of prefaces, therefore, was at this first stage conventional.

Just as there were some exceptional, unprefaced works, not all early prefaces were prosaic. Some prefaces not only theorized the subsequent pages, but were also intended to appeal wittily to readers—even if most were in fact formally rather straightforward. Johann Gottfried Schnabel, under the pseudonym Gisander, can still joke in his 1738 preface to *Der im Irr-Garten der Liebe herum taumelnde Cavalier* [The Cavalier Staggering Around in the Garden Maze of Love] that prefacing was too pervasive a fashion, yet he continues to preface: "Diese Vorrede habe ich nicht der Gewohnheit oder der bloßen Mode wegen hierher gesetzt, indem man selten ein Buch bei heutigen Zeiten zum Vorscheine kommen siehet, dem es an einer Vorrede fehlet, nein!"[32] [I have not placed this preface here because of convention or mere fashion, which nowadays dictates that a book seldom appears lacking a preface, no!] The irony is that Schnabel's prefatory assertions actually reiterate the conventional prefatorial topos for early German novels of commenting on how historically true their narratives might be and whether fictional elements in fact render a work more universally true beyond the historical events they purport to narrate. However, he represents these ideas comically inasmuch as he also draws attention to their possible inaccuracy, emphasizing that he is in any case unable to personally vouch for, or verify, the story's (fictive) author or source. In his parodic preface's self-reflexivity, however, Schnabel stands out as an exception.

After the invention of print, then, we witness limited prefatorial creativity such as parodic prefacing or—occasionally—prefatory absence, although the latter may be simply a pragmatic choice. Parodic prefacing thematizes the very preparatory text at hand. It is a stock strategy of many who start what de facto becomes a speech at an informal event or on an entertaining occasion to say that they will not give a speech at all, or that they dislike standard speeches. Once print culture took off, it was only natural that this age-old technique was transposed into the preface as a textual trope. But prefatory creativity in German was hardly prolific or formally provocative at this point; indeed, the satirical, self-reflexive preface in the early modern period corresponded to genre expectations. The fact that it is Schnabel who prefaces satirically is unsurprising given that he satirizes contemporary letters throughout the aforementioned novel. Hence we can summarize that German literature and its theoretical underpinning could be controversial in the first half of the eighteenth century, but the preface as a form conceived to an apologetic and intellectual end for literature—especially for an ever more creative novel genre—was generally not called into question.

The status of the preface changed in the latter half of the eighteenth century, when the convention of prefacing itself was popularly contested. The preface was now a problem; and in that problem authors saw potential. That is, in the second half of the eighteenth century the preface became particularly, formally creative, and less contingent on genre classifications or disciplinary boundaries. In 1789, Johann Arnold Ebert wrote that one topic was generalizable to all types of writer, scholarly and scientific, literary and philosophical: how or whether to preface. Speaking for all authors, Ebert asked: "Braucht er besonders darauf zu sinnen, wie er seine Vorrede anfangen wolle? Braucht er überhaupt einer Vorrede?"[33] [Must he reflect especially on how he might want to begin his preface? Does he need a preface at all?] "Crisis" is a popular term for historians of the eighteenth century, but such doubt or crisis in the conceptualization and suitability of front matter led to more ponderous self-reflexivity than Schnabel's earlier example, and as much to the preface's absence as to its proliferation. Prefaces, if they were composed at all, could now go on forever; and they were in this second stage first and foremost about prefacing, unless they were dispensed with altogether. In fact, Ebert's lines of 1789 preface his *Episteln und vermischte Gedichte* [Epistles and Miscellaneous Poems]; indeed, they preface his prefacing of this collection (and concern the questionable starting point of such a project)—in a preliminary, theoretical discourse that runs to no fewer than sixty-nine pages. The prosaic, prefatory caterpillar of the early eighteenth century had begun to form into its elaborate cocoon, retreating into itself: inasmuch as it was either away from view, or self-generative.

Hans Ehrenzeller choses an alternative—and suitably reproductive—metaphor for such prefaces that problematized themselves, calling their writers "incestuous" (identifying a "Vorreden-Inzucht"), and members of "a cult of prefacing for prefacing's sake" ("ein Kult der Vorrede um der Vorrede willen").[34] What Ehrenzeller observes as the inbred preface in German letters had occurred already in other European contexts, such as preface narratives in English or French after the rules of the writing game had been re-established, following the beginnings of printing. "As the function of the prologue grows in importance in the course of the Renaissance," writes Deborah N. Losse, "the *préfacier* becomes increasingly conscious of the problematic role of the preface";[35] and from the end of the sixteenth century, French writers became skeptical of the merits in prefacing—"a cynicism that becomes commonplace in later centuries in the works of such authors as Flaubert, Gautier, and Mallarmé."[36] Genette declares "playacting of the prefatorial activity . . . one of the truths of the preface,"[37] delineating between "elusive" prefaces and "the self-referential preface: a preface about prefaces" within his subcategory of preface "dodges."[38] But for the German tradition, both history and the history of eighteenth-century print, literary, and intellectual cultures are pertinent to the story of the preface in its larval, transformative, "second" stage. Ehrenzeller notes that the incestuous preface was in part a fashion imported from England, via the contemporary German craze for the prose of Laurence Sterne, whom we shall encounter time and again throughout this book. For Ernst Weber, the renaissance of self-reflexive prefaces to German novels around the 1760s, in what was simultaneously an age of prefatory decline, occurred because the major poetological changes affecting the novel in particular themselves required explication.[39] The preface continued to be exploited by novelists who were especially artistically aware, or Sentimental.[40] The latter, new celebration of Sentimentality in the German book market was often derivative of English models, which had to be explained to the foreign audience; and the genre entailed an explicitly affective appeal to a reader prior to a work. Sterne was the most significant influence both on this movement and in prefatory creativity more broadly into the nineteenth century. Jean Paul takes his cue from a specific line of Sterne's second novel, *A Sentimental Journey through France and Italy* (1768), as we shall see in chapter 2.

The alternative to a long, self-reflexive preface—to do without one altogether—in truth had been developing subtly over the course of the century. In introducing short, untitled verse in 1733, Christian Ludwig Liscow's preface ("Vorbericht") simply states: "Eine lange Vorrede vor einer kleinen Schrift stehet nicht wohl"[41] [A long preface before a short piece of writing does not sit well]. Without much further prefacing, he adds a Horatian epigram before charting a synopsis in prose form of the poem that follows, as a separate, subsequent summary of contents ("Inhalt") section, which runs to just over three pages. Similarly, the *Vorrede des Herausgebers* [Editor's Preface] to Luise Gottsched's on first publication anonymous work, *Die Pietisterey im Fischbein-Rocke* [Pietism in a Whalebone Skirt] (1736), acknowledges the necessity to preface at that time, but appears to disregard all conventional prefatorial topoi. Yet it justifies their absence by proceeding with other prefatory matter, notably fictive letters, which situate the work relative to convention, after all. For we first read: "Weil es doch eine hergebrachte Gewohnheit ist, daß ein Buch eine Vorrede haben muß; Ich aber dem Geneigten oder Ungeneigten Leser nichts anders zu sagen weiß, als was in folgenden beyden Briefen enthalten ist: So will ich dieselbe ohne fernere Weitläuftigkeit mittheilen"[42] [Because it is certainly customary that a book must have a preface, but I do not know what else to say to either the receptive or the unreceptive reader other than what is written in the following two letters, I wish to convey them without expounding on them any further]. By the time of Christian Fürchtegott Gellert's novel *Das Leben der schwedischen Gräfin von G**** [Life of the Swedish Countess of G***] in 1747–1748, though, which was also originally published anonymously, we genuinely encounter no preface—which we could call a "zero preface." Admittedly, Gellert's story was brought out in periodical form, but contemporary journals did not preclude prefacing. The absent or radically shortened preface gained "critical mass" in the 1770s, becoming more common and more brash in the German Storm and Stress movement.

The German literary preface lost its overtly pragmatic functions in the latter half of the eighteenth century, therefore, and ended not just in self-reflexive humor, but above all in conspicuous absence or a hypertrophic presence against theoretical conceptions of writing that were hostile to prefaces—and yet prefaces could be harnessed for such works all the same, perhaps because they were no longer obligatory. Especially the prefaces to German novels developed, in Ehrenzeller's trajectory, from being rhetorical set pieces into more autonomous, fictional, literary forms;[43] and above all in Jean Paul's works, they became an end in themselves. The present book seeks to explore this third phase properly, in depth, and to extend it to philosophy. In other words, stage three of the eighteenth-century German preface was the transition from an incestuous, self-referential, or absent, preface to an *incorporated* one around 1800. The subsequent chapters examine Goethe, Jean Paul, and Hegel, and these three authors each wrote one incorporated preface that was particularly generative for their wider prefacing in general: namely the preface to *Die Leiden des jungen Werthers* [The Sorrows of Young Werther] (1774) and its revisions and alternatives, the preface to a fictive second edition of *Quintus Fixlein* (1797), and the preface to the *Phänomenologie des Geistes* [Phenomenology of Spirit] (1807) respectively.

The start of this third stage in German literary prefacing has a comparatively similar backstory across Europe, but occurred much earlier in Britain and France than in German territories, on the whole, as we have noted above. But the incorporated preface was in vogue throughout Europe by the late eighteenth century, in any case. The fashion was not entirely original: as noted in chapter 1, metapoetic poetry is an older variant of the modern, "embedded" prose preface. And in French literature—and undoubtedly in other literatures, too—the latter phenomenon had been popular earlier in history, in the Renaissance, though it had then subsided. As Losse observes for writing in French, "with the advent of the seventeenth century, the preface no longer narrates but anticipates or comments on the narrative to follow. It loses its narrative function."[44] Indeed, according to Genette, the more objective preface Losse identifies was itself a belated result of the invention and increase of printing, since Genette takes the openings of the *Iliad* and the *Odyssey* to be indicative of an incorporated preface.[45] Yet this incorporated preface later re-emerged in print. In the eighteenth century, the dedication to Henry Fielding's *Amelia* (1751), addressed to Ralph Allen, promises the dedicatee, as primary reader, what we have termed a zero preface above, stating that there will be no "Preface concerning the Work";[46] yet the subtitle to the first chapter of Book 1 reads "containing the exordium &c."[47] The introduction is subsumed within the start of the narrative. Similar jokes recur throughout the novel, not least to chapter 1 of the tenth book: "to which we prefix no preface."[48] Weber has claimed that as the eighteenth century progressed, the preface for German novels is more integrated into the plot of the novel itself;[49] and after Fielding's *The History of Tom Jones, a Foundling* (1749), many reflections are displaced into the opening chapters of novels.[50] Genette calls the prefacing strategy for *Tom Jones* an "internal" preface.[51] But as late as the end of the century, authors and readers were still wise to this tendency as a conscious strategy, hence it could not neutralize or eradicate the preface as a form entirely, and the practice was satirized. Of "Vorrede" to the fragment *Biographische*

Belustigungen [Biographical Amusements] (1796), Jean Paul begins: "Ich schreibe sie bloß, damit man nicht das erste Kapitel für eine nimmt und nicht dieses überhüpft, sondern diese Vorrede" (SW, 1.5: 249) [I am writing it only so that the first chapter is not taken to be one (a preface) and skipped over, but instead this preface is skipped over]. In the 1790s and into the early nineteenth century, the incorporated preface won out especially in German writing, as Weber states. Uwe Wirth, like most critics, agrees.[52] This had to do with the greater theoretical autonomy of a literary—or indeed, philosophical—work, as we shall see in the next section.

A rare precursor to this third phase of incorporated preface writing in German literature is Schnabel's (Gisander's) satirical preface to *Wunderliche Fata einiger See-Fahrer* [Strange Fates of some Seafarers] (1731). Weber points to the meandering style of Schnabel's preface and its narrative content, which is embedded within the novel itself—and so the preface is quite creative.[53] In fact, Schnabel uses the status of *Wunderliche Fata* as his first publication and appeals to his alleged youth in order to excuse his liberal appropriation of prefatory form. (Schnabel was actually at least forty-two at the time of publication.) The insincere appeal to the author's age, Ehrenzeller observes, was particularly common in early eighteenth-century prefaces: we are inclined to turn a blind eye to the follies of the young.[54] Anna Richards notes that Schnabel's prefatory wit is otherwise atypical, perhaps a little scandalous, in that he questions the authenticity of his own work, inviting the reader to decide to what extent it is based on either history or fantasy.[55] But Schnabel ends the preface by assuring his readers that he knows to keep his humor in check: he and his preface may be funny, but he is not always a joker.[56] Only his preface, then, is truly radical, and an apology for this prefatory freedom as exceptional is the premise on which he hopes to secure his literary readership. Readers can immediately enjoy the playfulness of his novel's prose, but are reassured that it is not in the end immoral—after the preface. Although the preface might be a radical form in Schnabel's instantiation of it, and hint at a work that is to be taken on its own terms, this text is at the same time a nod to convention, insofar as it seeks to shape the reader's presuppositions about the whole work.

What is so Romantic about the prefaces and authors examined in the thrust of this book is that they are similarly, in actual fact all the more resistive and self-contradictory. The limits of the text, standing in for those of the world, are embraced precisely in order for the author and his work to try and go beyond them. Across the channel, Wordsworth wavered in writing an exposition of his and Coleridge's poetic purpose as a preface. For as he prefixes his megapreface to the second edition of *Lyrical Ballads* (1800), "adequately to display the opinions, and fully to enforce the arguments, would require a space wholly disproportionate to a preface."[57] And yet—or precisely because of this awareness—he prefaces at length anyway, up to the acceptable confines of the form. He elaborates "as far as the limits of a preface will permit."[58] The fact that the preface was appropriated was counter to Coleridge's taste, but it is nevertheless fitting for the project. Because completion—which a preface might be understood to confirm—is to the Romantic mind in any case preliminary. Friedrich Schlegel states in an aphorism at the onset of the nineteenth century: "das goldene Zeitalter der Literatur würde dann sein, wenn keine Vorreden mehr nötig wären"[59] [the Golden Age of literature would be if prefaces were no longer necessary]. Here he is idealistic, and disingenuous. With this statement, Schlegel means that literature is ideally always provisional, since a conventional preface connotes completion. But Schlegel does in fact preface, as we read in chapter 2. The preface ("Vorerinnerung") by him and his brother August Wilhelm to the debut issue of their journal *Athenaeum* in 1798, for example, is a programmatic as well as an immanent part of the publication. Although the pair begin by saying that the first contributions will be sufficient for the reader to understand the periodical's purpose, their preparatory explanation can contribute to that comprehension all the same.[60] Romantic writing relies on a notion of totality that can be demonstrated only by the enactment—and transgression—of textual limitation.

PARATEXTUAL THEORY AND TEXTUAL AUTONOMY

Prefaces are most commonly understood in contemporary scholarship as "paratexts," following Genette's seminal study in 1987 of the same title. Indeed, the preface is taken to be an example of a paratext par excellence, for Genette's book devotes no less than three lengthy chapters to an examination and further classification of the form.[61] But the preface is nevertheless subordinate within Genette's system of paratexts, which is admittedly a slippery and playful set of examples: the paratext as a whole is "a convergence of effects," which is "more important than their diversity of aspect."[62] Like many paratexts, the preface is considered paradoxical because it is conceived as a part of the work, and yet set apart from it; as a threshold, a transitional structure ("between text and beyond-text," in Genette's words),[63] the preface is also a specific, transactional situation. Genette surveys a dizzying array of examples across time, but comes to the conclusion that there is only one historical "distributional feature": that the most dignified and "Realist" writers tend *not* to preface.[64] (Though this does not mean that they never prefaced—see the present study's conclusion). The paratext—and with it the preface—has since been historicized in much more detail. According to Frieder von Ammon and Herfried Vögel, for example, a traditional "paratextual culture" increasingly came in for criticism in the eighteenth century, especially among German authors.[65] We have traced the history of the eighteenth-century German literary preface above—for the first time in English, and for the benefit of Anglo-American scholarship. But throughout the historical analysis of this book, it should become ever clearer that typologizing around 1800 was as much a practice of Enlightenment enthusiasm as it was an activity that Romanticism resisted: cataloguing logically, after all, was a major topic of Romantic critique. Genette's schematic reasoning, as lively as it is, insufficiently identifies the tension German writers of the late eighteenth century found in typologies of texts and not least of paratexts—including those of their own schematization.

Georg Christoph Lichtenberg states in an aphorism that to preface, for him, is to broach material that is of simultaneously immediate and long-standing relevance to writing. That content is peculiar to the preface; he implicitly classes the form alongside indexes, footnotes, or dedications—we could simply say "paratexts"—but the preface is also somehow distinct from them:

> Es gibt Materien in der Welt die sich am füglichsten in Registern, andere die sich in Noten, wieder andere, die sich fast allein in Dedikationen sagen lassen. Andere nehmen sich im Vorbeigehen gesagt am besten aus. Zu einer Vorrede habe ich diejenige für die schicklichste befunden, die ich sogleich abhandeln will und gewiß allemal abhandeln werde, sollte ich auch noch hundert Vorreden schreiben.[66]

> [There is material in this world that is most appropriate for a glossary or index, other matter suited to footnotes, and other material still that can almost only be said in a dedication. More matters are best said in passing. I have found the most fitting subjects for a preface to be those that I want to treat straight away, and yet they are also those which I will certainly always want to treat, were I to write another hundred prefaces.]

Lichtenberg does not hint at what is specifically prefatorial about prefatory material. But what it meant to preface around 1800 was not only an important question relative to other text types at this time. It was the most pressing and basic issue posed for writing itself.

Lichtenberg's contemporary Gottlieb Wilhelm Rabener is more explicit in coining an overall category of what we would today term the paratext. In 1745, Rabener published his satire *Hinkmars von Repkow Noten ohne Text* [Hinkmar of Repkow's Notes without Text]: a mock dissertation by a gentleman scholar ("Gelehrter"), a figure whom Rabener equates with an author of notes ("Notenautor").[67] His humorous nontext comprises only explanatory notes to notes. The sorts of notes which Rabener thematizes are usually found, if not in the footer of a page, then as other subtypes of the paratext than footnotes: dedications, authorial commentaries ("Abhandlungen")—or as prefaces. Asserting that his own notes are the most distinguished and important parts of his (fictive) works, the character specifies: "ich beziehe mich auf die Vorreden, so man vor diesen Büchern findet, und worinnen mein Satz allemal, nur auf verschiedene Art, behauptet ist"[68] [I refer to the prefaces that one finds in front of these books, and in which my proposition is always asserted, only in a different form]. In effect, scholarly "notes" were simply the broader term for Rabener's "paratextual" apparatus, though he turns out to be concerned chiefly with the preface. Despite his common concept that encompasses diverse types of (para)text—notes—Rabener is actually concerned with one particular text type, and in uncovering its contradictions.

For Rabener there was a particular, threefold problem about the preface that does not hold for other paratexts. First, there was the charge of false, rhetorical modesty, which we shall explore in the next section. Second, he accused the preface writer of appearing to think only of himself when preface writing: "Die Vorreden schreibt der Verfasser wohl nicht leicht um des geneigten Lesers willen, sondern seinetwegen"[69] [The author probably does not write prefaces easily for the well-disposed reader's sake, but rather for his own]. This is founded on a contemporary, emergent ideal of textual autonomy, as we shall see.[70] And third, to preface was in Rabener's view commensurate with continuing rather than commenting upon a work, and prefaces lengthened such a work in an irrelevant way. That is to say, "der Herr Verfasser darf sich gar kein Gewissen machen, wenn er darinnen Sachen sagt, die zum Buche gar nicht gehören"[71] [the author need not be concerned if he mentions matters in them that do not pertain to the book at all]; and wherever the word "explicated" ("erläutert") occured, Rabener surmises that it must have been a printing error, and should read "extended" ("erweitert") instead.[72] The book invites a hypertrophic preface that metastasizes from itself (either preface or work, for in this conception the one becomes the other). This is a joke that Rabener's contemporary, Friedrich Justus Riedel, enacted with greater extremity: the scholarly satire *Umständlicher Beweiß, daß im heiligen Römischen Reiche viele Narren sind* [Comprehensive Proof that in the Holy Roman Empire There Are Many Fools] (1765) has a preface so long that nothing remains to be said in the work itself: "Ich habe mich in der Vorrede so erschöpfet, daß ich keine Beweise mehr schöpfen kann, meinen Hauptsatz zu unterstützen, die ich nicht schon, wiewohl zu einem andern Endzwecke, angeführet hätte"[73] [I have exhausted myself so much in the preface that I cannot come up with any more proofs in support of my main proposition which I have not posited already, albeit for another purpose]. Riedel plays with the potential paradox in this line, viz. that the preface extends proofs for a book's thesis, but to a separate end such that they are relevant and irrelevant at once.

If emphasizing the particularity of the preface—notwithstanding the plausibility of the paratext as a more general analytical category—was a common stance in the eighteenth and early nineteenth centuries, it should also not surprise Anglo-American scholars today. Anthony Grafton's *The Footnote: A Curious History* is a playful and profound interrogation of scholarly notes since the Enlightenment, in which Rabener takes a lead role and Jean Paul a cameo.[74] Significantly, Grafton disrupts disciplinary specialization and examines philosophy, too, as part of a general study of *writing*: around 1800, Kant mastered the form of the footnote, whereas Hegel resisted it. He rebelled "against the idea that a philosopher's text should use footnotes to exemplify and carry on a dialectical argument."[75] The present book on prefacing likewise extends into Hegel's philosophy. But it is author-based, and in this respect it is inspired by Peter J. Burgard's examination of Goethe and the essay, which argues that the German author's essays on art are self-reflexive, antisystematic, playful and, as such, paradoxical. If this sounds familiar, for Burgard essays might be introductions (and vice versa): the *Einleitung in die Propyläen* [Introduction to the Propylae] (1798), for example, is apparently both an essay about essays and an introduction to introductions.[76] The essay form thereby appears to stand in for Goethe's nonfictional prose writing per se; the author's autobiographical project, for instance, "reveals an essayistic consciousness."[77] The essay and introduction can also be ascribed more formal, separate specificity, though, and this book takes the perspective of the "preface" (broadly construed). Beyond German

Studies, Giancarlo Maiorino has written on titles, Frank Kermode on endings, and A. D. Nuttall on narrative beginnings.[78] Such studies are scholarly close readings, but soon become reflective and theoretical, thinking with writers on specific paratextual forms or textual parts as an excuse for an exploration of writing itself.

A set of German scholars approach the paratext the other way around: from a more abstract perspective. They primarily include the "Siegen school"—Georg Stanitzek, Remigius Bunia, and Till Dembeck—and Uwe Wirth.[79] Wirth and Dembeck have both applied Genette to German literature written around and after the 1790s particularly, not least to works by Goethe and, to an even greater degree, Jean Paul. While Wirth's examples are all paratexts of novels, Dembeck's are taken from literary works, broadly understood (though they are de facto from novels, for the most part). The thrust of their theoretical concern is literary and indeed textual "framing" in general, and both apply the thought of not only Genette, but also (and to a greater extent) Derrida and post-Structuralists—read against an historical context of the late eighteenth century in which "autonomy" was the guiding concept. Literature (like philosophy) was emancipated from scholarship in the eighteenth century—as we shall see in the next section—and was emboldened by popularity, and the loss of scholarship's prestige. Niklas Luhmann has famously theorized literature of Weimar Classicism and Early German Romanticism as an autonomous subsystem of contemporary art, which was itself an autonomous social system in an increasingly specialized modern age—and in contrast to Enlightenment and Sentimental literary works, which had been understood as a branch of general learning.[80] Marianne Willems has integrated the Storm and Stress movement into this story of literary autonomy.[81] Literature was written and read for literature's sake, and had social purchase as such. Philosophy's purpose was to philosophize. Within this context, a work had to stand on its own, and in its own terms. Not only the preface, but the concept of textual framing was fundamental to writing. Thus Dembeck offers the theoretical equivalent of Weber's literary-historical analysis of the incorporated preface, coining the terms "extrinsic" and "intrinsic" framing ("extrinsische" and "intrinsische Rahmung") for the era around 1800. Intrinsic framing was the child of literary and intellectual autonomy. Its birth gave rise to a liminal paratextual zone that not only instantiated textuality, but was also conceptually constitutive of a whole work's aesthetic autonomy. Yet intrinsic framing is of course otherwise contingent on an artwork, without independent value—as another artful aspect of that work. Dembeck's point about internal and external framing as broader concepts is well taken. But the preface within the major historical and intellectual paradigm shift around 1800 was of special consequence for the authors studied in this book, and so deserves more particular interrogation.

The autonomy of literature and philosophy is unquestionably evident from the historical rupture within another paratextual form: dedications and dedicatory prefaces, which decreased dramatically over the course of the eighteenth century. Their prime had been in the earlier sixteenth and seventeenth centuries.[82] By 1759, Johann Georg Hamann's preliminary pages to his *Sokratische Denkwürdigkeiten* [Socratic Memorabilia] dedicated the work to an impersonal communicative sphere, in which free thinking, skepticism, and supposed common sense circulates: "An das Publikum oder Niemand, den Kundbaren"[83] [To the public or nobody, the notorious one]. The period of patronage in German literature was diminishing in practice, and the desire on the part of authors to keep dedicating their works to authority was also waning. While the dedication as a convention did not disappear entirely, its appropriation became more personal, toward a present-day acknowledgment of an emotional debt; or it was used as a playful, fictional device. Anomalies continued, of course. Goethe's preface to the sixth volume of his published correspondence with Schiller in 1829 is presented as a "Dedication" to Ludwig I of Bavaria, and as such is a surprising exception to the modern tendency. Goethe's contemporary, Christian Dietrich Grabbe, was appalled, reading it both as poetically disingenuous and as a sign of shocking servility toward court society.[84] The reasons for the dedication, and for Goethe's having dedicated this work specifically, were actually pragmatic: as Crown Prince, Ludwig had visited Schiller's grave in 1806 before he met Goethe in person, in 1827. And prior to writing the dedication in 1829, Goethe had received a bust of a son of Niobe from the king in celebration of the Weimar writer's eightieth birthday, together with a personal letter.[85] Nevertheless, the dedicatory epistle was received as antiquated by, and inappropriate for, the reading public.

Prefaces were equally problematic, but tolerated all the more. Perhaps because they could be, and indeed were, far more playful. Authors presented their interpretation of their newfound autonomy through intricate fictional strategies that readers, not least scholars, have reflected upon for centuries; and writers reconceptualized their own now autonomous form through a range of radical metaphors. If, as Rabener jokes, preface writers wrote for themselves, then their writing could be autoerotic—creating its own imagined readers, and reproducing itself with desire and frustration alike. Most authors were not so extreme, though Jean Paul was—as was Derrida, too, in the twentieth century.

In fact, this study excavates the prehistory of such post-Structuralist thinkers as Derrida, rather than making a systematic case for a specific conception of the preface around 1800—or presenting to readers some sober, academic typology. In adopting this historical and "Romantic" theoretical approach, the book follows a range of American scholars since the 1980s who have explored the affinity between German Romanticism and deconstruction. As Azade Seyhan claimed in 1992: "The [then] current debates in literary theory are not-so-distant echoes of the critical voices that informed Jena Romanticism."[86] In *The Dark Interpreter* (1980), Tilottama Rajan loosens traditional German periodization and refers to Jean Paul as a Romantic theorist, claiming that he tacitly encourages deconstructionist criticism.[87] Alice A. Kuzniar contends in *Delayed Endings* (1987) that Novalis and Hölderlin foreshadow critical thinkers of the late twentieth century, notably Derrida; these two authors "are less our ancestors than our contemporaries."[88] She contextualizes them among Schlegel, Jean Paul, and Heinrich von Kleist—all of whom are Romantics. Tantalizingly, she writes that for Novalis "the ideal form of writing is prefatory, provisional."[89] Moreover, Burgard posits an affinity between Goethe as essayist and Derridean deconstruction.[90] Now that the high tide of post-Structuralism in the academy has retreated, and the critical debate is no longer about the application of post-Structuralism to the period around 1800 per se, we can look back historically: not just on Derrida and his peers, which the latter parts of chapters 2 and 3 of this book seek to do, but into the late eighteenth and early nineteenth centuries in order to uncover archaeologically, and compare across time, a specific sort of paratext—the preface—on its own terms, in each instantiation. As a result, this book emphasizes recurring and contradictory conceptions and conceptual, sometimes antagonistic metaphors for prefaces and works. Together, these recurrences and above all their repeatedly resistant character allow us to think of the period around 1800 not only as Romantic, but as engendering pretexts for writing and a resistance to—alleged—"reductive" reading that we can call the attitude of Romanticism. The Romantic disposition is both historicizable and, in its formal and rhetorical flourish, influential on later, historically important thinkers in their own especially resistive moments—and intellectual movements—in time.

RHETORICAL CAESURA: COMPREHENDING ROMANTICISM

Although the history of the preface within print culture can be charted with a trajectory similar to footnotes, for example (and a long view on prefatorial form is sketched in the first section, above), the preface is also unusual among paratexts in being a stock part of a cultural tradition that predates printing, whose rules have been codified since antiquity. In classical times through to the early modern period, the literary preface or prologue (*prooemium*, *praefatio*, or *prologos*) had a bifurcated genealogy, stemming from ancient rhetoric as well as more general cultural myth or—later—Christian faith. Hence, literary front matter also attested the source of a poet's inspiration, through the *invocatio*. Around 1800, cultural assumptions about the preface *and* unconventional prefatory strategies were both still grounded in the reception of age-old, especially rhetorical practice. Rhetoric has continued to shape the ways in which we have thought about writing, reading—and prefacing.

Although rhetorical theory was founded upon the presumption that good speakers were moral men (Quintilian privileges the ideal of "vir bonus dicendi peritus"), its emphasis was the more pragmatic art of persuasion or, especially in Roman rhetoric, simply speaking well (which entailed the verbal proof of good character).[91] Various topoi of the *exordium*, or introduction to a speech, were deployed persuasively and eloquently in order to excuse or justify a work: the speaker professed modesty, claiming inexperience or reluctance to bother his listeners; he stressed the importance or relevance of his topic; and he summarized his material, explaining its genesis.[92] Weber explains the end of prefacing as a distinct part of the novel in the eighteenth century, in his interpretation of prefatorial history, by reference to a widespread recognition that a preface constitutes mere empty rhetoric.[93] For Weber, the preface in this period departed from its rhetorical heritage as an exordium, inasmuch as the age-old prefatory topoi became redundant as the novel and its readership turned increasingly pluralistic, and the genre was newly theorized.[94] But significantly, Ehrenzeller—unlike Weber—suggests that the traditional function of the exordium in gaining the positive attention of an audience (called *captatio benevolentiae*) continued in the prefaces of Jean Paul, for example, albeit in a new form: although an explicit podium was discarded, and listeners became inaudible, the rhetorical framework still existed in a different set-up.[95] Indeed, Dirk Niefanger describes the transition from Baroque to Enlightenment examples of the preface as characterized by a newly "implicit" rhetorical efficacy.[96]

Current histories of rhetoric in the long eighteenth century have similarly posited not an abrupt end of rhetorical theory, but rather its cultural transformation.[97] The hold of classical rhetoric over poetics largely became indeterminate, though its principles—the notion of necessary natural talent or genius (*ingenium*), for instance—were indispensable to a theorized fashion for textual naturalness over affectation, even if this was in practice an artful, affected naturalness. This is an important point, for it is often assumed that genius banished rhetoric, and with it the preface, from its repertoire. As England's Shaftesbury remarks in *Advice to an Author* in 1710: "Other artists have substituted the practice of apology or extenuation. For the anticipating manner of prefatory discourse is too well known to work any surprising effect in the author's behalf, 'preface' being become only another word to signify excuse."[98] True originality meant a zero preface, and therefore no prefatory rhetoric. The most convincing metaphor for this discursive change is that rhetoric as an ancient theory, explicated in handbooks and passed down by pedagogical means, receded from view, went underground, and henceforth grew rhizomatically.[99] This paradigm shift toward a rhetorically grounded antirhetoric has been termed "rhetorica contra rhetoricam." To say that this idea applies not least to the writing of Goethe, Jean Paul, and Hegel is uncontroversial.[100] And so it is hardly a stretch to claim that it applies also to the rhetorical practice of their prefacing.

Resistance within rhetoric to rhetoric, with the type of rhetoric that was contested being conceived traditionally, and as the topoi required in prefaces, was not unique to German letters around 1800. Kevin Dunn claims that, for British literature, it "was at its most complex (if not its height) during the early modern period"—a heyday of the English preface, when the preface explored its own form.[101] But more interestingly, drawing on Aristotle's accusation that introductions are preferred by those whose case is weak (and to this end, Aristotle cites Euripides problematizing the preamble),[102] Dunn recognizes: "Classical rhetoric houses in its very presuppositions a decided prejudice against its own project."[103] Quintilian's *The Orator's Education* hints that many were flouting norms even in classical speeches. Presenting his pedagogical work as descriptive rather than prescriptive, he admits of the orator in training: "Nature herself will then guide him to the knowledge of what has to be said first." Yet Quintilian continues with a contradiction: "Nowadays, on the other hand, people think any sort of beginning a *Prooemium*, and anything that comes to mind, especially if some clever epigram [*sententia*] beckons, a proper *exordium*."[104] The latter, for Quintilian lamentable, fashion of ad hoc prefatorial reflection with passing quotation is precisely the kind of phenomenon that re-emerged in the long eighteenth century. To speak of remarkable prefatorial creativity around 1800, in sum, is not to suggest that this subject was the preserve of modernity or its print culture. But as printed texts, modern prefaces are different from ancient rhetorical ones; and for German literary writing, their prevalence and formal play is most distinct around 1800, as sketched above, in this introduction's first section.

The abbreviation of some German prefaces in the 1730s and 1740s already, which we have noted also in this introductory chapter, could be interpreted as a strategy to avoid derision on account of an author's miscalculated ambition or excessive commentary, which readers increasingly interpreted as a rhetorical, affected, and learned indulgence. Ironically, the modesty mid-eighteenth-century German writers professed as their excuse for not prefacing much is itself a rhetorical prescription for the preface. Rhetoric was overcome through rhetoric. Gellert begins the preface to the 1747 edition of his comedies by stating that he will not delay his readers' entry into the volume with a long preface, because he neither wants to praise nor admonish himself.[105] Hagedorn similarly wanted to keep his prose about himself to a minimum. In 1752, he responds to the fact that his *Moralische Gedichte* [Moral Poems] were better received than his accompanying notes—although he thought the notes of his preface ("Vorbericht") sufficient—asking: "Wie wird es mir aber gelingen, lange von mir selbst zu reden?"[106] [How shall I successfully speak about myself at length?]. The risk of vanity or the pursuit of fame was too great. Hagedorn addresses the need for a protracted defense by advancing this comment not in another preface, but in a fictive and seemingly personal *Schreiben an einen Freund* [Letter to a Friend] instead. Personal correspondence with a (fictive) friend takes the place of the discredited preface, and the presumption of frankness that of specious rhetoric. In his 1757, succinct preface to *Geistliche Oden und Lieder* [Spiritual Odes and Songs], meanwhile, Gellert appeals to evidence from a third party in absentia, in order to defend his character: his friends would attest to his dutiful improvement of his poetry, he asserts—yet he lists neither them nor their opinions.[107] The purported existence of witnesses also excuses Gellert's omission of explanatory notes, which would have tracked his changes in composition and extended his preface.

Gellert and Hagedorn were prepared to shorten their prefaces out of an apparent faith—however misplaced—that the burgeoning number of reviewers would secure a work's reception on their behalf. Gellert suggests in the preface to his comedies that in any case an author has little control with a preface over how his work is received; its fate is determined by the taste of the reading public, and especially its connoisseurs. Moreover, if the author is of clear conscience, as a *vir bonus*, "so kann er auf die Billigkeit der Critik hoffen"[108] [then he may hope for the courtesy of the critics]. This model of literary reception is predicated on a trust in readers and a concomitant confidence that the quality of a writer's own work is such that it will stand the test of time. Both assumptions, in Gellert's view, make a lengthy preface redundant, and save the author from the sin of self-love. And even if the author comes in for criticism—as Gellert did before he prefaced—it was now better to appear friendly than to win fame through skirmishing rhetorically, in so-called "Streitschriften."[109] Hagedorn shares essentially the same view of the preface as Gellert, although he is somewhat less confident of immediate popularity. He ultimately commits himself to the idealized, and supposedly impartial, judgment of posterity. This is a strategy the older Goethe will employ, too, over half a century later.

A shift in the preface's form from a place of persuasion, facilitated by learned, rhetorical skills, into a more popular and less conventional space became the butt of a prefatory joke in 1771, in Wieland's preface ("Vorbericht") to the first edition of *Der Neue Amadis* [The New Amadis]. Wieland asserts that whereas Hagedorn had to defend the inclusion of extensive technical, prefatory commentary on his own poems ("Anmerkungen"), he himself did not have to excuse his own explanatory, "protective" guidance (via a "Schutzrede"), because he anticipates that his mass readership—unlike Hagedorn's implicitly small, educated reading public—makes no pretense to either know anything about poetry or to remember whatever it had been told about literature's concepts before. Readers have the right "ohne Beschämung nicht vieles zu wissen"[110] [to not know much, without being ashamed], and his poems, unlike Hagedorn's, were not written "für die Gelehrten, die alles wissen"[111] [for the scholars who know everything]. His quip is in part disingenuous: annotations attest to the fact that Hagedorn thought his readers would not already know enough to understand his poems. But it is true that he also expected the readership to care about the context of poetic composition. Wieland closes by remarking that the brevity of his own prefatory notes would now give the critics ("Kunstrichter") a free hand to do their job. Thus Wieland's disassociation of his prefacing from Hagedorn's suggests that his rejection of the preface complements his rejection of a perceived *pedantry*. In this age, rhetoric was widely and pejoratively equated with pedantry and the received, static wisdom that was standard in formal, school education (usually reserved for men).[112] In late eighteenth-century German literature, therefore—the new age of textual autonomy—the preface was also understood in contrast to pedantic, scholarly as well as overtly (that is, negatively) rhetorical prose.

Rabener mocks pedantic preface writing in the satires of his ten-part series *Der Autor* [The Author] (August 1743–May 1744), which in its entirety is an exposition of a writer's subjectivity and self-projection through a preface. In the ninth satire, Rabener's authorial persona defends himself against the accusation that as a writer he too precisely and insistently, pedantically refers to his own character;[113] and by the time this figure does offer a preface—at the end of the final, tenth part—he jokingly complains that the editors of *Belustigungen des Verstandes und Witzes* [Amusements of Reason and Wit], in which the series appeared, had cut his preface short, so that his scholarly skirmishing was censored. Evidently, the editors had no idea of "was zu einer Vorrede gehöret"[114] [what belongs in a preface]. Even when a new type of preface emerged in place of rhetorical-style pedantry, though, the charge was leveled that it was no different from its pedantic predecessor. In his preface to *Schöne Spielwerke* [Beautiful Musical Movements] (1763), Johann Matthias Dreyer complains that both old and new prefatory fashions are the same. Writers used to labor the point that they did not publish out of self-interest; later authors, by comparison, gallantly declared that they wrote in order to become famous or earn money: "diese neue Gewohnheit ist unstreitig eben so pedantisch und unangenehm, als die alte, weil sie eben so affectirt ist"[115] [this new convention is indisputably as pedantic and disagreeable as the old one, because it is just as affected]. The preface was therefore often set up in opposition to pedantry, as a sort of "straw man" argument. Literary (and as we shall see, Hegel's) authorship was helped in this regard by recourse to a tradition of scholarly satire. Cervantes' preface to *Don Quixote* at the beginning of the seventeenth century expresses a wish for a zero preface and is pitted against the pedantic Latin eloquence of prefacing, in a Golden Age of vernacular literature and, in fact, a Spanish heyday of preface discourse.[116] Cervantes influenced the German literary preface at its own point of crisis and creativity, as did Sterne's *The Life and Opinions of Tristram Shandy, Gentleman* (1759–1767): in "The Author's Preface," Tristram exclaims, "I hate set dissertations."[117]

In 1795, the German book dealer and publisher Johann Georg Heinzmann wrote a tirade against contemporary "Gelehrsamkeit und Schriftsteller" [scholarship and writers], as part of his *Appell an meine Nation: Über die Pest der deutschen Literatur* [Appeal to My Nation: Concerning the

Pestilence of German Literature]. Heinzmann reminisces about bygone books and prefaces, particularly their description of the author's character:

> Wie wohl thut es dem Mann von gutem Herzen wenn er einen Schriftsteller aus dem Anfang dieses Jahrhunderts ließt, und die größte Genauigkeit und Gewissenhaftigkeit findet; ja sogar seine Familien-Bekanntschaft aus seinem Buche machen kann, weil sie immer auch von ihren Verhältnissen als Mensch—in den Vorreden sprachen.[118]
>
> [How much good it does the man with a good heart to read an author from the beginning of this century! And to find in him such great precision and conscientiousness. Indeed, from the book he can even become acquainted with the author as if he were a family friend, because these past authors also always talked about their lives, as people—in the prefaces.]

Heinzmann's nostalgia is of a sort that is satirized in Theodor Gottlieb von Hippel's earlier novel *Lebensläufe in aufsteigender Linie* [Biographies in an Ascending Line] (1778–1781). Here the pastor, as the bastion of individual propriety, and the protagonist's father, as a representative of the older generation, consider the preface essential to the publication of a book. To behave in a socially acceptable way, the author must provide a preface because that is the space in which the writer makes a plea, displays gratitude, and prays: he shows his moral credentials, social standing, and faith as a rhetorical *vir bonus*.[119] Intriguingly, however, Heinzmann proceeds to accuse authors of the late, not early eighteenth century of being pedantic. He defines the pedant as a man "dem die Wahrheit fern ist"[120] [who is far from truth]: a person who loses himself away in a sea of theory (especially if awash with Kant) and who has no regard for the practical world on land that is immediately visible to him. No writer proclaimed pedantry for himself. Thus the reconceived literary prefaces from the mid to late eighteenth century onward can be defined in their intentions (however they were received) negatively: as unpedantic notes.

It is hardly surprising that the ridiculed or lamentable pedant was represented as a preface-writing figure, since writers reinvented themselves not only in relation to print, but more obviously also in it. The mid to late eighteenth century was a transition period for authorship, in which authors distanced themselves from a learned tradition that was still in evidence around them. The emergence of the modern writer toward 1800 was facilitated not only by the role of editorship and, as Wirth theorizes, the fiction of the editor ("Herausgeberfiktion"); it was aided, too, by the earlier rise of the scholar.[121] We see this in the published prefaces to the first and second editions of Schiller's *Die Räuber* [The Robbers], for example. The first preface of 1781 was signed by the editor ("Der Herausgeber"), with the obvious implication that the editorial persona was the author himself; the preface to the second edition the following year appeared under the author's actual name, but also with Schiller's doctorate acknowledged through an academic prefix: D. Schiller.[122] An author and his name emerge from a preface, and the preface writer of the not so distant past had been editorial and explicitly scholarly, "pedantic" even.

The literary and philosophical ideal of scholarship had been eroded by the rise in literary scholarly satire (such as Rabener's or Riedel's). And satire's attack on such "pedantry" in the Enlightenment should be understood, according to Alexander Košenina, in complementary relation to the establishment of classical and biblical philology as a university discipline in German lands around 1800. (Note that the German word *Philologie* includes literary scholarship, whereas the English term has usually—but not always—been restricted to historical linguistics.) For with the jokes came, in all seriousness, a new model of textual interpretation. Košenina points out that many of those who satirized pedantry were themselves trained in philology and went on to promote the careful understanding of creative texts, even hermeneutic modes of literary interpretation.[123] These men were exemplary of neither a Baroque *polyhistor* nor a pedant, but rather a *virtuoso* or *gentleman scholar*. The emergence of a professional philologist was aided, for Košenina, by the ability of those in and around the academy to also see the funny side of the academic enterprise. Although it does not follow that the more serious model of inquiry depends on satirical self-criticism in order to counterbalance its pedantic potential—Košenina claims the latter quality is an essential competence of philology—it is helpful to consider a discourse against pedantry alongside an emergent institutional discipline of closer textual comprehension. For as much as literary prefaces of this period were conceived contra scholarly prefaces, and as non- or implicitly rhetorical, they nevertheless sought to engage not only appreciative, but also more attentive readers. Rhetoric was rehabilitated in a medium that was now about written, textual exegesis. Reflecting on the characterization of his protagonist Fiesko in a retrospective *Erinnerung an das Publikum* [Notice to the Audience] about *Die Verschwörung des Fiesko von Genua* [Fiesco's Conspiracy at Genoa] (1783), Schiller contended that he had written "für den ruhigen Leser"[124] [for the quiet reader], wanting to write differently than "für den hingerissenen Hörer, der augenblicklich genießen muß"[125] [for the rapturous listener, who must enjoy for the moment]. These desired, deliberative readers should be attuned to the complexity of authors' works as unified entities. Such a readership was not only active in the universities, but schooled by popular philosophy that equally emphasized the unity of a book or oeuvre.

The idea of a hermeneutic circle was formulated around 1800, and is most frequently cited as a philological concept coined in 1808 by Friedrich Ast.[126] Contemporaneously, the preface became both an invitation and a challenge to receive a literary or philosophical writer's work as a whole as well as on its own terms, set out in the preface as a part of that unity. It should also exceed the binding of the book, elevating the reader and the book's ideas into a transcendental or spiritual realm. Novalis proposed a solution that at first sight might seem simple, but which belies much formal intricacy: "Der Gebrauch des Buches—die Phil[osophie] seiner Lektüre wird in der Vorrede gegeben"[127] [The use of the book—the philosophy of how to read it is given in the preface]. The preface is a theoretical part of a work—a potential it has always had—but in Romanticism, philosophy is also poetry. Novalis recognizes that paratextual elements of a book can have distinct functions: "Was soll eine *Vorrede*, ein *Titel*, ein *Motto*, ein *Plan*—eine *Einleitung*—eine *Note*, ein *Text*, eine *Beylage* (Kupfertafeln etc.), ein *Register* seyn—und wie werden diese eingetheilt und Classificirt"[128] [What should a *preface*, a *title*, an *epigram*, a *plan*—an *introduction*—a *note*, a *text*, *supplementary material* (copper plates, etc.), an *index* be—and how will these be subdivided and classified]. Although he then expands upon each of these text types, he does not actually distinguish between a preface ("Vorrede") and an introduction ("Einleitung"). The preface (and also perhaps the introduction) in his view must artistically encompass the work in its entirety—paradoxically, despite its distinctiveness. Its ideal is described, in a transdisciplinary move, not by reference to philosophy or even poetry, but to a musical genre. A preface should be "eine poëtische Ouvertüre"[129] [a poetic overture].

The formal impetus for such extreme creativity and an intellectual spirit in prefacing around 1800, then, is a conceptual one that concerned a rupture in textual interpretative method more generally. Rhetorical theory transformed, and opposition to pedantry gained momentum: fueled by authors' desires to be read more comprehensively and closely than for a prescribed effect—in traditional rhetorical terms, not simply for moral instruction (*docere*), to be moved (*movere*), or for light entertainment (*delectare*). Because in the eighteenth century, texts by the most intellectually ambitious, Romantic writers—literary or philosophical—became autonomous, as we have acknowledged.

WRITING TO WRITE

We have so far encountered the terms Enlightenment and Romanticism as rather elastic concepts. Romanticism is a countercultural or avant-garde mode, and yet it is also historicizable. Romanticism reflected upon itself (although German authors did not use a common term in their self-referential program); it was a self-reflection enabled by the Enlightenment. Clifford Siskin and William Warner have argued programmatically that the Enlightenment "was an event in the history of mediation."[130] A pan-European historical phenomenon occurring for "roughly a half century between the 1730s–1740s and the 1780s," it was a time of immense textual proliferation. Consequently, eighteenth-century print culture, as Siskin and Warner conceive it, became saturated; the material production of the Enlightenment "contained the formal conditions for its own demise."[131] In turn, European Romanticism built its discourse on the intellectual productivity of the Enlightenment: "The relationship of the Romantic period to Enlightenment is that of an eventuality to an event: Romanticism took shape as a contingent possibility, a coming to terms with what had just happened in the terms that event had platformed—had turned into a platform."[132] Further, Jochen Hörisch suggests for the German scene that the overproduction of literary as well as philosophical discourses from the Enlightenment into Romanticism caused three discursive reactions, which we typically equate with the time around 1800: hermeneutics, theories of self-consciousness, and philosophical systems that emphasized the paradoxes of knowledge—which were promoted, above all, by Hegel.[133] And so with regard to the preface, the proliferation of self-authored prefacing from the mid-eighteenth century, that is, the "Enlightenment," resulted in remarkable prefatorial, paradoxical, and self-reflexive play, which became ever more exaggerated and—crucially, in its third, "incorporated" historical phase described above—more complex from the 1790s onward in German letters (if also a couple of decades earlier with respect to Goethe's *Werther* of the Storm and Stress movement). In other words, the German preface became most intricate and creative at the high point of European Romanticism, of which the Storm and Stress of German literature was precipitative. With writers such as Goethe, Jean Paul, and

Hegel, Romanticism affirmed as much as it undermined the Enlightenment with new, idiosyncratic, inductive ideas of "objectivity" that were also skeptical, ambiguous, and performative—and in these respects, Romantic. Prefaces were part and parcel both of a new "politics" of (proto)philological reading, as we witness especially in the next chapter; and they were themselves part of philosophical method, as described below. This was not only because of a shift in persuasion, learning, and interpretation, as we have seen in the last section (or an idealized autonomy that affected a work's reception and production, as outlined in the section before that), but also due to the significant increase in *writing* itself. To put it differently, the radical Romantic preface in German writing was a media effect, an ironization of typical Enlightenment practice, and a cryptically inductive answer to the Enlightenment's textual overload that sought to "teach" thinking too obviously.

An emphasis on media and on textual mediation—the proliferation of not only ideas, but also writing that constituted the Enlightenment—necessitates a focus on form in the following chapters. Ehrenzeller astutely observes that, notwithstanding the preface's rhetorical schemata since the beginning of print, the "Vorrede," or preface, was never read aloud as a speech, as a "Vor-*rede*"[134] [pre-*speech*] might suggest; for him it is no coincidence that its first attestation in Grimm's dictionary comes from a time in which a work was beginning to be read more than it was heard. Genette turns back to the example of Isocrates's *Antidosis*, which has a foreword to the exordium, "a foreword the speaker undoubtedly was not meant to include in his public reading of the speech: here we see a difference in register that anticipates our thresholds of written presentation."[135] The norm for the social consumption of (particularly artistic) literature in classical antiquity was reading aloud, but we should note that silent reading was a scholarly default. Unlike in Romanticism, however, writing at that time did not reflect on being read. A. K. Gavrilov writes: "There would be no interest or dramatic value in the representation of someone perusing a long text for hours on end."[136] It is by having read the literary books of Romanticism that represent writing and its reception that we have become the types of general, critical, and scholarly readers we still are today. As Andrew Piper puts it for what Friedrich Schlegel called the "Zeitalter der Bücher"[137] [age of books] and criticism has since termed the European Romantic reading revolution, "one of the fundamental ways through which western cultures became bibliographic cultures was through reading literature"—and this paradigm shift occurred around 1800.[138] The preface from this era is a text that must be studied not only historically, intellectually (theoretically), and rhetorically but, as such, also as a textual *form* that reflects on all others from a point of remove, yet engenders them from an immersed perspective and through formal play.

Contemporary authors around 1800 and subsequent scholars have already proposed a type of media argument for changes in prefacing: chiefly that the preface changed so much at the close of the eighteenth century because its typical content was displaced into the periodical press, which was rising in popularity, or book reviews (as Gellert presumed), which were more widely circulated.[139] Edwin Zellweker suggests that the German prologue (and epilogue) became redundant in the late eighteenth century because of newspapers, pamphlets, and the program in the theater ("Theaterzettel").[140] Further, a speech given only on the occasion of the opening or closing of a theater or season ("Theaterrede") tended to supersede the need for individual plays to be contextualized within the institution or series in which they were being performed.[141] Goethe wrote many such opening prologues, not to plays but to venues—take, for example, the "Vorspiel" that inaugurated the new theater in Lauchstädt in 1802, entitled *Was wir bringen* [What We Bring].[142] New occasions and types of text therefore altered the form and function of the preface in general, just as the material conditions and authorial expectations of writing around 1800 affected the genesis of individual prefaces.

The present book claims instead that in European Romanticism the preface became perhaps more seldom and certainly less identifiable as such (since it was, after all, incorporated into the work), yet it presented itself—above all in German examples—as all the more significant poetologically and philosophically. The form was not only the *manifestation* of the literary imagination or conceptual thought concerning a work. It could also be said to *manufacture* such reflections through prefacing. An effect of the Enlightenment's textual overload was a Romantic sense that knowledge was mediated through, and created in, writing itself. In other words, Romanticism recognized that the act of writing encourages reflection on writing; and so the more we write, the likelier we are to write about writing, and to do so more reflectively. This observation in itself is far from new in scholarship, even with respect to prefacing, though until now it has been thought about in a more straightforward way. Ehrenzeller observes that—because of the suspect status of the preface—authors of the period "fühlen sich deshalb verpflichtet, die Vorrede, die ihr Werk entschuldigen mußte, selbst noch einmal zu entschuldigen. Diese Entschuldigung in der Entschuldigung, die sich gewöhnlich am Anfang oder Schluß einer Vorrede befindet, gibt gelegentlich Anlaß zu weiteren Reflexionen über Nutzen und Nachteil einer Form"[143] [feel obliged to excuse their preface, which is yet another excuse since the preface had to excuse their work. This textual excuse in an excusatory text, which is usually found at the beginning or the end of a preface, gives ample occasion for further reflections on the use and disadvantage of a form]. The preface thereby becomes an instantiation of writing not only with respect to the book it prefaces, but also to the preface itself. Reflective prefacing can lead to self-reflexive prefacing—prefaces about prefaces.

Literary writers around 1800 were aware of what we could call the "preface proliferation" effect, which we associated with the second and third stages of the German preface's historical development in the eighteenth century. Schiller wrote two prefaces to the first edition of *Die Räuber*, suppressing the initial draft before print and replacing it with the second. The original preface blatantly disregards the probable opinions of the author's public, and ends by truncating the preliminary text—conventionally for the Storm and Stress movement. However, Schiller did so because he implies that his preface, if conceived as an apology for the brevity of his play, otherwise could not have been exhausted, but would have gone on forever.[144] Indeed, Jean Paul later proves that a preface can soon spiral out of control.

The potential for a preface that continues to comment on and generate itself in a lively and intricate fashion was, by the 1790s and the early decades of the nineteenth century, manifest across German literary genres, whereas over fifty years earlier, witty self-referentiality and self-extension had been restricted to satirical prose fiction. It should be emphasized that such satire had mocked the philosophical as well as the literary preface. Riedel begins the preface to the first volume of his *Sämmtliche Schriften* [Collected Writings] (1787) with the opposite quip to Jean Paul's, which began this introduction. Some people progress no further than the foreword: "Da es Leute giebt, die, um gelehrt zu scheinen, viele Bücher kaufen und ihre Wände damit bekleiden, ohne, wenn es hoch kommt, etwas anders zu lesen, als Titel und Vorreden: so sind das zwei Hauptstücke der Autorsorge"[145] [For there are people who, in order to appear learned, buy many books and adorn their walls with them, without reading much more than their titles and prefaces at best. Hence these are the two main concerns of authors]. Riedel promptly goes in search of an adequate definition for prefacing. He first refers to metaphysics and then progresses through an extensive, empirical examination of as many prefaces as possible, "um aus der Vergleichung derselben durch den Abstraktionsweg den wahren Begriff einer Vorrede zu erfinden"[146] [in order to discover through comparison and via a path of abstraction the true concept of a preface]. He concludes that this text type is tantamount to self-satire, contrary to the author's knowledge or desire. Riedel's reflection on prefacing is amusing, and the joke associates preface writing with philosophical method in the vein of typical Enlightenment scholarly satire. But by the close of the eighteenth century, and more specifically with the invention of Hegel's system in the early nineteenth, the philosophical preface had begun to reflect on prefacing.

Although Hegel was a systematic rationalist, his form of expression was unusually sensitive to the written medium, and to literature in particular. In fact, he had written poems as a youth. To be sure, Jakob Fries ends his preface to *System der Philosophie als evidente Wissenschaft* [System of Philosophy as Evidential Science] (1804) with the claim that the same talent makes an artist as that which constitutes a philosopher, naming Klopstock and citing verse from Goethe's *Faust*; but the prose of Fries's preface is actually matter-of-fact, and the text is otherwise formally uncreative.[147] Hegel turned the preface into his own philosophical and textual program. Considering the time around 1800 to be finally ripe for a philosophically rigorous and thoroughgoing exploration of self-consciousness, Hegel gave his textual work that first advanced the idea of "Selbstbewußtsein"—*Phänomenologie des Geistes*—a self-reflexive turn from its preface onward, a strategy that was typical of his literary contemporaries. For Hegel, thinking about and through texts was not an aesthetic act, nor only a physical logic of the page. It was also an abstract one of the mind.

Taking the long—and literary—view, Hegel's preface that problematizes prefacing is an unsurprising development. Alongside contemporary philosophers, though, Hegel's concern is unusual. While we can trace the story of its emergence, there is no threefold tale as there is for the history of the German literary preface in the eighteenth century. Hegel appears rather suddenly, but his prefacing strategy nevertheless has its philosophical precedents. Kant's *Kritik der reinen Vernunft* [Critique of Pure Reason] was originally published in 1781, with a preface. In 1783, Kant then published *Prolegomena zu einer jeden künftigen Metaphysik, die als Wissenschaft wird auftreten können* [Prolegomena to Any Future Metaphysics that Will Be Able to Present Itself as Science] in order to summarize the First Critique's principles and the legitimacy of positing them, which he additionally applies to metaphysics more generally. And so he describes his 1783 introduction as being sent in advance of future work, clarifying the conditions that would make science reality. Kant therein reflects on the form of a prolegomenon itself, stating that it comprises "Vorübungen"[148] [preliminary exercises] for critical philosophy; and its method—in contrast to that of a main, synthetically reasoned work—is analytic (whereby predicate concepts of propositions are contained in the subject concepts). A prolegomenon, then, can analytically present what is already there, or Kant's existing critical conclusions. It cannot fundamentally create new insight into philosophy itself. But it can reveal or preview, and summarize, existing knowledge so that the preconditions are fulfilled in order for philosophical insight to become reality for the reader.[149] Further, Kant's revised edition of his First Critique in 1787 was again prefaced with analytic judgments, and he rewrote its introduction in order to differentiate between empirical beginnings (expressed through the verb "anheben") and transcendental origins (with the verb "entspringen").[150] His prefaces thereby become an explanatory, auxiliary epiphenomenon, not a primary or even parallel, originating one in its own right that would begin by discussing and devising its own discourse. Kant's prefaces advance practical, not philosophical points—albeit about the practice of philosophy. It was a metaphilosophy that would be contested, not least formally.

The philosopher who truly paved the way for Hegel, and with whom Hegel actually skirmished the most, was Fichte. In setting up a presentation of his *Wissenschaftslehre* [Science of Knowledge] in 1801, Fichte sought to preclude interruption that would demand he further prefaces (or introduces) his introduction, although he does not reflect explicitly on the form of introducing itself.[151] In effect, however, Fichte continued to revise his introductions and publish more prefaces. (Prefaces and introductions are here essentially the same, conflated in Kant's term *prolegomenon*.) For Fichte, introducing appears to have been only an abstract, not also a textual problem, though this preoccupation with how to begin with absolute knowledge had a formal effect, of course. The post-Kantian preface was thus becoming less epistemological (a question of what we can know, or justifiably write about in a philosophical work), and more ontological: what is a preface's place in the material, textual world, and in relation to a philosophical system? Ontology came to the fore after Fichte had placed the subject at the center of philosophy, and also following the renaissance of Spinoza in the late Enlightenment and resultant philosophical monism. It was left to Hegel to make the implicit philosophical problem of the preface explicit.

Philosophically and textually, Hegel's preface was bound to become hypertrophic. Philosophy was now as autonomous as literature was. With the onset of modern German philosophy, philosophical discourse had no grounds outside of philosophy, and became grounded only within discourse itself[152]—unless it were to ultimately defer to the rules of religion or, less dogmatically, would turn into a theological form of free thinking ("Nichtphilosophie," or "Non-Philosophy," in Carl Eschenmayer's terminology).[153] An autonomous and self-reflexive intellectual work requires a demonstration of its own argument, if its precepts are not derivative. Romantic prefaces must introduce inductive reading, then, and govern it in and on their own terms. This formal principle was theoretical and practical, inasmuch as it arose from the practice of writing itself, as well as from the thoughts that led to a writer putting pen to paper. Unlike the Early German Romantics, Hegel, Jean Paul, and Goethe—also as Romantic authors—sought to establish their own notions of "objectivity" in prefacing, as a preventative cure for the potentially infinite amount of prefatory fragments that Fichte, the Schlegel brothers, Novalis, and others could introduce, which Hegel, Jean Paul, and Goethe understood as unbridled, self-consuming thought. Throughout this book, we shall explore these three writers' prefaces, their adversaries, and some of the thinkers they have inspired to make a problem out of prefacing.

Each of the subsequent three chapters reads German Romantic prefaces historically, theoretically (but on their own terms), rhetorically, and formally. This introduction has begun with each of these methods, and sought to combine them. Above all, prefaces that ask to be pondered, not perused are revealed to be paradoxical. Taken together, Goethe, Jean Paul, and Hegel exemplify the following three "Romantic" preface paradoxes, or traces of the form's resistance to its tradition or very existence. These ironies are also broadly true of the (post)modern, post-Structuralist text type that encompasses various terms such as introduction, preamble, foreword, and so on. Preliminarily, this trio of preface paradoxes is abstracted and tabled below, but it becomes concrete over the course of the three canonical case studies. And as we shall learn, a "table" is a very unprefatory metaphor if a preface is to be understood as autonomously literary or philosophical. Since the present work is one of commonsense close readings that are inspired by German Romanticism, however, rather than a work of fiction or philosophy proper, the three preface paradoxes proposed are summarized for simplicity's sake here:

(1) Prefaces initiate works by being both immanent and procrastinatory, determined by and deferring the main texts. Thus we can ask: are prefaces (im)pertinent? A foreword could go on forever, as much as it might be omitted.

(2) An author's own preface is predicated on an act of address to a person external to the work's poetics or thought—but the desired addressee, whether a peculiar or popular readership, is imagined by the writer, and so is integral to his conceptual or creative work. To preface is therefore autopoetic and even, in its exaggerated form, autoerotic.

(3) Prefacing always retains its textual-rhetorical functions, regardless of whether it attempts to flout them by problematizing prefacing, philosophically or fictionally. Even at its most creative and intellectual, prefacing remains a pragmatic act. Such pragmatism, in turn, may become paradoxical: ingratiating by not ingratiating—or less paradoxically, by a willingness to forgo the easy applause of the many in favor of the approval of the few.

CHAPTER ONE

Goethe

A Playful and Resistive Set of Preface Strategies

THE PREFACE WAS once conventional, became controversial, and was especially intricate by around 1800. Turning to Goethe's case, we might think that he consistently circumnavigated the form. For "zero prefaces" appear to recur over the course of his literary career, regardless of any publisher with whom he collaborated. Early examples include his twelve poems under the title *Annette* in a one-off, calligraphical copy by Ernst Behrisch (1767); his *Neue Lieder* [New Songs] collection for a musical score by Johann Breitkopf (1769); and the play printed at his own expense, *Götz von Berlichingen mit der eisernen Hand* [Götz von Berlichingen with the Iron Hand] (1773). All abstain from much front matter: there are merely title pages and, in the last instance, a character list. Moreover, many of Goethe's later literary writings are apparently unprefaced—including his most significant. *Wilhelm Meisters Lehrjahre* [Wilehlm Meister's Apprenticeship] (1795–1796), first published by Johann Friedrich Unger, was fundamental to what became, or was already the founding model for, the German Romantic novel (depending on how we define Romanticism). Yet whereas Friedrich Schlegel's *Lucinde* (1799) has a prologue and Brentano's *Godwi* (1800–1801) begins the narrative proper after a dedication, an untitled preliminary text, and a preface (to name just two paradigmatically Romantic novels), Goethe's masterpiece seemingly needs no introduction. Nor is the final version of *Wilhelm Meisters Wanderjahre* [Wilhelm Meister's Journeyman Years] (1829), this time brought out by Johann Friedrich Cotta, set up by any sort of preamble at all. But if it seems counterintuitive to say that Goethe was especially concerned about prefacing, on closer inspection his creative—and critical—work best exemplifies a *pluralism* in preface writing in the third, incorporated stage of the form's German development toward the end of the eighteenth and at the beginning of the nineteenth centuries (for an historical sketch, see the introduction). Absence of an explicit strategy can of course be an implicit one, concealed by Goethe and revealed only by comparison with his other means of prefacing. As he put it poetically in a prologue ("Prolog"), read aloud in Weimar on May 7, 1791: "Der Anfang ist an allen Sachen schwer; / Bei vielen Werken fällt er nicht ins Auge" (FA, 1.6: 875) [The beginning is difficult in all matters / In many works it does not catch the eye]. And so the following chapter categorizes Goethe's six principles of preface writing, which often overlap; and they arise out of stages of Goethe's career as much as they cut across them. For the Romantic preface—in the broadest, European terms—is, as we have already seen, peculiarly difficult to pin down in a formal, fixed description.

ZERO PREFACES

Goethe's genuinely zero prefaces seem to form a systematic strategy for his drama of the 1770s through to the early 1790s, in *Götz* (1773), *Clavigo* (1774), *Claudine von Villa Bella* (1776), *Die Geschwister* [Brother and Sister] (1776, published 1787), *Prosperina* (1778), *Iphigenie auf Tauris* [Iphigenie in Tauris] (1787), *Egmont* (1788), and *Torquato Tasso* (1790), among others. These works list the dramatis personae and, at times, briefly describe an opening scene. Changes to their front matter tended to clarify a drama's title. The first, 1771 draft of *Götz von Berlichingen mit der eisernen Hand* was entitled *Geschichte Gottfriedens von Berlichingen mit der eisernen Hand dramatisiert* [The Dramatized History of Gottfried of Berlichingen with the Iron Hand], and this previous version was prefaced by a motto from Albrecht von Haller's novel *Usong. Eine Morgenländische Geschichte* [Usong: An Oriental History] of the same year—lines which emphasized the ambiguity between writing empirical history and narrating a fictional story (FA, 1.4: 125). The motto was replaced by the simple subtitle *Ein Schauspiel* [A Play] in Goethe's second draft, and the main title was shortened (that it is a dramatized narrative, for example, was deleted). As Ulrike Landfester notes, this paratextual alteration placed a revised emphasis on Götz as a maverick individual over a tale told, as fiction, out of historical interest.[1] Her point notwithstanding, classifying a work's genre more clearly was typical of Goethe's method for setting out his early plays, even when they were revised much later. The original subtitle to *Stella. Ein Schauspiel für Liebende* [Stella: A Play for Lovers] (1776), for instance, became *Ein Trauerspiel* [A Tragedy] in 1816.

Thus the only justification Goethe perceived as necessary for his juvenile dramas was their categorization: the controversial *Der Triumph der Empfindsamkeit* [The Triumph of Sensibility] (1778) was subtitled *Eine dramatische Grille* [A Dramatic Satire]; *Götter, Helden und Wieland* [Gods, Heroes, and Wieland] (1774) was labeled *Eine Farce* [A Farce]. All were otherwise unprefaced.

Although this technique was consistent throughout Goethe's earlier plays, it was not exclusive to them. His 1809 poem "Johanna Sebus" is preceded by a note comprising just one sentence in prose: the poetic subject was not a remarkable historical or contemporary character, but rather, as Goethe writes, an ordinary seventeen-year-old girl who had drowned that January (FA, 1.2: 271). This brief prefatorial context for Goethe's creativity is, interpreted next to *Götz* or *Egmont* (both of which are based on historical personalities), merely an extension and explication of the title—which is, typically for Goethe, a proper name. His verse epic *Hermann und Dorothea* [Hermann and Dorothea] is not subtitled as such, perhaps because to do so would have conflicted with the work's primary label from print culture: the poem was brought out in 1797 as an annual magazine, a modus that signals its intended popular readership (*Taschenbuch für 1798. Hermann und Dorothea von J. W. von Goethe*). What is more, the two proper names—Hermann and Dorothea—stand equally alongside one another, irrespective of social class or other categorizations, reflecting the poem's own argument. However, the first canto is suggestively called after Calliope, the Greek muse of epic poetry, and is of an introductory (if not a prefatory) nature: "Kalliope. Schicksal und Anteil" (FA, 1.8: 807) [Calliope: Fate and Sympathy]. Furthermore, a prose text was published in 1828 without any prefatory content whatsoever, but its genre can be inferred immediately from its title: *Novelle*. The reason for this generic title lay in its recent history as a genre in German letters, and in Goethe's attempt to become paradigmatic for the short-story form—it was not, as he wrote to Wilhelm Reichel, to be prefixed with the indefinite article, "eine" (FA, 1.8: 1063). Within Wieland's earlier frame narrative *Das Hexameron von Rosenhain* [The Hexameron of Rosenhain] (1805), a short fiction is introduced (in what we could call an "embedded," untitled preface) with the claim: "daß meine Novelle sich von allen andern, soviel ich weiß, dadurch unterscheidet, daß sie keinen Titel hat"[2] [to the best of my knowledge my novella distinguishes itself from all others in having no title]. This novella is apparently "das erste in seiner Art" [the first of its type], so is entitled "Die Novelle ohne Titel" [The Novel without a Title], although to title a work as one without a title actually had an eighteenth-century precedent.[3] Goethe shortened his own title all the more, surely staking his claim for his text being the very definition the form. And in general, Goethe embraced genre- and character-based classification, often at the expense of prefacing.

Alongside his preference for concise and classificatory titles and an absence of prefaces, though, the author also wrote prefaces—including prefatorial commentary that historicized his preferred alternative: abstention from the form. But he does not acknowledge the predominant genre specificity of his genuinely zero prefacing. Since Goethe offers no hint, we can only conjecture on why he opted not to preface most of his youthful theatrical works in particular. One probable explanation is that unprefaced drama was common among other young, brash authors of the Storm and Stress movement. Jakob Michael Reinhold Lenz is a good contemporary example, whose plays *Der Hofmeister oder Vorteile der Privaterziehung. Eine Komödie* [The Tutor, or the Advantages of Private Education: A Comedy] (1774), *Der neue Menoza oder Geschichte des cumbanischen Prinzen Tandi. Eine Komödie* [The New Menoza, or The History of Prince Tandi of Cumba: A Comedy] (1774), *Die Soldaten. Ein Schauspiel* [The Soldiers: A Play] (1776), *Die Freunde machen den Philosophen. Eine Komödie* [Friends Make a Philosopher: A Comedy] (1776), and *Die Engländer. Eine dramatische Phantasey* [The English: A Dramatic Fantasy] (1777) all appeared with categorical subtitles and without prefaces. Johann Anton Leisewitz and Friedrich Maximilian Klinger, too, often opted for zero prefaces. Wieland had published his early plays unprefaced and suitably categorized, such as *Lady Johanna Gray, oder der Triumph der Religion. Ein Trauerspiel* [Lady Johanna Gray, or The Triumph of Religion: A Tragedy] (1758) or *Clementina von Porretta. Ein Drama aus Richardsons Geschichte Sir Karl Grandisons gezogen* [Clementina of Porretta: A Drama Derived from Richardson's *History of Sir Charles Grandison*] (1760). But contemporary to the Storm and Stress, his dramas *Rosamunde. Ein Singspiel in drei Aufzuegen* [Rosamund: A Musical Piece in Three Parts] (1779) and *Pandora. Ein Lustspiel mit Gesang in zwei Aufzügen* [Pandora: A Comedy with Music in Two Parts] (1779) both have a preface ("Vorbericht")—and the former also includes a "Nachtrag zur Geschichte der schönen Rosamunde" [Afterword on the History of the Beautiful Rosamund]. This was more than coincidence, for Wieland sought to distance himself from a younger, brazen generation of playwrights and their tendency not to preface. Indeed, when the Storm and Stress of German literature was at its height, Wieland satirized the zero preface of this younger generation by, paradoxically, writing one: he prefaces

Geschichte des Philosophen Danischmende [The History of the Philosopher Danischmende], published as a series in the *Der Teutsche Merkur* [The Germany Mercury] in 1775, with a short text called *Keine Vorrede* [No Preface]. He exclaims: "Nein, bei allem was gut ist, ich werde *keine Vorrede* dazu machen, es erfolge auch daraus was will!"[4] [No, by all that is good, I shall not write *any preface*, come of it what may!]. But for those who seriously dropped the practice of preface writing, the daring strategy often had to be a total, all-or-nothing one to succeed. Brief or partial prefaces could be flawed: as Wieland's nonpreface as preface jokes, for the reader who comprehends, even the shortest preface is too long; for the reader who does not understand the work, a preface three times the length will not help.[5]

However, it is not accurate to say that all authors of the Storm and Stress movement avoided the preface: Heinrich Wilhelm von Gerstenberg composed one (a "Vorbericht") for *Ugolino* (1768), though it comprised only three lines citing the source of, and briefly setting the scene for, the drama.[6] Heinrich Leopold Wagner placed a one-paragraph description of Voltaire's costume before *Voltaire am Abend vor seiner Apotheose* [Voltaire on the Eve of His Apotheosis] in 1778, referring the leading actor to specific, published images of the protagonist for sartorial guidance.[7] Schiller, too, prefaced *Die Räuber* [The Robbers] (1781). Thus prefacing, although popularly abridged even to the form's absence, to some extent remained a personal, authorial choice even within the avant-garde. But it was undoubtedly an unpopular one.

Above all else, Goethe sought unity in art. His later, what are termed here "embedded" prose prefaces are seamlessly written into their works. His major dramatic project in maturity has multiple prologues that mirror its form: both the preliminary and the main parts to *Faust* are in verse. If prefacing in his youth seemed superfluous, then once he decided to preface—in prose, poetry, and criticism—Goethe formally conjoined his front matter with the subsequent texts. A prose preface to dramatic dialogue, by contrast, would surely jar with the form of what is to come. But it can contradict the form to a lesser extent than we might think: August Wilhelm Iffland wrote the middle section of his short preface ("Vorbericht") to *Figaro in Deutschland* (1790) as a pair of questions in quotation marks with authorial answers pertaining to the composition of the work.[8] This preface is thereby a scene enacted between the writer and an imagined reader. Goethe's zero prefaces to plays are comparatively uncreative.

One type of preface that Goethe composed from early on, and consistently throughout his career, tells of the genesis and intention of a work in retrospect; and he provided such "belated" prefaces for criticism as well as for his scientific treatises. At the end of 1772, a *Nachrede statt der versprochenen Vorrede* [Afterword in Place of the Promised Preface] appeared in the *Frankfurter Gelehrte Anzeigen* [Frankfurt Scholarly Notices], written by Goethe on behalf of Johann Heinrich Merck, Johann Georg Schlosser, and himself as they resigned as editors and reviewers from the publication. The title of the afterword is already a concession that the writers would justify their project with a sort of preface after all, albeit now after the original publication. But the text defies the expectation of that title, for it is playfully contrite about the offence these personalities caused. Goethe and his co-editors repeatedly lament that, as reviewers, they were misunderstood, but they do little to correct the public's error of judgment other than offer the afterword as a short, rhetorical exercise in damage limitation. They only assert: "Wir wissen uns rein von allen bösen Absichten" (FA, 1.18: 108–109) [We know we meant no ill whatsoever], promising to end their lives as critics as the closest they come to conceding that their actions were wrong. Although this example is a one-off rehabilitation of prefacing for the young Goethe, after the fact, it is not yet a creative reconception of the form. Indeed, we can still read a palpable resistance to it.

Goethe's creativity in such belated prefacing emerged only later on, though even then some of his prefaces remained prosaic and resistant to the necessity of their existence that Goethe came to admit. His later introduction ("Einleitung") to *Noten und Abhandlungen zu besserem Verständnis des West-östlicher Divans* [Notes and Essays for a Better Understanding of the *West-Eastern Divan*] (1819) is a prime creative example, as we shall see later. It begins by acknowledging the absence of prefaces from his early works in greater detail, beyond mere allusion in a title: "Ich habe die Schriften meiner ersten Jahre ohne Vorwort in die Welt gesandt, ohne auch nur im mindesten anzudeuten, wie es damit gemeynt sey; dieß geschah im Glauben an die Nation, daß sie früher oder später das Vorgelegte benutzen werde" (FA, 1.3.1: 138) [I sent the works of my first few years out into the world without prefaces, without implying in the slightest what they were meant to be. I did so because of a belief in the nation, that she would use, sooner or later, what I had laid before her]. In his maturity, Goethe made the transition from a youthful, avant-garde presumption of the public's appreciation of his purpose to the realization that he needed to encourage the reception, and participate in the understanding, of his writing himself. By the 1810s and 1820s, his writings had proliferated and had become ever more diverse. What is more, it was the Early German Romantics, notably Friedrich Schlegel, who flushed Goethe out of hiding his authorial influences and intentions, and forced him not to withhold prefaces—the covert practice of his youth. The Romantics' discussion of his work antagonized him. But even when Goethe belatedly added a foreword, his inner tension about this type of text at times remained tangible. In an *ältere Einleitung* [Older Introduction] drafted at some point prior to 1816 in order to preface supplementary material to the 1810 edition of *Zur Farbenlehre* [On the Theory of Colors], he addresses why previously he had not responded to his critics as an author. Originally, he had not wanted to preface, "weil hinter einer Vorrede gewöhnlich eine Mißhelligkeit mit dem Leser versteckt sei" (FA, 1.25: 732) [because a misunderstanding with the reader is usually hidden behind a preface]. As we shall see, *Zur Farbenlehre* in fact already had multiple prefaces. They must have been inadequate, because Goethe's point is now this: to preface is usually and at worst to misapprehend the reader, just as the reader misunderstands the author—though the implication in this piece, by virtue of its planned presence despite such criticism, is that the preface might be rehabilitated more positively, and clear up the problems Goethe's treatise had encountered to date. He finally published the belated introduction as a standalone defense of his theory of colors in the first volume of *Zur Naturwissenschaft überhaupt* [On the Natural Sciences in General] (1822). This "preface" is foreshadowed in its strategy by his afterword from 1772.

Since Goethe's earlier abstinence from prefacing was not unusual (though by no means his only approach), we must ask again: what was so wrong with the preface in the late eighteenth century? Authors' objections were not only that they would be misunderstood, as Goethe suggests; as his afterword from 1772 implies, they also thought themselves above submitting their works to scrutiny. Many of Goethe's peers, who shared his youthful, antiprefatory sentiments, blamed the book reviewers for their bad reception. Georg Christoph Lichtenberg, for example, quips of bad reviews sometime in the late 1780s or early '90s: "Man hat häufig versucht, ihnen durch Amulette von Vorrede und Dedikation vorzubeugen oder sie gar durch eigene Urteile zu inokulieren, es hilft aber nicht immer"[9] [One has frequently attempted to prevent them through the amulets of a preface or dedication, even to inoculate them with one's own judgments—but it does not always help]. We have witnessed that not all authors were as charming, nor their prefaces as precautionary, as Lichtenberg indicates. Beyond the case of Goethe, while Johann Timotheus Hermes begins his preface to the opening volume of the first edition of *Sophiens Reise von Memel nach Sachsen* [Sophie's Journey from Memel to Saxony] (1770) with a modest address to the judges of art ("Kunstrichter"), he soon becomes provocative: scolding them for the scarcity of literary genius. The critics may be the gatekeepers, or the anterooms ("Vorzimmer") of a book's reception—but it will soon reach the chamber of his true readers, Hermes asserts. The women judges will read him at their dressing tables ("Putztisch").[10] The critics were indeed an easy group to charge with being uncooperative, but they were a contingent which was in effect so heterogeneous that they must be let off the hook. Criticism burgeoned in the late eighteenth century, yet it is impossible to claim that as a discourse it was either more or less destructive in the Age of Goethe than in any other period. And as much as some critics around 1800 skirmished under the name of serious criticism (as is inevitable in any era of book reviewing), the activity as a whole was in one abstract regard already on an author's side—whether he met with agreement or was attacked. As Anni Carlsson points out, the critical readership was mainly hacks who were also literary authors themselves.[11]

As the critical profession developed, it was increasingly annexed, and incorporated into, authorship and literary understanding—rather than being a part of a more generalized, argumentative Enlightenment discourse of common reason (such as the criticism, or "Kritik," that developed into Kant's thought and emerged from a learned culture of debate—"Streitkultur"). According to Sulzer's definition in the mid-1770s, the "wahre[r] Kunstrichter"[12] [true judge of art] should be so talented and wise that he is likely to be as rare as "ein guter Künstler"[13] [a good artist]. In this respect, the two roles were as exceptional as each other, though not yet one of a kind. By the time of the Early German Romantics, criticism and creativity were combined in the idealized figure of the self-reflexive, literary-critical artist who no longer wished to be improved by the reasonable criticism of a third party or exterior discourse. Steffen Martus interprets this shift from an ideally constructively *negative* mode of correction in the early Enlightenment, somewhat simplistically, as a movement toward (proto)philological, *positive* textual appreciation that is promoted by the writer himself.[14] Wherever prefaces continued to be written, they were no longer primarily composed for the critics, nor as a submission to the judgment of others. For Martus, they instantiate a new textual politics of a desired (proto)philological interpretation. He is broadly right. But Goethe's prefaces were not written just for such ever more specialized readers (which we could say, accepting the concept of criticism around 1800, would be to increasingly write for writers themselves, and ultimately for oneself—hence the Romantic topos of auto-prefacing, explored in chapter 2). Prefaces were presented to everyone: the public. Recall that where Goethe refused to preface in his youth, in maturity he claimed that this was due to a misplaced faith in the nation as a whole, and its use of his work.

The claim that Goethe addressed a *general* readership, but in the hope of converting it into a specialized set of critical readers, in a positive sense, is borne out in his most explicit critique of prefacing: in the thirteenth book of *Aus meinem Leben. Dichtung und Wahrheit* [From My Life: Poetry and Truth] (1814). Reflecting on his formation as a writer, and on the initial reception of *Die Leiden des jungen Werthers* [The Sorrows of Young Werther] (1774), he scathingly describes the preface as a pointless text type. The publication of his first novel confirmed what he had apparently suspected all along, namely that prefaces are futile in an author's effort to condition his readership's response. Writing about himself in the third person, he expresses frustration at the popular reaction to his debut novel:

> Auf diese Weise bedrängt, ward er nur allzu sehr gewahr, daß Autoren und Publikum durch eine ungeheuere Kluft getrennt sind, wovon sie, zu ihrem Glück, beiderseits keinen Begriff haben. Wie vergeblich daher alle Vorreden seien, hatte er schon längst eingesehen: denn je mehr man seine Absicht klar zu machen gedenkt, zu desto mehr Verwirrung gibt man Anlaß. Ferner mag ein Autor bevorworten so viel er will, das Publikum wird immer fortfahren, die Forderungen an ihn zu machen, die er schon abzulehnen suchte. (FA, 1.14: 645)
>
> [Inflicted in this way, he became all too aware that authors and their public are separated by an immense chasm of which neither party fortunately has any conception. He had long ago understood that all prefaces are pointless: the more an author takes care to make his intention clear, all the more occasion he offers for confusion. Besides, an author may preface as much as he likes, but the public will continue to make precisely those demands on him which he has already sought to prevent.]

The divisive agent that alienated Goethe was criticism—a common lament among his contemporaries, as we have learned. But Goethe employs a loose sense of this concept; it includes more than Enlightenment scribblers, though does not yet mean sympathetic, philologically inclined readers. As an author he had prepared, he tells us, for intellectual interrogation. But instead, "das forschende Publikum" (FA, 1.14: 644) [the researching public] insisted on debating the extent to which *Werther* was based on its writer's empirical experiences, or those of his associates. This was the culmination of the "unerträgliches Geschäft" [insufferable business] of a "sondernde Kritik" (FA, 1.14: 644) [divisive criticism]. Intrigued not least by the novel's parallels to people of Goethe's acquaintance such as Charlotte Buff and Johann Kestner, or by the famous case of Karl Jerusalem, readers industriously called the fictionality of each part of the sensational text into question, and investigated the supposedly real incidents that lay behind it.[15] Importantly, Goethe here attacks his readership in general, rather than as comprising critics specifically—albeit under the name of a type of "Kritik." For he sought to change the public's very sense of criticism. He recalls his dismay at those everyday, indeed ubiquitous readers—he exaggeratedly refers to "jedermann, der mich nur ansah" (FA, 1.14: 645) [anyone who even looked at me]—who reduced his novel to a prompt for their fact-finding mission that sought to reveal the man behind the work. In this context, an author apparently prefaces in vain.

Goethe was correct in writing of a public response to his work, rather than a particularly, professionally critical one. Iffland also conceived the general public as the chief respondent to his later drama *Die Jäger* [The Hunters] (1785), though he encouraged precisely the interpretation of literature as representative of real-life characters that had become so problematic for Goethe. Iffland, in other words, told his readership to search for characters' equivalents in their everyday existence. He employed his "Vorbericht an Schauspieler und Leser" [Preface to Actors and Readers] as an appeal for such empirical engagement, requesting excerpts from court proceedings from everyone in public office who observed such a course of events and witnessed similar characters. Indeed, he measures the success of his reception on the receipt of material from readers: "Binnen Jahr und Tag hoffe ich manchen Beitrag erhalten zu haben—wenn anders meine gegenwärtige Arbeit nicht mißfällt"[16] [Within a year and a day I hope to have received many a contribution—that is, so long as the present work does not displease]. That the public had reacted in a similar way to *Werther*, assuming that the prose must be based on traceable case studies, is in this light not so unusual (unless Iffland was capitalizing on the reception of *Werther* specifically, and there is no evidence to confirm that he was). And so, too, is the typical reader's response to *Werther* all the more understandable. It was an attitude to which Goethe later objected and which he initially misunderstood, provided we grant that Goethe's mature protests are a genuine retrospective account of his postpublication shock.

But is it in fact the case that the early works in general, and *Werther* in particular, are unprefaced? Beyond his plays or the short and singular prose piece *Novelle*, the answer is not as clear-cut as Goethe's retrospective narrative of 1814 would suggest. The controversial little book of 1774 might be read as actually a prefaced work, despite there being no heading to this effect. On the other hand, in discussing this text and his unwillingness to explain it biographically upon its reception, Goethe describes its unity as poetic ("poetische Einheit"; FA, 1.14: 644). Is there, then, an ambiguity here: a prosaic preface that is a part of this literary whole? In fact, it is with *Werther* that Goethe truly began experimenting with the preface, and throughout this novel's revisions Goethe's experimentation took many different forms. And so we should turn to the prefaces to *Werther*, which prompt our next strategy of Goethe's prefacing, and—in the work's later editions—produce further types within Goethe's prefatory repertoire.

AMBIGUOUS PREFACES

Werther is succinct, striking, and ambiguously arouses either our sympathy or our suspicion from the start. None of the novel's editions, unlike Goethe's dramas or *Novelle*, has a categorical subtitle or title, such as "novel." The initial three sentences present an unidentified narrative voice: he is sure that readers will thank him for collecting and presenting the young protagonist's story, or history ("Geschichte"), despite its undetermined source and an implication that the background research was necessarily incomplete. For he has undertaken the task to the best of his ability, but not to perfection: "Was ich von der Geschichte des armen Werther nur habe auffinden können, habe ich mit Fleiß gesammlet und leg es euch hier vor, und weis, daß ihr mir's danken werdet" (FA, 1.8: 10) [I have made efforts to collect whatever I could find out about the story of poor Werther, and I present it here to you in the knowledge that you will thank me for it]. It is then stated that the readership, with reference to a personal plural form, will admire the protagonist's intellect and character, and will be moved to tears for his fate. And readers, who in the third sentence are now a collective soul ("Seele") addressed individually through the singular personal pronoun, will apparently find the little book ("Büchlein") consoling—as a friend. These three sentences are divided into two paragraphs (and in early editions, onto two pages), before *Werther* begins properly with its first letter, as an epistolary novel. The opening threefold claim is not labeled as a preface or any particular text type, nor is it undersigned with a name, pseudonym, or initials: the declarative words are not obviously attributable to an empirical or fictional author, editor, or any other character whom we might already know. Goethe was evidently content with this ambiguity: he revised *Werther* substantially in 1787, but the preface, as also part of the fiction, remained more or less the same. There were only orthographical changes, and an exclamation mark was inserted at the end of the third sentence.

The most significant alterations and additions to the novel in its revised form instead affected the fictional commentary entitled "Der Herausgeber an den Leser" [The Editor to the Reader], which was included toward the close of the book. In fact, a famous criticism of the first version of *Werther* was leveled at its ending: Lessing wrote to Johann Joachim Eschenburg on October 26, 1774, in a commonly cited response to the original publication that Goethe should include a sober, even cynical concluding speech, or "Schlußrede," to compensate for the work's passion.[17] Subsequent critics have responded to the remaining underspecification of the opening lines by assigning the apparently preparatory text their own categorical term of choice; and like Lessing, they assume that the novel's frame should be somehow external to the main story. In German, the initial lines have been called an epigraph, preface, or dedication ("einstimmendes Motto," "Geleitwort," "Vorbemerkung," "Vorrede," "Vorspann," "Vorspruch [an die Leser]," "Vorwort," "Zuschrift an den Leser," or "Widmung").[18] In English criticism, they have been labeled both a "prefatory comment" and, more substantially, a "preface" by the same scholar.[19] These many different terms by contemporary and present-day critics demonstrate that in reading a work we are guided as much by our preconceptions of its form as by an inductive reading of the book itself. But inductive reading is what Goethe and authors around 1800 more generally were surely all about.

Jürgen Nelles points out that we are inclined to read the initial lines to *Werther* as a preface in the first instance, because the book is otherwise so underdetermined: it was first published anonymously, without an identified genre, and its title is not a reference to a known personality of the same name. At first sight, the three sentences are simply clarification of the title page, delivering instructions for reading the work.[20] But as instructions, they are hardly unequivocal. They only fleetingly adhere to the topos of a confessional work of personal truth suggested by the "sufferings" or "sorrows" ("Leiden") of the novel's title. The narrator, who has allegedly assembled the tale from collected manuscripts, is a stock character of the Sentimental novel specifically. But unusually, Goethe does not assert the general historical probability of his writing, even if aspects of it are actually made up; nor does he contend that his story is empirically true for a particular case. He refuses to refer to provenance. As Erdmann Waniek acknowledges, therefore, the prefatory lines resist the initial presumption that *Werther* is either a Pietist (auto)biography or a Sentimental novel, and so they may arouse suspicion in the reader.[21] However, it was equally possible that unsuspecting contemporary readers were unperturbed by the preface, and assumed the conventionality of the subsequent prose all the more. Given the glut of novels in the traditions of Pietist confession and Sensibility around 1800, readers of Goethe's day could be forgiven for having overlooked the preface's nuance to which Waniek is attuned. On publication, then, many people might just as well have thought that the familiar framing was implied in this case, too, and could be left unsaid. Partial omission is a risky strategy: silence, after all, can be as affirmative as it is noncommittal.

Notwithstanding this ambiguity about whether the opening to *Werther* invites interpretation as a typically eighteenth-century book (or preface), there is a crucial omission among the prefatory topoi to which Goethe pays lip service. Underpinning the second paragraph's idea of the readership finding solace in literary friendship is Goethe's presumption of consensus with a grateful recipient.[22] In this respect, he boldly surpasses the prefaces of his European counterparts. The fictional editor of Defoe's *Robinson Crusoe* (1719), for example, first—if insincerely—states the historicity of his fiction: "The Editor believes the thing to be a just History of Fact; neither is there any Appearance of Fiction in it"—before claiming of his readers that "he does them a great Service in the Publication."[23] Goethe's fictional editor as preface writer shares such confidence, without offering the assurance of facticity. The editor character to Rousseau's French novel *Julie: Or, The New Heloise* (1761), though self-confident, accepts that his public might disapprove; but if a man is dissatisfied, he should not share his negative opinion with the preface writer: "let him proclaim it to the world if he pleases, but let him not come tell me: I feel that I could never in my life have any regard for such a man."[24] The later epistolary French novel *Dangerous Liaisons* (1782) by Choderlos de Laclos likewise accepts that some will receive the book critically. Despite this, the author, as editor, decides not to forestall any negative reaction in the preface, and so cuts the preliminary text short:

> I frankly admit that these strictures may all be justified; I also believe that it would be possible for me to reply to them, even within the limited space of a preface. But people are bound to think that if

> it seems necessary to provide an answer to everything, the work must be inadequate to provide any answer itself; and that if I had held that view, I would have dispensed with this preface and with the book as well.[25]

In this context, Goethe's prefatory logic becomes all the more comprehensible and controversial. To apologize for a work at the time of publication provokes the question why it was not withdrawn at that opportunity, prior to print. An apology seems to have little point; but abandoning a conventional apology might appear rude. Goethe—unlike Choderlos de Laclos—does not apologize for his lack of apology. And what further distinguishes *Werther* is that Goethe does not publicly allow for any dissent at all. Like *Robinson Crusoe*, his preface persona is self-assured—but unlike Defoe, Goethe does not provide a cause for conviction upfront. His first page(s), in short, express(es) a sense of election without excuse, evidence, or external authority.

Indeed, the preface becomes authoritative only once it is revealed who is speaking: the editor character, whose three footnotes we read as we progress through Werther's letters and whom we explicitly encounter at the end of the novel. Reaching the end of the work entails renewed reflection on the start of the story. This necessarily careful reading and rereading in order to better comprehend the initiation of *Werther* throws up more questions than it answers, though. Comprehension remains open-ended, despite repeated (re)interpretation. The editor's prefatory (and later, properly narrative) voice is almost omnipotent: in the words of Martin Swales, it is "masterly"; for Nelles, it is "sovereign."[26] But it remains unclear whether the character of the editor is a mask of the author, Wilhelm (Werther's correspondent), or Werther (perhaps as a fictional Goethe). All have been proposed.

If the editor controls the reader's experience of the narrative from the start, then surely his role is akin to that of the author. Uwe Wirth contends that the narrator of *Werther* and the modern author-function arise in tension with, and as a replacement for, the character of the editor in literature around 1800, who is subsumed by an epic superiority ("epische Überlegenheit").[27] The only persona who governs this work's narrative for the reader as a known entity is the editor figure, but here he is like no other. He is the implied author. Insofar as *Werther* was first published anonymously, this argument makes sense. But as Goethe's literary career progressed, he became personally associated with—and, moreover, aware that his writing was continually defined by—his debut novel. Ilse Graham understands the fictional editor as Goethe himself, and as a fictional expression of his relationship toward his own works of fiction.[28] In this sense, the fiction of an editor figure gave rise not so much to a single discursive category of authorship, but rather enabled specific writers to develop authorial dimensions alongside, separate from but in complementary relation to, their empirical identities, which were likewise lived out both physically and discursively.

Understanding the editor as the implied or, as Goethe, the literary-empirical author can be further complicated by interpreting the editor's perspective not as an outsider's, but as an intradiegetic viewpoint: as either Wilhelm's or Werther's (which in turn might be Goethe's). Christoph E. Schweitzer, for example, posits that the preface is written by Wilhelm, the correspondent to whom Werther's letters are addressed, because the friendly "Büchlein" to which the third opening sentence refers, "tries to compensate for his failure to rush to Werther's side in time by creating a monument to his memory in the form of the book."[29] Wilhelm's hope in writing the preface—apparently that the little book, *Werther*, might act as a friend for the reader—admits, according to Schweitzer, "his not having been the close friend for Werther he should have been . . . . Wilhelm does not want to confess openly to his sense of guilt but hides it in the "wenn" clause that concludes the preface.[30] Deirdre Vincent, meanwhile, argues that the editor's report as the final fiction of *Werther* is in fact an account from the perspective of Werther himself. In closing the novel's second version, the editor authentically depicts the protagonist's inner state in a way that only Werther could achieve with authority; and the "dispassionate objectivity" of the editor's words elicits more sympathy for the protagonist.[31] Vincent concludes: "Here the narrative voice is not that of any Editor, but quite simply of Werther."[32] Significantly, she introduces her identificatory argument by reminding us that Goethe did not change the preface, which she understands as written with passion so typical of the protagonist, yet composed by the editor: "not once, but twice Goethe produced this preface to his work without any alteration in the wording, the second time long after he had supposedly left the emotionalism of his earlier years behind."[33] Although the editor takes on the role of Werther's "biographer," it is Werther who emerges as the "hidden author" of the work—which is, by implication, his autobiography.[34] And this life story, for Vincent, is actually Goethe's, since she pursues biographical criticism.

All of these interpretations result from rereading the text (and, in the latter instances, turning to Goethe's life, too). A hermeneutic circle is initiated by the preface, and continues throughout the work, because each stage of narration is so underspecified. Further, the overall prefatorial ambiguity and indeed *Werther* as a whole also gives rise to another set of contrary readings, alongside the question of who is behind the narrator's editorial mask (if anyone). Michael Bell summarizes a bifurcation in criticism of this book more broadly, whereby the tale has been received as either a "Romantic tragedy" or "neurotic case history." That is to say, *Werther* has been read as *identificatory* or *ironical* material.[35] The same can be said of scholarly interpretations of the preface—if, indeed, the opening piece can be called a preface at all. And both interpretative modes are, once again, deferred until the novel is reread, and even then they remain equivocal.

If the preface to *Werther* is thought to be composed as part of a broader subjective, sympathetic account of the protagonist, or as emerging from Wilhelm's guilt, then we will read the odd opening as a way of eliciting as much empathy with the protagonist as possible. But even so, an identificatory reading should not be interpreted as an invocation to mimic Werther's end. On first publication, the third prefatorial claim that *Werther* extends friendship to its readership as a little book was especially understood as an invitation to identify with the protagonist in an extreme fashion. A young fellow named Hartmann imparted to Johann Caspar Lavater that on reading the novel ten times, it had become his friend; and he wanted, above all, to match Werther's tragic fate.[36] In Karl Philipp Moritz's *Anton Reiser* (1785–1790), the protagonist thinks of the friendly prefatory line every time he takes Goethe's first novel from his pocket. Moritz's Anton could relate to *Werther* more than he could converse with any friend—which is apparently equal to identifying with Goethe's protagonist.[37] However, the interpretation Moritz advances for his character is no longer tenable after Goethe's revision to *Werther* in 1787, for Nelles reminds us that Goethe's sentence proposes the book as *whole* should be the reader's friend, not Werther the character of the narrative (and even if Werther is the implied author, the latter instantiation would include his editorial, sober [self-]reflection).[38]

In contrast to reading the *Werther* preface—insofar as it is an actual preface—as evoking personal sympathy, others have suggested that the first two paragraphs ironically hold readers at a distance, and simultaneously draw them in. The second paragraph, in this reading, has a more subtle effect than the first. Namely, Goethe initially seeks to distance the reader, since there is a token, unsubstantiated claim to historical authenticity, but without enough detail for us to empathize or believe completely; whereas the second paragraph, offering friendship, establishes an ironic intimacy after distance from the manuscript has been demarcated. For both Waniek and Landfester, a "distanced identification" wins out as the overall effect of the opening three sentences to *Werther*.[39] As Landfester explains, the reader recognizes from the first paragraph the alterity of the novel as the narrated experience of someone else; and while the reader who personally identifies with *Werther*, as suggested in the second paragraph, finds a friend—if only in the book—Werther does not. He dies alone in the world. This prefatorial play enables the reader to become compassionate and understand, but not identify outright with the protagonist. Thus the reader can feel empathy, without that compassion turning pathological.

Ironically, however, Erich Meuthen has observed that acknowledging such difference can itself morph into greater identification with Werther. For the second paragraph of the opening to the novel introduces a rhetorically ironic idea: in marking out the book as unnatural, or as an example of art (*ars*) that is meant to affect the reader, it lays claim to a prosthetic function and tacitly acknowledges its suboptimal support for anyone suffering suicidal thoughts—especially someone who seeks a close connection with nature, such as Werther. The preface undermines its very purpose to appeal to the reader as comforting, because it is fiction and foregrounded as such; *Werther* cannot authentically replace any genuine friend, in spite of the preface's promise. Readers who feel similar to its protagonist will find real solace neither in their friends, nor in the book, and so they remain as lonely as Werther was.[40]

An addition to the 1787 version of the work states that the task of the editor in assessing Werther's life must be extremely attentive; even "das kleinste aufgefundene Blättchen" (FA, 1.8: 199) [the smallest piece of paper that is found] cannot be considered closely enough. But such close, additive reading of *Werther* as a novel cannot result in a robust, closed argument for the reader because the book, from its preface onward, is and remains chronically underspecified. Each snippet of text that is interpreted only emphasizes the necessity of radical interpretative openness. We can search—as contemporary readers did—for more material and bring this to bear on Goethe's writing; and we can find scraps of evidence to substantiate both identificatory and ironical readings of the preface, and indeed the book as a whole.

With regard to the preface, while the wording of the original two-paragraph opening remained the same in subsequent revisions, its layout did not. Attending to pagination is one such subtle "scrap" of evidence readers might consider. Published with Georg Joachim Göschen and reproduced in the collected works brought out with Unger and Cotta, the initial two paragraphs of *Werther* were, from 1787 onward, assimilated onto the same page. In 1774, by contrast, the first two sentences appeared on one page, whereas the third, which is the more personal after the previously established distance between work and reader, with its shift to the familiar second-person singular pronoun from its plural form, appears on another. Setting these sentences on the same page arguably further increases the distancing effect of the two paragraphs taken together, with the jolt between plural and singular pronouns more obvious. A paginal separation for each respective paragraph, with differing pronouns, turns first to the entire readership, and then homes in on the individual. The material caesura perhaps suggests a trajectory toward greater intimacy that will continue as one leafs through the book. A direct appeal to the soul ("Seele") in closer proximity to a line that does not authenticate the source of the story, on the other hand, might encourage an observant reader to take solace in the book more critically from the outset, with greater awareness of the paragraph that precedes it on a single page. But the contrasting argument is also plausible: Waniek proposes that turning a page offers a choice whether to continue, and emphasizes the increasing, paradoxical, and physical "identificatory distance."[41] In this reasoning, the second edition's limitation of the preface to one page decreases the distance that for Waniek is observable as the three prefatory sentences progress, thus making the beginning less reserved, more passionate, and all the more identificatory, which would undermine the changes undertaken to the end of the novel that invoke the narrative voice of the editor. Nevertheless, as noted above, to argue that the second edition increases the distancing effect, even if it thereby reduces the number of pages, is equally plausible. We soon find ourselves going round in interpretative circles.

There is no evidence that the page breaks were Goethe's decision, though there is nothing to suggest that they were not. The preface and alterations to its content across editions, which we shall consider shortly, were certainly of Goethe's choosing. Common to both identificatory and ironical interpretations of *Werther* is that they are not so much unlocked by the novel's first few lines, but that that these lines lock readers into the text. A mere three lines are enough to resist any definitive conclusion, other than the inconclusive resignation that the opening to *Werther* is ambiguous. Goethe's resistance to the preface for fear or distain of readers' misinterpretation turns, in *Werther*, into a preface that resists easy or conclusive interpretations of the book by readers. And so within a contemporary context of prefatorial crisis, Goethe as the author of *Werther* opted not so much for a radical rewriting of the form, but for an intriguing—or, less positively, perplexing—innovation that resists that which a conventional preface surely sets out to do: he flouts critical foreclosure. In terms of the book's initial reception, he did so at its peril. In the longer term, though (and above all among scholars), Goethe's strategy has ensured the critical debate surrounding *Werther* continues.

The global effect of the preface to *Werther* enacts a suggestion that—surprisingly—Johann Joachim Schwabe already advanced in the preface he wrote for Johann Christoph Gottsched's first, 1736 collection of poems. Addressing the reader in the guise of the editor, he writes:

> Du wirst es zwar gewohnt seyn, daß die Vorreden der Herausgeber fremder Werke von deren Vortrefflichkeit, Nutzbarkeit, Wichtigkeit und Vorzügen, vor vielen andern Schriften ihrer Art, viele Worte machen. Allein, ich habe mich jederzeit gewundert, daß sie sich nicht gescheut, in ihrer eigenen Sache ein Zeugniß abzulegen. Es ist mir immer verdächtig vorgekommen, wenn man seine Leser durch Anzeigung vieler guten Eigenschaften eines Werks zum Voraus einzunehmen gesuchet hat. Lies und beurtheile es selbst, ohne meine Vorschrift. Ich traue dir schon so viel Verstand und Einsicht zu, daß du wirst unterscheiden können, ob diese Gedichte von der gemeinen Art sind, deren du vielleicht genug gelesen hast; oder ob sie zu einer höhern Gattung gehören, die bey uns eben noch nicht gar zu bekannt ist. Mich dünkt, ich würde dir und dem Herrn Verfasser derselben viel Unrecht thun, wenn ich etwas entscheiden wollte.[42]
>
> [You will be familiar with editors' prefaces to works by others having much to say about their greater merit, usefulness, importance, and other advantages over many similar writings. But I have always been surprised that these have shied from letting works be a testament to their own worth. It has always seemed suspicious to me to capture readers by advertising many a good quality for a work in advance. Read it and judge for yourself, without my prescription. For I trust your understanding and insight very much, such that you will be able to distinguish whether these poems are of the common sort (of which you have perhaps read enough), or whether they belong to a higher genre, which is not quite known to us yet. I consider I would do you and the author a great disservice if I were to decide.]

Ironically, Schwabe did not practice what he preached: his original preface is lengthy, and the second edition of 1751 included another preface by him. Goethe's first novel, by contrast, demands to be read on its own terms, inductively: from inside the fiction, outward, and back into the fiction again. This demand is not dogmatic, because (for the time being) it is not formulated as an explicit instruction for readers. It is rendered literary or is, as Thomas Wegmann puts it, an intricately aestheticized paratext.[43]

Two of Goethe's other preface strategies adopted throughout his career were also tested out on *Werther* in the experimentalism of its various editions, and these likewise require inductive reading rather than a preparatory gloss. Goethe introduces readers to his writing, and *Werther*, through emblematic lyric or metapoetic poems and embedded prose prefaces, alongside especially ambivalent prefacing. These two later alternatives for introducing *Werther* similarly pull in opposite directions, ambiguously presenting an identifactory mode of reading and ironizing the little book's reception all the more.

As the novel went into a second print run already in 1775, with Christian Weygand, Goethe replaced the two prefatory paragraphs with a pair of poetic mottos, one motto presented before each half of the work. Both verses are as presumptive as the previous prose preface, and they match the sequence of address in the prose opening: a plural sentiment in the second original sentence is transposed into rhyme in the first motto, followed by the poetic apostrophe in the second verse that is a development of the singular pronoun in the prose preface's third sentence:

Jeder Jüngling sehnt sich so zu lieben,
Jedes Mädchen so geliebt zu sein;
Ach, der heiligste von unsern Trieben,
Warum quillt aus ihm die grimme Pein?

Du beweinst, du liebst ihn, liebe Seele,
Rettest sein Gedächtnis vor der Schmach;
Sieh, dir winkt sein Geist aus seiner Höhle:
Sei ein Mann und folge mir nicht nach. (FA, 1.8: 917)

[Every young man yearns to love so,
And every girl to be loved just the same;
But O! Out of the most sacred of impulses,
Must spring such brutal pain?

> Dear soul you cry for him, you love him,
> You save his memory from disgrace;
> Look, his spirit points to you from the corpse's cavity,
> And says: Be a man, don't follow me.]

Together, the mottos address the identificatory mode of reading negatively: the last line even personifies the protagonist, who appeals directly to the reader. Here, the prefatory voice does in fact become (a poetic version of) Werther; the previous hints at the contemporary Sentimental and epistolary topos of an editor figure, or at historical truth, are entirely absent. The first motto is rather facile verse, almost trivializing the narrative. The second is an overt call to no action: it urges the readership not to follow in Werther's footsteps as the voice of the protagonist speaking with hindsight, back from the dead. If the first verse debases the literary quality of the narrative by encapsulating half of it within a ditty, the second turns Werther into a moralizer. According to Benjamin Bennett, this verse is a didactic plea on Goethe's part; the motto's last line "is the ethical message; but the book, in this sense, is not an ethical teaching so much as an ethical training."[44] The word "training" here is key. The motto was too teacherly: both verses were deleted in 1787, "probably as representing rather too specific a moral imperative."[45] Regardless, Goethe's addition of poetry about the following prose—prefatorial poetry, in other words—remained his strategy for subsequent copies of *Werther* issued with Weygand.

The jubilee edition of 1825 appeared, according to the title page, as a "neue Ausgabe, von dem Dichter selbst eingeleitet"[46] [new edition, introduced by the poet himself]. The introduction is the initial poem that occurs before the first letter and in lieu of the original, two-paragraph preface in all of Weygand's subsequent reprints of *Werther*. In Goethe's collected works with Cotta, however, this introductory poem is subsumed among the author's lyric: in 1827, titled as "An Werther" [To Werther], it began the poem cycle *Trilogie der Leidenschaft* [Trilogy of Passion]. Goethe applied a principle of strict categorization to his Cotta editions, such that forms were grouped according to their kind: poems appear alongside poems, and are prefaced by verse; prose is preceded by prefatory prose; early dramas have zero prefaces, and so on. In any case, "An Werther" discloses Goethe's unease. The poem is presented not as an appeal to a group of readers, nor to an individual recipient. Nor is it, in the end, really an address to Werther. The poem is not so much about the reception of writing or Werther's character, as ultimately about Goethe's authorial creativity. A few of the images in Goethe's prior dedicatory poetry return: the poem starts by addressing Werther as a "vielbeweinter Schatten" (FA, 1.2: 456) [much-wept shadow], and reminisces—just as, in the "Zueignung" [dedication] to *Faust*, "schwankende Gestalten" (FA, 1.7.1: 11) [wavering shapes] remind the poet of earlier times, raising "manche liebe Schatten" (FA, 1.7.1:11) [many beloved shadows]. In both cases, life or passion is depicted as a labyrinth (FA, 1.2: 457; 1.7.1: 11). But "An Werther" closes by shifting perspective, away from Werther and speaking about the author in the third person:

> Und wir verschlungen wiederholter Not,
> Dem Scheiden endlich—Scheiden ist der Tod!
> Wie klingt es rührend wenn der Dichter singt,
> Den Tod zu meiden, den das Scheiden bringt!
> Verstrickt in solche Qualen halbverschuldet
> Geb' ihm ein Gott zu sagen was er duldet. (FA, 1.2: 457)
>
> [And we, devoured by distress recast,
> Part we must, at last—parting is to die!
> How stirring it sounds when the poet sings,
> To escape the death that parting brings!
> Half indebted, and in such anguish ensnared,
> Grant him a god to tell of the life he bears.]

Over fifty years after the novel's first publication, avoiding death—associated here with parting—refers to Goethe's continued republishing of *Werther* as a paradoxical will to keep a fictional dead man alive so that he, as empirical author, need not yet die also. The poem begins with a reunion of Goethe and Werther, and identifies the poet, as introduction writer to *Werther*, as the protagonist's friend. But unlike Wilhelm, the authorial companion shared real-life moments with Werther, rather than merely narrated, epistolary ones. The first stanza suggests that while the protagonist departed life and the world of literature, Goethe remained: "Zum Bleiben ich, zum Scheiden du erkoren" (FA, 1.2: 456) [I am chosen to remain, as you are to part]. The third and fourth lines of the stanza above expose Goethe's idea of writing, and of having written *Werther* in particular, as substitution for self-violence: instead of shooting (or stabbing) himself, as he tells us in the thirteenth book to *Dichtung und Wahrheit*, the author put pen to paper (FA, 1.14: 636). But while this is moving for the reader, the survivor is left as the sufferer. "An Werther" thus addresses the identificatory mode of reading *Werther*, yet Goethe's, not the reader's identification with the book is now his primary concern. Hence the closing couplet: since the poet, too, is partly afflicted, his suffering should also be written about, and characterized, in addition to him being able to sing to the effect that he is stirring for the readership.

In this version of *Werther* introduced by the author himself, the writer is deferring, at the end of the poetic introduction, the proper introduction to somewhere else, into his fiction and criticism. For the closing line is a prayer that Goethe would receive a muse to reflect on his own life that leads to his work. But since he has already done this elsewhere, the poem is ironically concealing, through its implicit reference to *Torquato Tasso*—Goethe's drama on authorship with autobiographical aspects—or *Dichtung und Wahrheit*, a critical revelation that is to be found in a separate book (or series of books), which can be read as a dismembered, fictional or semifictional, "hypertrophic" preface, as we shall see. And his strategy of prefatory poetry imbued with the poetics of the work at hand, yet which points the reader somewhere else in his life and writings for interpretative guidance, was one that Goethe had been working out for some time. He had earlier deployed it through rhyming verse placed before *Noten und Abhandlungen zu besserem Verständnis des West-östlicher Divans*, in 1819. Here, Goethe wrote, the reader should travel to the "country" of poetry, in line with the exoticism of the work under discussion. Through a parallel grammatical structure in the next couplet, completing the motto, that place is equal to the land of the poet:

> Wer das Dichten will verstehen,
> Muß in's Land der Dichtung gehen;
> Wer den Dichter will verstehen,
> Muß in Dichters Lande gehen. (FA, 1.3.1: 137)
>
> [Whoever wants to understand writing poetry,
> Must go to the land of poetry,
> Whoever wants to understand the poet,
> Must walk around in the poet's country.]

Goethe's prose and poetic prefaces to *Werther* play not only to readers' passions, then, but also to their critical faculties, which in the later poetic prefaces are directed toward the author's life and broader work as the only relevant interpretative sources outside the text. The preface as a place of readerly voyeurism and—Romantic—authorial self-desire is explored at length in the next chapter, through the example of Jean Paul. In Goethe's case, guiding readers to sources for greater understanding is not a matter of writing prefatory "instructions," since his prefatorial guidance refuses to satisfy any interpretative question by itself. In this sense, Goethe's openings *induce* investigation and informed appreciation, rather than offering information upfront.

The prose revisions to the prefacing of *Werther*, meanwhile, appeared in editions printed by Cotta. Goethe included the original two-paragraph, two-page opening, now on one page, in an 1808 edition with this publisher. He also rewrote these three prefatorial sentences at the start of an insert to the whole story, which he appended after the work. This supplement was part of Goethe's general attempt to emphasize the status of *Werther* as fiction; in the words of Hans Rudolf Vaget, the fragment altogether "provides additional proof of his continued efforts to minimize the potentially harmful effects of the earlier book."[47] It portrays Werther's journey to Switzerland before the events of the novel, and the protagonist is unquestionably depicted unsympathetically, even satirically—as narcissistic. Goethe personally called the text *Werthers Reise* [Werther's Journey] on writing it in 1796 (FA, 2.4: 172); in the 1808 appendix to *Werther*, it was entitled *Briefe aus der Schweiz. Erste Abteilung* [Letters from Switzerland: Part One].

The closing fictional addition, then, is actually a new beginning to *Werther*. As Vaget contends, we read not a continuation, but "what in today's terminology would be called a 'prequel.'"[48] Landfester emphasizes that its opening paragraph, which we might term a preface of sorts, calls into question the (limited) authority of the original preface to the previous—but within the logic of this story, subsequent—novel. Consequently, it develops the distancing devices of the primary prose preface.[49] But this new prefatory paragraph, separated from the insert's main prose through additional spacing, is more extreme than a suspicion of its predecessor. It is a disavowal. For it actually negates, as a quasi-preface, the point of prefacing *Werther* per se:

> Als vor mehreren Jahren uns nachstehende Briefe abschriftlich mitgeteilt wurden, behauptete man sie unter Werthers Papieren gefunden zu haben, und wollte wissen, daß er vor seiner Bekanntschaft mit Lotten in der Schweiz gewesen. Die Originale haben wir niemals gesehen, und mögen übrigens dem Gefühl und Urteil des

> Lesers auf keine Weise vorgreifen; denn, wie dem auch sei, so wird man die wenigen Blätter nicht ohne Teilnahme durchlaufen können. (FA, 1.8: 594)
>
> [When copies of the following letters came into our possession several years ago, the individual who supplied them said they had been found among Werther's papers, and claimed to have information that Werther had been in Switzerland before he became acquainted with Lotte. We have never seen the originals, and in any case we in no way wish to anticipate the feelings and judgment of readers. For whatever their provenance and reception, it is impossible to read through these few pages without sympathy.]

The editorial character does not want to pre-empt the feelings and judgments of readers, which will emerge from, or be induced by, the text itself—though he still presumes to know their basic impact. And yet the editor prefaces such a stand-alone narrative with a paragraph explaining why he explains the bare minimum. Like the moralizing ditty that Goethe added to the second edition with Weygand, this 1808 prose revision is more instructive than the original work. In finally rejecting their own form explicitly, the initial sentences to the prequel of *Werther* are actually more helpful to readers and more of an unequivocal incitement for them to make up their own minds than the equivocal opening to the original text. The only dogma here is an antidogma: readers must decide for themselves. The preface, in Cotta's editions, becomes not only a site of overt deferral, but also an abdication of immediate interpretative responsibility.

Although the supplement adds greater critical distance to our perspective on the protagonist of *Werther*, the additional fragment is also, in part, based on Goethe's autobiography. However, the material taken from the author's empirical life is again as ironic (satirical, even) as it is identificatory. Goethe had traveled to Switzerland after the original 1774 publication of Werther, in 1775 and 1779. He presents the prequel writer, if not as an explicit double of himself, then at least in playful, biographical relation to his authorial image. Given Werther's antics and concluding visit to a brothel, this is surely as comic as it is controversial. Moreover, Manfred Link reads the first letter of this appendix-as-prequel as a travel narrative in the style of Laurence Sterne's *Sentimental Journey Through France and Italy* (1768), in which Goethe mocks *Werther* spin-off stories ad absurdum.[50] Sterne's work was phenomenally successful around 1800, and its fictive locations extended, in German copycat novels, to Germany and, in Johann Friedrich Schink's supplement ("Nachtrag") of 1794, Switzerland, too.[51] If "An Werther" suggests a more identificatory reading between the author and his written creation, then the appended pre-story—as an alternative afterword to the poetic introduction—ironizes that relationship.

Werther, the prose, and the poetry that prefixed the novel as well as the prose that followed it, beginning its prequel, all span the course of Goethe's writing career. As ambiguous, poetic, and embedded prefaces, the prefatory material to his most famous story introduces three of Goethe's prefatorial strategies, which develop greater depth over the course of his life. They all can be comprehended only after inductive reading (although even then not fully), but their comparison reveals Goethe's contradictory urges: irony versus instruction, to effect identification or distance, and so forth. Indeed, his poetic prefaces uncover precisely such underlying "contradiction" as central to his conception of writing, and so we consider them next.

POETIC PREFACES

Goethe's poetic prefaces to his poetry similarly resist foreclosing criticism or facilitating an immediate understanding of his literary creativity, and its causes. Instead, they are intriguing: they form part of the verse they precede, and as such invite as much close reading and careful reflection as his poetry collections as wholes. Interpreting the *Römische Elegien XX* [20 Roman Elegies], Kevin Hilliard stresses the traditionalism of Goethe's addition of metapoetic poems to individual poem cycles more generally, since "many collections of his own and earlier times contain proemia and poetic epilogues."[52] It is true that the sort of introduction ("Einleitung") Brockes composed and chose to front his poetry collection of 1738, for example, itself took the form of poetry; but this was in turn prefaced (and edited) by Friedrich von Hagedorn. By comparison, Goethe's prefaces to poetry are more thoroughly formally consonant with the composition they preface. Moreover, in Hilliard's words on Goethe's metapoetry, "what we are being presented with in such poems is not a plain account of the poet's actual motives and procedures, but their transposition into a fictionalizing and symbolic key." He continues by stating that Goethe's examples are unique in each case. Indeed, Goethe's prefatorial poetry consistently complements the theme of the given work, too. Recall that the poetic introduction to the jubilee edition of *Werther* is linked to the author's own creative death drive, and the introductory motto to *Noten und Abhandlungen zu besserem Verständnis des*

West-östlicher Divans sets up the idea of the prose introduction that the poet is a traveler to the East. Since such poetic contemplation is apt for its context, then, it is *pragmatic* rather than *poetological*, inasmuch as it does not, as Hilliard rightly says, "overtly seek some fundamental, philosophical clarification of the nature of poetry."[53]

Nevertheless, there is an overarching characteristic of Goethe's prefatory poetry. It sought, paradoxically, to explicitly hide—or at most hint at—rather than illuminate the sources and production of his writing. As Olaf Kramer observes, the final poem to his juvenile *Neue Lieder* collection of 1769 begins with a covering up of the technical artistry deployed in the previous songs: "Da sind sie nun! Da habt ihr sie! / Die Lieder, ohne Kunst und Müh" (FA, 1.1: 95) [There they are! You have them! / The songs, without art or effort].[54] This closing strategy of *dissimulatio artis* then introduces the thematic remainder of Goethe's first dedication titled as such, at the end of the cycle: the poet reminds young boys in this "Zueignung" [dedication] that life is not all play, for soon they will have to marry. The final lines contain a cheeky, sexual pun in keeping with the anacreontic verse, as the poet is mocked as a bitter old fox that has lost its tail. This dedication, therefore, conceals the toil of writing but reveals the prosaic side to life, thus offering an analogy if the reader wishes to take up the clue that poetic composition, like life, has its everyday obligations.

Paradigmatic for Goethe's verse as a whole, for which the *dissimulatio artis* of the 1769 "Zueignung" prepares the way, is the paradoxical image of a veil of truth in a later "Zueignung" poem that prefaces most versions of Goethe's collected works. This piece is the one true preface of *poetological principle* that Goethe conceives. The poem opened the first volume of *Goethe's Schriften* [Goethe's Writings], which appeared with Göschen between 1787 and 1790, and was the epigraph for initial volumes of the Cotta editions, which in any case began with volumes of Goethe's poetry, in 1815–1819 and 1827/1828–1830. (The first Cotta edition of 1806–1810 relegated "Zueignung" to the fragments of Goethe's incomplete "Die Geheimnisse" [The Secrets], for which it originally had been conceived.) It presents a contradictory gift to the poet, contending that poetry by its very character is concealing, and thereby an act of revelation: "Der Dichtung Schleier aus der Hand der Wahrheit" (FA, 1.1: 11) [The veil of poetry from the hand of truth]. This conception of truth emerging from the concealment of art—of artifice presenting itself as natural, lest it should appear affected, as it naturally is, and therefore be assumed to be false—is an age-old idea on which the ancient rhetorician Quintilian remarks.[55] Within scholarship, it has become canonical to apply

Goethe's poetological paradox, first formulated in 1784 in terms of the veil and as generally applicable to poetry, to his writing as a whole. As Emil Staiger noted in 1952, it spans over sixty years of Goethe's career;[56] and it has led to an understanding of Goethe's works as an *open secret*.

Goethe's "Zueignung" poem is rightly read as so important because its fundamental contradiction is reflected in other prefatory poems—and perhaps even his prefatory prose. On August 9, 1799, Schiller recommended to Goethe that he should explain his guiding principles for the readers of poems revised for the seventh volume of the *Neue Schriften* [New Writings] brought out with Unger (1792–1800), "in einer Vorrede oder wo es schicklich ist"[57] [in a preface or wherever it is appropriate]. For his next edition of collected works with Cotta, which was published from 1806 onward, Goethe opened with lyric, which Martus understands as promoting the metapoetic function of Goethe's poetry in general, and so as Goethe's answer to Schiller.[58] Goethe's first poem of the section is entitled "Vorklage" [Preliminary Complaint]. It begins with a couplet expressing the same truth as the "Zueignung" poem that, exceptionally, does not preface this edition: "Die Welt ist voller Widerspruch, / Und sollte sich's nicht widersprechen?" (FA, 1.2: 11) [The world is full of contradiction / And ought it not to contradict itself?]. When in later editions Goethe's favorite epigraph, "Zueignung," is reinstated, "Vorklage" follows it: a contradictory conception of poetry progresses into a paradoxical perception of the world. What is more, the opening essay in prose to the fiftieth volume of Goethe's *Ausgabe letzter Hand* [Final Authorized Edition], in which the author's collected scientific writings were published posthumously, complements this guiding idea: nature is described as a play, yet as a play it is nature (FA, 1.25: 11). The authorship of this essay is uncertain, however, and the person responsible for its inclusion and position in the volume of 1833 is unclear. (It was first published as an anonymous fragment in an issue of *Das Tiefurter Journal* [The Tiefurt Journal] in 1782–1783, and Goethe denied having composed the piece at the time; paratextual alterations in 1833, such as a change of title, were undertaken by Friedrich Wilhelm Riemer and Johann Peter Eckermann.)[59]

As a public piece of private knowledge, the revealing veil of poetic truth is a remarkably underspecified idea that wholly depends on what is being hidden, hinted at, and what can be uncovered in any particular poetic form. In this sense, Goethe's poetological principle can be deployed only pragmatically; the figure becomes meaningful once it is embedded into a specific poetic context. In terms of determining a work's interpretation, such underdetermined prefacing—whether as poetic pieces, ambiguous ones to

Werther, or (as we shall see shortly) embedded examples in prose—has several advantages. It encourages close reading on the part of readers, for they cannot jump to premature conclusions so easily. Underspecified prefacing also enables the author to engage in self-commentary elsewhere, perhaps at length and at a later point: in critical treatises or an autobiography, for example. Once again, the revisions to *Werther* exemplify this possibility, whereby the preface acts as a placeholder, deferring the material we would normally expect of a preface until another occasion. And with respect to the composition of the following work, and the possibility of its future revision, Goethe's underdetermined prefacing that is also formally appropriate both preserves the unity of a creative piece and allows for its playful continuation at a later date—through supplementation, rather than substitution. A metapoetic poem that is appropriate but general allows for expansion through ever greater particularity, and adjustment to a work's details.

A primary example of both unity and potential continuation is Goethe's final version of *Wilhelm Meisters Wanderjahre*. It ends with the bracketed line "(Ist fortzusetzen.)" [(To be continued.)], appended to the closing poem "Im ernsten Beinhaus war's" (FA, 1.10: 774) [It was in the solemn bone-house]. Especially in the mid-1940s, a debate raged in *PMLA* concerning whether Goethe here refers to the continuation of the *Wanderjahre* as a narrative whole or of the individual poem. Karl Viëtor defended as the most positivistic and conservative interpretation a reading of the final sentence as a reference to the continuation of a future poem cycle. That is to say, Viëtor contends that the form of the present poem is closed, but that its idea remains open—to be substantiated, exemplified.[60] Consequently, the poem at the end of the *Wanderjahre* would present a preliminary stage of the poem ("eine Vorstufe").[61] This technique would not have been unusual. Goethe appended the line "Die Fortsetzung folgt" (FA, 1.1: 485) [The continuation will follow] to his second epistle published in the second issue of Schiller's journal *Die Horen* [The Horae] (1795); on the reprinting of it and the prior poem of the planned cycle in his final collected works with Cotta, the *Ausgabe letzter Hand*, Goethe prefaced the two epistles with the admission: "Gerne hätt ich fortgeschrieben, / Aber es ist liegen blieben"[62] [I would have liked to have continued writing it / But it remained unfinished]. In effect, "Im ernsten Beinhaus war's" that closes the *Wanderjahre* constitutes metapoetic poetry to a project that was to be extended, and so was left incomplete at the end: the novel finishes with what is potentially a poetic preface. Such a closing, moreover, formally complements the novel's initiation in the earlier version of 1821, which begins with a motley, seemingly fragmentary collection of verses.

Poetic, prefatory underspecification has the advantages for writing, then, that Goethe could carry on where he left off (without beginning all over again and without too much overwriting), while presenting his work to the world as a poetic unity. But there are two potential counterexamples. The first can be excused as a juvenile exception: the untitled verse before his libretto *Erwin und Elmire. Ein Schauspiel mit Gesang* [Erwin and Elmire: A Play with Song] in 1775 is a straightforward dedicatory ditty to Goethe's betrothed: "Belinde," or Lili Schönemann (FA, 1.4: 503). The second is more vexing, and a major case: *Faust.*

The *Vorspiel auf dem Theater* [Prologue on the Stage] before *Faust* pokes fun at an author producing a work as a whole ("ein Ganzes") that is picked apart by the public, or audience; and so the cynical theater director of the comic prologue suggests that a work might as well be presented in pieces (FA, 1.7.1: 17). This *Vorspiel* is preceded by a *Zueignung* [Dedication] and followed by the *Prolog im Himmel* [Prologue in Heaven], all published in front of the first part of *Faust. Eine Tragödie* [Faust: A Tragedy] in 1808. At the very least, the play and its prologues constitute a formal unity: they are all in verse, and a draft "Abschied" ["Valediction"] comprising a couple of verses survives along with a more lighthearted planned "Abkündigung" ["Proclamation"], both of which would have complemented the beginning of the play at its close if they had been included (FA, 1.7.1: 731–732). But as Peter Michelsen points out, in the first edition the reader must pass over thirty-one pages to reach the title *Der Tragödie. Erster Theil* [Of the Tragedy: First Part], and the *Zueignung*, *Vorspiel*, and the *Prolog* each have their own title page.[63] Formally, we could say that the three poetic prefaces enact the tension that the poet and theater director stage in the second prefatory poem: that a whole must be presented, and is read, in parts, though it is produced as a whole and intended to be interpreted as such.

Establishing the thematic unity of *Faust* and its front matter is far more difficult. The prefatory poems originated for different purposes, and the context for which the *Vorspiel* was penned has been disputed in particular (as a continuation of Mozart's *Die Zauberflöte* [The Magic Flute] [1791], for example, or for the reopening of the Weimar Theater in 1798).[64] But let us not forget that the "Zueignung" to Goethe's collected works was originally composed for a different, abandoned work, too: "Die Geheimnisse." Calvin Thomas concludes about the "Zueignung" to *Faust* in 1892 that it is "occasional lyric": in his view, Goethe has written a dedication to his playwriting, not to his audience.[65] As such, it is an introduction that is perhaps akin to his poem "An Werther." The *Vorspiel*, according to Thomas, is connected to the dedication inasmuch as it allows Goethe to present different masks of himself: as director, poet, and as a fool. But how might these then relate to the third prologue, and to *Faust* as a play? Werner Keller suggests that the *Zueignung*, *Vorspiel*, and *Prolog im Himmel*, taken together, are three distinct veils Goethe can wear to the same end: to expose and exemplify the contradictory nature of art.[66] For Douglas F. Bub, the crux of *Faust* is indeed the contradictoriness of life and poetry: the "central theme is that of the poet's special gift and mission of bringing cosmos from chaos, of grasping the labyrinthine contradictions of human experience in an aesthetically conceived totality."[67] True as this may be, though, we can read the majority of Goethe's poetic prefaces as foregrounding such abstract paradoxicality, which is so essential for his art in general. The specific settings of at least two of the three prefatory poems to *Faust* remain resistant to the usual pragmatic function of Goethe's prefacing, in that their connection to what follows is most obscure, if evident at all.

Goethe's categories of the preface are therefore fuzzy at best, and are *tendencies* rather than—indeed, they are resistant to—a *typology*. However, as much as *Faust* is a problematic case among Goethe's poetic prefaces, it is also in its genesis paradigmatic of his shift toward greater prefacing in general, and the development of his prefaces as his career progressed. Referring to the *Zueignung* that introduces *Faust*, Goethe remarks in a letter to Karl Friedrich Reinhard on June 22 of the publication year, 1808: "Soviel habe ich überhaupt bei meinem Lebensgange bemerken können, daß das Publicum nicht immer weiß wie es mit den Gedichten, sehr selten aber, wie es mit dem Dichter dran ist. Ja ich leugne nicht, daß, weil ich dieses sehr früh gewahr wurde, es mir von jeher Spaß gemacht hat, Versteckens zu spielen" (FA, 2.6: 324) [This much I have been able to notice in the course of my life generally: that the public does not always know what the point of the poems is, and very seldom what the poet's concern is. No, I will not deny that because I became aware of this very early, I have long had fun playing hide and seek]. Goethe had long liked to hide his creativity from his readership, as we have witnessed; and the poem he is referring to here is vague about the nature of the play it precedes. But the fun of hide and seek for the hiding party depends on eventually being found. Significantly, Goethe's letter to Reinhard not only identifies the poet's literary game but also records the author's frustration that his readers did not always, as he saw it, play fair. While he confesses that Friedrich Schlegel's reviews of his work initially pleased him, he became less satisfied once he realized why some parts of it were held up to the light and others remained in the shadows (FA, 2.6: 321–322). Goethe suspected that Schlegel reviewed his work as a means to convey his own ideas to the public, in the guise of an "Apostel einer veralteten Lehre" (FA, 2.6: 321) [apostle of an antiquated teaching]. If Goethe was to conceal himself from his readers and be revealed in the way he had intended—and not be appropriated by the high priests of a new, Early German Romantic criticism as part of their poetic dogma—then he would need to set a more explicit trail for his readers to discover him. In other words, Schlegel and his contemporaries flushed Goethe out of hiding.

In the 1810s and 1820s, he began to preface much more overtly, with respect to his explicit purpose, alongside his poetic prefacing. Poetry frequently remained in pride of place, however: the prose introduction that prefaces the notes to his poetry collection *West-östlicher Divan* (1819), for instance, follows two couplets about poetic composition; and the four parts to *Dichtung und Wahrheit* present a preface about a preface and next a motto, a motto, and then a preface in turn. Nevertheless, the explanatory prose that followed resulted from Goethe's new acknowledgment that revealing was now as important as concealing.

EMBEDDED PREFACES

Following the early example of *Werther*, Goethe fictionalized his prose prefaces, such that they became more embedded within his texts. The simplest example of this strategy is the start to the second part of *Die Wahlverwandtschaften* [Elective Affinities] (1809), at the beginning of which, after the title "Erstes Kapitel" [First Chapter], the narrator of the whole novel remarks that in everyday life—and in the imminent action of the narrative at hand—marginal characters take center stage as protagonists recede. It is as if they were brought to the fore by the artistic interference ("Kunstgriff") of the epic poet (FA, 1.8: 394). Goethe, via his fictional narrator, thereby implicitly compares his work to a classical genre, the epic ("Epopöe"), and so his opening classifies the subsequent prose—but it is an opening that is already clearly part of the fiction. Indeed, unlike *Werther* this is a novel that is subtitled definitively, as *Ein Roman* [A Novel]. The text as a whole is here more clearly categorized, but its initiation is all the more blurry.

Another embedded preface of this type—that is, a text conceived as introductory, but comprising immanent material and characters, governing the narrative as an obvious part of it—is the preamble to the cycle of short stories *Unterhaltungen deutscher Ausgewanderten* [Conversations of German Emigrants] (1795), published as a six-part series in *Die Horen*. Goethe derived the idea of a series of texts, undivided without titles and set within a narrative frame, from Boccaccio's *Decamerone* from the mid-fourteenth century. Goethe starts without an explanation of his purpose in the first half of what we might call the *proem*: he begins with the beginning of a preparatory tale, before the first "novella," if we can call it such, which is the second part of the work. The preface-cum-frame fiction is much longer than the editor's opening to *Werther* or the narrator's first paragraph to the second part of *Die Wahlverwandtschaften*, and so its preliminary status is noted toward the end of this preparatory text, the first part of the series—by a fictive character. In the course of a dialogue, the baroness exclaims to the narrating clergyman: "Ihre Einleitung erregt den Wunsch, bald ein Probestück zu hören" (FA, 1.9: 1015) [Your introduction arouses the desire to soon hear a sample piece]. The first story subsequently commences, and the constituent stories segue from one into another, with mini-introductions facilitated by the characters of the preamble, which become as much a part of the overall fiction as the individually narrated tales.

The prefatory prose to "Die neue Melusine" [The New Melusine], by contrast, turned increasingly fictional as Goethe's framing of the narrative changed. First partially published in Cotta's *Taschenbuch für Damen* [Women's Annual] as a short story in 1817, with another installment in 1819, it was there prefaced by a brief, prosaic explanatory note to the effect that the tale had been written decades earlier.[68] This prefatorial comment was deleted in 1821 as the text was incorporated into the middle of *Wilhelm Meisters Wanderjahre*, a novel comprising, and preceded by, prior versions of stories in periodicals, many of which were originally prefaced with a prosaic line or two. (The embedded preface of the first part to the journalistic *Unterhaltungen deutscher Ausgewanderten*, and the lack of explanatory pieces to the subsequent parts, is unusual.) These prior prefaces to the texts incorporated into the *Wanderjahre* serve as pointers: they situate a text in relation to its previous or planned publication. Accordingly for Andrew Piper, the *Wanderjahre* constitutes not a repository of Goethe's creativity, a "discursive archive," but instead the historical transformation from the idea of a unified, single book into—borrowing a concept from media theory—a "network."[69] But within the *Wanderjahre* in its final form (which Piper would read as still in flux), prefaces are no longer pointers. Effaced and made fictional, the lines originally prefacing "Die neue Melusine" are rewritten as a part of the novel as two paragraphs from the perspective of its fictive editor, who is also the first-person narrator of the subsequent story. He refers to a preference for not prefacing, and implicitly back to Goethe's default prefatory absence: "Da mir bekannt ist, daß Sie vorläufige Reden und Einleitungen nicht besonders lieben, so will ich ohne weiteres versichern, daß ich diesmal vorzüglich gut zu bestehen hoffe" (FA, 1.10: 633) [Since it is known to me that you are not particularly fond of preliminary speeches and introductions, I want to assure you without further ado that I hope to hold my own this time, most splendidly]. This opening does not clarify its subsequent story—although in introducing it (and excusing that introduction), it presents to the public a work based on the idea of concealment that contains the possibility of public discovery through the interpretative process. The preface brashly promises the greater truth and satisfaction that will be derived from reading this tale over the others offered thus far in the *Wanderjahre*. In this presumptuous regard, the two-paragraph prefatory piece is reminiscent of the beginning to *Werther*; and since it appears in the middle of the novel that frames this specific story, it is unambiguously part of the wider fiction.

BELATED PREFACES

Goethe's scientific works, his literary criticism, and his autobiography are generally—unlike his drama, fiction, and poetry—presented to the public with prose prefaces, titled as such. In the 1810s and 1820s especially, Goethe prefaced explicitly: in spite of the form's alleged problems. He did so most obviously because an ordinarily prosaic form is not as threatening to explanatory, less creative works. E.T.A. Hoffmann, for example, wrote to his publisher Kunz in 1813 that the only type of preface ("Vorrede") he could personally stand was "als Prolegomena zu einem wissenschaftlichen Werke"[70] [as a prolegomenon to a scientific work]. Goethe seems to have shared this bias at times; and he was frustrated about the need for forewords at others, when his criticism was supposed to be literary. As he admits in his self-authored advertisement for *Zur Farbenlehre* in Cotta's *Morgenblatt für gebildete Stände* [Morning Paper for the Educated Classes] on June 6, 1810, a writer is allowed, "in einer Vorrede oder in einer Rekapitulation, von seiner Arbeit, besonders wenn sie einigermaßen weitläuftig ist, Rechenschaft zu geben" (FA, 1.23.1: 1043) [to give an account of his work, especially if it is reasonably extensive, in a preface or summary]. Oddly, Goethe writes that in more recent times, it is not considered improper to publish an "Ankündigung" [announcement] for a work, and that his advertisement is to be simultaneously read as a “Vorrede” or “Rekapitulation.” He must be referring to the relative acceptability of prefacing nonfictional works: the proper sort of preface to fiction or poetry was still contested in the 1810s—and given such controversy, was a source of greater creativity.

Perhaps it was because Goethe’s nonfiction was among his most controversial writing (alongside *Werther*), and certainly the most disputed, that prefacing as an explicit strategy became necessary and appropriate. For however badly the public may receive a book, an author can at least defend himself by subsequently maintaining in a preface that any misunderstanding was not for want of the efforts he made, and even in spite of attempting to explain his intention. This is an age-old ploy that preceded, and has continued well beyond, the Age of Goethe: whatever you think of my work, we say, I tried my best. Jeremias Gotthelf placed such a *Vorwort* before his novel *Uli, der Pächter* [Uli the Tenant Farmer] (1849):

> Der Verfasser behauptet nicht, das Rechte getroffen, sondern blos das: mit ehrlichem Willen nach dem Rechten gestrebt zu haben. Ob das Publikum billig und damit zufrieden ist, weiß der Verfasser nicht. Mag es aber nun so oder anders sein, so ist das sein Trost, daß ihm, so Gott will, nirgends ein gedankenloses oder feiles Segeln mit herrschenden Winden wird nachgewiesen werden können.[71]
>
> [The author does not claim he has achieved what is right, merely that he has aspired to what is right with honest determination. Whether the public approves and is satisfied—now that the author does not know. But however the book is received, it is his consolation that, God willing, he cannot be found guilty of sailing thoughtlessly into, or taking easy profit from, prevailing winds at any point.]

Goethe’s earlier critical prefaces are short introductions to long treatises, defending them and outlining them once again. But the more he prefaced, the more extensive his prefaces themselves became. Goethe recognized early on that a foreword can go on forever, as much as it might be omitted. In the middle of his 1773 fictional essay *Zwo wichtige bisher unerörtete biblische Fragen zum erstmal gründlich beantwortet, von einem Landesgeistlichen in Schwaben* [Two important Biblical questions, hitherto untreated but here answered thoroughly for the first time by a rural Swabian clergyman], the narrator exclaims: “Doch alles das wollt’ ich nicht sagen. Beikommende Auslegungen fordern einen Vorbericht” (FA, 1.18: 132) [But I didn’t want to say all of that. Interpretations in passing demand a preface]. The more that is written by the by, the more pertinent prefacing either those incidental comments or the entire, longer text becomes. In the introduction ("Einleitung") to the first volume of Goethe's journal *Propyläen* [Propylae] (1798), the transition between the preliminary text and the work itself is marked by the moment in which the introduction draws attention to, and enforces, its provisional status—a provisionalism, incidentally, already implied by the title (which is the Greek term for a monumental entrance to a building): "Doch es wird Zeit, diese Einleitung zu schließen, damit sie nicht, an statt dem Werke bloß voranzugehen, ihm vorlaufe und vorgreife" (FA, 1.18: 474) [It is time to end the introduction so that it does not get ahead of the work or anticipate it, instead of simply preceding it]. Here, self-reflexivity functions to keep the introductory text succinct. The notion of the preface as a textual forerunner or anticipatory moment that gives part of the plot away, or already begins the actual work, is the very objection which the prefaces to "Die neue Melusine," as part of the *Wanderjahre*, and the prose supplement to *Werther* raise against their own form. Goethe's later criticism works in the opposite direction, however. *Zur Farbenlehre* already had a foreword ("Vorwort") before the advertisement declares itself to be a recapitulation of the whole, or another preface ("Vorrede"). His "Ankündigung" for the initial volume of *Über Kunst und Altertum* [On Art and Antiquity] extended across three issues of the *Morgenblatt für gebildete Stände* (1816: 60–62). An essay of 1824 announces a planned volume of *Serbische Lieder* [Serbian Songs], the first paragraphs of which are implicitly a preface: "Verweilen wir aber nicht zu lange im allgemeinen Vorworte und treten unser Geschäft ungesäumt an" (FA, 1.22: 125) [Let us not pause too long in a general preface and promptly assume our task]. In turn, the forthcoming volume under discussion is of course prefaced by this very essay; and apparently it will be introduced again, more thoroughly, because the present preface merely introduces the subject in a provisional way. Once Goethe began to advertise, introduce, and preface critically, in other words, he prefaced profusely.

Intriguingly, he began to do so in a way that partially—but not entirely—complements his poetic and creative prose prefaces. Goethe prefaces *Zur Farbenlehre* with a criticism of the popular notion that experience should be examined without a theory, or a theoretical volume ("ein theoretisches Band"); rather, a scientist or author should acknowledge his implicit theory explicitly. In this preface ("Vorwort"), he proposes preliminary theorizing, "mit Selbstkenntnis, mit Freiheit, und um uns eines gewagten Wortes zu bedienen, mit Ironie" (FA, 1.23.1: 14) [with self-knowledge, with freedom, and to use a bold word: with irony]. This contention of an ironic relationship between theory and practice emerges from the fact that theorizing is already an act of applying practical knowledge, albeit in a more abstract regard; and practice is informed by theory (if sometimes intuitively). After all, an objection to theory is itself—and ironically—a theoretical standpoint. Thus Goethe's preface chimes with the paradoxes of his ambiguous, poetic, and embedded prefaces: it is theory, but already also a part of his scientific investigation. Similarly, his prefaces to literary criticism—like his literary criticism—become literary; and his preface to an autobiography about his life writing fiction becomes partly fictional, just as his autobiography does.

The rhetorical arguments Goethe employs in his critical prefaces are—with one notable introductory exception, to the notes for the *Divan* in 1819—hardly especially creative. On the contrary, and typically for a discursive preface, they are rather hackneyed. The belated *ältere Einleitung* [Older Preface] for *Zur Farbenlehre* mentioned earlier, which Goethe composed some time before 1816 and eventually published separately in 1822, demonstrates the author's penchant for multiple prefacing, and his conventional appropriation of prefatory topoi. He conceived the text in order to defend his particularly controversial work within scientific discourse that, as is well known, contested Newton with flair and—to be fair to the latter—a good deal of misunderstanding on Goethe's part. This introduction is partially concerned with why *Zur Farbenlehre* should be read within a scientific context at all. Goethe's line of defense is threefold. First, he begins with the assertion that his friends prompted him to write a preface, though he was usually historically disinclined toward the form. This was a reservation he had evidently already overcome, for the advertisement of 1810 is to be understood as a kind of "Vorrede," and the edition itself had a "Vorwort." Nevertheless, we are apparently to grant that the present introduction is for those whom he cherishes, and who cherish his work. Granted, it may be true that Goethe had kept relative silence compared to the hefty criticism his work received, and he had his supporters. The prefatory gesture corrects the historical record, as Goethe sees it; its dedication notes that, as disputed as his theory of color certainly was, it also had its admirers. As a second defense, Goethe writes that he had not previously prefaced the treatise with pre-emptive justification because he preferred to continue his endeavors in his own direction, and simply ignore the many objectionable reviews that would ensue. He thereby places himself above petty skirmishing; he can claim to have "niemals Gegner gehabt, Widersacher viele" (FA, 1.25: 732) [never had opponents, but many adversaries]. Remarkably, both of these moves are highly conventional: that others have persuaded him to speak out, and so he is not excusing himself out of egotism; and that he does not think the counterarguments too significant. If one way to win an argument is to signal toward one's supporters, and a second is to resist participation in critical discourse altogether, a third is to adjourn it for another day. And so Goethe's third argument is that it is simply too early to tell the real worth of his thesis: the jury must still be out on the topic, and thus readers of the age cannot adequately comprehend the book's contribution to knowledge.

In other words, Goethe ostensibly defers an adversarial position, leaving judgment to futurity: "Ein Autor, der mit etwas Ungewöhnlichem auftritt, appelliert mit Recht an die Nachwelt, weil sich ja erst ein Tribunal bilden muß, vor dem das Ungewohnte beurteilt werden kann" (FA, 1.25: 732) [An author who appears with something unusual rightfully appeals to posterity, because of course a tribunal must first be formed before which the unfamiliar can be judged]. Such a court hearing takes time to come about, allowing him to delay a protracted defense. In doing so, Goethe seems confident that, in the end, he will secure a positive scientific reputation. He draws comparison with reviews of his aesthetic works over the previous three decades, and points out that critical judgment has improved through practice. He reminds his readership of the initial reception of his *Metamorphose der Pflanzen* [The Metamorphosis of Plants] (1790), too, and that any provisional skepticism, aside from that of linguistic purism, has since been revised. In twenty years, then, Goethe reasons, a tribunal will be formed that will hear his case, "vor welchem die Sache ventiliert und mit gerechter Einsicht entschieden werden kann" (FA, 1.25: 733) [before which the matter will be aired and can be decided with just discernment]. Our author of stature does not offer his readers rational evidence for why judgment day will balance out his reputation, though, other than his own conviction and personal precedent.

Although Goethe conceives the forum for his critical evaluation as located at some point in the future, once science has sufficiently developed in order to be in a position to properly assess his thought, he is not actually addressing readers in posterity. Rather, Goethe asks the readership of his own day to pre-empt a deferred judgment not of the substance of his contribution, but (as Gotthelf would request) of its intention. That Goethe expects his readers to put themselves in his shoes in order to understand his work in a preliminary ("vorläufig") way, before the advancement of science and the ability to judge from a retrospective, more informed vantage point—if not to judge the work itself, then at least its means of presentation ("Vorstellungsart") (FA, 1.25: 734)—is as presumptive as his youthful, partly fictional preface to *Werther.* But unlike his first novel, Goethe here gives his readership no affective, let alone aesthetic cause to support him, other than to plead for his envisaged future (i.e., for sympathetic foresight). The imagery Goethe employs is hardly creative: he transposes us to an imagined, prosaic courtroom. We are left with a self-decree, but no evocative description.

Goethe once again proposes to postpone judgment until the future in 1826, and similarly he does so without much inspiration. In his foreword to Eckermann's essay *Ueber Goethe's Recensionen für die Frankfurter Gelehrten Anzeigen von 1772 und 1773* [Concerning Goethe's Reviews for the *Frankfurt Scholarly Notices* in 1772 and 1773], published in *Über Kunst und Altertum*, he proposes to leave critical opinion to an educated youth. However, while he admits that over the course of his life his reception has been both positive and negative, he presumes that his image will at worst be balanced, not harmed (FA, 1.22: 274). Only posterity can be the eventual judge of that, but the preface's readers are addressed as Goethe's contemporary, if younger friends, who know his intentions; and they are expected to be able to begin understanding him, prior to the final word. As Klaus Berghahn notes, in later life Goethe's critical writings became concerned with conditioning the sympathetic, friendly, and loving understanding of his ideal readership.[72] His prosaic prefaces rely on a reader's pre-existing and continuing affection for his literary works, instead of themselves renewing that enthusiasm.

The introduction ("Einleitung") to *Noten und Abhandlungen zu besserem Verständnis des West-östlicher Divans*, by contrast, is more aesthetically arresting. It was written for the 1819 book edition of the poetic collection, after some of the constituent poems had previously appeared in journals, and was originally called *Besserm Verständniß* [For a Better Understanding]. The revised title was adopted for the *Ausgabe letzter Hand.* The notes are introduced with the professed intention of fulfilling a need for critical assistance, with questions and objections from German listeners and readers ("deutsche Hörende und Lesende")—presumably as preliminary reactions to the work's journalistic prepublications (FA, 1.3.1: 139). Goethe's "Einleitung" thus stresses his purpose of facilitating direct understanding ("ein unmittelbares Verständniß"), for those unacquainted with poetry from the East (FA, 1.3.1: 138). But the introduction is also a partial defense of the poetry that precedes it, and which the subsequent notes explain. For Goethe foregrounds his creative process in having made the *Divan* accessible: he attempted, we learn, to phrase his language in its simplest form so that it could be comprehended most easily. The idea that clarity was a duty and that Goethe had to try and write in a way we can understand naturally is the very opposite maneuver of his metapoetic poetry, which attempts to cover up the artistry behind his works. In his 1819 introduction, then, Goethe emphasizes the fact that he has brought his artistic talent to bear on making his poems seem effortless: contrary to *dissimulatio artis*. His poetry of the *Divan*, if we accept the premise of this (post)introduction, should not have been an enigma; and if we read the notes which adjoin it, after this "Einleitung," the artificial composition of its naturalness will no longer be enigmatic, either.

In professing "zu erläutern, zu erklären, nachzuweisen" (FA, 1.3.1: 138) [to recount, to clarify, to show], Goethe evokes the senses of sound, sight, and physical gesture in his 1819 introduction. Asking us to read him as a traveler throughout the notes—a metaphor he had already adopted in his 1816 advertisement for some of the poems in *Morgenblatt für gebildete Stände* (FA, 1.3.1: 549)—he excuses his infelicities in language by figuring himself as a foreign-speaking, nonnative, accented author. It is an aural metaphor. In a visual analogy, this introduction reveals Goethe's poetic sources as a trader ["Handelsmann"] would lay out his wares. Preliminary understanding is repeatedly depicted as insight ("Einsicht"), and the poet wants to uncover "dunkle Stellen" ["dark spots"]. What is more, we are asked to imagine Goethe's material as revitalizing for his poetry, in a pun on literary and intellectual sources: as "Quellen und Bäche . . . , deren erquickliches Naß ich auf meine Blumenbeete geleitet" (FA, 1.3.1: 138) [springs and streams . . . , whose refreshing water I directed onto my flower beds]. Taken together, this introduction and these notes fortify Goethe's poetic self-presentation as a naïve poet of an unmediated, sensuous nature that followed from the writer's relationship with Schiller, as Angus Nicholls observes.[73] But they simultaneously undermine precisely that image, too, in their explanatory endeavor that Goethe professes was effortful—and thus artful. The very effort of a secretive poet to disclose himself as effortless can be interpreted ironically, as yet another artistic, prefatorial mask: this time for literary (self-)criticism.

In two further senses, too, the introduction of 1819 can be aligned with Goethe's alternative prefatory strategies apart from his belated, critical (and autobiographical) prefacing. The introduction is surely Goethe's most inventive, and to a reader of literature most interesting, among his critical prefaces—unlike the conventionalism of his abandoned, belated introductory draft to the second part of *Zur Farbenlehre* or, as we shall soon see, his prefaces to *Dichtung und Wahrheit*. Matthias Buschmeier argues that Goethe's notes to the *Divan* as a whole constitute a literary struggle against academic, prosaic classical philology.[74] Moreover, whereas the prose preface to *Werther*, say, can be understood only after the novel is completed, Goethe's introduction to the critical treatise appended to the *Divan* literally follows the last poem, and precedes criticism that is itself arguably poetic. It is thereby part of inductive understanding, too, and invites repeated reading of Goethe's work. But for some contemporaries it was simply confusing. In a review of August 12, 1820, Adolf Müllner found this sequence of texts perplexing: "Alsdann kommt—man denke! Mitten im Buche, S. 244—eine Einleitung, und wozu?"[75] [Thereupon follows—imagine! in the middle of the book, on page 244—an introduction, and to what?]. His confusion is understandable: only in the *Ausgabe letzter Hand* did the notes constitute a separate volume, explicitly titled as explanatory material. For Müllner, the self-reflexive introduction was a "Rätsel ohne Schlüssel"[76] [puzzle without a clue]. Read alongside Goethe's other preparatory pieces, published before or after the works to which they refer, but comprehensible only within the whole of the respective work, Goethe's introduction of 1819 is as ironic, intriguing, and immanent as his other types of prefaces.

Embracing prefacing with contextual, incidental details on the activity of writing literature also meant continuing to preface. In fact, a late section of the *Divan*'s *Noten und Abhandlungen* is entitled "endlicher Abschluss!" [final conclusion!], while the final one is called "Revision" (FA, 1.3.1: 283 and 292). This does not mean that Goethe's critical thoughts, unlike his poetic ones, were inherently disunified or unsystematic. Rather, it has to do with their greater degree of content, the environment of their genesis (including their at times reactive nature), and the fact that they categorize his own poetic creations. A systematic mindset, as some of us will know first-hand, produces not only order, but also provisional chaos, often: the result of thinking systematically is as much a desire to perpetually readjust the system. In Goethe's case, collecting and contextualizing his own works is especially paradoxical: he organizes his literary products as self-critic, yet at the same time continued to write, add to, and—with his short stories which became the *Wanderjahre*, for example—rewrite them by virtue of still being a literary author. When Goethe reflects on his readerly role in receiving himself as a current writer, he constantly needs to reposition himself. The most provisional method of doing so is not so much a complete autobiography, but to preface, after all—autobiographically.

A HYPERTROPHIC PREFACE

The text preceding the first part of *Dichtung und Wahrheit* (1811) is untitled, but begins with an acknowledgment that the subsequent work requires a preface ("Vorwort") more than any other (FA, 1.14: 11). There is also external, positivistic evidence for labeling this preliminary prose a preface: Goethe's diary states that he wrote the "Vorwort zum l. Teile" (FA, 2.6: 701) [Preface to the First Part] on September 8, 1811. The lengthy story of Goethe's childhood and early literary career clearly demanded justification, even though the infamous author of *Werther* and man of the Weimar court was already a towering figure of German letters at this point in history. Autobiography is a necessarily self-centered genre, and Goethe's would have risked being interpreted as an egotistical endeavor if he had left it unexplained. Ulrich Bräker quips in his "Vorrede des Verfassers" [Author's Preface] to *Lebensgeschichte und natürliche Ebentheur des Armen Mannes im Tockenburg* [The Life Story and Natural Adventures of the Poor Man in Tockenburg] (1789) that life writing is an act of self-love, and so for him self-confession and reasoning through prefacing is all the more important:

> Obschon ich die Vorreden sonst hasse, muß ich doch ein Wörtchen zum voraus sagen, ehe ich diese Blätter, weiß noch selbst nicht mit was vor Zeug überschmiere. Was mich dazu bewogen? Eitelkeit?—Freylich!—Einmal ist die Schreibsucht da. Ich möchte aus meinen Papieren, von denen ich viele mit Eckel ansehe, einen Auszug machen. Ich möchte meine Lebenstage durchwandern, und das Merkwürdigste in dieser Erzählung aufbehalten. Ist's Hochmuth, Eigenliebe? Freylich! Und doch müßt' ich mich sehr mißkennen, wenn ich nicht auch andere Gründe hätte.[77]
>
> [Although I otherwise hate prefaces, I must nevertheless say a little word at the start, before I cover these pages in goodness knows what (not even I know). What moved me to do so? Vanity? For sure! All of a sudden the compulsion to write is there. I would like to take an extract from among my papers, many of which I look at with revulsion. I want to stroll through the days of my life and preserve the strangest bits in this story. Is it arrogance, self-love? It is indeed! And yet I would be a stranger to myself if I did not also have other reasons.]

Bräker excuses his autobiographical work by claiming that he has written it for God, and for his children. And Iffland, who like Goethe was a dramatist of high standing around 1800, exclaims as his opening to *Ueber meine theatralische Laufbahn* [On My Theatrical Career] (1798) that he wrote the subsequent autobiographical reflections after the encouragement of friends: "Einige Männer, deren Meinung mir schätzbar ist, haben mich aufgefordert, bey Gelegenheit der Herausgabe meiner Schauspiele über meine theatralische Laufbahn etwas zu sagen"[78] [Several men whose opinion I value have asked me to say something about my theatrical career on the occasion of publishing my plays]. Composing an autobiographical account of literary creativity should not, it seems, be an author's own idea—no matter how important a writer may be. Goethe was no exception to this rule.

Thus in the initial pages before Book 1 of *Dichtung und Wahrheit*, readers experience the writer as the recipient of, and respondent to, a letter from his contemporary readership. According to Hans Ehrenzeller, its fictionality renders the preface literary; and the form thereby cancels out the author's later antiprefatory criticism of the thirteenth book, published in the third part of his autobiography in 1814.[79] If the letter is a literary device, however, by 1811 it was surely the most hackneyed one available to authors: for life writing generally, as well as for prefacing in particular. In Landfester's view, the epistolary construct was so commonplace that it cannot have been meant to add authenticity to Goethe's work.[80] Indeed, in the light of satire of the mid- to late eighteenth century, it is impossible to take Goethe's preface seriously as an original, literary opening. Johann Arnold Ebert begins his preface to *Episteln und vermischte Gedichte* [Epistles and Assorted Poems] (1789) with mock nostalgia:

> Es war doch eine gute Zeit, da ein Autor, der seine Werke—oder Werklein, entweder einzeln, oder gesammelt, herausgab, gleich im Anfange seiner Vorrede noch sagen durfte, daß er dieses bloß auf inständiges Bitten und anhaltendes Zureden seiner Freunde gewagt hätte; und da der gutherzige Leser noch diese Versicherung, ohne weitere Untersuchung, auf Treu und Glauben annahm.[81]
>
> [Those were good times when an author publishing his works, however significant and either individually or as a collection, could still say right at the beginning of his preface that he dared to do so because of the incessant request and continual encouragement of his friends; and these were times when the kind-hearted reader still took this assertion in good faith, and without thinking anything more of it.]

Initially, people apparently trusted not only an author whom they perhaps did not yet know, but also his anonymous friends who offered him support and credibility. Once the fictionality of these pleas and recommendations from peers and readers became evident, so goes Ebert's joke, cynicism about the author's motives set in. These writers considered the figure of the friend to be, in Ebert's words, "eine verzeihliche Nothlüge"[82] [a forgivable white lie]; yet the reading public got wise to the stock prefatory trick:

> Das Schlimmste war, daß endlich auch solche Schriftsteller, die sich mit gutem Gewissen hätten rühmen können, daß sie von ihren Freunden als gültigen und zuverlässigen Richtern, zum Schreiben oder Sammeln ihrer Schriften aufgefordert wären, nicht mehr damit Glauben zu finden hoffen konnten, und daher nun entweder allen Muth dazu, oder wenigstens—einen bequemen Eingang zu ihrer Vorrede verlohren, und auch in Absicht auf diesen Anfang das alte Sprichwort wahr befanden, da aller Anfang schwer sey.[83]
>
> [The worst thing was that in the end even writers who could have claimed with a clear conscience that they were called on to write or assemble their writings into a collection by friends who were legitimate and reliable judges had no hope of being believed. They therefore either lost heart, or at the very least lost a ready way into writing a preface; and with respect to this new beginning the old saying rang true: all beginnings are difficult.]

Johann Matthias Dreyer, too, amusingly reflects on both old and new types of preface writing in his own preface to the 1763 collection *Schöne Spielwerke* [Beautiful Musical Movements]. The outdated fashion was allegedly for an author to labor the point that he did not publish for his own financial gain, or out of egotism. He writes: "Freunde, welche sich erbauen oder die Zeit vertreiben wollen, hätten ihn so lange gebeten, bis er sich zu der Herausgabe seines Werks, nach vielen Weigerungen, entschliessen müssen" [Friends who wanted to edify themselves or pass the time would plead with him until, after refusing many times, he would have to resolve to publish his work].[84] Thus if there was one prefatory cliché of German letters around 1800 that was popularly presented comically, it was the claim of Goethe's 1811 preface that he wrote *Dichtung und Wahrheit* because "dieses so freundlich geäußertes Verlangen erweckte bei mir unmittelbar die Lust es zu befolgen" (FA, 1.14: 12) [this insistence, expressed in so friendly a fashion, immediately awakened a desire in me to submit to it].

Goethe's *Dichtung und Wahrheit* preface is not only a literary exercise; it is also one of self-historicization. We could conclude that the author chose such a conventional preface in order to commence this synoptic project from its very start, appropriating a typically eighteenth-century topos for himself before describing the period and his own trajectory in greater detail. His autobiography as a whole was an effort to capture not only his early life and work, but also his historical moment. However, in contrast to either Goethe's prefaces to *Werther*, in which the writer had seemed so confident of a positive reception, or his critical prefaces that presume vindication in the future, there is a hint of desperation in Goethe's autobiographical prefacing. And he had good reason to be worried: Schlegel and the young Early German Romantics were overtaking him in a nineteenth-century literary scene in which Goethe was no longer the sensation he had once been, at the close of the previous century. He had expressed annoyance in his letter to Reinhard of 1808; the 1806–1810 edition of Goethe's collected works, the first of three to be printed by Cotta, was hardly a runaway success; and the public had reacted in ways that are genuinely depicted in the prefatory, fictive letter of Goethe's composition, as most commentaries attest. Some people did in fact find it difficult to believe that his output was so multifaceted, asking whether the works really were by the same, single author. In addition, there had been complaints that the twelve volumes of Goethe's oeuvre did not cohere, and a call for the author to provide a chronology of his writings. These were the precise readerly needs to which *Dichtung und Wahrheit* was intended as an answer.

Vincent has emphasized Goethe's desire to (re)connect with readers as his reason for embarking upon an autobiography. As she explains, the mature or what we have come to term the *Classical* Goethe (after his departure for Italy in 1786) may be a man of stature in our literary histories, but he was no longer especially popular in his day. Nothing could match the success of *Werther* in his youth. Of *Dichtung und Wahrheit*, Vincent asserts that "the chief reason for writing it seems to have derived, if only gradually, from a cumulative, complex mixture of negative emotions in Goethe—a sense of hurt, disappointment, anger, and fear, as well as the awareness of personal transitoriness."[85] She cites a letter from the author to his publisher, Cotta, written in May 1811 after Goethe had begun writing his autobiography, in which he hoped: "das was ich bisher allenfalls [habe] thun und leisten können, besonders für meine Freunde abermals zu beleben und interessant zu machen"[86] [to once again revive, especially for my friends, that which I have at best been able to do and achieve]. The prefatory letter of that same year, which Vincent calls "a significant fiction," reflects Goethe's wish to appeal to a sympathetic audience, and especially, as she elucidates, his friends.[87] In the first instance, then, Goethe wrote for a close, appreciative circle, and hopefully a wider readership thereafter. For his prefatorial letter placed before the first volume of *Dichtung und Wahrheit*—as if in response to genuine feedback—entices Goethe to devote himself to "einem engern Kreise, vielleicht entspringt daraus etwas, was auch einem größern angenehm und nützlich werden kann" (FA, 1.14: 12) [a narrower circle; perhaps something will spring forth from that, which may be appealing and useful to a larger circle]. This small group would rehabilitate him within the positive opinion of wider readers, since the preface offers the perspective for recipients through which Goethe's writing can be "am besten genossen, genutzt und am billigsten beurteilt" (FA, 1.14: 14) [enjoyed in the best way, made use of, and judged in the most approving fashion].

Readers writing to Goethe in his fictive letter require supplementary tuition ("Nachhülfe") in their reception of his work, via authorial, friendly reflections; they have not, we are told, given up "Nachforschung" (FA, 1.14: 11) [supplementary research], because the writer's difficulty has its appeal. Goethe responds to this apparent request by affectionate means, in order to support and encourage those who wish him well (FA, 1.14: 12–13). We here witness an idealized reciprocity of critical attentiveness to an author. In fact, Goethe's ideal mode of reception became reciprocal in two senses. The poet produces literature, which is read; and reading himself, he must preempt his readership's close and contextualizing study of his productions. This desired mode of reception conditions the framing of *Dichtung und Wahrheit* beyond the first part. The preface to the fourth part of his autobiography no longer stages correspondence, but is written using the inclusive first-person plural pronoun (FA, 1.14: 727). The first preface has reconnected with these broader readers—which is once again a presumed plurality by the time of the second preface—via Goethe's friends and admirers. But the fact that the initial exchange is presented as fictional, and as such a stock fiction, evokes a sense of his clutching at straws. Though friendly readers existed, Goethe had no empirical letter that he could cite and perhaps embellish with literary flair. He used older epistolary comments from Schiller in 1797; and after Schiller's death in 1805, there was no one in sufficient esteem whom he could address publicly. His relationship to Ludwig I of Bavaria, attested in print through the "Dedication" to the sixth volume of Goethe's and Schiller's correspondence, developed later. And unlike the "Einleitung" to the notes of the *Divan*, Goethe here seeks to recapture his readers' attention in such a remarkably tried and tested way.

This preface to the first part of his autobiography reveals that which his writing in the twelve volumes of his collected works, brought out with Cotta, conceals. Martus contends that in his creativity more broadly, Goethe's work leaves spaces for commentary and interpretative leaps;[88] he purposively planted puzzles for his (proto)philologists to solve. Goethe's ambiguous, poetic and embedded prefaces are commonly underspecified and defer the sort of information which *Dichtung und Wahrheit* now provides. By 1811 at the latest, readers could conceive Goethe's literary works and autobiographical criticism as parts of a jigsaw. The readership, ventriloquized in the preface by Goethe, observes that his oeuvre presents, "manches Rätsel zu erraten, manches Problem aufzulösen" (FA, 1.14: 11) [many a puzzle to work out, many a problem to solve]. The preface is the site in which Goethe admits his intention to fill some of the elusive literary gaps in his existing publications and that which is known about him (FA, 1.14: 13). In another image, the preface is the place in which the private author enters the public sphere. An act of self-staging, the esoteric Goethe is from here on worldly, and exoteric. His writing becomes correspondence, as a short *Erklärung und Bitte* [Explanation and Request] in *Über Kunst und Altertum* of 1821 makes clear: the author says he will not respond to letters from readers individually, but rather through his volumes ("Hefte") to which his interpreters should turn (FA, 1.21: 203). The *Dichtung und Wahrheit* preface may be less innovative than Goethe's introduction to the notes of the *Divan*, but it complements that critical preface and his other creative prefaces inasmuch as it conforms to the central poetic idea of an interchange between concealing and revealing.

Moreover, his autobiography can itself be understood as prefatory: in the preface to the first part, the work is set up as provisional (a "vorläufig[e] Arbeit") to his life already lived and his writings already published (FA, 1.14: 12). Importantly, this claim can be interpreted in a double sense. Most simply, *Dichtung und Wahrheit* includes what we would normally consider prefatorial material. The line that explains Goethe's exposition of *Werther*, which begins in Book Twelve of his autobiography, follows a contextualization of the author's first play, *Götz von Berlichingen*. The autobiographical reflection on *Werther* might be read as a retrospective, embedded preface, since Goethe begins his examination: "Von der historischen Vorbereitung zu der ersten Arbeit habe ich bereits gesprochen; die ethischen Anlässe zu der zweiten sollen gegenwärtig eingeleitet werden" (FA, 1.14: 588) [I have already spoken about preparing for the first work historically; the ethical causes of the second will be introduced presently]. Hence the following passage is belated introductory, prefatory content that we do not find before *Werther* as a book; it is instead incorporated within, and is auxiliary to, the larger life story of the poet.

The other sense in which *Dichtung und Wahrheit* can be read as a preface is more formally intriguing. It is hypertrophic, explicating the first preface paradox of the present book:

> Prefaces initiate works by being both immanent and procrastinatory, determined by and deferring the main texts. Thus we can ask: are prefaces (im)pertinent? A foreword could go on forever, as much as it might be omitted.

As we have begun to see with Goethe's prose prefaces to criticism, contentful prefacing demands further prefacing. In this sense, *Dichtung und Wahrheit* remained provisional, ever extended until it was cut short by Goethe's death. It remained unfinished. But it was also based on previous, at times comprehensive advertisements and essays ("ausführliche Anzeigen und Erklärungen") (FA, 1.14: 12–13) on Goethe's compositions and their individual histories, and so *Dichtung und Wahrheit* already—as a preface—required prefacing. Goethe's opening claim that the 1811 preface is more necessary than most was not only an acknowledgment of expected modesty before an egotistical enterprise, but was also due to the nature of the very project it prefaces, which is itself prefatorial. His autobiography began and continued as a type of preface, because in its form this historical-critical project is perennially prefatory.

The 1811 preface was reprinted as the four parts of *Dichtung und Wahrheit* were extended and bound together, as four volumes, in 1833—although they remained unconcluded. The interpretation of Goethe, we gradually realize, is inevitably incomplete: it was to be furthered by us after his own day, and will last for as long as we can trace and reread every aspect of his oeuvre and life. Before his autobiography, Goethe pursued such an aim in fragments ("Bruchstücke"), as he tells his readers in the second part, and to realize his ambition by means of the little book ("dieses Büchlein") is daring (FA, 1.14: 310). Indeed, the preface to the fourth part of the autobiography clarifies the fact that it "nicht gerade ans Ende des vorigen Buches anschließt" (FA, 1.14: 727) [does not exactly follow on from the previous book], but instead "sowohl Personen als Gesinnungen und Handlungen in einer redlich gründlichen Folge vorzuführen beabsichtigt" (FA, 1.14: 727) [intends to relay people, attitudes, and events in a fairly sound order]. Goethe implicitly invites his close readers to similarly go beyond the structure of the book and fill in the gaps, adding details in the spirit of the structure he lays out. *Dichtung und Wahrheit* is only the preface to his creativity and its critical documentation, outlining merely—as its preface states—the "Hauptfäden" ["main threads"] of both.

In 1819, Goethe appended to the twentieth, final volume of the second Cotta edition of his collected works what he at the time called a "summarische Jahresfolge Goethescher Schriften" [summarizing year-by-year list of Goethe's writings], which was combined with an explanation for the edition as a whole—that had previously appeared as an advertisement in the *Morgenblatt* [Morning Paper] in 1816.[89] Goethe continued to list all his writings to date, also referring to it as a "summarisch-chronologisches Verzeichniß" [summarizing, chronological register] (FA, 1.20: 625). But such a lifeless table was meant to be only provisional, though it was also empirically complete. The sympathetic reader should be able to continue such categorization discursively, yet still refer to the list. Or as Goethe puts it rather ambiguously and pseudo-modestly in 1819, for the time being it was a good enough general thread, "an welchem auch künftig der freundliche Leser einer ausgeführteren Darstellung folgen möchte" (FA, 1.20: 625) [whereupon the friendly reader, even in the future, might follow a more elaborate representation]. While he still hoped to flesh out the skeleton story himself, he made sure to leave space for (proto)philologists to do so in his stead, after his passing. As such, the table is both like and unlike Goethe's prefaces. His prefaces were of course less tabular because they were a more discursive—and at their best, more literary—way to help readers. They can be categorized into six sorts of strategy: zero prefaces as well as ambiguous, poetic, embedded, belated, and hypertrophic ones. But Goethe's prefaces also resist this typology, indeed they are resistant to being rendered tabular. All of his prefatorial categories are necessarily underdetermined, either conceptually or in terms of content, and so—ironically—are in that sense not dissimilar to Goethe's final table, after all. His prefaces are playful, though; and for the inattentive reader, their price can be incomprehension. Goethe wrote in a letter to Wilhelm Reichel on February 12, 1827, "daß ich meine Intentionen niemals, wie es Autoren sonst vorsichtig und zweckmäßig in einer Vorrede oder in Noten thun, genugsam ausgesprochen, wodurch denn gar manche Mißverständnisse veranlaßt worden" (WA, 4.42: 53–54) [that I have never spoken sufficiently of my intentions, as authors tend to do carefully and with purpose in a preface or in notes, and it was due to this that many misunderstandings came about]. To secure a full understanding of a work before the beginning proper with conviction, if this were possible at all, would require prefatory induction in and of itself that would be so long it would become an extensive and unfinished (and thus likely still insufficient) preface—the *Dichtung und Wahrheit* project, in other words.

Nonetheless, some prefaces have less detail than others. Goethe's prefatorial variants to *Werther* are comprehensible only after the book has been read in its entirety, and are generative of a literary unity that can be reread and continually questioned as a whole. Many of Goethe's poetic or embedded prefaces are placeholders, pleasurable in themselves and postponing information typical of a preface until further into the poems or fictions at hand, or until Goethe's belated, critical, and autobiographical prefacing. Delay, diffusion, and deferral, as well as dispersion, are the key descriptors for Goethe's prefatorial program, which acknowledged the pointlessness of the form early on—only for the author to then preface, anyway. For if it is pointless to preface, this truth equally applies to zero prefacing. Arbitrarily, there is as little or as much point in prefacing.

In this line of thinking, Goethe was not unusual. For example, Wieland launched his *Sämmtliche Werke* [Collected Works] with Göschen in 1794, and thought necessary a programmatic preface ("Vorbericht") that depicts his authorial development and careful editing of his writings. But in this preface, he also professes his hope that the purpose and material of a complete works "verstehe sich von selbst"[90] [would be self-explanatory]. However pointless the preface may seem, it is also somehow pertinent—if only as an attempt to make an author's creativity or editorial choice appear self-evident. Goethe, though, marks the point at which the preface ceases to be salient or significant as such, yet remains remarkable as a form.

Such a tension suggests that Goethe's prefacing should both be read as singularly important for the interpretation of his work *and* simply as creative as all his other prose writings, poems, critical works, and so on. The latter reading is supported by recent scholarship on Goethe's concept of a printed body of work. For Martus, for example, prefaces have the same constitutive status as all other texts by Goethe. The author apparently advanced the very interpretative mode in which he has become canonized: philological reading as a form of sensitive, contextualizing, and apparently nonselective attention that is exerted on an individual and his expansive work. Thus Goethe fictionalized and poeticized his prefaces because they were just as important to him and his desired reception as his other literary productions—no more, no less—although his poetry assumed a particularly poetological status in collected editions of his writings, as it did more generally in "collected works" at the beginning of the nineteenth century.[91] Martus therefore talks of Goethe's politics of interpretation that takes effect through the totality of his life and work (and the latter should be read with reference to the former), for which Martus coins the term "Werkpolitik."

Landfester, meanwhile, reads Goethe's writing as always already points of crossover and poetic continuation, which she calls his "Grenz-Werk." A perpetual work-in-progress, it is instantiated by his paratexts, not least his prefaces, which are partly literary texts like any other, and particularly sites of self-reflection; and Goethe's work is incessantly destabilized by their revision.[92] For Landfester, Goethe's creativity refuses the idea of closure, even the Romantic idealization of it. Her conception is similar to Martus's understanding insofar as all of Goethe's texts become intertextual. And the paradigm she posits is similar, too, to Piper's notion of a Goethean textual network. Piper rightly observes that the *Wanderjahre* is unbound and, as such, exemplary for Goethe's literature as print object: "When taken together, Goethe's uses of print, publication, and narrative, far from establishing and solidifying the regulatory system that was emerging in the nineteenth century, in fact strongly resisted this program."[93] But to speak of resistance is too strong if it is supposed Goethe conceived some kind of fixed, alternative idea. Ambivalence, or inherent, incessant resistiveness, is surely more appropriate.

Precisely the fact that Goethe struggles with prefacing and seeks ways to overcome, revise, and play with prefaces, introductions, prologues, and so on throughout his career proves that prefacing cannot be subsumed into, nor read as paradigmatic of, his oeuvre in any straightforward sense, although arguments to this end can be convincing. And so Goethe's work as a whole is not uniformly resistant toward conventional print culture, just as it is not a conformist physical remainder of that culture. Instead, it appropriates and alters, as much as it antagonizes and elevates conventional notions of a "book" and its constituent parts—notably the preface. In this vein, Goethe shares a prefatorial affinity with other authors of his age, most notably Jean Paul and Hegel. His ambivalence toward prefaces in particular holds for the three major authors in the present book, and indeed many more writers around 1800. Especially his frustration and the eventual, potential infinity of his forewords, and their fictionalization, becomes a familiar story when read against Jean Paul.

CHAPTER TWO

Jean Paul

Autoprefacing

JEAN PAUL'S WRITINGS humorously reflect on what it means to write. In this regard, he self-consciously followed the most popular satirical authors of the German Enlightenment in the late eighteenth century. Parts of Friedrich Nicolai's *Das Leben und die Meinungen des Herrn Magister Sebaldus Nothanker* [The Life and Opinions of Master Sebaldus Nothanker] (1773–1776), for example, which sold more than twelve thousand copies in no fewer than four printings, satirize the European book trade.[1] Nicolai's protagonist moves to urban Leipzig, a center of bookselling activity, whereas Jean Paul's fictional commentary adopts a provincial perspective (and includes a specific nod to Nicolai). Jean Paul's country schoolmaster Wutz reads "nur Ein Buch . . . , den Meßkatalog" (SW, 1.2: 412) [only one book . . . , the trade catalog] at home and then writes out the listed stories from his own imagination, in order to fill his personal, rural library with all the titles of his times. Comically, Wutz's engagement with the outside world of books is entirely self-involved. Reading is equal to writing the imagined thoughts and words of others, by oneself.

Leben des vergnügten Schulmeisterlein Maria Wutz in Auenthal [Life of the Cheerful Little Schoolmaster Maria Wutz in Auenthal] became an appendix to Jean Paul's first novel, *Die Unsichtbare Loge* [The Invisible Lodge] (1793). This book inaugurates his mature oeuvre, which, as Till Dembeck recognizes, is of singular status for paratextuality around 1800.[2] Of particular note within Jean Paul's insatiable, idiosyncratic and, all in all, willfully incoherent writings on writing are not only the writer's paratexts in a broad sense, but his prefaces in particular. In Timothy J. Casey's words on Jean Paul's literary productions: "The digressions, the appendices, and the prefaces are central in this eccentric work, above all perhaps the prefaces."[3] In 1786, Jean Paul proposed a preface for *Mixturen für Menschenkinder aus allen Ständen* [Mixtures for Children of All Social Classes] that was to open with the brash and disingenuous self-reflection: "Wahrhaftig dieses Leben ist zu wichtig als daß ich lang an der Vorrede künsteln und zimmern dürfte; zumal da ich sogar schon eine Viertelstunde über ihren Anfang nachgesonnen"[4] [in truth this life is too important to be spending a long time crafting some artful preface, particularly as I have already spent a whole quarter of an hour reflecting on how to begin it]. Was Jean Paul's life really too short to pay much regard to prefacing? Nothing could have been further from the truth. Prefaces preoccupied Jean Paul like nothing else, and his own pieces problematize prefatory form, function, and paradoxicality in the period through a presentation of *autoprefacing.* They are as self-involved as Jean Paul's novels and short stories (such as *Wutz*), yet also have a special status as prefaces. In fact, his published prefaces—for this draft from 1786 was declined by the publisher—are markedly contemplative, if also mischievous works of art.

Although the phenomenon of prefatorial deliberation and irony was not in itself atypical around 1800 (quite the contrary), Jean Paul's prefaces are nevertheless exceptional, not least because they are prefaces to, as well as about, prefaces. This strategy materially expanded his books and was extended as he returned repeatedly to his previous book projects: lengthening, revising, and reprinting them for the public during his lifetime. But Jean Paul's penchant for prefacing began early on. The initial volume of the writer's earliest satires, *Grönländische Prozesse* [The Greenland Trials] (1783), concludes with a section that he explicitly presents in place of a preface and, simultaneously, as the preface to the introductory pages of his second volume, which was brought to market the following year. A "Beschluß" [conclusion] thus becomes "eine Vorrede zu einer Vorrede" (SW, 1.1: 104) [a preface to a preface]. Such self-reflexivity, and the concomitant self-proliferation within and of a textual space, is characteristic of Jean Paul's prefaces from his juvenile attempts into his maturity: the unpublished draft of *Geschichte meiner Vorrede zur zweiten Auflage des Quintus Fixlein* [History of my Preface to the Second Edition of Quintus Fixlein] (1797) is entitled *Vorrede zur Vorrede* [Preface to the Preface]; and in 1801, he wrote a *Vorrede zu Vorreden* [Preface to Prefaces]. What over time becomes a stock Jean Paulish joke is set up in his earliest prefaces.

Jean Paul's prefaces over the course of his life do not trace only the author's own literary development, however. Through them, a Romantic concern with the form and its contradictory character emerges, which becomes the source of complex conceptual and creative productivity. Thus Jean Paul's maturity moves us into the high point of European Romanticism, within which Jean Paul is a remarkable and textually radical writer. It was around 1800 especially that the proliferation of the German preface in Enlightenment satire turned into such intricate and original self-critique.

And yet, Jean Paul is generally thought to have been the most significant literary outlier around 1800. As Heine puts it, he was isolated in his time.[5] Goethe's junior by fourteen years, nine years older than Friedrich Schlegel, and a preface writer for E.T.A. Hoffmann, he is categorized in German literary history as the creator of an oeuvre that is independent from, but informed by, Weimar Classicism and Early German Romanticism as well as a satirical, Sternean Sentimentality. His best-selling novel was *Hesperus* (1795), which rivaled Goethe's *Werther* in its popularity. Once Jean Paul had met with both acclaim and disdain in intellectual circles, and once he had experienced mass appeal with the reading public, his prefaces began to satirize canonical practices adopted by his peers for framing their books, and for promoting themselves as authors. In doing so, Jean Paul also creatively exaggerated an increasing formal concern in this era with the fictionality of the preface, and exploited the motif of the double, or "Doppelgänger," for which he has become so famous. He is thus as important as he is idiosyncratic among authors concerned with prefacing around 1800. The peripheral form of the preface brings Jean Paul into the center of literary creativity at the end of the eighteenth and the beginning of the nineteenth centuries, notwithstanding his exceptionalism.

BAROQUE BEGINNINGS: THE PREFACE AS BROW, MORSEL, AND PORCH

In his earliest satirical works, Jean Paul wittily acknowledges that to preface is an historical, hypocritical, and hackneyed practice. He justifies his choice of a *conclusion* to the first volume of *Grönländische Prozesse* (1783) because of prefatory affectation (SW, 1.1: 103)—although he then subverts this claim by prefacing the following volume of 1784, which, he jokes, is prefaced by the previous part's conclusion. The main reason a preface appeared affected to Jean Paul, like so many an author around 1800, was its writer's disingenuous humility ("die heuchlerische Demuth des Schriftstellers"). His 1784 preface explicitly adheres to prefacing as an age-old custom, and he praises it as such (SW, 1.1: 119); but it also professes to reinvigorate the historic preface with humor. For as the young writer quips in *Auswahl aus des Teufels Papieren* [Selection from the Devil's Papers] (1789), to preface had become extremely laughable (SW, 1.1: 229). Johann Arnold Ebert agreed, writing that the preface (like a verbose title) is superfluous and "sogar lächerlich"[6] [even laughable] in his lengthy preface to *Episteln und vermischte Gedichte* [Epistles and Assorted Poems] (1789). Satirizing prefacing alongside an ostensible dismissal of the form as trivial was a commonplace strategy in late eighteenth-century German writing. Jean Paul's innovation was to say that if the form's very existence is laughable, then his examples should make us laugh all the more. And, more Sentimentally, we should smile with emotion.

Although Jean Paul's metaphors for prefaces are funny, they are hardly fresh. Indeed, they began in the Baroque period. We can follow their well-trodden path of negotiating textuality and the preface as a text type from shortly after the invention of print in English literature, for instance; and early writers who employed them influenced the Anglophile Jean Paul. Further, according to Deborah N. Losse, for the French context: "Recycling metaphoric expressions—putting old wine in new bottles—was a favourite trick of Renaissance *préfaciers*, who sought not only to establish familiar ground for the readership but to stake their own claims for innovation."[7] The ingenuity in traditionalism of Jean Paul's early conception of prefacing becomes clear once we consider three metaphorical source domains: the body, food, and architecture.

The oldest trick in the book for conceiving of a book is to compare it to the human corpus: we need only think of a volume's *spine* or *footnotes*. Writing as bodily was a popular metaphor as early as twelfth-century humanism, and, for Ernst Robert Curtius, gave rise to the analogy "of a man's face to a book, from which his thoughts can be read."[8] In the 1740s, Gottlieb Wilhelm Rabener equated prefaces with an author's countenance ("Die Vorreden sind gleichsam das Antlitz des Autors") in order to satirize contemporary physiognomic analysis: an author's literary physique could be judged, he jokes, from his prefaces.[9] In his satires of the 1780s, Jean Paul related the preface to the head as well as, more specifically, to the forehead of a book, although he also goes beyond the human body and describes a preface as the distinguishing feature of the head of a unicorn ("Einhorn"), the mythical creature of classical and medieval times (SW, 1.1: 30–31). And Rabener's physiognomic analogy continued in humorous asides about paratexts more broadly throughout the century: Novalis later remarks, "Oft ist der Titel selbst physiognomisch lesbar genug. Auch die Vorrede ist ein subtiler

Büchermesser"[10] [Often the title itself is enough for a physiognomic reading. The preface, too, is a subtle measure of books].

A second prevalent trope for prefacing around the invention of print was, as William H. Sherman writes, "a table furnished with tasty morsels."[11] Prefatory formulations, Jean Paul proclaims, satisfy the reader's initial hunger (SW, 1.1: 119), and they facilitate the social norms of table talk. His 1783 conclusion can be interpreted as "ein Freundschaftgespräch oder bildlich, eine Schüssel Krebse . . . , die man bei Landleuten nach der Mahlzeit giebt und die wenig Fleisch und viel, auch wol schöne Schale haben" (SW, 1.1: 104) [a conversation between friends or, visually, a bowl of crabs . . . , that one dishes up among country folk after a meal; crabs that have little meat and lots of shell, which can be quite beautiful]. Ebert similarly employs the metaphor of a titbit ("magre Bissen") in order to mock prefatorial convention.[12] But Jean Paul employs this stock source for a joke in thematizing an ancient rhetorical instruction for the exordium. Quintilian states that "there is also a certain tacit approval to be won by proclaiming ourselves weak"; and the speaker can apparently then astound his audience by enacting, rather than proclaiming, his strength.[13] Jean Paul dutifully and playfully reiterated the point in 1784:

> Die erste Satire, zu welcher diese Vorrede dich begleiten wird, ist die schlechteste in diesem Buche. Dieses sag' ich deswegen, damit du nicht Messer und Gabel bei dem Gerichte weglegst, das seinen bessern Nachfolgern nur den Weg bahnen sollen. Der Rath, den man in den alten Rednerschulen den Rednern gab, die Rede mit einer schwachen Stimme anzufangen und mit einer verstärkten fortzusezen, verdient Befolgung. (SW, 1.1: 120)
>
> [The first satire, to which this preface will accompany you, is the worst in the book. I'm saying this so that you do not put down your knife and fork during the dish that is only supposed to clear the way for the better ones which follow. The advice given to orators in the ancient schools of oratory to start with a weak voice and continue with a strengthened one deserves to be followed.]

The act of eating socially thereby provided Jean Paul with a model for the reinterpretation of classical rhetoric in a conventional preface, which was otherwise so often composed and interpreted like a formulaic recipe. But the etiquette of dining properly cannot be relied upon; Jean Paul does not assume automatic obligation on the part of his readership to be well-mannered toward him, if the literary palate feels cheated. Thus the preface functions as the menu ("Küchenzettel") (SW, 1.1: 103) for the dishes to come which, Jean Paul quips, may or may not turn out to be actually available.

Third, in the conclusion to the first part of *Grönländische Prozesse*, Jean Paul compares the prefatory transition into a book to a doorway. Although this renders the author its guard or porter ("Leibwache"), the conversation in the prefatorial transition from the outside to the inside of a work should be congenial, as if it were with a friend (SW, 1.1: 103). Perceiving prefacing as a threshold had a learned heritage. Francis Bacon refers in *De augmentis scientiarum* (1623) to:

> those parts of speech which answer to the vestibules, back doors, ante-chambers, withdrawing-chambers, passages, &c., of a house; and may serve indiscriminately for all subjects. Such are prefaces, conclusions, digressions, transitions, intimations of what is coming, excusations, and a number of the kind. For as in buildings it is a great matter both for pleasure and use that the fronts, doors, windows, approaches, passages, and the like be conveniently arranged, so also in a speech these accessory and interstitial passages (if they be handsomely and skilfully fashioned and placed) add a great deal both of ornament and effect to the whole structure.[14]

But even Bacon had a precedent, preprinting—an influence that was equally important for Jean Paul in the latter half of the long eighteenth century. Pindar figured his sixth Olympian ode as "a splendid palace"; to build it, he says, he and his listeners must raise "golden columns to support / the strong-walled porch"; "for when a work is begun, it is necessary to make / its front shine from afar."[15]

These three Baroque metaphors of a book's preface recur throughout Jean Paul's mature preface writing. His preface to the second edition of *Hesperus* in 1797 is conceived as a plan ("Entwurf") for the preface itself, and in terms of a building metaphor: as "Architektonik und Bauholz für die Vorrede zur zweiten Auflage des Hesperus" (SW, 1.3: 9) [Architectural drawings and timber for the preface to the second edition of *Hesperus*]. But we encounter an inversion. The preface, contrary to our usual assumptions about the form, now becomes the major as well as the preliminary part of a book's text. Jean Paul's 1801 *Vorrede zu Vorreden* portrays a main work as an ancillary building, a "Wirtschaftsgebäude" (SW, 1.9: 506) [estate building], and thus by implication a preface is the grand house. But his preface to prefaces then proceeds to present the prefatorial, textual object as a dome, or "Kuppel" (SW, 1.9: 507). In other words, the preface is paradoxically also a late, decorative addition. Furthermore, Jean Paul introduces his prefaces for the third edition of *Hesperus* in 1821 as a suite of anterooms on the way to the gallery of historical portraits ("die Gasse von Vorzimmern zum historischen Bildersaale") (SW, 1.3: 3), and he jokes that the reader dies along the way to the book. Prefaces are therefore texts that have been added on to the main frame of the book; and they are also conceptualized as miniatures of the literary work, both integral and secondary to the overall architecture. This sort of irony was a hallmark of Romantic prefacing, which—as Jean Paul's chronology suggests—properly emerged in the late 1790s.

For Jean Paul's contemporary Friedrich Schlegel, the preface is expressed using a different metaphorical domain, but to a similar end. A preface is already the fabric of the fiction, and the work as a whole is figured as a single room. In Schlegel's *Prolog* to his novel *Lucinde* (1799), the author acknowledges a debt to Petrach, Boccaccio's typical entrance ("Eingang") to a text, as well as Cervantes's prefacing; "das bunte Schauspiel der lebensvollen Werke"[16] [the colorful drama of the work that is full of life] is here dressed "mit dem kostbaren Teppich einer Vorrede, die selbst schon ein schönes romantisches Gemälde ist"[17] [with a sumptuous tapestry that is itself already a romantic painting]. In this image, the preface envelops the walls of the book, but it is also a part of those walls, decorating the novel into which the reader has entered, rather than functioning as a separate space altogether.

Jean Paul's book on poetic theory, first published in 1804, might in its entirety be read as preliminary, and so as both under construction and completed, since it is also ornamental. *Vorschule der Ästhetik*, he reminds the reader in the preface to the second edition (1813), borrows in its title the construct of a decorative, preparatory chamber for his architecture of aesthetic thought (SW, 1.11: 7): it translates as *The Proscholium of Aesthetics*, and is not dissimilar in its title image from Goethe's earlier journal *Propyläen* [Propylae] (1798). Such a hall or foyer would be added to a venue last, but it evokes a sense of grandeur that is still to come. Although Jean Paul's later prefacing seems to break from the past—through the paradox of prefaces as preliminary matter to works whose prefaces can be interpreted as also being the main part—there remains, at least in the title to his treatise, a Baroque precedent to his framing of texts. Sherman notes for the Renaissance that a "common textual edifice, particularly for didactic or polemical titles, was the schoolhouse,"[18] and in the mid-seventeenth century there was a fashion for porches "to represent entryways in the most general sense: the great educator Comenius, for example, called one of his introductions to the Latin language *Vestibulum Novissimum Linguae Litinae; Or Joh. Amos Comenius his Last Porch of the Latin Tongue* (1647)."[19]

Jean Paul must have been well versed in these previous *loci communes* of and for prefacing, for a later configuration of the preface as a site of gustatory and religious celebration hints at his wide, early modern reading habits.[20] In the preface to the second volume of *Hesperus* (1795), he ironically refers to the Catholic doctrine of transubstantiation in order to invite critics to take the prefatorial text for the body of the work itself: "Und dieser kühle ernste *hocus pocus* von Vorrede—ein Ausdruck, den Tillotson für eine Verkürzung von der katholischen Formel *hoc est corpus* hält—sei für gute Rezensenten auf Universitäten genug" (SW, 1.3: 241) [And this cool, serious *hocus pocus* of the preface—an expression that Tillotson understands as an abbreviation of the Catholic formula *hoc est corpus*—suffices for the good book reviewers in universities]. This scathing, satirical attack implies that such academic reviewers who read the preface as the whole work itself are lazy. In its topic, it is a familiar Jean Paulish joke: in his "Beschluß" of 1783, he laments that book reviewing is predicated on the rhetorical figure *pars pro toto*, since critics apply their impression of an excerpt, such as the preface, to an entire work or oeuvre (SW, 1.1: 103); and in the fifth chapter of *Hesperus*, he proposes to establish a complete collection of all German prefaces and titles as a lending library for reviewers and girls, so that users would not have to read an entire book (SW, 1.3: 312). The example from the preface to *Hesperus*, however, is historically charged. John Tillotson had cited the Latin phrase as the source of the magic words "hocus pocus" in his 1684 *Discourse against Transubstantiation*. Although the jibe had caught on among Jean Paul's Protestant peers (notably Goethe and Hegel), only he reminds us of its early modern, textual origin.[21]

Jean Paul's modern, and especially his Romantic prefaces supersede this early modern pre-story. On the one hand, as Bettine Menke remarks, Jean Paul assembles textual excerpts in humanist fashion. But as she also says, he collects them as *written* thoughts.[22] In other words, he is all the more self-aware of their place in the history of the book, and of his appropriation of them within his own contribution to that history. Jean Paul yokes so many of his historical references not to questions of religion, or learning in general, but to the problem of the book market, and especially of prefacing. In addition, Jean Paul's mature prefaces are more clearly, and most creatively, paradoxical.

REVIEWERS AND READERS

The preface to Jean Paul's second volume of *Grönländische Prozesse* graciously belittles itself as indistinct from any predecessor, on account of being superfluous; yet it simultaneously, insincerely proclaims that it is in one way distinguished from any precedent: "Bis hierher hat, wie ich hoffe, meine Vorrede alles Ueberflüssige vorgebracht, was alle Vorreden vorzubringen haben, nämlich ein Selbervertheidigen . . . . Nun aber geh' ich meinen eignen Vorredenweg und versichere gerade zu, daß ich hier nicht ein einziges mal auf die Rezensenten losfahre" (SW, 1.1: 124) [Up until this point my preface has, I hope, exhibited all the superfluous things that all prefaces have to exhibit, namely a defense of oneself . . . . But now I shall embark upon my own prefatory path and I positively assure you that I won't at any point start attacking the reviewers]. Jean Paul's mature prefaces indeed become more ambitious works of textual art. And as we saw in chapter 1, writers in the second half of the eighteenth century had witnessed an explosion of literary criticism. The preface was an opportunity for authors of this age to forestall negative judgment of their works or react to reviewers' opinions—or refuse either normative option. More creative authors condensed or circumvented their prefatory texts, or made them more complex; Goethe was the last chapter's case in point. Jean Paul's prefaces first seem as if they simply satirize the contemporary reception of literature among and beyond the book reviewers. But closer inspection reveals the intricacy and intelligence of his prefatorial humor. In particular, we return time and again to three themes about the consumption and comprehension of literature along Jean Paul's prefatory path: the pluralism of the readership, satirized self-love, and doubling of the authorial persona.

Critical as well as general readerships became more diverse as our period progressed, so it was especially unclear with whom writers should skirmish, if anyone at all. In his first-ever preface, Jean Paul already admits that to focus on the present-day reception of a work can distort a longer-term perspective, just as a fly that passes too close to the nose might appear to be an eagle (SW, 1.1: 107). In the preface to his first novel, *Die Unsichtbare Loge*, he quips that bookbinders read his writing before they cut it to size and compress it, whereas the opposite holds true for ostensibly good reviewers—but that these reviewers are not the same as the critics.[23] Whereas he likens the former to appeal judges, the latter rule on the basis of a work's first hearing (SW, 1.2: 19). Instead of pandering to these critics, Jean Paul addresses his everyday readers and aligns himself in this preface of 1793, albeit hesitantly, with belletristic authors (SW, 1.2: 19). He begins the preface to the first edition of his next novel, *Hesperus* (1795), by stating that he had wanted to rage against unwelcome readers at the start, standing at the front of his book as prefatorial "Pförtner" [porter] or, employing a medical metaphor, a "Prosektor" [prosector]. But he reconsidered, asking why he did not address in his opening line those readers to whom he would give a free copy if only he knew where they lived, and take them by the hand (SW, 1.3: 15).

The homely imagery Jean Paul uses in imagining himself as a friendly visitor to readers' houses turns out to be significant as he sought to capture and captivate a section of the reading public for himself. His first preface to *Quintus Fixlein*, published the next year in 1796, is presented as a *Billet an meine Freunde* [An Address to my Friends] and is especially friendly: authors, like tradesmen, girls, and Quakers, apparently call everyone their friends (SW, 1.5: 3). The preface takes the place of a personalized inscription, on the initial blank pages of a book; and Jean Paul adds his middle name Friedrich for the first time, revealing his full name ostensibly in order to conform to epistolary convention (SW, 1.5: 7). Most importantly, he describes a familiar, intimate conception of writing that is at home as much in readers' domestic experience as in high art. The genius—categorized together with heroic men, republicans, or reformers of the church—is a man who acts purposively and passionately, governed by an idée fixe (SW, 1.5: 4–5). Determination or frenzy supposedly separates him from everyday folk at the kitchen table, since like a bird of paradise he will instead soar to idyllic heights. But although this image figures such a writer's creativity as sublime, Jean Paul simultaneously introduces this type of author as oblivious to the traumatic events of the real world. The genius, then, is self-absorbed, though Jean Paul jokes as consolation that at least few people can be placed in this category, and those who can be defined as such are so often bitten by fruit bats, which he glosses as vampires. By contrast, he asserts that he is himself able to move from the lofty realm of creativity to that of the ordinary person. The artist becomes the artisan. Through use of the verb *einbeugen*, he indicates that he does not reject one literary domain for the other, but instead occupies both spheres, progressing from privileged poetic genesis into the milieu of readers, from military accomplishment to appraisal in the kitchen:

> Der siegende Diktator muß das Schlacht-Märzfeld zu einem Flachs- und Rübenfeld umzuackern, das Kriegstheater zu einem Haustheater umzustellen wissen, worauf seine Kinder einige gute Stücke aus dem Kinderfreund aufführen. Kann er das, kann er so schön aus dem Weg des genialischen Glücks in den des häuslichen einbeugen: so ist er wenig verschieden von mir selber, der ich jetzt—wiewohl mir die Bescheidenheit verbieten sollte, es merken zu lassen—der ich jetzt, sag' ich, mitten unter der Schöpfung dieses Billetts doch imstande war, daran zu denken, daß, wenn es fertig ist, die gebacknen Rosen und Holundertrauben auch fertig werden, die man für den Verfasser dieses in Butter siedet. (SW, I.5: 7)
>
> [The victorious dictator must plough the battlefield, the field of Mars, and work the land for flax and beet; he must turn his theater of war into a parlor theater in which his children can stage some good pieces from *The Children's Friend*. If he is able to accomplish that, then he can turn from the happy path of genius onto a happy, homely track; and in this regard he is little different from myself, for I am about to—although modesty ought to prevent me from saying this—for I was even now, I tell you, even in the middle of writing this *Billett*, able to think about the roses and elderflowers that will be ready when I've finished, which are being blanched and buttered for the author of this work.]

In flouting the rhetorical, prefatory precept of modesty, Jean Paul here suggests that he possesses the ability for literary combat, which is typical of the genius's fate and presumably common to the reviewers or critics; and yet he writes in the expectation that he will also appeal to a domestic public, which will prepare food in his honor. At this point, the preface's title becomes all the clearer: one historical sense of a "billet" is a note given to a soldier permitting him to take up quarters with a specified civilian.[24] Moreover, cookery connects Jean Paul to his readers; and this connection is not additional, but essential to what might begin, as literary prose supposedly does, as a crisis. A powerful genius is like the sort of dictator who was appointed in times of emergency in ancient Roman culture. This character traditionally returns to private life once normality is reinstated. Jean Paul thus implies that after his creative fervor, he can address his readers as a homely, useful subject, following the example of Friedrich Eberhard von

Rochow, whose enlightened journal *Kinderfreund* [The Children's Friend] was published for a domestic audience between 1776 and 1779.

By the close of the eighteenth century, reading had become a private, everyday pastime among the German middle classes, though writers evidently hoped that within this habitual practice their creations would be received as extraordinary. In the preface to the first edition of *Siebenkäs* in 1796–1797, Jean Paul positioned himself appropriately. Whereas in ancient rhetoric and typically throughout humanist poetics there were three styles of speech based on the speaker's goal—to instruct (*docere*), entertain (*delectare*), or move (*movere*) the recipient—our author now distinguishes between three types of reading publics: the "Kauf-," "Lese-," and "Kunst-Publikum" (SW, 1.6: 8) [purchasing, reading, and artistic publics], which correspond to "Leib," "Seele," and "Geist" (SW, 1.6: 8) [body, soul, and mind], respectively. The three rhetorical styles ascend from the lowest form of writing to the most elevated, and so too do Jean Paul's categories. He does not expand upon the last: reading material which was written under cosmopolitan influence, and so includes works by Lessing, Wieland, Herder, and Goethe. According to Jean Paul, the corresponding style was too refined, so that by the 1790s works of this kind were seldom read (as we saw for the late Goethe in chapter 1). The "Kauf-Publikum," on the other hand, apparently determined the literary market and was typified by the merchant characterized in this preface, Jakob Oehrmann. Such a readership bought what Jean Paul describes as the heftiest and most bodily works ("die größten und korpulentesten [körperhaftesten] Werke"), which the women used as if they were cookbooks, looking up recipes and "working" from them (SW, 1.6: 8). He writes that these readers knew nothing loftier in the world than bread; and empirically, around 1800 they comprised an increasingly significant consumer sector.

Indeed, the burgeoning trend for cookbooks had been thematized just one year earlier in Goethe's *Episteln* [Epistles] (1795). The second poem of this collection implies that the staple customers of the book trade as a whole, namely women, not only found series of recipes practical, but began to turn to them for reading material, too; cookbooks were apparently churned out onto the market in their hundreds (FA, 1.1: 484). As its etymological root suggests, reciting a *recipe* is about more than giving a list of instructions: cookbooks contain elements of storytelling; recipes can be read as narratives.[25] Indeed, contemporary volumes of recipes also contained short stories, poems, etc.; and Jayne Elizabeth Archer argues that cookbooks in early modern Britain transformed housewifery so that it was auxiliary to the literary sphere.[26] Further, Fichte's preface to *Einige Vorlesungen über die Bestimmung des Gelehrten* [Several Lectures on the Definition of the Scholar] in 1794, two years before Jean Paul's preface, fears that "der gröste Theil der übrigens rechtlichen, ordentlichen, und nüchternen Leute"[27] [the largest proportion of people who are otherwise proper, orderly, and sober] will judge his work to be useless. He mocks those readers who cannot raise their ideas to a higher realm of genius as demanding "daß alles Gedruckte sich als ein Koch-Buch, oder als ein Rechen-Buch, oder als ein Dienst-Reglement solle gebrauchen lassen"[28] [that everything which is printed should be able to be used like a cookbook, accounting ledger, or rules of service].

None of this, of course, was positive. If one set of readers was too spiritual and high-minded, the other was basely utilitarian and coarse. For Jean Paul that left the middle category: those with "Seele." The readership that constitutes the "soul" class had leisure time and read for pleasure. Its representative character in the *Siebenkäs* preface, Johanne Pauline, is already aware of most of Jean Paul's literary corpus, which he calls "die halbe Blaue Bibliothek" (SW, 1.6: 11) [half of the Blue Library]. This term alludes to the French entertainment genre *Bibliothèque Bleue*—volumes with blue covers. Thus Jean Paul's prefaces confront a moderate, middle group of readers who turn to books for enjoyment, emotional engagement, and an enlightened but accessible worldview.

The first theme to predominate across Jean Paul's prefacing, then, was an acknowledgment that the conception of critics or readers as homogeneous entities was false. The period around 1800, with its emergent commercial literary market, was one of increasing differentiation in the authorship and reception of books. Addressing a more narrowly defined target audience was tactically preferable to trying to win readers with some generalized goodwill. Jean Paul himself makes this point in his 1807 preface to *Schmelzles Reise nach Flätz* [Schmelzle's Journey to Flätz], in which he praises the function of footnotes for addressing a multifaceted readership. An author, he reasoned, could write a book, "indem er, statt ein ekles gärendes Allerlei für niemand zu brauen, blos dahin arbeitet, daß er Notenlinien oder Demarkationslinien zieht und so auf dem nämlichen fünfstöckigen Blatte die unähnlichsten Köpfe behauset und bewirthet" (SW, 1.13: 5) [simply by drawing lines between notes, or demarcation lines, so that on a sheet of namely five rows the most dissimilar minds are housed and fed—instead of brewing a disgusting, fermenting mishmash for nobody]. Prefaces address not a vague public, but Jean Paul's perspective on specific publics, for the section of the general public that constituted his desired readers.

The specific set inclined to receive a writer's work positively became, in Jean Paul's poetics, those readers who reflected the authorial self. Hence his alter ego Johanne Pauline in the *Siebenkäs* preface. The second theme observable across his prefaces, therefore, was the mock-defense of self-love as a motive for writing, which meant that his prefaces displayed vanity—the satirical inversion of their standard rhetorical function of demonstrating modesty. A pragmatic strategy to this end was to write a review of one's own work as a preface. In his second satirical collection, *Auswahl aus des Teufels Papieren*, Jean Paul humorously justifies prefaces as "die ächtesten *Milchschwestern* der Selbstrezensionen" (SW, 1.1: 415) [the truest *sisters by the same wet nurse* to self-reviews]; among other arguments, an author's praise of himself is permissible, because readers can reasonably hope that he is more likely than a reviewer to have really read the book (SW, 1.1: 416). The analogy of the self-authored preface to a book review written by the writer himself recurs across Jean Paul's mature prefaces, to both his own writings and those of others. His preface to Hoffmann's *Fantasiestücke in Callot's Manier* [Fantasy Pieces in Callot's Manner] (1814–1815), for instance, is presented as a review by a fictive critic called Frip, because "die eigenen Vorreden der Verfasser ordentlicherweise nichts sind, als offene Selberrezensionen"[79] [authors' own prefaces are regularly nothing other than explicit self-reviews]. And in the preface to his *Kleine Bücherschau* [A Little Overview of Books] (1825), Jean Paul writes: "Alles ist im Buche Rezension; denn Vorreden sind theils außerhalb des Buches stehende, theils an dieses geheftete Rezensionen, entweder vom Verfasser selber (wie diese) oder von einem fremden Lobredner" (SW, 1.16: 267) [everything in the book is a review, for prefaces are reviews—partly external to a book, in part bound into it—and are either by the author himself (as in this case) or are by a third party who sings the work's praises]. As a prefatory practice, Jean Paul's "Selbstrezensionen" were more satirical than serious. In the preface to the fourth volume of *Hesperus* (1797), he is comically wary of reviewing his own work and, moreover, attacks the critics' readings of his prefatorial self-interpretation. If an author lightly chastises himself in this space, the book reviewers will seize on the flaw, and double it. But if a writer promotes praise of his own writing, "so wird dieses gar nicht akzeptiert, geschweige verdoppelt" (SW, 1.4: 197) [this will not even be accepted, let alone doubled].

Instead, Jean Paul plays with prefatorial personae as reflections on, and doubles of, himself—the third notable theme of his prefacing. He prefaces the second, third, and fourth volumes of *Siebenkäs* that same year (1797) by regretting in jest that no writer had yet asked him to write a preface, or "Vorerinnerung," for a book as an apologist on the author's behalf. Jean Paul must therefore continue to write his own prefaces to works (or rather, his own works to prefaces) in order to maintain his existence as a preface writer: "Es hat mich oft verdrüßlich gemacht, daß ich jeder Vorrede, die ich schreibe, ein Buch anhängen muß als Allonge eines Wechselbriefes, als Beilage sub litt. A–Z" (SW, 1.6: 129) [It has often made me annoyed that I must append a book to each preface I write, as a slip for additional endorsements attached to a bill of exchange, as a supplement under the headings A–Z]. Such prefaces by a third party traditionally resulted from correspondence between an author and a scholar or more established writer, whose preface would promote the work on the younger party's behalf. Jean Paul proceeds, with mock earnestness, to assert himself as a renowned author who had been asked to preface the current narrative, *Siebenkäs*, and thereby splits his writing personality into two roles: a writer and preface writer ("Vorberichtmacher"). Jean Paul pens the preface as "Hr. Verfasser des *Hesperus*" [Mr. Author of *Hesperus*] (SW, 1.6: 130), since his previous novel of 1795, which he had published and prefaced under his own pseudonym Jean Paul, had become a bestseller throughout German lands. But the first and subsequent volumes of *Siebenkäs* were published under this pseudonym, too, and so the signatures below the fictive and the framing prefaces are the same: "Jean Paul Fr. Richter" (SW, 1.6: 135). His witty doubling was obvious to all readers from the work's and preface's first appearance.

Jean Paul's prefatory characters served to do more than deliver a funny commentary for or on contemporary readers, or on book reviewers who were accused of not actually reading books. They are poetologically key to unlocking his ideas about writing. The introduction to the present book began with an interpretation of Jean Paul's intricate, comically monstrous prefatorial persona—the monoped ("das Einbein") in *Die Unsichtbare Loge*. Even in his conclusion to the first volume of *Grönländische Prozesse* a decade earlier, Jean Paul already employs this odd image of one-leggedness. Here, he concedes that his metaphors can be convoluted, because they are formed by ideas that occur to him in passing while he writes "in der Hitze der Arbeit" (SW, 1.1: 107) [in the heat of work]. For this reason, their frames of reference cannot always be grasped by readers; and in this way, we write for ourselves before we write for others. Indeed, we write for others as if they were ourselves—but they are nevertheless not the same as us. The first person to receive a work is the one who writes it, yet that person is not its only recipient. Writers, therefore, must neither wholly depend on nor relinquish their critical reception. Jean Paul then appends an obscure metaphor to this discussion: "Schreiben ist empfangen, empfangen geniessen; aber im Genusse gleichen wir alle dem Papagai, der während seines Fressens auf Einem Beine steht" (SW, 1.1: 107) [Writing is to receive, to enjoy receiving; but in that enjoyment we are all similar to the parrot who stands on one leg while eating]. Parrots perch on a single leg in order to conserve their heat; presumably, an author should not expend all of his energy on being grounded within the public sphere (which, yet again, is presented in gustatory terms). He also writes for writers—and so, in some regard, for himself. At the same time, solipsistic enjoyment is not enough for human life: it is better to be able to stand on two legs, and so the writer should think of his readers' pleasure as well. Jean Paul's ideal reader, Johanne Pauline, is thus both not Jean Paul and Jean Paul.

WRITERS AND PREFACE WRITERS

Jean Paul's major breakthrough as a mature writer, we will recall, was the publication of *Die Unsichtbare Loge* in 1793. After his juvenile false starts, this proper beginning to what would become a successful writing career was founded upon his literary connections: the first novel appeared following a productive exchange of letters with Karl Philipp Moritz the year before. Subsequently, Jean Paul became personally acquainted with all the prominent writers of the period around 1800, though his most congenial relationships were with Wieland and Herder. And consequently, especially from the turn of the century onward, his prefacing was as much concerned—for the most part, still satirically—with canonicity in contemporary literary circles and the literary afterlife as it was with a more general critical and popular reception.

Most notably, in 1801 he composed his preface about prefaces, the *Vorrede zu Vorreden* from the perspective of the "Literaturgeschichts-Forscher" (SW, 1.9: 505). The literary historian's primary interest is apparently biographical; Jean Paul calls him a "Meuselische[r] Literator" (SW, 1.9: 506), thereby evoking Johann Georg Meusel, who compiled short summaries of authors' lives and the order of their works in a volume that went through many editions, the fifth in 1796: *Das gelehrte Teutschland oder Lexikon der jetzt lebenden teutschen Schriftsteller* [Learned Germany, or Lexicon of Authors Alive in Germany Today]. But while Jean Paul expresses mock sympathy for the historian's task, he humorously suggests a distinction, just as he had distinguished between the critic and the reviewer in his preface from 1793: the reviewer is "der Vorläufer und Gazettier des Literatur-Historikers" (SW, 1.9: 506) [the forerunner of, and gazette animal to the literary historian], and so deserves all the more pity. There is a familiar Jean Paulish joke: both the "Literaturgeschichts-Forscher" and implicitly also the reviewer require only the preface for their studies, which deal merely with "die Geschichte, nicht . . . die Textur des Buchs" (SW, 1.9: 506) [history, not . . . the texture of the book]. They are more interested in the preceding summary of, and background information to, a work than "[das] materielle Buch" (SW, 1.9: 506) [(the) material book]. Frustratingly for them, this is often attached to the book itself, hence the author (falsely) claims that his preface is available from booksellers in discrete form, neatly bound, so that literary historians or reviewers do not have to purchase and read the book in its entirety, gleaning their contextual details from the preface instead. He also (once again jokingly) tells of lending libraries in literary towns such as Jena or Erlangen which, he writes, merely circulate the prefaces to works for historical-critical judgment.

This 1801 preface about prefaces also prefaces the author's wider commentary on writing for a public, past and present. It is placed before a volume of two short prose texts, *Das heimliche Klagelied der jetzigen Männer* [The Secret Lament of Today's Men] and *Die wunderbare Gesellschaft in der Neujahrsnacht* [The Marvelous Society on New Year's Night]: the first satirizes a literary backwater, the second a watershed for authors on the edge of the commercial age of the book. Both texts gently mock traditional types of authorship as outmoded, and anxiously imagine the course of the new century, as well as literary history beyond it. *Vorrede zu Vorreden* comically thematizes prefatory practices within these contexts; and rather than the witty introspection of self-review, we are concerned here with a parody of a classical-cum-Enlightenment writer's presentation of his historical self-development. Accordingly, the preface is "der historische Theil des Werks" (SW, 1.9: 507) [the historical part of the work], and Jean Paul quips that "Vorher, am ersten Tage—im Buche—wird Licht geschaffen, am letzten—in der Vorrede—der Mensch, der Autor" [Beforehand, on the first day—in the book—there was light—and on the last, in the preface, man, the author, was made]. It is a space in which the writer summarizes the story of the subsequent work as well as the history of how and why it was written; and so the preface also offers the author the opportunity to tell of his own genesis. That is to say, preface writing historicizes a work's creation and the authorial image. In this regard, Jean Paul cites Lessing's 1759 *Vorrede zu den Fabeln*

[Preface to the Fables] in describing the preface as "die 'Geschichte des Buchs'—wie Lessing die Vorrede definiert" (SW, I.9: 505) [the "history of the book"—as Lessing defines the preface]. Lessing's preface recounts what motivated the author to compose his collection of fables as well as, crucially, the reason he took pains to revise them: "Und so nahm ich mir vor, was ich erst *verwerfen* wollte, lieber so viel als möglich zu *verbessern.*—Welche Arbeit!"[30] [And so I took it upon myself to instead *improve* as much as possible that which I first wanted to *discard*—Oh, the work!]. However, he goes on to jokingly flout his own maxim, by acknowledging that he exceeds the stated remit of writing a history of the book by proceeding to engage with existing critical opinion of his work.

Steffen Martus coins the term "Verbesserungsästhetik"[31] [aesthetics of improvement] to denote the poetics, and particularly the prefacing, of Friedrich von Hagedorn, Christian Fürchtegott Gellert, and Wieland, who all followed the examples of early Enlightenment writers such as Friedrich von Canitz, Albrecht von Haller, Benjamin Neukirch, and Christian Wernicke. Lessing, and especially his preface of 1759, forms part of the trajectory in a self-aware and humorous manner—which is further exaggerated by Jean Paul. Martus's argument is twofold. First, he claims that time-intensive extension and continual revision of a literary work became a German ideal in the eighteenth century, in part through the reading of Horace. In *The Art of Poetry*, Horace had praised effort and condemned error; art should be smoothed over with a file, and improved many times over.[32] The import of this poetological principle into German letters can begin to be seen, for example, in *Die römische Octavia* [The Roman Octavia] by Anton Ulrich, Herzog von Braunschweig-Wolfenbüttel. This prose romance was first published in three volumes in 1677, albeit incompletely; extended and revised editions appeared in 1712 and 1713. In the 1712 "Vorbericht an den Leser" [Preface to the Reader], the author admits that the present work was completed with haste ("Eilfertigkeit"), not patient labor—but the purpose of the preface was in part to clarify to the reader why it was reprinted in an improved ("verbessert") form.[33] Second, Martus observes that a relationship is established in the early eighteenth century between the autobiography of an author and the development of his literary output—which later develops into Goethe's *Dichtung und Wahrheit* project, as we witnessed in chapter 1. This connection emerged out of an environment of self-historicizing prefaces. In other words, German writers began to historicize their careers as authors in relation to their sequences of published works, for the benefit of general readers and the critics. Simultaneously, they promoted revisions to subsequent editions of their work as improvements for posterity and future understanding.[34] In the first quarter of the nineteenth century, this attitude to authorship fell out of fashion; and Jean Paul, from his mid-career onward, continues the tradition in a tongue-in-cheek way.[35]

In and of his preface to the second edition of *Die Unsichtbare Loge* (1822), the author notes: "Bei allen neuen zweiten Ausgaben wird es dem Verfasser, der sie so gern zu recht verbesserten machen möchte, von neuem schmerzhaft, daß keine seiner Dichtungen ein um- und eingreifendes Kunsturteil über Charaktere und Geschichte und Sprache jemal hat erobern können" (SW, 1.2: 11) [With each new second edition it pains the author all over again to see that while he would like to really improve his books so much, none of his works has ever managed to overcome an invasive and all-encompassing artistic judgment about his characters, stories, or language]. Consequently, Jean Paul humorously complains about the care with which he should attend to his revisions, since prefacing a second time is likely to be as pointless as any previous attempt. Hence he presents the convention of detailing the development of, and changes to, his works comically. He jokes that his satirical phase from nineteen years old to the age of twenty-eight, until 1790, was "ein ganzes horazisches Jahrneun" (SW, 1.2: 7) [a whole Horatian nine years], referring to the Horatian maxim in *The Art of Poetry* that poetry should be kept from the public eye for nine years before being offered for critical judgment.[36] In this way, Jean Paul suggests that his earlier material, which was not widely received and was not published under his own name or mature pseudonym, was such that it was like not being published at all, and thus was not until now part of his oeuvre in print—though his "Beschluß" [conclusion] of 1783 was signed with the initial of his surname, "R." (SW, 1.1: 116). Here, in the 1822 preface to *Die Unsichtbare Loge*, he refers to the preface of the second edition of the satires of his youth, *Grönländische Prozesse* (SW, 1.2: 8).

Further, although for his *Sämmtliche Werke* [Collected Works] of 1826 he reverses changes undertaken throughout his career that had purged contentious content from his early satirical writings such as *Auswahl aus des Teufels Papieren*, Jean Paul writes in the prefatorial "Vorerinnerung" [Prior Reminiscence] to their final republication that he had applied "Schminkquecksilber zum Verbessern der Farbe" (SW, 1.1: 219) [mercury make-up for improving the color] to his juvenile work nonetheless. This commitment to stylistic improvement but retention of the basic ideas is consistent with his earlier, second preface to *Hesperus* (1797), in which he notes that he has corrected typographical errors, spelling mistakes, linguistic dissonances, semantic blunders, and infelicities of content: "die Einfälle aber und die poetischen Tulpen hab' ich selten ausgerissen. Ich sah, wenn ichs thäte, so bliebe vom Buche (weil ich die ganze Manier ausstriche) nicht viel mehr in der Welt als der Einband und das Druckfehler-Verzeichnis" (SW, 1.3: 11) [but I have seldom pulled out the ideas or the poetic tulips. I saw that if I were to do so, not much of the book would remain in the world (because I would efface its whole manner) other than the binding and the register of printing errors]. In other words, the editing process is necessarily limited and does not imply perfection, for the latter ideal might result in a dearth of pages and demand an entirely new book. And according to the third preface of *Hesperus*, a later change to a completed work might actually disrupt it: "Der spätere Mensch hält zu leicht das Aendern am jüngern für ein Bessern desselben; aber wie kein Mensch den andern ersetzen kann, so kann auch nicht einmal derselbe Mensch sich in seinen verschiedenen Alterstufen vertreten, am wenigsten der Dichter" (SW, 1.3: 6) [Man in his late years too easily takes a change to his younger self to be an improvement on it; but just as no man can replace another, so the same man, and least of all an author, cannot represent himself as he was at different stages of his life]. Jean Paul's final preface to *Hesperus* thereby historicizes his writing in the extreme, in order to satirize the ideal of successive revisions of a work. What is more, such prefaces are also satirical presentations of the constant, pedantic revision of, and historicizing self-reflection on, prefaces themselves rather than the works to which they are appended (prefaces which, in the aforementioned 1822 preface to *Die Unsichtbare Loge*, are figured as implicitly scholarly: "Studierstubenfeste" (SW, 1.2, 6) [parties in the study]). For Jean Paul quips in his preface to *Politische Fastenpredigten während Deutschlands Marterwoche* [Political Lent Sermons During Germany's Holy Week] (1817) that the history of the preface to the fifth part of the work, as well as the history of the work itself, will be summarized (SW, 1.14: 185).

Jean Paul's ultimate act of prefatory and satirical self-historicization occurred toward the end of 1824 or early the following year. As he neared the end of his life, he wrote *Vorbericht zu dem Kranken und Sekzion-Berichte von meinem künftigen Arzte* [Preface (or Preliminary Report) to the Report on the Illness and Dissection of My Future Patient]. The text was dictated by the author and transcribed by his wife, Caroline, since Jean Paul was losing his sight by this time, and it was signed by him with his honorary doctor title (from Heidelberg, which had been awarded on Hegel's recommendation). It is a self-diagnosis written in the form of a pseudoscientific document that ends with a wish to remain alive, specifically "um meine *opera omnia* herauszugeben und zu vermehren" (SW, 2.10.1: 414) [to publish and expand my *opera omnia*]. The "Vorbericht" is a satirical, ostensibly objective medical history of Jean Paul's subjective, authorial persona, from his early satires in the 1780s onward; and it establishes an individual Jean Pauline disease as his namesake. It confirms that he aspired to publishing, increasing, and completing his body of collected works into his final days, which he was editing at the time of writing. And significantly, one of Jean Paul's last pieces of prose presents itself as a preface or provisional report. He consistently figured his existence as a writer as prefatorial, and mock-historicized himself prefatorily as desiring continual improvement.

In this satirical yet serious, self-historicizing, and self-prefacing endeavor, the preface becomes a playground of the authorial Doppelgänger, a term whose coinage literary history attributes to Jean Paul: in *Siebenkäs*, he defines the word as depicting "Leute, die sich selber sehen" (SW, 1.6: 54) [people who see themselves]. In his 1825 supplementary afterword to his (preliminary) aesthetic theory, *Kleine Nachschule zur ästhetischen Vorschule* [Small Extension to the Aesthetic Proscholium], he suggests that through characterizing the self in the form of another, an author attains "eine reine Ironie mit weniger Mühe" (SW, 1.16: 433) [pure irony with less effort], since he overcomes the conflict inherent in offering an objective representation of his own subjective perspective. Irony, Jean Paul reminds us, is already an invention of rhetorical theory. He then cites the exemplary German writer Wieland (and his *Geschichte des Agathon* [History of Agathon], 1766–1767, specifically) as well as the most famous example of a preface-writing double as two masters of a pure, fictionalized irony, though Wieland is better: "Sogar der Meister Cervantes ironisiert in seiner Vorrede zum Don Quixote nicht so unverfälscht als dieser in seinen Selbgesprächen" (SW, 1.16: 433) [Even the master Cervantes does not ironize as purely in his preface to *Don Quixote* as he (Wieland) does in his monologues]. With this reference to Cervantes, we encounter a common influence on Enlightenment humor (such as in the young Wieland's *Don Sylvio*, 1764) and Early German Romantic thought (recall the prologue to Schlegel's *Lucinde*).[37]

If the literary artist must be objectively knowledgeable about his subjective art, he needs to be a practitioner and theorist at once. This dual demand became a tenet of literary writing about literary writing around 1800. Herder begins the second part of *Kalligone* [Calligone] (1800) with the wordplay that whoever has knowledge without creative capacity is a theorist, whereas whoever has creative capacity without knowledge is a practitioner, a craftsman: "Wer *kennt*, ohne zu *können*, ist ein Theorist, . . . wer *kann* ohne zu *kennen*, ist ein bloßer Praktiker oder Handwerker."[38] The true artist ("Künstler") must possess both. Jean Paul helped Herder to write this work during stays in Weimar between 1798 and 1800. He had already begun to draft his own theoretical treatise, *Vorschule der Ästhetik*, in 1794. The preface to the first, 1804 edition contends that writing on aesthetics must itself have an aesthetic quality; theoretical prose must be literary, too. Beauty can be identified and evoked only by beauty (SW, 1.11:16). This prescription dovetails with the Early German Romantic idea of transcendental poetry, formulated around 1798. Accordingly, in their transcendental material literary authors should develop a poetic theory of literary art, so that there is "überall zugleich Poesie und Poesie der Poesie"[39] [poetry everywhere, and poetry of poetry as well]. As a corollary claim, Friedrich Schlegel writes in his "Brief über den Roman" [Letter Concerning the Novel] in *Gespräch über die Poesie* [Conversation on Poetry] (1800) that a theory of the novel itself must take the form of a novel.[40] Jean Paul's affinity to this recent movement is clearly stated in his *Vorschule* preface: "Meine innigste Ueberzeugung ist, daß die neuere Schule im Ganzen und Großen Recht hat" (SW, 1.11: 19) [It is my most deeply held conviction that the new school is, on the whole, correct]. It makes sense, in this light, that discussion of a preface during the onset of the nineteenth century should occur in a preface. The form can only be theorized within its reproduction.

Jean Paul expresses his ideal, one that is akin to transcendental poetry, through a more comic, if crude metaphor in the preface to the second, 1813 edition of the *Vorschule*. For his presentation of aesthetics is funnier as well as more applied—and, therefore, more practical—than that of the Early German Romantics as they are traditionally categorized. As he emphasizes in his first preface, aesthetics should rightfully be written by someone who is both a literary writer ("Dichter") and a philosopher at once (SW, 1.11: 15). In the second preface, he compares post-Kantian philosophers, who are not simultaneously poets or literary prose writers, to capons, "welche sich dadurch über alle Haushähne erheben, daß sie sich niemals mausern, sondern immer die alten *Federn führen*" (SW, 1.11: 7) [which soar above the backyard cockerels not because they lose their young features, but because they always write with the old feathers]. Castrated cockerels do not molt. This jibe refers to Jean Paul's conviction that too many, purely philosophical writers of aesthetics advance the same juvenile point. They do not reproduce it organically, in the language of genuine literary genius—which would also give birth to new, beautiful writing—but instead retain the same original down. Figuratively, they all write with the same old sort of quill. The implication is that philosophers, unlike literary authors who share a philosophical bent, cannot achieve greatness, since the idiom "sich mausern" approximates the English phrase "to blossom." To theorize fiction entails fiction writing; to theorize preface writing to and about fiction entails prefacing fictionally and theorizing it as such, in the act of its (pro)creation.

Jean Paul thus occupies a literary position between a classical-cum-Enlightenment model on the one hand, and an Early German Romanic mindset on the other—and he comments on both through his humor. His satirical yet serious stance was developed contemporaneously with the emergence of these two opposing yet deeply related movements, which he ironizes. Jean Paul's immanently ironic critique places him in a broad Romantic position rather than, as Heine later assessed him, as an isolated ironist. Jean Paul transcends these two poles of what we might call an ultimately Goethean, self-historicizing prefatory poetics (though Goethe shared an affinity for the fragmentary and for irony, as we have learned), and what we shall see is Romantic irony at the other extreme. He does so through a specific sort of Sentimentality that he imported from mid-eighteenth-century England—specifically, from Laurence Sterne's writings—and domesticated as his own.

PREFATORY PROCRASTINATION AND TEXTUAL FOREPLAY

Jean Paul's prefaces to the first editions of two early novels are presented as travelogues and, as such, are descriptions of the (semifictive) author's leisurely diversions from his intended preface writing. The preface to *Die Unsichtbare Loge* recounts the horse-drawn journey taken by the narrator through the Fichtelgebirge; it is entitled *Vorredner in Form einer Reisebeschreibung* [Prefacer in the Form of Describing a Journey]. Originally, he tells us, he had intended to write the text in nearby Sichersreuth or Alexandersbad, but saved the preface for his excursion in order to experience the scenery in a more meaningful way. Aiming, as preface writer ("Vorredner"), to compose his preface on a portable tablet while riding in the carriage, he thereby sought to receive nature "in die aufgeschlossene Seele" (SW, 1.2: 14) [into my soul opened up to the world]. This idea of drafting on the spot is similar to the stock metaphor of drawing used by prefaces to later, nineteenth-century French travel writing: the spontaneous, private sketch serves as proof of personal and creative authenticity, securing prefatorial goodwill (*captatio benevolentiae*).[41] However, Jean Paul appropriates the practice in order to narrate his digressive adventures. In this sense, the preface's style follows, as Eric A. Blackall notes, "the fashion of Sterne's *Sentimental Journey*";[42] indeed, for Rüdiger Scholz it evokes the fictional preface of this English novel that was comically claimed to have been written in a carriage.[43] Jean Paul's prefatory travels, then, are undertaken by a *sentimental traveler.* Jean Paul's preface, he himself tells us, should have occupied his attention for the duration of the trip, reaching completion once he was on top of the highest mountain in the area, the Schneeberg, and in proximity to the second-highest peak, the Ochsenkopf. But the author is constantly interrupted by a variety of characters and a precarious passage through the countryside.

Another preface describing how it did not get written is that to the first edition of *Siebenkäs* in 1796. However, the preface is here procrastinatory primarily because of sublimated eroticism. Jean Paul depicts a scenario in which, traveling in a post chaise, he stops at the nearby, mid-Franconian town of Scheerau, the location of the invisible lodge of his fiction three years earlier (though the "unsichtbare Loge" is never actually explained, let alone revealed). Having traveled from Berlin, where he had seen his publisher, the author arrives frozen; and he had apparently not given a thought to his preface along the way. He pauses at the merchant Jakob Oehrmann's house in order to deliver Wiener Briefe ("Vienna Letters") for Oehrmann to sell: presumably, copies of Johann Friedel's *Vertraute Briefe zur Charakteristik von Wien* [Confidential Letters Characterizing Vienna] (1793). The reference to Friedel projects an affinity with both contemporary travel and Sentimental literature. In a gesture toward the latter category, Jean Paul the preface writer becomes distracted by Oehrmann's daughter, figured as a "Vorrednerin" (SW, I.6: 7) [female prefacer]. He jokes that no reasonable preface writer such as himself (in the masculine form) could continue working. Throughout the prefatory text, he once again humorously reflects on his (lack of) progress with the preface he is supposed to be completing, and yet proposes to continue it: "Die Vorrede will so bis morgen währen" (SW, I.6: 12) [The preface can last until tomorrow]. The deferral, which prolongs prefacing rather than really putting it off for another day, has an illicit subtext: Jean Paul describes how he reads *Hesperus* aloud to Oehrmann's daughter while her father is asleep. But as soon as Oehrmann awakes, the writer is hounded out of the house. His listener is his ideal reader such that he wishes the book reviewers could see them together on the sofa; and she, as Johanne Pauline, is his alter ego. Thus the self-authored preface is not only an act that is concerned with one's own representation. It also desires the reception of oneself as an author. For Jean Paul, preface writing is a form of satirical self-love.

In the 1796 preface to *Siebenkäs*, the journey that meanders across the provincial German landscape and is halted by sexual arousal both explains why the planned preface did not get written and is a metaphor for the digressions and delays of preface writing. The same conceit is at work in another preface the following year, ostensibly intended for a second edition of *Quintus Fixlein*. Jean Paul called this preface *Geschichte meiner Vorrede zur zweiten Auflage* [History of my Preface to the Second Edition], though its draft title was *Vorrede zur Vorrede* [Preface to the Preface].[44] This self-reflexive preface was the only prefatorial piece that Jean Paul brought out as a separate book in its own right, in isolation from the literary work, thereby enacting one of his favorite jokes. At ninety-six pages, it is by far his longest preface; and ironically, the publication is an exception within Jean Paul's oeuvre for being a book without a preface—because it is itself exclusively an explicit, hypertrophic preface. The second edition of *Quintus Fixlein* that this book, as a preface, prefaces was drafted in the same year as Jean Paul submitted *Geschichte meiner Vorrede* to his publisher, 1796, but the edition was not immediately accepted for print and eventually appeared in late 1800 (though it was dated 1801). Consequently, on the appearance of *Geschichte meiner Vorrede* in 1797, and on account of its literal severance from *Quintus Fixlein*, we can read the text as a fictional preface to a fictive second edition.

Jean Paul begins the preface by suggesting that the process of drafting a preface is essentially the same as planning a book chapter, only shorter: the present example takes a journey via just three coaching inns, instead of a half-day excursion. But we proceed to read of a perennial delay in tackling the task at hand. Though there are (just) three public houses along the way, the preface is prolonged. Traveling by foot, the author character walks from the Upper Franconian town of Hof to Bayreuth, and attempts to write his preface as a prefacer ("Vorredner") on the go. But once again he is continually disturbed, and the preface is interspersed with asides that the task of prefacing was therefore impossible ("an Vorberichte war nicht zu denken" (SW, 1.5: 14) [there could be no thinking about prefaces], and that it was unlikely he would ever finish the piece. Consequently, the text repeatedly returns to structural subheadings, which attempt to help him get back on track with his prefatory composition. They fail. "Vorrede zur zweiten Auflage" (SW, 1.5: 24) [preface to the second edition] and "die Fortsetzung der Vorrede folgt" (SW, 1.5: 24) [the continuation of the preface will follow] are both repeated twice, but Jean Paul still digresses; the subheading "fortgesetzte Vorrede zur zweiten Auflage" (SW, 1.5: 24) [preface to the second edition continued], meanwhile, is footnoted with the advice that the reader should refer back to the previous continuation of the preface, in order to remind himself of the context. And so this preface mocks the notion that the preface tells a coherent history about the genesis and development of a particular literary work—otherwise so usual, as we have seen, for a preface to a second (or subsequent) edition.

As preface writer, Jean Paul is primarily distracted in *Geschichte meiner Vorrede* by a vis-à-vis carriage that stops before him to pay the road toll at the start of the text. He abandons his thoughts about the preface in order to run in a vain effort to see the face of its female passenger. The coach disappears into the forest and Jean Paul is left standing alone on the open road. Although his mind returns to the preface at hand, it does so only fleetingly: he asks himself whether he should instead focus his attention on the magical carriage "mit dem gebildeten Kopfe" (SW, 1.5: 14) [with the educated head] that had passed in front of him. Thus, from the beginning of this preface, reflecting on the vis-à-vis takes equal place to the task of writing a preface, vying to occupy Jean Paul's imagination as he chases the carriage to the village of Gefrees, and then on to Berneck, where it draws up at the "Suppenschüssel" [Soup Bowl] inn. There, the mysterious woman alights and her identity is exposed to the reader as Johanne Pauline, whom we recognize from Jean Paul's preface to *Siebenkäs*: "eine Primadonna, die schon einmal in einer von meinen Vorreden agierend aufgetreten war" (SW, 1.5: 25) [a prima donna who has already played an active role in one of my prefaces]. The present preface develops her story, since her father is now deceased and she is under the control of another man—a husband. Jean Paul finally departs together with Johanne Pauline in the carriage, so that he "saß ihr im Vis-à-vis—vis-à-vis" (SW, 1.5: 27) [sat with her in a vis-à-vis—vis-à-vis]. Facing his muse, he writes furiously in order to read his preface aloud to Johanne once they reach Bindloch. A preface, however, has apparently become impossible, since his desire for Johanne is foreclosed. Instead, because of Johanne's personal situation, Jean Paul feels he cannot converse with her, and cuts off the preceding chatty, prefatorial context. In doing so, he buries his sexual desire—and ends his preface, changing his preferred text type. He first writes a genre typically composed for a bride on the way to her marital chamber, an "Epithalamium,"[45] and then significantly in an 1826 revision he calls this an epitaph, or "Grabschrift" (SW, 1.5: 31). Jean Paul's history of a preface becomes in effect the story of why this preface stops short.

Jean Paul the character is further distracted by another interpersonal tension within the fictive sketch: an art critic, Fraischdörfer, appears, who had apparently previously expressed an interest in reviewing Jean Paul. Our preface protagonist Jean Paul pretends to Fraischdörfer that he is the character of the novel's title—Quintus Fixlein. Consequently, this critic speaks candidly about Jean Paul's limited literary talent, using contemporary tenets of Weimar Classicism as his yardstick.[46] In mock irritation (for from the empirical Jean Paul's perspective, Fraischdörfer's dogmatism profitably differentiates the author from his Weimar contemporaries), the preface writer Jean Paul expresses authorial opinions that raise Fraischdörfer's suspicions about his true identity. The conflict between the two men continues until the female beauty riding in the vis-à-vis finally assumes an active role in the scene. For she knows Jean Paul, recognizes him, and upon confirmation of Jean Paul's real name (which is actually a pseudonym) the critic is embarrassed and becomes a figure of further mockery. But at the same time, Jean Paul implies that Fraischdörfer's presence is fundamental to his preface as a text type. The author takes time out from debating with Fraischdörfer to write just some of his prefatory pages, which was the same as arguing with the critic in person, and his colleagues: "weil es ja so viel war, als spräch' ich mit dem Kunstrat selber, da ich ihn darin meinte" (SW, 1.5: 25) [because it was really as if I were speaking with the art critic there, and it was he whom I meant]. The preface is equal not only to a vis-à-vis with an author's readers, but also a tête-à-tête with the book reviewers. However, the former equation is the more significant. Since Fraischdörfer diverts Jean Paul from his pursuit of Johanne Pauline while the critic drinks goat's milk, the preface writer complains that he has almost reached Gefrees "ohne irgend etwas Schönes gesehen oder geschrieben zu haben (ich rede von dem Vis-à-vis und der Vorrede)" (SW, 1.5: 20) [without having seen or written anything beautiful at all (I am speaking of the vis-à-vis and the preface)]. He may have written a fragment of prefatorial discourse with criticism, but he has not yet properly produced aesthetic beauty.

Jean Paul's and Johanne Pauline's journey in the vis-à-vis—which is the moment of the preface writer's disappointment and abandonment of his preface—can be read as an intricate literary critique of marriage, a popular topic of intellectual debate in the 1790s.[47] But at the same time, it is an implicit argument about writing and, above all, preface writing in the period. The re-emergence of Johanne Pauline as Jean Paul's alter ego reaffirms that Jean Paul imagines his readers as fictive characters and, moreover, as extensions of an aspect of his authorial persona: the reading counterpart to his writerly self. Note that the readership for novels in this era mainly comprised women, and it is to them as well as his literary peers (who would undoubtedly pick up on references to their poetics) Jean Paul addresses the prefaces to his domestic-oriented, ridiculous yet learned, middle-of-the-road works. He defends this preoccupation with his own (masculine and feminine) Doppelgänger: "es muß überhaupt noch mehre Paulinen und Jean Pauls in Deutschland geben" (SW, I.5: 30) [in general there must be more Paulines and Jean Pauls in Germany]. Otherwise, there would be no demand for his writings in the first place, nor for their subsequent editions. On the one hand, then, the preface is a fictive scenario that ostensibly appeals to an addressee; but on the other hand, that person is conceived by, and as, the preface writer himself. Jean Paul's prefaces thereby become not only a self-reflexive, but also a narcissistic activity. Novalis, by contrast, advanced a similar but more objective idea. He first contends that: "Der wahre Leser muß der erweiterte Autor seyn. Er ist die höhere Instanz, die die Sache von der niedern Instanz schon vorgearbeitet enthält"[48] [The true reader must be an extension of the author. He is the higher authority that receives a matter that has already been prepared by the lower authority]. The writer, of course, is his own work's initial reader. But he must attempt to be impartial, because the work is at the same time no longer his own—and so the author can be creative and critical at once: "Durch *unpartheyeisches* Wiederlesen seines Buchs kann der Autor sein Buch selbst läutern"[49] [through *impartial* rereading of his book, an author can clarify his book himself]. Jean Paul, meanwhile, at this stage appears to be thoroughly subjective: for him, prefacing as a communicative act in order to connect with readers is paradoxically about the authorial self.

Geschichte meiner Vorrede was inspired by Sterne's *A Sentimental Journey through France and Italy* (1768): a work that had taken German readers by storm since its first translation into German, just one year after its English publication, by Johann Bode (and was playfully mimicked in Goethe's "prequel" to *Werther*, as we noted in chapter 1).[50] No commentator has yet noticed the significant and intricate influence of this novel on Jean Paul's *Geschichte meiner Vorrede* specifically. Toward the beginning of Sterne's novel, the character Yorick goes in search of a carriage in which to ride through Europe. In the corner of a hotel yard, a désobligeant takes his interest and so he climbs inside. While stationary, he writes the preface to the book he is simultaneously narrating. In contrast to Jean Paul, this preface writer completes the introductory manuscript, even though he was originally distracted by a female bystander. As the narrator re-emerges, having composed his preface, two onlookers ask him why the carriage moved: "'Twas the agitation, said I, coolly, of writing a preface.—I never heard, said the other, who was a *Simple Traveller*, of a preface wrote in a *désobligeant*.—It would have been better, said I, in a *vis-a-vis*."[51] This joke about prefacing is a double entendre. On one level, Sterne's wit depends on a difference in the two types of transport: a désobligeant seats one, whereas a vis-à-vis holds two passengers, who face each other. The vis-à-vis, like the preface, lends itself to a conversational style. Sterne is content with this joke, whereas Jean Paul acts upon it, writing a preface about a journey after, and then in, a vis-à-vis.

On a more risqué level, though, for Sterne the act of writing a preface is an autoerotic activity. The movement of the désobligeant while Yorick is alone inside is caused by both his prefatory and bodily creativity. For as the narrator stepped into the carriage, on seeing the lady he closed the taffeta curtain, suggesting subsequent action of a sensual and secret nature. He admits that he "took out" his "pen and ink."[52] Yorick later considers asking the lady to share his chaise, wondering "what mighty mischief could ensue?"[53] When they do in fact find themselves in the same coach, he "makes love" to her, meaning that he is flirtatious.[54] Unlike his English counterpart, Jean Paul cannot talk suggestively with his eventual traveling companion, because she is married: a fact of reality that disrupts the imaginative pleasure of prefacing, and precludes Jean Paul acting on any advance he might have made, let alone consummating his love with an ideal reader. Penning a preface, for him, is the pursuit of a sublimated desire; but because of Johanne's commitment to her husband, our German author in the end suppresses frustration, dismay, and a sense of loss. His preface is unlike Yorick's expectant fantasy. Hence the eventual "Grabschrift" ("epitaph") in place of a "Vorrede" ("preface").

Autoeroticism, implicit in Sterne's and Jean Paul's comic conceptions of preface writing, was an especially controversial topic across Europe around 1800. Thomas W. Laqueur conveys the point in the most racy manner, comparing masturbation in this age to drug taking: it was thought to be "prone to excess as no other kind of venery was, the crack cocaine of sexuality; and it had no bounds in reality because it was a creature of the imagination."[55] Adrian Daub interprets Jean Paul's *Clavis Fichtiana seu Leibgerberiana* (1800) as an autoerotic portrayal of Fichte's alloerotic understanding of marriage—though Jean Paul's purpose (or whether it is simply satirical) remains unexplained.[56] This raises the question: apart from being a topical piece of humor, is Jean Paul's conception of self-prefacing in *Geschichte meiner Vorrede* as unfulfilled, narrative desire significant for our appreciation of preface writing at this time, or in general? Metaphorically, it expresses the three preface paradoxes with which the present book was introduced (see the close of the introduction), and so Jean Paul is the centerpiece of this study.

To begin, in Jean Paulish fashion, back to front: according to the third preface paradox as outlined in this book's introduction, the preface is predicated on rhetorical theory even when it appears to rail against rhetorical prescription. For Sterne, the preface is associated with arousal: either the author's or the reader's. In "The Author's Preface," inserted into the middle of *The Life and Opinions of Tristram Shandy, a Gentleman* (1759–1767), he writes about "the first insinuating *How d'ye* of a caressing prefacer, stifling his reader, as a lover sometimes does a coy mistress, into silence."[57] Verbose digression can become a rhetorical, albeit not classically rhetorical, ritual;[58] in Sterne's and Jean Paul's prefaces it is a display of—at least linguistic and narratological—virility.[59] The preface is therefore paradigmatic of "rhetorica contra rhetoricam," to which we shall return toward the end of this chapter. The second preface paradox of the present book, meanwhile, proposes that:

> An author's own preface is predicated on an act of address to a person external to the work's poetics or thought—but the desired addressee, whether a peculiar or popular readership, is imagined by the writer, and so is integral to his conceptual or creative work. To preface is therefore autopoetic and even, in its exaggerated form, autoerotic.

Walther Rehm has concluded for Jean Paul's footnotes that the note writer writes notes for himself.[60] This is partially true for Jean Paul's prefaces, as he prefaces for his own pleasure. But to say that these prefaces are wholly for the writer's benefit is wrong. The middle group of contemporary readers, which Jean Paul describes under the heading of "Seele" ("soul") in his *Siebenkäs* preface, for example, constitutes part of his implied or intended readership.[61] This set may or may not be based on people he knew in real life, but they are presented as a fictive category in Jean Paul's prefaces which are, in any case, fictions. Thus to preface, for Jean Paul, is to address empirical readers within his own imagination. We should consider this second paradox of Jean Paul's prefacing—and of the preface in general—more thoroughly still, deferring the first preface paradox of the present study and its relevance to *Geschichte meiner Vorrede* until later in the discussion.

If literary prefacing is an act of autonomous creativity contingent on empirical existence, then it is somehow a real action that is dislocated from reality, in fiction. The character of Johanne Pauline in the prefaces to *Siebenkäs* and the second (nonexistent or belated) edition of *Quintus Fixlein*, however, appears more exaggerated in the degree of imagination the author employs—as much for entertainment as for complex, conceptual, and intertextual comedy. But Jean Paul's peculiar preface of 1797 about the relationship between himself as author and his reader (in the guise of himself) nevertheless expresses a fundamental and practical point about writing around 1800. In a seminal article entitled "The Writer's Audience Is Always a Fiction" (1975), Walter J. Ong suggests that the writer places an audience for whom he writes, in his mind, within a persona that readers must perform in order to participate in his work, so that readers fictionalize themselves: "A reader has to play the role in which the author has cast him, which seldom coincides with his role in the rest of actual life."[62] Literature in the age of Romanticism, broadly construed, apparently complicated the situation of the classical orator, who had a collective audience before him, or a rhetorical tradition of writing before modernity. The Romantics were paradigmatic moderns. The readers conceived by them did not have obviously real-life counterparts, nor were they specific individuals, though they may have had contemporaries familiar to the authors.[63] For writing, according to Ong, is an *indirection*. In his logic, the reader is generated by the writer in order to receive his own work. Although Ong is wrong, for the German context in any case, to assume that "as orality yielded to writing, the focus of rhetoric was slowly shifted, unreflectively for the most part, and without notice,"[64] he is quite correct in summarizing:

> If the writer succeeds in writing, it is generally because he can fictionalize in his imagination an audience he has learned to know not from daily life but from earlier writers who were fictionalizing in their imagination audiences they had learned to know in still earlier writers, and so on back to the dawn of written narrative. If and when he becomes truly adept, an "original writer," he can do more than project the earlier audience, he can alter it.[65]

W. Daniel Wilson has usefully drawn a distinction between these sorts of readers in texts as "characterized," and implied or intended ones.[66] In Jean Paul's *Geschichte meiner Vorrede*, Johanne Pauline is Jean Paul's extreme example of a characterized, even autoeroticized reader-construct.[67] And Jean Paul, of course, is also a fiction: a characterized author. As his pen name indicates, information Jean Paul attributes in prefaces to the identity of his authorial name is playful, and not necessarily empirically accurate.

One extreme option is to read Jean Paul's prefaces as part of a work's or the oeuvre's narrative and understand them only aesthetically, in terms of their effect. The locus classicus of the ongoing debate in narratology surrounding authorial intention suggests this strategy. For William K. Wimsatt Jr. and Monroe C. Beardsley, T. S. Eliot's notes to *The Waste Land* should be interpreted as part of the artwork: "whereas notes tend to seem to justify themselves as external indexes to the author's *intention*, they ought to be judged like any other parts of a composition."[68] Alternatively, we could overcome the "intentional fallacy" by employing Wayne C. Booth's concept of the "implied author,"[69] or competing conceptions of constructed, hypothetical-if-real writers, such as Alexander Nehamas's "postulated author," among many others.[70] These concepts would be invoked functionally. But either way, the resultant author-construct would be partially of our subjective making, and then applied to interrogate our author-as-another against our interpretation of him, under the guise of objective scholarship. Phrased in this way, scholarly activity sounds satirical and Jean Paulish. Indeed, the creative tension in Jean Paul's prefaces is their play with both intentionalist and aesthetic interpretative modes—attributing motivations to the author, as a fictional character, in a dramatized, affective scene. Such motivations are both for and not for himself. In essence, Jean Paul's autoerotic conception of (prefatorial) authorship and his (prefatory) readership is simply an exaggerated, exuberant representation of a writing and reading process in which we ourselves participate as general readers, critics, and scholars, albeit with varying degrees of subjective restraint.

The conceptual analogy of autoerotic desire and the autopoetic preface in *Geschichte meiner Vorrede* emerges from Jean Paul's first preface to *Siebenkäs*, and does not correspond to the first preface of *Quintus Fixlein*. However, *Geschichte meiner Vorrede*, as the latter novel's second preface, does present a second metaphor that complements the domestic imagery of its more obvious predecessor. Jean Paul describes the act of writing a preface as being confined "im Webstuhl der Vorrede" [in the loom of the preface], and progress with its composition as "mit dem Weberschiffchen werfend" (SW, 1.5: 11–12) [throwing with the weaving-shuttle]; he later writes of "die Weberei der Vorrede" (SW, 1.5: 12) [weaving mill of the preface]. Preface writing is thus still an activity that is connotative of craftsmanship and an idyll of domesticity, or at least cottage industry (consumerism may have arrived in late eighteenth-century German territories, but the industrial revolution really came later). That is to say, the preface artist is again introduced as an artisan. More important for Jean Paul's prefatorial satire and paradoxicality, however, is the potential of this fabric metaphor to mock the pseudosolidity with which contemporary writers projected their literary output as a unified work of art. Pulling himself together as preface writer ("Vorredner") and holding himself to account for his preface's lack, through the presence of a preface, the author jokingly asks himself: "Steht es dir denn nicht frei, wie Herr von Moser zu arbeiten (der Gevatter und Vorläufer deiner Zettelkästen), der in seinem Leben keinen zusammenhängenden Bogen geschrieben, sondern nur Aphorismen, Gnomen, Sinnsprüche, kurz nichts mit Flechtwerk?" (SW, 1.5: 14) [Are you not free to work like Mr. von Moser (the Godfather and precursor to your slip boxes), who hasn't written a cohesive block of paper in his life, but instead mere aphorisms, posies, mottos: in short, nothing with wickerwork?]. Jean Paul structured *Quintus Fixlein* not as chapters, but as "Zettelkästen" [slip boxes]. This term refers to an organizing principle of Johann Jakob Moser's autobiography;[71] and the above line from Jean Paul's preface was possibly meant to evoke if not a specific prefatory claim from a book by Moser's son, Friedrich Carl von Moser, then at least the sentiment of the latter's *Mannigfaltigkeiten* [Miscellaneous] from 1796, the year Jean Paul composed his preface. The younger Moser declares in his own preface: "Wenn sich der Buchhandel ebenso gut mit Journalen, Flugschriften, Almanachen und anderer kurzen Waare treiben lässt, wer will es den Starosten der Literatur verargen, wenn nur sie sich bey diesem Handel wohl befinden!"[72] [If the book trade can carry on just as well with journals, pamphlets, almanacs, and other short wares, who can hold it against the guardians of literature if they are quite content with this type of trade!]. Concurring with this sort of logic, Jean Paul continues his incongruous preface "bandfrei" (SW, 1.5: 14) [free from a volume]: that is, without a (revised) volume of *Quintus Fixlein* attached. And yet Jean Paul still lays claim to craftsmanship, to weaving a text as if it were a textile—or wicker.

In addition, he alerts readers to his unfinished works in progress: Fraischdörfer, the art critic, comes from "Haarhaar" (SW, 1.5: 15) [Hair Hair], which according to a footnote is the principality in which Jean Paul's future *Titan* will be set, a novel that was eventually published in parts between 1800 and 1803. In response to Fraischdörfer's irritating comments throughout the prefatory fiction, Jean Paul plans to write "ein kritisches Werkchen" (SW, 1.5: 22) [a critical little work], in which he will demonstrate that aesthetic humor is the fruit of a long-standing culture of reason. This treatise becomes his *Vorschule der Ästhetik* (published in 1804 and revised in 1813); at the time of *Geschichte meiner Vorrede* in 1796, he had been drafting the work for two years already. His later preface to the first volume of *Komet* [Comet] (1820) exaggerates this potential for prefacing as yet unpublished, even (partly) unwritten material. It introduces two volumes: the one at hand and one that will hopefully appear in the near future. Significantly, "die Vorrede zu dem andern, das erst erscheinen soll, hat vielleicht desto mehr zu sagen, da sie sich noch auf nichts Vorhandenes steuern kann" (SW, 1.15: 4–5) [the preface to the other one that is yet to appear perhaps has all the more to say, since it can still guide itself toward nothing that exists]. A preface to an absent work contains more imaginative, free play: certainly, *Geschichte meiner Vorrede* frames an initially nonexistent and then belated edition, and is one of Jean Paul's most creative prefaces.

Although *Geschichte meiner Vorrede* is open-ended, as an eventual epitaph ("Grabschrift") the preface, at the end, is also dead and buried. This paradox enables a foreword to go on forever or—and consequently—to be cut-off prematurely, as was the case for Goethe's autobiography *Dichtung und Wahrheit* [Poetry and Truth]. Moreover, as much as Jean Paul's digressions and discontinuities run counter to the notion of a coherent life's work, they also attempt to contain it—for the memory, perhaps, of future generations. *Geschichte meiner Vorrede*, as we have seen, positions itself relative to Jean Paul's other published works and prefaces (if also unpublished ones): the character Johanne Pauline is borrowed from the *Siebenkäs* preface; and as a second preface, *Geschichte meiner Vorrede* also partially continues the symbolism of its predecessor. The subtitle to the book edition specifies Jean Paul as "Verfasser der Mumien [*Siebenkäs*] und der Hundsposttage [*Hesperus*]" [author of the mummies and the dog-post days]. The second prefaces to both *Siebenkäs* (1817) and *Die Unsichtbare Loge* (1822) refer to Jean Paul's prefaces to further editions of another, third work—*Hesperus*. In weaving together other titles and prefaces of his ever-expanding oeuvre, Jean Paul's prefaces might be understood, like his writing as a whole, as hypertextual.[73] Following Genette's phrasing, their pages are palimpsests.[74] To be sure, the final preface to *Hesperus* (1819) claims each published work is already the prior edition of a future version if an author appropriates what Martus has called "Verbesserungsästhetik," or an aesthetics of improvement; in Genette's terms, each such pre-work would constitute a "hypotext." In a comical reference to Methuselah, in myth the oldest man to have ever lived, Jean Paul writes:

> Aber Himmel, wie oft muß nicht ein Schreibmensch an sich bessern, der kaum über ein halbes Jahrhundert alt ist! Lebte er sich vollends in ein Methusalems-Jahrtausend hinein und schriebe dabei: der Methusalem bekäme so viele Bände von Verbesserungen nachzuschießen, daß das Werk selber ihnen nur als Vorwerk, Anhängsel oder Ergänzblatt beizugeben wäre. (SW, 1.3: 5)
>
> [But heavens, how often must a writing person not improve himself when he is scarcely more than half a century old! If he continues to live on through a complete century of Methuselah, and if he writes while doing so: then Methuselah would receive so many volumes of improvements to his writing, one after another, that the work itself would be attached as mere pre-work, appendix, or supplementary sheet.]

He here suggests that a book is akin to an appendix, supplement, or "Vorwerk": a work that is always a prequel. This coinage is also a pun. It returns to Jean Paul's typical source imagery for prefaces, architecture, since a "Vorwerk" is an outlying building on an estate. But crucially, the author does not actually liken a preface ("Vorrede") to a work—it remains distinct. Prefaces are a part of Jean Paul's writings, and as such they are digressive and hypertextual appendices, or supplements. Yet read as a preface, *Geschichte meiner Vorrede* simultaneously seeks to be a stand-alone piece of art, separate from other forms of textuality—and it leads to its own cessation. There are contradictions, then, between Jean Paul's preference for the tangential and incomplete on the one hand—thereby resisting the idea of a coherent history to his works, authorial image, or indeed prefaces—and a cataloguing enterprise on the other, which contributes to greater coherence; or between a yearning for continuation and the paradoxically lively wish to bury desire, to stop it short in its tracks, to cease prefacing: if only to recommence with the opportunity of a new work, volume, or edition.

In this latter respect of (repeatedly) moving toward closure, too, Jean Paul's prefacing is paradigmatic of general emplotment. Peter Brooks proposes that: "One could no doubt analyze the opening paragraph of most novels and emerge in each case with the image of a desire taking on shape, beginning to seek its objects, beginning to develop a textual energetics."[75] Brooks posits a teleology of desire, a libidinal drive directed at an end point. But this end is arbitrary: "Any closure of our subject would be artificially imposed: the story of plot may be interminable, the examples calling for attention are legion, and any terminus reached suggests the need for a revisionary epilogue, another perspective, a different narrative."[76] These lines would seem to characterize the way Jean Paul's autoerotic, autopoetic prefaces close in on themselves; yet in order to understand their operations fully, we must also admit that they concurrently aim to open themselves up to, and contain, other, associated works. They are works of both private introspection and public inventory of Jean Paul's authorial self.

For this reason, and as we read of Goethe's prefacing in chapter 1, a preface can be extended ad infinitum, or it can be omitted altogether. Jean Paul thus also exemplifies the first preface paradox identified in the introduction to the present study, as Goethe does. And so we finally return to the third way in which Jean Paul is central to the present study. His prefaces, most notably *Geschichte meiner Vorrede*, demonstrate that a preface itself can be prefaced in perpetuity—or killed off. Self-reflection necessarily expands the preface, whereas revision to a work does not necessarily enlarge the revised text: the former is a forethought to prefacing that is left as a trace of its drafting. In *Geschichte meiner Vorrede*, Jean Paul jokes that authors should append, for the reviewers, a complete list of all the fatuous thoughts which might have shaped previous, unpublished drafts, since he reasons: "Der Kritiker sieht freilich nur, wie viel der Autor behalten hat, aber nicht, wie viel er weggeworfen" (SW, 1.5: 18) [Of course the critic can only see how much the author has retained and not how much he cast away]. He takes the last edition of Voltaire's collected works as his inspiration, which includes "hinten für feinere Leser einen Lumpenboden des Auskehrigs der ersten Edizionen" (SW, 1.5:18) [at the back a floor of rags from the refuse of the first editions, for more refined readers]. The equation of rags and refuse with refinement is comical, but for Jean Paul also conceptual. Admittedly he does not enact this idea for the work in its entirety, but his commentaries on preparing his prefaces—left, for the reader, as prefaces—fulfill a similar function.

Furthermore, the metaphor of leftover rags is indicative of his conception of writing as a whole. Previously in this preface, Jean Paul had expounded on a problem of literary reception: contemporaneous works are soon forgotten, and lose out to the ancient classics. He proposes that the older, wise recipients remember whatever they heard and read in their youth, but fail to recall books which they encounter in maturity, even in the past hour. Employing another contemporary material metaphor, he explains: "Daher denn unsere Bücher den Lumpen in der Papiermühle gleichen, von denen sie genommen sind, unter welchen der Papiermüller die frischen allzeit früher zur Fäulnis bringt als die alten" (SW, 1.5: 17) [For this reason our books are like the rags in the paper mill, the rags from which they are made; and it is the fresh rags among them that the papermaker always lets disintegrate before the old ones]. In the late eighteenth century, rags of cloth still constituted the raw material for making paper; wood pulp was an invention of the mid-nineteenth century, by Friedrich Gottlieb Keller in 1844.[77] In Jean Paul's time, bleach probably would have been introduced only recently, so newer rags were preferable because they were more easily cleaned and their fibers were likely to be of better quality. Although this joke initially seems to be an aside, albeit relevant to the period's book market of which the preface is a constituent, Jean Paul notes: "Im Grunde hätt' ich das als einen abgesonderten Satz in der Vorrede zur zweiten Auflage aufstellen können" (SW, 1.5: 17) [Essentially, I could have set that apart as a sentence all on its own in the preface to the second edition].

All paper is a recycled product; writing is rewriting. But in Jean Paul's oeuvre, it is recognizable as such. In his preface ("Vorrede") to *Leben Fibels* [Life of Fibel] (1811), which precedes the "Vor-Geschichte oder Vor-Kapitel" [Pre-History or Pre-Chapter], he quips that if he were to receive his small work from a third party, he would perceive it as "ein gefundenes Essen" (SW, 1.13: 348) [a piece of food he found] that would bring life into him. It would nourish his soul as he would relax inside, insulated from the cold outside; he "würde Mitleid mit jeder Kutsche haben, die zum Thee führe" (SW, 1.13: 348) [would have sympathy with every carriage that drove to tea]. He laments that he cannot receive his work in this way, because he wrote it himself: yet again, the author poses as his ideal reader. The turn of phrase that his writing is a morsel that he would find and eat is a linguistic play on the idiom "gefundenes Fressen," which means "grist to the mill" in English. This saying precisely formulates Jean Paul's idea of the writing process: everything that exists can be used for new production, but as a remake of the old. Thus further editions to Jean Paul's novels could be exploited for producing more prefaces to prior prefaces. The author notes in *Geschichte meiner Vorrede* that he is writing his preface to the second edition of *Quintus Fixlein* on the recycled paper of the first, which, like contemporary literature and in contrast to the classics, has already fallen into obscurity. Rather than simply rewriting the original preface, though, he remarks on the very fact that he is rewriting it, and comments on its own genesis. The preface is in this respect not only a palimpsest in authoring a previous text anew; it is also the hypotext of itself. Self-reflexivity, prefacing about prefacing, is the trace of the preface writer's forethoughts.

And yet the opposite is also true: self-reflection is the addition of a thought that arrives in the act of writing a preface, an afterthought, and thus prefacing gives rise to further reflection. This is an argument about the generative function of writing for writing's sake, which is substantiated in the following section. But as a preliminary point, in Jean Paul's poetics the preface is an opportunity to extend a text with originality, for even in a revised edition its inclusion adds new introductory pages to a book. Such prefaces permit creativity in a work that is otherwise an act of reiteration. Jean Paul's *Herbst-Blumine oder gesammelte Werkchen aus Zeitschriften* [Autumn Flora, or Collected Little Works from Periodicals] (1810), for example, comprises a selection of the author's previously published prefaces—to his own works and to a couple by other writers—and reviews. Introducing the volume (in a preface), he exclaims: "Der Leser findet hier, diese Vorrede, die Zueignung und den Schluß ausgenommen, lauter wiedergedruckte Sachen. Wie schwer fällt dieß einem mehr Vor- als Abschreiber!" (SW, 1.17: 8–9) [The reader will here find a load of reprinted matter, aside from the preface, the dedication, and the ending. How difficult this is for someone who is more preface writer than copyist!] In other words, a preface to a series of reprinted pages is one of the few spaces in which the writer is not necessarily a copyist, but can write down fresh ideas. Alternatively, the prefatorial content in a second preface may simply be livelier than the first time around, since the work has secured at least enough attention to merit a reprint. In the second preface to *Vorschule der Ästhetik* (1813), Jean Paul admits that he repeats the arguments of the initial preface, but permits himself to do so more jovially: "Diese zweite Vorrede will nur die heitere Paraphrase der ersten sein, welche ihr nachfolgt und sogleich so viel Ernstes mitbringt, daß nachher der Uebergang leicht ist in den wissenschaftlichen Ernst des ganzen Werks" (SW, 1.11: 12) [This second preface is meant to merely paraphrase the first one more jovially; the first preface follows shortly and is accompanied by such seriousness from the start that the ensuing transition into the scientific sincerity of the whole work is easy]. Indeed, according to Jean Paul's second preface to *Die Unsichtbare Loge*, repetition of the form is liberating: without the strict rule of modesty, if this still held sway at the time (and Jean Paul is mocking the retreat of an obviously rhetorical tradition), an author can be more triumphant in a second preface, "ungebundener und heiterer" (SW, 1.2: 6) [less restrained and more jovial].

The irony across Jean Paul's prefaces to further editions is that, in reality, they are for the most part far from original texts. Even though the structures of prefaces to first editions are similar to each other (such as the pseudo-travelogue), their manifestation across texts is in the main more individual and inventive. The repetitive impression of Jean Paul's prefaces to subsequent editions is exemplified by a comparison of the prefaces to the revised editions of *Hesperus* (1797 and 1819), as well as the second editions of *Siebenkäs* and *Die Unsichtbare Loge*, respectively. In the second prefaces to *Hesperus* and *Siebenkäs*, Jean Paul notes not only the improvements ("Verbesserungen"), but also the additions and enlargements ("Vergrößerungen") to the following works, true to the norm of an aesthetics of improvement. And then, as is usual for his second or subsequent prefaces, he satirizes that convention. In his second preface to *Siebenkäs*, he is skeptical of the extent to which his efforts in these editorial respects help his reputation. Readers may buy and read the improved edition, but they will hardly study it and come to a considered judgment. In the second preface to *Die Unsichtbare Loge*, Jean Paul logs the same complaint. All these prefaces then turn this grievance into a common joke. Since holding two editions side by side is annoying, Jean Paul states in his second preface to *Siebenkäs* that he has left a copy of the former edition at the Berlin "Realschulbuchhandlung" ["high school bookshop"], in which he has marked up subsequent corrections and changes in ink, so that the reader will make the comparison and be suitably astounded (SW, 1.6: 5). In his third preface to *Hesperus*, he wishes that a certain Herr Kolbe would travel to see such a copy (SW, 1.3: 4); in his second preface to *Die Unsichtbare Loge*, he claims that if an art critic ("ein Kunstrichter") were to view it, he too would be amazed (SW, 1.2: 11–12). Although this sort of satire against "Verbesserungsästhetik," or an aesthetics of improvement, is found in the second preface of *Quintus Fixlein—Geschichte meiner Vorrede* (1797)—as well, this preface's narrative is by comparison extraordinarily creative. And in its paradoxicality, it is also all the more amusingly problematic. The preface, published as a stand-alone and thus as an autonomous work, is autoerotic and autopoetic, while being an act of address. And as we shall explore further, it is also about opening and closing, as well as an example of antirhetorical rhetoric.

THE LOGIC OF LENGTH; OR, DIGRESSIVE FRAGMENTATION

If the moment of writing a preface offers the opportunity to reflect on prefacing, the obvious question is why this should be so extreme in Jean Paul's writings, compared to those of his peers. Prefacing about prefacing was an activity engaged in by all kinds of literary writers (and as we shall see, philosophers) around 1800, whom we could together class as Romantics. Jean Paul, though, is our most copious case in point. In his 1822 preface to *Die Unsichtbare Loge*, he observes with respect to himself that: "ein Autor wie er auf diese Weise am Ende mehr Vorreden als Bücher macht—z.B. zu Einem dreimal aufgegangnen Hesperus drei Vorreden als Morgenröthen—und daß folglich beinahe des Redens mehr ist als des Machens" (SW, 1.2: 6) [in this way an author like him in the end produces more prefaces than books—for example, three prefaces as dawns to a *Hesperus* that has risen three times in the sky—and so consequently there is almost more of speaking than there is of doing much]. Since he assumes that each act of literary revision requires an introduction, he writes a new preface; and this habit gives rise to reflection on the proliferation of his prefaces more generally. Thus the structure of revising a publication—at least according to Jean Paul's interpretation—not only adds to the number of the author's prefaces and leaves traces of his prefatory forethoughts, but also multiplies their levels of reflexivity with afterthoughts that occur in the act of composition itself. The key to understanding the latter is the logic of length in a preparatory text or the cumulative extent of prefatory material. This logic arises from writing itself, specific to the prefatorial text type. It reveals why Jean Paul's prefaces appear to write themselves, and why they become autopoetic, even autoerotic.

As observed in the introduction to the present book, and through the example of Goethe in chapter 1, German writing around 1800 gave rise to both the hypertrophy and the degeneration of preface writing. In his 1813 preface to *Museum*, Jean Paul jokes that, should one decide to begin a preface, there is no necessity for the example to end:

> Da ich aber immer jede Vorrede mit dem närrischen Gefühle anhebe, daß ich sie ganz gut weglassen könnte, oder auch eben so gut hinschreiben, wie denn mein ältestes Werk, die grönländischen Prozesse, eben so schicklich eine hätten haben können, als dieses neueste keine: so verspürt man sich in einem so behaglichen Elemente, daß man die goldnen Worte des Vorberichts gern übermäßig wie in einem metallischen Walz- oder Streckwerke ausdehnen und kaum ablassen möchte, besonders weil ohnehin da, wo keine Notwendigkeit des ersten Worts war, schwerlich eine des letzten zu erweisen ist; daher sind denn Vorreden so lang. (SW, 1.16: 3)

> [But since I always begin every preface with the foolish feeling that I could just as well omit it as go ahead and write it, just like my oldest work—*The Greenland Trials*—would have been as proper with one as this new work would be without a preface, one finds oneself in such an easily agreeable mood that one gladly lengthens the golden words of a preface excessively, as if they were metal in a rolling or stretch mill, especially because where there is in any case no necessity for the opening word, it is difficult to prove the necessity of a closing one. It is for this reason that prefaces are so long.]

The freedom from function "auf der vorredenden Schwelle" (SW, 1.16: 5) [on the prefacing threshold], as Jean Paul goes on to call it, enables self-fulfillment and consensus with oneself, or "Selber-Konsens"; here again, an author writes a preface for his own gratification. Phrased in this way, Hans Ehrenzeller's analysis, as outlined in this book's introduction, is proved right: prefatory form depends on the presence or absence function; and without strict adherence to rhetorical handbooks (flouting modesty, trying readers' patience, etc.), Jean Paul freewheels along his prefatorial path. Let us, however, consider the issue of length. As a result of literature's newly gained autonomy—and, with it, the preface's recently independent status as no longer just a place of textual-political pragmatism, but of unconstrained creative fiction as well—there was no need to put down the pen. In theory, a preface can continue to infinity and beyond ("ins Unbestimmte") (SW, 1.16: 5). This entails ever greater levels of reflexivity, because at some point a writer will have to preface his prefatorial remarks, and preface his prefatory comment to a preface, and so on. In this sense, the more words there are on a printed, prefatorial page, the more likely it is that these will need to be set up, introduced—prefaced. Logically, a longer preface necessitates greater reflection on the prefatory act; it demands more organizational thought. Jean Paul's witty theorization in the above passage, though short, takes place in a preface. *Geschichte meiner Vorrede* is notably long. Would such digression maintain readers' attention as a preface, would it even be possible without defense of, or at least commentary on, its prefatorial status? Readers need reminding about what they are reading, or why they are reading it, if a section is not self-evidently relevant to a work—even if such a reminder only amuses (or jovially antagonizes) them.

Jean Paul hints that this relationship between length and self-reflexivity is a facet of human communicative interaction that also applies, for example, to the conversational preamble. Fittingly, as so frequently in Jean Paul's writing, he points this out in a preface. In the second preface of 1817 to his educational manifesto *Ergänzungsblatt zur Levana* [Supplementary Sheet to *Levana*], he declares: "Zu dieser *Vorrede* schreib' ich nun hier (der neuen Auflage wegen) die zweite, nach der Gewohnheit von uns Menschen, die wir sowol im Staat- als im übrigen Leben immer Vorreden zu Vorreden machen" (SW, 1.12: 411) [To this preface I am now writing another here (because of the new edition), as is our habit as people who in civic life and in other aspects of our lives always ramble preliminarily before preambles]. Once the textual preface became a less controlled and contrived, more delightfully discursive space around 1800, Jean Paul's prefacing became the printed form of conversational rambling, and also of self-centered speech.

The way to end such perpetual self-depiction is to cut the preface short. In concluding the (untitled) preface or introduction to *Gespräch über die Poesie*, for instance, Schlegel abruptly finishes his preliminary text: "sonst wäre des Vorredens kein Ende"[78] [otherwise there would be no end of prefacing]. Had he continued to preface, he eventually would have had to preface his preface. Significantly, the author uses the gerund, "prefacing," in his joke: perhaps he feared continual prefacing as a layering of prefaces, as well as, or rather than, simply a long preface. For once we have a thought, there is always something else we can say to better clarify and contextualize that idea. Enough said.

Just because a writer professes to finally begin—or stop—with a point does not mean that he honors the promise. In fact, a reason for suspicion of the preface around 1800 was its alleged insincerity. Just as Jean Paul could earlier be contextualized alongside writers of the German Enlightenment—though his appropriation of an aesthetics of improvement, not least to comic effect—the fragmentary and ironic nature of *Geschichte meiner Vorrede*, together with the above logic of length, connects him to his Romantic contemporaries.

Heinrich von Kleist, for example, expounds an argument about the oral and intellectual construction of thoughts during speech in a fragmentary essay that he drafted in 1805–1806, *Über die allmähliche Verfertigung der Gedanken beim Reden* [On the Gradual Production of Thoughts Whilst Speaking]. The text comprises one long paragraph and ends with the promise of its continuation. For Kleist, thinking happens in tandem with the process of speaking: "Die Sprache ist alsdann keine Fessel, etwa wie ein Hemmschuh an dem Rade des Geistes, sondern wie ein zweites, mit ihm parallel fortlaufendes, Rad an seiner Achse"[79] [Language is not a chain, it is not like a breaking block on the wheel of the mind; it is rather like a second wheel that runs parallel to the mind on the same axle]. He permits spoken language conceptual play and constitutive power over ideas, too, in reasoning that is similar Jean Paul's prefatory logic: that the physical activity of (preface) writing conditions thoughts and writing on (preface) writing.

Friedrich Schlegel, perhaps the most paradigmatic Early German Romantic, reflected on the preface as a fragment. But Schlegel did so more literally than Jean Paul, in the most fragmentary way. In a critical aphorism of 1797, he writes ironically: "Eine gute Vorrede muß zugleich die Wurzel und das Quadrat ihres Buchs sein"[80] [A good preface must be both the root and square of its book]. This witticism encapsulates a significant point about prefacing and poetics around 1800. It metaphorically demonstrates the value of examining the preparatory form relative to an entire work: the book can be extrapolated from the ideal preface (everything that is in the book should be there in nuce in the preface); and the preface also takes the book to a higher level of reflexivity, which would also be a reflection on prefacing: recall that Schlegel's "Prolog" to *Lucinde* is in part a preface about a preface.

Exponentiation was a key concept in Early German Romantic poetic theory. Novalis claims that "Romantisiren ist nichts, als eine qualit[ative] Potenzirung"[81] [Romanticizing is nothing but a qualitative exponentiation]: a being attains self-improvement through multiplying a prior state of itself. And Schlegel writes in an *Athenaeum* fragment of 1798:

> Die romantische Poesie . . . kann . . . am meisten zwischen dem Dargestellten und dem Darstellenden, frei von allem realen und idealen Interesse auf den Flügeln der poetischen Reflexion in der Mitte schweben, diese Reflexion immer wieder potenziren und wie in einer endlosen Reihe von Spiegeln vervielfachen.[82]
>
> [Romantic poetry . . . can most of all, free of all real or ideal interest and on the wings of poetic reflection, hover in the middle between the represented and that which is representing, raising this self-reflection again and again to a higher power, as if multiplying it in an endless row of mirrors.]

The Early German Romantic preoccupation with mathematics derived, more specifically, from a contemporary combinatorial school in the wake of J. L. Lagrange's *Théorie des fonctions analytiques* [Theory of Analytic Functions]

(1797), of which there had been prepublications. The upshot, as Hans Jahnke explains, is that "since the eighteenth century, it was widely held that all functions could be represented by power series . . . mathematics was no longer to be a mere science of numbers and quantities, but rather the science of all combinatorially producible forms."[83] But in strict mathematical logic, Schlegel's two statements on the preface cannot both be true. Thus the aphorism above might also dismiss the preface as a desired impossibility, negating a workable formula that produces a predicted outcome. Schlegel wrote in another aphorism, as mentioned in the introduction, that "das goldene Zeitalter der Literatur würde dann sein, wenn keine Vorreden mehr nötig wären"[84] [the golden age of literature would be once no preface is necessary any longer]. Novalis confesses in his incorporation of Schlegel's fragment on prefacing from 1797 into his own fragment the following year that writing "eine gute Vorrede"[85] [a good preface] is "schwerer wie das Buch"[86] [more difficult than the book]. Around 1800, in the creative heyday of prefacing, the preface should be presented as incalculable if it was to be used at all.

In a letter dated July 20, 1798, Novalis comments that Schlegel's fragments as a collection are unfinished, and he wishes that they were completed: "Es sind freylich nur Früchte einzelner Augenblicke—unter andern Titel eurer Fragmente. Es könnten auch noch zu einigen Vorreden hinzukommen—denn man muß sie als Bücher behandeln und das Fehlende ergänzen"[87] [They are of course only fruits of particular moments—under the other title of your fragments. Some prefaces could also be added, for one must treat them as books and complete (or supplement) what is missing]. For Novalis, prefaces would turn the set of fragments into a coherent whole (of incoherent fragments), a book; with the addition of a unifying preface, they would be finished. Jean Paul, on the other hand, shows us that a preface, even as a book, can also signal a project that either is still unfinished or has not yet properly begun. And so—*pace* Novalis—prefaces can instantiate fragmentation as much as they can be considered its antidote. Furthermore, Novalis's conception of the incomplete as inconclusive must be revised, after reading Jean Paul, to include that which remains uninitiated. If we were to change our understanding of the preface accordingly, it would no longer necessarily complete Schlegel's project as Novalis thinks it would. It would continue, destabilize, or simply start his fragments more fully. Jean Paul therefore radicalizes, through his application of Shandean humor, an Early German Romantic conception of the preface and, or as, a fragment. By contrast, Novalis understands fragmentation, the book, and the preface in the above letter all in a way that is conventional, commonsensical, and thus as surprisingly un-Romantic. In the sense that the preface is fundamentally fragmentary and ironic, Jean Paul is more in tune with Schlegelian poetics than Novalis. Friedrich Schlegel's brother, August, places irony in the antechamber of poetry ("Vorzimmer der Poesie"); Jean Paul literally places it in the preface, which he so often describes as such a "Vorzimmer," in any case.[88]

Jean Paul's more differentiated, fragmentary prefacing is concerned with interpretative opening and closure to equal, expansive, and paradoxical effect. It progresses forth as much as it pauses for thought about itself. This is achieved through a continual humor that in its contradictoriness achieves an always incomplete state on a more abstract, yet apparently finite level, or what Jean Paul calls in his *Vorschule der Ästhetik* "der Humor, als das umgekehrte Erhabene" (SW, 1.11: 112) [humor as the inverted sublime]. Novalis actually shares with Jean Paul a conception of irony as "ächter Humor" [real humor]; but Jean Paul theorizes humor much more thoroughly, and turns theoretical irony into witty literary practice.[89] Proof of humor's ironic potential is a short section of the *Vorschule* in which Jean Paul contends that humor is directed "zum leersten Ausgange" (SW, 1.11: 118) [to the most empty exit], into infinity and in an implicitly verbose way; whereas seriousness, or the most important matters, are expressed concretely, succinctly and epigrammatically. As evidence for the latter, he lists "z.B. der Schluß der Vorrede zu Mösers verteidigtem Harlekin" (SW, 1.11: 118) [for example, the close of the preface to Justus Möser's defended harlequin]. The concluding lines to Justus Möser's preface for *Harlekin oder Vertheidigung des Groteske-Komischen* [Harlequin; Or Defense of the Comic Grotesque] (1761, second edition 1777) are as follows: "Wenn ich nicht irre, so wollte ich eine Vorrede schreiben. Meine Leser werden es aber meinen Jahren verzeihen, daß ich darauf vergessen bin"[90] [If I am not mistaken, I wanted to write a preface. My readers will forgive my age and that I forgot about it]. Möser's epigrammatic closing, attributed to the fictive preface writer Harlekin, is a joke: it ends the preface ("Vorbericht") to this text that is titled as such. In saying he forgot to preface, Möser's preface-writing character actually prefaces. In his *Vorschule*, then, Jean Paul performatively proves and subverts his own theory on abstract, sublimely inverted humor with a counterexample offered in support of his point—a devious, if deliberate contradiction. Here and in his writing more generally, Jean Paul performs his paradoxes, including his preface paradoxes. Consequently, Jean Paul not only exceeds the Early German Romantic theorists in the extent of his textual fragmentation: he adds to, and complicates, our appreciation of the fragment as a Romantic form in the abstract—and above all, on the page.

An interpretation of Jean Paul that aligns him with the Early German Romantics might be received as controversial, indeed as a categorization error. In his own terms, Jean Paul argued against what he identified as a contemporary poetic *nihilism*, a "gesetzlose Willkür" [lawless arbitrariness], with which Novalis apparently shared an affinity in his being and on the page (as "ein Seiten- und Wahlverwandter": SW, 1.11: 22–23). In *Geschichte meiner Vorrede*, published in the same year as Schlegel's first fragment on prefacing but written the previous year, Jean Paul makes mocking reference to Friedrich Schlegel's journalistic publications (SW, 1.5: 21). Paul Fleming distinguishes between Jean Paul's humor and a Schlegelian, Early German Romantic irony, because, as he puts it, the former is concerned not with infinite progress, but instead with the impotence of finitude.[91] Jean Paul explains in the *Vorschule* that humor, or "das romantische Komische" (SW, 1.11: 111–112) [the romantically comic], results from finitude ("Endlichkeit") being deployed in subjective contrast with the philosophical idea of infinity ("Unendlichkeit"), which results in an unending applied finitude, or an inverted sublime, rather than the sublime as an applied form of infinity. However, such ironic inversion can reproduce itself continually, so is somehow as subjective as Schlegel's writings, even more so.

On the one hand, therefore, Jean Paul, Friedrich Schlegel, and Novalis are all predicated on a basic, textually ironic commonality which came to characterize all of these authors as they emerged alongside, and in competition with, each other. Indeed, Jean Paul *materializes* Schlegelian irony to a more extreme and humorous degree. That is to say, the authorial, ironic interplay between finitude and freedom in prefacing, rather than aphoristically in more conventionally fragmentary form, gives rise to textual self-reflexivity and reproduction more radical than anything we read in Schlegel or Novalis. For Schlegel, even materiality is abstract; as Leif Weatherby correctly observes, it is the "intermixture of possibility and the arrangement of concrete matter: it is a formal notion of material."[92] Jean Paul would not disagree, yet he is able to ironize all the more because he is happier to also linger in the sphere of the literal.

On the other hand, then, Jean Paul's humor is different from Early German Romantic irony inasmuch as it relies on the finitude of our subjective being and the world around us, as Ralf Simon points out.[93] The recurrence of such finitude makes Jean Paul's humor more objective. And so Simon thinks that Jean Paul's humor is a "Stoppregel" for Romantic irony, or a means to cut it short. Conceptually speaking, that may be so, though textually such a contention does not work. But Simon's phrasing that Jean Paul grounds self-reflexive philosophy in everyday life, making it a counterintuitive *thing*, is surely productive.[94] Jean Paul turns Romantic irony into written material and, in doing so, writes more and more material. Reflection on "Reflexionsphilosophie" is an example, perpetuation, and exaggeration of the latter—and it is a humorous, ironic terminological maneuver on Jean Paul's part to declare a return to finitude through his writing that keeps ending never-endingly. What could be more Romantic than contradictorily negating Romanticism with a self-negating process of continual prefacing? For Jean Paul does indeed seek to negate the thought and writing of Schlegel, Novalis, and others, as Fleming observes. To this end, as Simon proposes, Jean Paul adopted a dualist philosophy—influenced, in part, by a close relationship with Jacobi, which has been examined in properly philosophical terms by Oliver Koch.[95]

As Koch demonstrates, the positive, finite, and objective element of Jean Paul's humor—a positivity that is missing from Romantic irony—resides, ironically, in subjective feeling: in our finite, core individuality, as expressed in the beautiful and the sublime.[96] Jean Paul's conception of beauty, which is based on Sentimental feeling, is that which can transcend humor.[97] Thus humorous reflection—the infinite play with finitude—is only half the story. Feeling and beauty provide the positive side that grounds an individual in the world, and lends objectivity to such subjective humor that reproduces itself.[98]

This second tenet of Jean Paul's philosophy, as Koch describes it, has two consequences for Jean Paul's *Geschichte meiner Vorrede* preface, which is his most complex and creative preface of all. Here, he deploys what is generally understood as (Schlegelian) Romantic irony as radical ironic enactment, an *argumentum ad absurdum* that affirms the logical operation of Romantic irony, but demonstrates its comical outcome. Taken on its own terms, by itself in its materiality, Jean Paul's humor is akin to Romantic irony—albeit as an immanent critique of it, as Koch notes.[99] It is an amusing equivalent to rational, commonsense, or (Hegelian) systemic criticism.[100] Jean Paul's positive resolution is to then turn to subjectively individual, but objective feeling. And it is with this aspect of his thought that Jean Paul concludes his preface.

Geschichte meiner Vorrede ultimately ends as an epitaph ("Grabschrift"), or in its earliest version as a celebratory wedding poem ("Epithalamium"). The concluding text is appended not so much in place of, but as a part of the preface. For although Jean Paul calls it a substitute for the reader, as recompense for the impossible conclusion of the preface (SW, I.5: 31), he signs with his name and the date, so typical of a preface. In a typically Jean Paulish reference to contemporary print culture, the concluding piece is entitled "Die Mondfinsternis" [The lunar eclipse], thereby referencing an entry on the preface ("Vorrede") in the fiftieth volume of Zedler's *Grosses vollständiges Universal-Lexicon aller Wissenschafften und Künste* [Great Complete Universal Encyclopedia of All Sciences and Arts] in 1746. This lemma on prefacing states that the effect ("Würkung") of prefaces written and inserted by the booksellers ("Buchführer") is "in general not great, hence they appear as seldom as a visible lunar eclipse" ("insgemein nicht groß; daher erscheinen dieselben nicht öfters als die sichtbaren Mondfinsternisse").[101] Jean Paul's preface perhaps adopts and adapts this joke: the effect of the preface is frustrated, and so this commercial author instead presents the reader with a "Montfinsternis" that is rendered visible, literary, and Sentimental. Before he begins this closing, evocative description, Jean Paul describes alighting from the carriage with Johanne Pauline and showing her the pila on a column that depicts a young bride having fallen under the wheels of a wagon, which explains the vague illustration on the title page when the preface was first printed on its own, as a book.[102] This object strikes his companion's "weiches Herz" (SW, 1.5: 31) [soft heart]; she cries, and dries her tears only after he finishes reciting "Die Mondfinsternis," which is also intended for the reader (whom his alter ego, Johanne Pauline, depicts). The story, then, is an example of the beauty that makes the nihilistic fragmentation of Romantic irony *Sentimentally wholesome*. This closing fiction, significantly, is called a "kleine Dichtung" (SW, 1.5: 32) [small poetic piece]. It develops, structurally, the strategy of the "Mustheil für Mägden" [A Sugary Delicacy for Young Ladies] that followed the first preface to *Quintus Fixlein*, and which comprised two Sentimental, poetic prose pieces—the second of which begins as a "Dedikation" [Dedication]. But more specifically, "Die Mondfinsternis" is poetic prose as part of a preface in place of a preface, and under a title that subtly references precisely the definition of exceptional prefacing.

As we shall see in chapter 3, Hegel nevertheless accuses Jean Paul of being whimsical—not, in the end, objective (via our subjective, infinite feeling within our concrete, mortal identity). This is for two reasons. First, until we reach ultimate self-consciousness (if we ever do), for Hegel we remain organic, self-constituting creatures capable of continual change relative to our emergent knowledge and environment. Our identity does not have such a stable core. And second, Hegel operates within monist logic, whereas Jean Paul implicitly adopted a dualist perspective. Jean Paul's humor was ironic in a Romantic sense, though critically deployed for a more abstract agenda. But because such nihilism, as he himself calls it, can be fully rectified only outside of textuality, in personhood, Hegel will say that Jean Paul's writing is still too subjective. Hegel raised contradiction to a method and means of objective truth in a single system, in and through writing.

COUNTERING *CAPTATIO BENEVOLENTIAE?* BEYOND ELOQUENCE

One word commonly deployed by literary critics in discussing Jean Paul's prefaces is "play."[103] Ehrenzeller correctly notes that Jean Paul honed the wit of his prefatory pieces through the reception of Sterne, but then contends that compared to his English model, the German author conceives and achieves a greater reciprocity between his own authorial (preface-writing) persona and his readers. The urbane Sterne, by contrast, writes in polite, ironic condescension toward his readership.[104] While confessing his predilection for prefatorial play, Jean Paul implies in his *Appendix des Appendix* [Appendix to the Appendix] to *Der Jubelsenior* [The Jubilant Old Man] (1797) that this habit makes him happy. Crucially, he is happier than the reader, and liberates himself—for he refers to the Phrygian cap of the French revolution:

> Ich glaube nicht, daß ein Autor etwas lieber schreibt als seine Vor- und Nachrede: hier darf er endlich reden, was ihn letzt, seitenlang von sich, und was am meisten labt, von seinem Werk—er hat aus dem Raspelhaus und Sklavenschiff des Buchs den Sprung auf diese beiden Spielplätze und Luftlager gethan und hat zwanzig akademische Freiheiten bei sich und eine Freiheitsmütze auf dem Kopfe und lebt da froher als den Leser. (SW, 1.5: 516)
>
> [I believe that an author enjoys nothing more than writing his preface and afterword: here he can finally speak for page after page about himself, which amuses him, and about his work, which enlivens him the most; he has made the jump from the prisoners' workhouse and the slave ship that are the book onto these two playgrounds or spaces in which he has room to move freely—having twenty academic freedoms in his pocket and a Phrygian cap on his head, here he lives more happily than the reader.]

Of course, we cannot tell how happy Jean Paul really was, in comparison to us, and to what extent this is a fictive claim; and for him we are, as readers, also a fiction. The problem with Ehrenzeller's interpretation is that our writer is put on a pedestal and can do no wrong. In Ehrenzeller's view, even

Jean Paul's occasional disregard for his readers can count as evidence for his particular closeness to them, teasing them—and it is precisely this tension that creates his unique relationship with them.[105] For Ehrenzeller, the historical disrepute into which *captatio benevolentiae* had fallen, as part and parcel of the rejection of Baroque eloquence, led to the preface's demise in the later eighteenth century. But with Jean Paul's innovative approach to convention in his post-1793 works, this decline now halted and the maxim of winning goodwill was positively rehabilitated by playful provocation and ironic pandering. (Ehrenzeller does not discuss the prefaces to Jean Paul's early writings.) To be sure, Jean Paul released rhetorical prescription from scholarly pedantry into what he himself calls, in the above passage, "academic freedoms," and in a way that was not simply that of the scholarly satires by Rabener, Riedel, and others—as explored in the introduction to the present book. Yet his tactics were more complex than Ehrenzeller suggests. We should ask more precisely: what does Jean Paul's playful prefacing mean for the tradition in which winning the goodwill of an audience (or readership) was conventionally contained—namely, rhetorical theory?

Jean Paul's prefaces are only secondarily acts of cheery confrontation with criticism (for his responses are never caustic or cynical) and apologetic address. Primarily, they establish an ad hoc, conversational context for the author alone—and hence, in Jean Paul's conception, for others as well. Prefacing (and prefacing prefacing) equates with rambling preambles to preambles of speech. In this chapter, then, Jean Paul's written prefaces have been compared with orality as well as being described as textually specific. Their comedy, eclectic references, and nonce, at first glance nonsense, metaphors surely charm good-humored readers, setting them at ease through their chatty style. Their unexpected connections to so many branches of learning, and their innovative use of topoi in this regard, must impress as much as they baffle many a reader.[106] If this efficacy seems equal to the age-old rhetorical, oratorical function of the preface or exordium (*captatio benevolentiae*), though, it cannot be understood as such in any strong, strategic sense. Jean Paul's free-form conversation openers are not traditional or obvious gambits. First and foremost, they humorously gratify himself as a preface-writing figure.

Nevertheless, a Jean Paulish preface is undoubtedly a platform for prefatory play in which readers are invited to participate. As Ehrenzeller argues, a preface's instrumental purposes ("die Zweckfunktionen") are sidelined to make room for a comfy get-together with readers;[107] but the "unverbindliches Spiel" ["nonbinding game"] (in Ehrenzeller's words) of

Jean Paul's prefatorial method characterizes a strikingly autonomous text that is about imagined personal togetherness, not empirical persuasion (not to mention calculated attack).[108] This argument against an overt rhetoricality complements the broader idea that, in the latter half of the eighteenth century, rhetorical theory became ostensibly irrelevant and largely invisible for literature more generally: rhetoric mutated; or the paradigm went underground and, therefore, can be conceptualized as a rhizome (see introduction). If Goethe concealed and revealed the artifice of his natural creativity coyly (see chapter 1), then Jean Paul gleefully dug up rhetorical tradition and held it up to the light, as outdated, and for his own, brand new textual-conceptual discoveries.

Although we can admit that the preface, in Jean Paul's time, was not as pragmatic or goal-orientated as a classically rhetorical schema might suggest, and thus its rhetoric was revised, it would be wrong to say that rhetoric was superseded in the preface. Even if we allow that Jean Paul wrote or prefaced without purpose—and surely he did not, since to amuse and to analogize is to advance both entertainment and knowledge, possibly in a moving, and as Jean Paul would have it, in an inversely sublime way—prefacing can become a pretext for, or a purpose of (preface) writing. That is to say, self-reflexive, apparently self-governing prefaces are also intentional, though their intention may be discovered in the writing process itself.

Moreover, rhetorical theory has never been so systematic that it had to be accepted or rejected in its entirety. Indeed, its history is in one sense a list of attempts to systematize the protean discipline, if rhetoric is read as a series of proper names such as Aristotle, Cicero, Quintilian, and so on, who each assembled handbooks, organized according to their own conception of the subject. So we should not be reductive in our understanding of Jean Paul's rhetorical heritage. If, of the three classical genres of oratory, the *forensic* and the *deliberative* modes declined around 1800, that still left plenty of scope for the third genre: the *epideictic* genre of verbal displays at ceremonies, for example. Satirists of the Second Sophistic, a late heyday of Greek rhetoric and oratory, composed *prolaliae*. Lucian's are frequently texts which came before his main performances—though the latter are seldom extant—and these preliminary pieces are sometimes self-referential. His *forechats* were intended, in some instances at least, to be entertaining in and of their own right. He ends *A Slip of the Tongue in Greeting*, for example, with the request that his composition "be such that all may see it as a starting point of a display, not as a defence."[109] Such displays had to win the goodwill of audiences, of course, but their strategies to this effect could be off the beaten track, and they would sometimes satirize those rhetorical topoi which contemporaries used forensically or deliberatively. After all, orators who are too conventional and strictly prosaic do not successfully entertain, though they may be taken seriously in a court of law (forensic rhetoric) or in politics (deliberative rhetoric). Lucian himself emphasized the importance of originality to previous Greek writers in the fifth century B.C., a stress on novelty that made covert use of rhetorical theory.[110] Jean Paul's perpetual prefacing and its contrary, abortive fragmentation is similarly rhetorical: with a purpose not to persuade, but to display ingenuity.

Jean Paul's individual prefatory path therefore has a rhetorical precedent. But it is remarkably contrary to Quintilian's rhetorical advice against unusual words, overbold metaphors, and a whimsical attitude: "people think any sort of beginning a *Prooemium*, and anything that comes to mind, especially if some clever epigram beckons, a proper *exordium*."[111] Quintilian himself had to admit, however—as supporters of Apollodorus contended in Athens—that the respects in which the mind of a judge might be prepared and won over can be categorized beyond the given description, ad infinitum, which must give some license, at least in theory, to exordial exaggeration.[112] In sum, Jean Paul is another case of "rhetorica contra rhetoricam," with his traditional rhetorical underpinning referenced most overtly in the juvenile satires.

In his later aesthetic theory, Jean Paul is explicit about his employment and subversion of rhetorical precepts for a style of writing that he conceives as nonrhetorical, inasmuch as it is not intended for the purpose of public oratory, but for silent reading and individual pleasure instead. In *Vorschule der Ästhetik* (1804), he reasons: "Der Schreiber ist kein Sprecher, und der Leser kein Zuhörer; und deshalb darf der langsame Schreiber schon dem langsamen Leser so ausgedehnte Perioden vorgeben als Cicero, der Feuer-Redner, einem Feuervolke" (SW, 1.11: 300) [The writer is no speaker, and the reader is not a listener, and because of that fact the slow writer may give the slow reader such elongated sentences as Cicero, the fiery orator, gave his people of fire]. This is an argument about the generative potential of writing that defends long, digressive sentences over a series of shorter ones. The ancients, the English, and also earlier Germans, Jean Paul notes, all wrote convoluted sentences. The fashion for concision occurs in times that have pretension to taste, and succinct sentences were recently the rage in German letters following Gellert and Rabener, who were influenced by the new French norms—unlike the Anglophile Christian Ludwig Liscow: "Was ist ein Rabenersches Perioden-*haché* gegen einen Liscovschen *roast beef*!" (SW, 1.11: 300) [How can a *haché* of Rabener's sentences be compared with Liscow's *roast beef*!]. In fact, since the works of Johann Christoph Gottsched, anti-Ciceronianism had gained ground, and with it a dismissal of the associated periodic style typical of ancient and Baroque rhetoric, a style in which sentences are not grammatically complete until the final clause. A so-called Senecan style, or *style coupé*, had taken hold in Enlightened debate instead, and the idea that one should write as naturally as one speaks in everyday conversation had become commonplace. So far, this summary is familiar ground for language criticism around 1800, a discourse on which Jean Paul wrote far more technical thoughts than those offered here. But by rejecting the latter maxim, Jean Paul returns to an alternative, classically rhetorical and Ciceronian style for his prose, including his intricate prefaces. He does so precisely, he says (or rather, writes), because he considers writing not to be like speech. Ironically, only through a medial dissimilarity between literary and spoken exchange can rhetoric become useful in what is otherwise a nonoratorical, not obviously rhetorical context of eloquence and wit, in order to appeal to an audience's (or readership's) affects.

The invocation of Cicero is pertinent not least to Jean Paul's prefaces. Cicero, like Jean Paul, produced a book of only prefaces, the *volumen prohoemiorum*; unlike Jean Paul, though, they were all to manuscripts that existed elsewhere.[113] Jean Paul comments on this book in *Hesperus* (1795): "Wer hätt' es von Cicero gedacht (wenn ers nicht gelesen hätte), daß ein so bejahrter gescheiter Mann sich in seiner Johannis-Insel hinsetzen und *Anfänge*, Eingänge, präexistierende Keime im voraus auf den Kauf verfertigen würde? "(SW, 1.4: 109) [Who would have thought it of Cicero (if he had not read it) that such an old and clever man would sit down on his island of St. John and assemble *beginnings*, introductions, pre-existing seeds for sale in advance?]. Jean Paul was as ancient as he was modern; or he was modern because of his attempt to grapple with the ancients, their thoughts, and their texts in a novel, self-aware way—conceptually and textually.

In the preface to the second volume of *Titan* (1801), Jean Paul expresses irritation about his observation that: "Über den gegenwärtigen Vorredner wird seit einiger Zeit fast mehr gesagt als gedacht" (SW, 1.8: 403) [For some time now, almost more is said about the present prefacer than is thought about him]. We have thoroughly interrogated not only Jean Paul but above all else Jean Paul as prefacer; and we rest assured that his own reflections not only on himself but on his role as preface writer ("Vorredner") through preface writing are as conceptual as they are verbose. The present investigation becomes more conceptual still, however, in the next chapter: in its consideration of Hegel. For the paradox that antirhetorical prefacing is still rhetorical is equally remarkable in his philosophization of prefacing.

CONCLUSION: PREFACE TO PREFATORIAL PHILOSOPHY (AND THEORY)

In the preface to the first volume of Hoffmann's *Fantasiestücke in Callot's Manier* (1814), Jean Paul laments a perceived absence of ancillary notes, indexes, and prefaces to contemporary works—the loss of an explanatory framework within or attached to a text. Goethe is apparently to blame for this disregard for prefacing, because he addresses his contemporary readership (his "Mitwelt") as a posthumous one ("Nachwelt"). What is more, authors are nowadays, Jean Paul laments, all too impolite by not helping their readers out:

> Verzeichnisse des Inhalts—(oft der Druckfehler)—Kapitel—erläuternde Noten—Anführungen nach Seitenzahlen—Registerfache ohnehin—auch Vorreden (z.B. diesem Buche) und Absätze (wie hier) fehlen neuerer Zeiten gewöhnlich und der Leser helfe sich selber.[114]
>
> [Tables of contents—(often of the printing errors)—chapters—explanatory notes—quotations with page numbers—indexes and glossaries in any case—prefaces also (like the one to this book), and paragraphs (such as here) are all usually missing in more recent times, and the reader must help himself.]

Jean Paul assigns to what we would now call paratexts, and prefaces among them, a common function. The inclusion of a preface is apparently polite, because the form facilitates understanding, assisting the reader with literary instruction. Structurally, however, we might infer that the preface belongs to a higher order of reflexivity than the other textual framing devices he mentions, since the various elements of the paratext, including prefaces, are here grouped together and discussed within the preface itself. Moreover, the above preface is also a preface to a preface, because Hoffmann inserts the short essay "Jaques Callot" as the first piece of the collection, which he called a "Vorwort" in a letter to his publisher Kunz on July 20, 1813.[115] But such formal self-reflexivity of Jean Paul's prefacing also occurred in his other sorts of paratext, too: in 1797, for example, he appended the "Appendix des Appendix" to the appendix *Der Jubelsenior*, in which he reflected on the nature of appending (a paratext that Derrida later emphasizes). Thus, Jean Paul's prefacing is part of his wider concern with what we now call the paratext in its different, individual instantiations, as well as with the texture of writing itself. His is a focus on framing that has since been taken up by thinkers such as Derrida, Genette, and others, and examined in recent literary-historical scholarship, too (see introduction). However, so far Jean Paul's prefaces in all their particularity have not been a significant part of studies on the genealogy of deconstruction, or the "paratext." Telling their afterstory here reveals how their jokes, literary games, and conceptual maneuvers have been appropriated since, as both conscious echoes and silent inspiration. And so the present chapter closes, and prefaces a more philosophical examination of Hegel, with a consideration of the theoretical legacy of Jean Paul's prefaces.

In 1844, Søren Kierkegaard published *Prefaces: Light Reading for People in Various Estates According to Time and Opportunity*, an amusing work under the pseudonym Nicolaus Notabene. It is a collection of eight forewords to unwritten books, framed by a preface; a selection of satires—or, as the title suggests, easy reading—that implicitly but obviously mocks Copenhagen intellectual politics as well as German intellectualism. Primarily, *Prefaces* makes fun of Hegel's philosophical system and his chief Copenhagen follower, Johan Ludvig Heiberg. Kierkegaard figuratively connects a preface to a book as the preface writer is wedded to his wife; and he quips that in the wake of Hegel and Hegelians, "if the preface and the book cannot be hitched up together, then let the one give the other a decree of divorce."[116] But the starting joke that Kierkegaard's *Prefaces* severs a preface from a subsequent *book* as well as a philosophical system is immediately revealed to be insincere, since this witticism is formulated in a foreword to a book—of forewords. If this seems a Jean Paulish sense of humor, then it is unsurprising that scholarship confirms Kierkegaard is otherwise indebted to our German humorist, who was translated into Danish, incorporated into Kierkegaard's more serious philosophy, and is explicitly mentioned in Preface 8.[117] Kierkegaard subverts and appropriates Jean Paul's preface strategies.

Prefacing, as Kierkegaard interpreted it, not only prescribes that the preface writer—ostensibly as an author, we note, of prefaces alone—must be funny. He should also be a writer of untruth: "The preface as such, the liberated preface, must then have no subject to treat but must deal with nothing, and insofar as it seems to discuss something and deal with something, this must nevertheless be an illusion and a fictitious motion."[118] He glosses this definition as *lyrical*, and insofar as he equates poetic prose with nothing he surely negates a higher meaning of literary-style prefaces (if nothing here means nothing of philosophical note, as a commonsense understanding of the word). Thus Kierkegaard directs a jibe toward creative as well as philosophical prefacing.

Yet despite this comic attack, he proceeds to appropriate an array of metaphors for creative prefacing that can be read as an allusion to the literary prefaces penned by Jean Paul. Kierkegaard compares composing a preface to the start of falling in love, secretly observing a woman an author desires; and the male preface writer is apparently a happy, nonchalant, and self-content character.[119] Above all:

> Writing a preface is like arriving by stagecoach at the first station, stopping in the dark shed, having a presentiment of what will appear, seeing the gate and then the open sky, gazing at the continually receding road beyond, catching a glimmer of the pregnant mystery of the forest, the alluring fading away of the footpath; it is like hearing the sound of the posthorn.[120]

Moreover, in Kierkegaard's model—as in Jean Paul's—the imaginative act of prefacing is suggestively masturbatory. As Mads Fedder Henriksen points out, Kierkegaard employs images for preface writing which evoke male autoeroticism: the author sharpens his scythe, spits out of the window, or lashes his cane in the air, for example.[121] The preface to *Prefaces* thereby becomes erotic, but it is an arousal that cannot be acted upon. Of the writer's home situation, we later read that Notabene tussles with his wife, who resents his authorship. The prefatory chit-chat and abandoned prefatorial self-stimulation we examined in Jean Paul's prefaces similarly becomes, in Kierkegaard's, frustrated private fantasy and domestic interaction (including conflict).

The core argument of the present chapter was that Jean Paul's prefaces are governed by a concept of *autoprefacing*, which can be understood in a subliminally erotic sense: interpersonal desire on which a preface is traditionally predicated becomes a masturbatory gesture, and so the preface turns into an act of self-exploration. Autoprefacing can be comprehended rhetorically, too, and with respect to writing itself. In the twentieth century, Derrida develops a concept of "autoinsemination" (similarly a partially sexual image) in "Outwork, Prefacing," the opening essay to his *Dissemination* (1972). His theory about textual framing in this prefatory chapter is chiefly a response to Hegel's preface to *Phänomenologie des Geistes* [Phenomenology of Spirit] (1807), Hegelian and—more broadly—philosophical method. But Derrida explicitly invokes literary writers and thinkers of Enlightenment satire and European Romanticism in his effort to counter Hegel's systematicity with deconstruction. Most obviously and in greatest depth, he includes Novalis's poetics of the encyclopaedia. Further, Derrida cites Jean Paul supporting his own idea that the preface is a "simulacrum" of the "postface": paradoxically, "the recapitulation and recurrent anticipation, the auto-motion of the concept, it is another text entirely, but at the same time, as an 'attendant discourse,' it is the 'double' of what it goes beyond."[122] Significantly, he introduces Jean Paul in the corresponding footnote as needing no introduction; he "hardly needs to be identified as the master of the double."[123] The core preface paradox, in Derrida's model, is described as "self-effacement." The preface is as irrelevant as it is relevant and, as such, "prefaces, along with forewords, introductions, preludes, preliminaries, preambles, prologues, and prolegomena," cancel themselves out, leaving a remainder.[124] In this regard, Derrida reiterates the first preface paradox of the present book that Jean Paul and, less explicitly, Goethe evince in such an exemplary way—and Derrida gestures toward this late eighteenth-, early nineteenth-century creative debt.

There are two further correspondences between Derrida and Jean Paul in particular—though in Derrida, unlike Jean Paul, this pair of ideas is not paradoxical. In outlining the main preface problem at the beginning of "Outwork, Prefacing," Derrida intriguingly and implicitly describes the preface as proof that the writer is the first reader of his own work. Since the preface announces a text already written (a past proposition) in a future tense (as a book that will be received), it is "thus sufficiently *read* to be gathered up in its semantic tenor and proposed in advance."[125] The authorial act of writing and then reading the preface becomes autoerotic—as it does for Jean Paul and, following him, Kierkegaard. The preface, for Derrida, is a "seed" and "semen," and so it is also a masturbatory form of self-love—which, he seems to imply in a long footnote, is why classical rhetoric was apparently against prefacing.[126] Philippe Lacoue-Labarthe and Jean-Luc Nancy later apply and adjust this idea of autonomous regeneration apart from any function to the fragment in 1978—though the fragment, for them, is not "a dissemination, but is rather the dispersal that leads to fertilization and future harvests . . . the organic is essentially *auto*-formation."[127]

Dissemination turns into a Derridean literary game, "the preface is a fiction,"[128] and the preface is paradigmatic for writing per se. As such, prefaces, like all texts, become sites of sexual pleasure, because of their acts of opening and closing, their fragmentation, their foreplay, climax, foreclosure:

> Where does pleasure take *place* if it is practically literary in essence? If the foreplay, the "bonus of seduction," the "preliminary pleasure (*Vorlust*), the formal moment of literature, reaches satisfaction only at the *end* of pleasure, then the climax of pleasurable fulfilment [*jouissance*] would never be anything other than the instance of seduction, the supplementary bonus of nothing else. Pleasure would always be a formal, threshold phenomenon.[129]

The author as preface writer as self-reader is unproblematic in this logic because Derrida understands writing as unrhetorical (or rather, as replacing rhetoric). He charges metaphysical discourse with operating with dualistic oppositions which ultimately settle on presence over absence, or speech over writing. "Logocentrism" and "phonocentrism," as he calls these biases, are overcome by the Derridean (non)concepts of *différance* and *dissemination*; and so a preface should no longer connote the exordium of a speech. Rejecting the word "preface" because of its etymological oral connection, Derrida instead privileges the term "protocol," thereby solving the form's perceived tense problem, and emphasizing its proximity to the written, not spoken word (unlike the German "Vorrede," say).[130] A protocol does not have such an obvious addressee as a preface. In a further—to readers of the present chapter, by now familiar—metaphor, the preface can be understood as an illustrative, penned "sketch." In half the same way as Jean Paul, then, Derrida advances a sexually animated argument concerned with writing (about writing . . .). But Jean Paul also admits a rhetorical dimension nonetheless.

Moreover, Derrida's prose style, by his own comparison, is similar to Swift's, Rousseau's, and Jean Paul's. He summarizes: "Dissemination would propose a certain theory—to be followed, also, as a marching order quite ancient in its form—of *digression*."[131] Oddly though, he also employs an analogy from speech for our text type under consideration: prefacing in particular is "the site of a kind of chit-chat external to the very thing it appears to be talking about"; it is the "gossipy small talk of history."[132] In this sense, too, Derrida is akin to Jean Paul.

"Outwork, Prefacing" is primarily about prefatory, introductory material. But in the course of writing, Derrida at times enlarges his scope: "The staging of a title, a first sentence, an epigraph, a pretext, a preface, a single germ, will never make a beginning."[133] One of Jean Paul's paratexts to which Derrida refers in his footnote frames the appendix *Der Jubelsenior* as an appendix (1797), and it is cited by Derrida in order to posit the more particular point that a preface, or his "Outwork would then, for example, be the hystero-colic sketch of an *appendix*."[134] Derrida here also likens the preface, via Kierkegaard, to the postscript; and his categorization of a particular form soon explodes into a much broader preoccupation. In this way, Derrida's thought concerns what we, post-Genette, call the paratext (encompassing postscripts and appendices), and predominantly the preface within that category. His preface is not just about prefaces. But the preface initiates that paratextual discussion.

The quotation Derrida selects from Jean Paul is later reiterated by Genette, who follows Derrida in his own study of the paratext as a paradoxical threshold.[135] Derrida suggests that scholars should follow his "Outwork, Prefacing" with an exploration of extant prefaces rather than their internal principles, which he examines in his essay. "Oughtn't we some day to reconstitute their history and typology?" he asks.[136] Genette's canonical (Structuralist) *Paratexts* (1987) might be received as an answer to this (post-Structuralist) rhetorical question, especially as Genette acknowledges Derrida's essay, and particularly its interpretation of Hegel, in his very introduction to prefacing.[137] Genette's reply to Derrida is even less about prefaces in particular than "Outwork, Prefacing," though—prefaces that were the single topic of the specific Derridean question to which Genette responds. And so the literature on paratexts was born. But for all its strengths and scope, the concept of the paratext leaves more particular conceptions of prefacing unaddressed, and the resistance of peculiar paratextual forms (such as the preface) to an albeit plausible, general category undisclosed—even if the more specific focus on the preface adopted by the present book soon implodes, once we examine forms other than mere commonsense prefaces. (Classificatory resistance and expansion is evident in the categorizations of chapter 1, which we were unable to pin down in too fixed a way, and which digressed, in the end, into autobiography.) Particular "preface problems" are worked through by authors repeatedly in the late eighteenth and early nineteenth centuries and since, despite the generality of the paratext as a concept. The fundamental nature of prefaces is somehow the same as for writing or framing itself, yet is still—and ironically—distinct. Jean Paul is a literary example to this end par excellence. Derrida's question on prefaces continues: "Can they be grouped according to the necessity of some common predicate, or are they otherwise and in themselves divided?"[138] This thought recurs throughout time, too, and was the question first posed by authors around 1800. Such inquiry is just one legacy of that era: of Jean Paul's prefaces, and of Hegel's as well.

CHAPTER THREE

Hegel

Prefatorial Polemic Becomes Philosophy

OF ALL PREFACES written around 1800, Hegel's preface ("Vorrede") to *Phänomenologie des Geistes* [Phenomenology of Spirit] (1807) has since been the most influential on what we could call "preface philosophy," or at least subsequent theories of prefacing—especially in post-Structuralism. But no commentator has suggested that its composition must have been influenced by the self-reflexivity typical of contemporary preface writing. Like Goethe and Jean Paul, Hegel discussed and dramatized prefacing most critically, conceptually, and creatively in his maturity: as he conceived, developed, and organized his system (just as literary authors worked on their oeuvres). Like his contemporaries, Hegel was aware that the public of his day might stop reading books after their prefaces, and he reflects on this problem in the preface itself (HGW, 9: 48). He is critical of those prefatory texts which he perceives as superfluous to, inappropriate for, and against the very point of philosophical works (HGW, 9: 9). In short, prefaces are usually at best simply historical (or empirical), not speculative; and at worst they are superficial. Rather than refuse to preface his *Phänomenologie*, though, Hegel writes a prefatory text that runs to ninety-one pages in the layout of the original edition—just five pages less than Jean Paul's *Geschichte meiner Vorrede* [History of my Preface]. To summarize in any conventional preface a system of thought that for Hegel should be understood in its entirety is as impossible and irrelevant as it is imperative, if the following work as a whole is to be taken seriously from the outset. And so Hegel's preface from 1807 had to become innovative and yet remain identifiable as a preface, in order to be both rhetorically pragmatic and, at the same time, philosophically respectable. This causes a problem of contradiction for Hegel, but then precisely contradiction is the core issue of his philosophy.

STARTING WITH STERNE? LITERATURE AND PHILOSOPHY AROUND 1800

Before we interrogate Hegel's preface through the prism of his own philosophy, he should be contextualized alongside his literary peers—and Laurence Sterne in particular. Sterne and Hegel are in most respects as different as chalk and cheese. But they share an underlying concern with the contingent and its relevance to conceptions of the self. Of course, this problem was of the widest possible philosophical interest around 1800. But in 1827, Goethe published a few paragraphs in an issue of *Über Kunst und Altertum* [On Art and Antquity] as a tribute to an apparently forgotten precursor of modern writing and subjectivity: "Lorenz Sterne." Sterne had shaped literature as well as thought about the human condition ("Menschenerkenntnis"). In Goethe's view, the anthropological merit of German letters (and presumably philosophy) owed a debt to the "Yorick-Sterne" of *The Life and Opinions of Tristram Shandy, Gentleman* (1759–1767) and, above all, *A Sentimental Journey Through France and Italy* (1768), who discovered "das Menschliche im Menschen" (FA, 1.22: 338–339) [humanity in the human]. Goethe simply means that Sterne was an initial influence on the period's greatest writers as they investigated selfhood. But in light of chapter 2, we can also say that within Jean Paul's works, Sterne inspired a literary reconception of beginning itself, beginning with prefacing. Recent criticism has advanced the claim that Hegel's philosophy, too, starts with Sterne: conceptually and textually.

The idea that Hegel's writing is influenced by *Tristram Shandy* or *A Sentimental Journey* is somehow comical, even Shandean. But the notion is as astute as it is absurd. Sterne's works were among Hegel's favorites, and Klaus Vieweg reminds us that Hegel and Hölderlin read Theodor Gottlieb von Hippel's Sternean *Lebensläufe in aufsteigender Linie* [Biographies in an Ascending Line] (1778–1781) together at the Tübingen seminary, alongside the thought of Plato, Kant, and Friedrich Heinrich Jacobi.[1] And as Hegel draws toward the close of what he interprets as Romantic art in his later aesthetic lectures (published posthumously), he praises the humor of Hippel and Sterne especially (HW, Ä 1: 231). For Vieweg, these two authors facilitate Hegel's transition from metaphorical to conceptual representation, and they are his bridge from literary into philosophical prose.[2] Vieweg understands Hegel's works of the Jena phase, including and most notably the *Phänomenologie*, within and as overcoming the tradition of the humorous novel. He suggests that the conceptual tenet of the *Phänomenologie* was a skepticism comically derived from Sterne, and this writer's contemporary currency. It is true that a comic attitude is skeptical in its view of the world; and Vieweg's analysis of Sterne as philosophically skeptical satire is so convincing because it is by now common sense. As Judith Hawley notes, *Tristram Shandy* reveals the "comic potential" of especially Locke's dismissal of associative thought.[3] In general, she observes, the satirical genre to which Sterne's first novel "partly belongs shows greater concern for academia than for adventure."[4]

More specifically, Hegel's admiration for Sterne and Hippel in his aesthetic lectures has to do with their depiction of incidental humor that hides (as he reads them) an underlying coherence. In Hegel's view, Sterne's humor is not subjective; and, implicitly, Hegel suggests that it is also not ironic in a Romantic sense. Having already criticized Friedrich Schlegel's conception of irony for both positing "nichts *an und für sich*" (HW, Ä 1: 94) [nothing *in and for itself*] and being entirely contingent on the subjectivity of the self, he attacks Jean Paul's humor for a similar subjectivism. Jean Paul is guilty of "barocke[s] Zusammenbringen des objektiv Entferntesten . . . , deren Beziehung etwas durchaus Subjektives ist" (HW, Ä 2, 230) [bringing together in baroque fashion that which is objectively so far removed, whereby the relationship between objects is thoroughly subjective]. Sterne and Hippel, by contrast, are more objective writers, whose wit may seem disorganized but is paradoxically orderly on a deeper level. Its coherence is undetermined by the authorial subject. Hegel wants to uncover the necessity within the apparently contingent, without Jean Paul's typical *authorial* self-reflexivity that is at its most intrusive in his prefaces.

Indeed, the fictional author's preface to *Tristram Shandy* begins with Tristram declaring that his book "must speak for itself" without prefatory comment—before he ironically proceeds with prefacing.[5] To the reader of Hegel's *Phänomenologie*, this act of disregarding prefaces only to then contradict the dismissal by prefacing sounds familiar. But the aim that a book and its ideas should be self-explanatory, and the inevitable failure that ensues, is appropriated and acknowledged by Hegel with great seriousness. Moreover, "The Author's Preface" to *Tristram Shandy* is placed in the center of the work—and understanding Hegel's preface, which ostensibly prepares the reader for the system it precedes, can be understood fully only once the reader has worked through that system. Derrida was right to compare Hegel and Sterne in this respect, but not to contrast them.[6] In a very abstract sense, Hegel begins in the middle of his main text; the beginning is already contingent on what is to come. We shall return to Derrida later. To remain with Sterne, Tommaso Pierini, a student of Vieweg's, is not wholly incorrect in claiming that *Tristram Shandy* is the structural basis of the *Phänomenologie*, though this is surely less an intention and more a necessity.[7] For there is less a planned structural affinity between Sterne and Hegel than there is a shared curiosity about contingency, and a rejection of its straightforward—linear and simple—interrogation as an obvious consequence. Pierini's and Vieweg's further contention that Hegel's philosophy is akin to a travelogue, or an adventure into knowledge, is comparatively far-fetched.[8]

The significance of writing itself is another, perhaps the most fundamental commonality between Hegel and Sterne, yet it is one that has not been remarked upon. Tristram, in narrating *Tristram Shandy*, exclaims: "—But this is neither here nor there—why do I mention it?—Ask my pen,—it governs me, I govern not it."[9] Around 1800, an explosion in printing and a concomitant popular book market caused increased reflections on texts, within texts, contemporary to philosophical self-reflection valorized by Fichte. Both these trends stimulated Hegel's philosophical emphasis on mediation. In his Jena notebooks of 1803–1806, he accuses Wieland of a paradoxical approach to composition: "Wieland, dem man sonst eben nicht Paradoxie vorwirft, hat den paradoxen Satz aufgestellt, daß es dienlich sei, von der Materie, worüber man schreibe, etwas zu verstehen, und man hat ihn probat gefunden" (HGW, 5: 491) [Wieland, whom we otherwise do not accuse of being a paradoxical author, has come up with the paradoxical proposition that it is useful to understand something of the material one is writing about—and he has been proved right]. Wieland's commonsense conception of the writing process is only a paradox once we conceive of writing as a way to understand our material and the world around us, rather than as a mere expression of that understanding. This point is significant for Hegel's desire to philosophize, on paper, *in-and-for-itself.*

Hegel writes about what he read, which is how he experienced the wider world. As Jeffrey Reid argues, his philosophy is bookish. Hegel's "philosophical science does not observe natural events, it reads texts. These are considered true and more objective than what we might be tempted to call the 'real' world, which for Hegel is merely natural and undetermined and, therefore, less real than the world as penetrated (determined) by thought and manifest in meaningful language."[10] According to Reid, thought is more objective than matter because of its intermediary: language. Jochen Schulte-Sasse proposes a similar significance of textual mediation in the *Phänomenologie*. For him, the book is work ("Arbeit") as a work produced ("Werk").[11] The written form is the result of mediation, not just conceptual reflection, and so what appears on the page is more objective as a result. In the *Phänomenologie* itself, Hegel maintains that truth is not lost once it is written down: "eine Wahrheit kann durch Aufschreiben nicht verlieren; ebensowenig dadurch, daß wir sie aufbewahren" (HGW, 9: 64) [a truth cannot lose anything by being written down, any more than by our preserving it]. (That the truth in question becomes stale is due to Hegel's conception of deixis, not writing per se.) The thoughts of others, then, are objective also once they are written by them and incorporated into Hegel's texts, because as published sources they are taken up as mediated reflections—and mediated yet again. Thus they can be sublated: as Ian Balfour summarizes, writing is "a privileged formula of the dialectic in general, and even of Hegel's signature concept of sublation, of *Aufhebung*."[12]

The importance of reading writing not as the result of Hegel's philosophizing, but as that which produces it, allows us to contextualize Hegel among his literary contemporaries without asking whether his work is truly "philosophical," or more "literary" in nature. Conceptually, there was much crossover in any case. Both literature and philosophy were as concerned with textual form as each other. Hegel's advertisement for the *Phänomenologie* that was placed in three periodicals in 1807 was categorized, in the *Allgemeine Literatur-Zeitung* [General Literary Periodical] of Jena and Leipzig, under *Literarische Anzeigen* [Literary Advertisements] (HGW, 9: 471). He had written poetry before his philosophical maturity, dedicating an ode ("Eleusis") to Hölderlin in 1796. But while Hegel later turned to philosophy and Hölderlin wrote literature, prefaces by both men aspired to being read in similar ways. Hölderlin's preface to the first volume of *Hyperion oder der Eremit in Griechenland* [Hyperion, or the Hermit in Greece] (1797) asks for the work to be understood as a whole, and to be interpreted in a comprehensive way. An ideal but unlikely reading of this novel would not be achieved, the author tells us, through a search for information, instruction, nor even "mere" contemplation (via "das bloße Nachdenken"), nor by a base desire or empty entertainment, yielding to "die leere Lust."[13] *Hyperion* is instead an effort to transcend the division between abstract thought and pleasure seeking. As Howard Gaskill points out, "in order to appreciate Hölderlin's novel we must respond as wholes [. . . and] take the novel as a whole without detaching form from content."[14] Form and content, concepts and concrete examples, sober reflection and curious enjoyment: preface and work. All aspects are bound to one another yet are independently remarkable in Hegel's *Phänomenologie*, too. They are not only ideally comprehended as living apart together. They are nonsensical if they are not interpreted as such.

Moreover, bons mots of Hegel's preface from 1807 were lifted from literary-philosophical debate, such that discourse was not subdivided by discipline. Hegel famously attacks the apparently dark intuitive method of Schelling's transcendental, philosophical system that tries to immediately and innately distinguish difference in an Absolute in which everything is one. He portrays such an approach as vacuous formalism: it is akin, he says, to drawing distinctions at night "worin, wie man zu sagen pflegt, alle Kühe schwarz sind" (HGW, 9: 17) [in which (as the saying goes) all cows are black]. This line is a comic allusion, evoking a humorous idiom uttered by Sancho Panza in Cervantes's *Don Quixote* (1605–1615): "by night all cats are grey."[15] And significantly, as Li Sui Gwee notes, Schelling employed the image of an indeterminate pure night as a parody of the well-known portrayal in Novalis's dithyrambic poem cycle *Hymnen an die Nacht* [Hymns to the Night] (1800), in order to inform readers how not to interpret his own work.[16] Hegel, in turn, appropriated Schelling's image against Schelling himself—or, as Hegel professed in his letter to Schelling on May 1, 1807, against Schelling's lesser followers—and in support of a new philosophical system.[17] Further, the variant from Cervantes, though it does not occur in the *Phänomenologie*, was attributed to Hegel in Heinrich Steffens's recollection written in 1841—as having been plucked from Schlegel's verbal mockery of Schelling.[18] Another prefatorial example of literature's and philosophy's fusion is Hegel's appropriation of Lessing's numismatic metaphor in discussing truth (HGW, 9: 30).[19] And moving on to his introduction, Hegel argues that nothingness is determinate (HGW, 9: 57). This claim was already the source of an English satirist's joke in 1751, when Francis Coventry wrote on nothing, thereby—paradoxically—rendering his subject something. He begged leave "to detain the Reader with an introductory chapter upon *Nothing*; being the most proper Subject I can recollect at present for such an initial Section" in *The History of Pompey the Little, or, The Life and Adventures of a Lap-Dog*: a book translated into German, and copied and adapted for the German market multiple times.[20]

What connected literary and philosophical authors was not only a culture of ideas, therefore, but most literally print culture. And so Hegel and contemporary philosophers devised their conceptual systems through intertextual references and—more importantly—textual metaphors, rather than specifically literary or philosophical ones.

In his first preface to *Kritik der reinen Vernunft* [Critique of Pure Reason] (1781), Kant presents metaphysics as "nichts als das *Inventarium* aller unserer Besitze durch *reine Vernunft*, systematisch geordnet"[21] [nothing but the *inventory* of everything we possess through *pure reason*, ordered systematically]. This is not to say that Kant physically laid out his philosophical writings in the form of systematic inventories, nor is it in fact his guiding metaphor for his First Critique, which instead emphasizes structures of knowledge: architectonics ("Architektonik"). Nevertheless, the inventory metaphor helped him conceptualize the purpose of his work in his preface. By contrast, Hegel writes in his 1807 preface that science can be organized only through the organic, actual life of the concept ("Begriff"). He mocks (implicitly Kantian as well as Idealist) schematizing by suggesting that "der tabellarische Verstand behält für sich die Notwendigkeit und den Begriff des Inhalts" (HGW, 9: 38) [understanding by categorical tables keeps the necessity and concept of the content to itself], so it must fail to know the actual content of *what is*—otherwise, it would philosophize more thoroughly, to get to the nub of the problem. Tabular understanding "gibt nur die Inhaltsanzeige, den Inhalt selbst aber liefert er nicht" (HGW, 9: 38) [offers only a table of contents; it does not supply the content itself]. A schematic kind of enterprise is never-ending: once cataloguing is completed, we can catalog catalogs. Consequently, the activity remains superficial. Hegel sought a way to stop this process sensibly, and scrutinize it, while still being systematic. And so he conceptualized his system and ideal understanding of it metaphorically, through a material text type: the preface.

Although the *Phänomenologie* had a contents page from its first publication onward (in which no fewer than nineteen subheadings list the preface's topics), the table assumes a conventionally pragmatic, and not a conceptual role in Hegel's work. Hegel favors the preface as his metaphor from the textual source domain. It is noteworthy that Hegel's first edition of the *Phänomenologie* in 1807 differs materially from previous and contemporary philosophical books, with respect to its layout: although the pagination is, as usual, in Roman numerals, the preface follows the contents page rather than precedes it. This strategy indicates through its physicality a greater proximity between preface and work. But Hegel's literal manifestation of the preface must redefine the form that Novalis compared to a "verrätherischer Inhaltsanzeiger"[22] [treacherous table of contents] in 1798. And Friedrich Schlegel was perhaps objecting to Hegel's sort of position in order to defend poetry and attack logic when he said that the latter was neither preface ("Vorrede") nor instrument, neither prescription ("Formular") nor an episode of philosophy—but instead a pragmatic, systematic conception of science that contrasts with the literary imagination ("Poetik") and ethics. In his typically fragmentary formulation, Schlegel takes aim at the way that parts of the book—such as a preface—were metaphorically appropriated to express philosophical method around 1800.[23]

In this chapter, Hegel's prefacing against prefacing is read as the textual manifestation of his philosophy, and this way of reading is in keeping with both contemporary philosophical and print cultures. In other words, the physical form of his philosophy is as important as the ideas behind it—they are one and the same—and this includes the preface. Such a contention should not be confused with philological scholarship, though the latter has also put the preface on a pedestal. Since Rudolf Haym's philological analysis in 1857 and especially in the mid-twentieth century, the disunity of Hegel's philosophy and particularly the *Phänomenologie* has been emphasized by one set of readers.[24] This school's interpretation of the 1807 work is, as Haym calls it, "palimpsestic": it proposes that Hegel changed course during the writing process of the *Phänomenologie*, making many revisions to the manuscript without unifying them as much as he had wanted.[25] He wrote hurriedly, after all, with the Battle of Jena on his doorstep and the suspicion of many that he would not amount to much academically. He also changed the work's title, confusing his publisher Joseph Anton Goebhardt.[26] Originally conceived as *Wissenschaft der Erfahrung des Bewusstseins* [Science of the Experience of Consciousness], it was then revised to its full title, *Wissenschaft der Phänomenologie des Geistes* [Science of the Phenomenology of Spirit] (HGW, 9: 52), a revision that became the subtitle to the work's appearance as *System der Wissenschaft. Erster Theil, die Phänomenologie des Geistes* [System of Science. Part 1: the Phenomenology of Spirit] (HGW, 9: 3). The irony for our present purposes is that Haym reads precisely Hegel's preface to his palimpsestic philosophy as systematic, because it was written last: if we master the preface's meaning, we apparently understand Hegel's philosophy as it would have been edited and perhaps rewritten.[27] In suit of Haym, Werner Marx has argued that the preface introduces Hegel's ambitions for the *Phänomenologie* and should be read together with the closing sections, whereas the introduction prepares the reader for the work as it was previously conceived (because it was written first). For Marx, the preface is thus a "supplement" to the introduction.[28] But regardless of the textual unity of the rest of the *Phänomenologie*, its broad conceptual coherence is beyond doubt—and is engendered by the preface. On that much, critics agree. And so it remains to read the preface from 1807 in its Hegelian context, and to ask just how philosophical it actually is: a question that soon becomes controversial.

DESCRIPTIVE INDUCTION VERSUS PERFORMATIVE PREFACING

Hegel's preface is paradoxical, like his philosophy is contradictory—because our very being is thought to be so. Contradiction is elevated to Hegel's method (the aim of which is the highest means of description), and this method takes on a material, printed form. The dialectical movement of Hegelian philosophy negates contradiction via *sublation* ("Aufhebung," or overcoming) that is itself a paradoxical procedure: negating, thereby positing. This process of annulment and preservation of a trace is the hallmark of Hegel's thought. He exceeds concrete, determinate contradictions through an abstract state of contradictoriness that he makes manifest as a speculative text, returning (in circular fashion) to physical particularity that is, this time around, better conceptualized. His *Phänomenologie*, once prefaced philosophically, can then proceed with an unproblematic introduction. The latter "Einleitung" starts by disputing our most general premises on the book's chosen topic of consciousness, yet to a metapurpose and from a philosophical perspective with which, having read the preface, we are already familiar. To call Hegel's preface, as counterpreface, somehow or partly philosophical is beyond question. But to say that it is thoroughly Hegelian—sublating prefatory convention—goes against the majority of notable scholars on Hegel, though their consensus arguably results from academic philosophy's neglect of textual form.

Most Hegel scholars, then, would interpret the preface to the *Phänomenologie* as merely declaring and explicating his aim and method for the work that follows, albeit in complicated prose. Erwin Metzke suggests that Hegel's prefaces in general, and his preface to the *Phänomenologie* in particular, are gateways into his philosophy. He admits the complexity of the philosopher's preliminary texts, their "closed" or autonomous argument, and yet their contradictory concision such that—read apart from Hegel's philosophical work—they are insufficient for full comprehension.[29] But Metzke argues that Hegel's system as a whole is gradated: there is not yet enough content in the preface from 1807 for Hegel to do justice to the preface's argumentative structure. Prefaces help the reader by telling him what to expect, albeit already in terms so individual and with such density that, in turn, he requires the commentator's assistance to understand Hegel's prefatorial help. However, Metzke is not concerned with how Hegel's preparatory text operates formally, in service to its assertions. Indeed, "literalist" readings tend to presume that the preface cannot be argumentatively or textually complex primarily because of its status as a preface—and they thus apply a priori a reductive, if conventional, conception of the preface to Hegel's radical text. Richard Schlacht, for instance, refers to the *Phänomenologie* preface as "*only* a Preface,"[30] in which we "should not expect to find arguments"[31]—even if this preface is "the best summary of philosophy" that Hegel ever wrote.[32] Hester IJsseling's doctoral thesis in Dutch imports Metzke's notion of a gradual transition into Hegel's philosophy, and also proposes that it must be read outside of any sublative operation.[33] Turning to Derrida, she argues that the preface prefigures a totality it cannot achieve, and so it is a fiction. On a larger scale, too, Hegel's totalizing system is apparently fictitious in its claim to absolute truth. And so for IJsseling, as for Metzke, Hegel's preface and his philosophy are different only in degree, notwithstanding the fact that according to their logic, no sublation takes place in the prefatory part of the *Phänomenologie*.[34] This cannot make sense: there must also be, in IJsseling's terms, a *principal* difference she otherwise denies between the text types if one can sublate and the other cannot.

Annette Sell affirms categorical difference: in the preface there is no dialectical operation.[35] And so this text is simply "ein nachträgliches Supplement"[36] [a retrospective supplement] that is explanatory—despite Hegel's dislike of explanation. Hegel, in this conservative account, achieves concision at the price of structural simplicity. At best, this unmediated beginning is conceived as deliberate: for Ardis B. Collins, logic begins with thought as both pure being and, as such, as a positive claim that the presuppositions of philosophical science—and precisely not our everyday, nonphilosophical presuppositions—are true, to be substantiated in the subsequent philosophical work.[37] At worst, as Walter Kaufmann is forced to admit, Hegel "casts aspersions on his own preface"—but presumably in this reading, Hegel's reservation is because his text is only a preface, anyway, to which he is not thought to have attributed much creative significance.[38] This leaves unexplained why Hegel would preface nonetheless, and for ninety-one pages. The critical consensus has continued all the same. In more recent commentary, Yirmiyahu Yovel tantalizingly introduces Hegel's preface to the *Phänomenologie* as "an enlightening (and tacitly ironic) text, which seems to negate performatively its own claim (namely, that truth lies exclusively in its full evolution). Hegel came to this decision because he considered that the Preface could work as a *pre*philosophical preparation to actual philosophizing."[39] Performatively ironic, but not systematic: would this not suggest that Hegel's preface is a mere curiosity, and thus superficial and unnecessary? Such a text is the very type to which Hegel objects. It would surely be simpler to say that Hegel makes the preparatory, prephilosophical space genuinely philosophical, Hegelian even. Although the preface cannot yet grapple with the big questions sufficiently, it can nevertheless philosophize about our attitude toward answering them.

An alternative interpretation of this problematic preface has a properly performative bias, and posits that Hegel dramatizes as he discusses his concepts preliminarily. Demonstration is the highest and liveliest form of description, which is what Hegel's philosophy should pursue. Indeed, in an exceptional article from 1977, John Sallis argues that Hegel's 1807 preface is remarkable for a "questionableness rooted in a basic conflict between the character of a preface as such and the demand under which philosophy stands."[40] The preface appears to be set up to fail, as if it must revoke itself. But Sallis continues: "in this self-revocation a certain content is preserved, namely, the determination of the nature of presentation; it is preserved inasmuch as it is carried over into *enactment*. The preface sublates itself; its fundamental movement is an *Aufheben*."[41] Sublation is a specifically Hegelian term that renders a concept or thing less immediate; that is, it becomes mediated, and so objective and ideal.[42] Recall that sublation means both canceling out a property yet also leaving a shadow, thereby elevating the thing or concept to a new form while nevertheless retaining something of its old shape. In this case, according to Sallis, the preface begins with a rejection of itself, but overcomes normal prefatory content through philosophical discourse that remains, nonetheless, on the page, in the book, in the form of a preface.

The interpretation that Hegel's preface to the *Phänomenologie* sublates itself complements a performative understanding of the text by Maurice A. Finocchiaro that is correct in principle, and yet has posited a problematic conclusion. Finocchiaro rightly observes that Hegel, "in the context of his initial qualifications about the character of prefaces to philosophical books . . . comments on what is perhaps the central datum of philosophy, namely the existence of a multiplicity of philosophical systems."[43] According to Finocchiaro, the philosopher's engagement with, and his preface that supersedes such pluralism employs the dialectic method it describes. But we encounter a difficulty: where is the negative methodological element that Hegelian dialectic necessitates? Finocchiaro concludes that the absence of a negative feature is, here, the required negativity. This reasoning must be wrong, since it would mean that anything else Hegel wrote in a for-and-against fashion while elsewhere being dialectical would also become, in Hegelian terms, dialectical.

We could concede that Hegel's preface only describes dialectic, after all—he does not enact it. Admittedly, in disassociating his own work from the commonplace philosophical assertion that the essence of truth exists solely in concepts, Hegel himself concedes in this preface that his explanation ("Erklärung") for his different approach—that truth instead inheres essentially in the concrete—can only be presented dogmatically, as an assurance ("Versicherung") (HGW, 9: 12). If we take him at his word in this passage, Hegel's preface is an act of telling, not showing. But there is good cause to read this particular prefatory concession as a piece of conventional prefatorial modesty, rather than as reflective of his method of preface writing. For in distinguishing himself from prefaces and philosophical diversity, and in presenting dialectical movement as the only rigorous route toward speculative philosophy (which is, for Hegel, the superior kind), the preface to the *Phänomenologie* is concerned not so much with, in Yovel's terms, "*pre*philosophy," but rather with *meta*philosophy—which is itself a branch of philosophy. For the preface attempts to sever itself from a fixed relationship to other studies, even disciplines, and in laying claim to the singularity of its philosophy it reveals the very interconnectedness of literary and philosophical discourses around 1800 that are unified and bound within the pages of Hegel's book. Thematically, the preface exceeds the topic of phenomenal knowledge with which the *Phänomenologie* is chiefly concerned; and it is also applicable to all branches of (Hegelian) philosophy. While the preface and introduction are both preparatory, discussion in the introduction refers more specifically to the Absolute and to consciousness, out of which a conception of truth emerges. This is a fundamental problem, to be sure, but not the primary one for setting up Hegel's system—which is what constitutes philosophical writing at all.

It would be perverse to suggest that the very framework for Hegelian thinking must be accepted as a given, when his thought, as Allen Speight says, "no longer sees itself as being on a search for an "incorrigible" or indubitable Given."[44] To interpret the preface to this corrigibilist philosophy as a dogmatic, if gradated description of itself would be counter to Hegel's words more generally. For Hegel, texts—whether literary or philosophical, and however plausible—are philosophical, corrigible content when taken up by his system as a whole, and because in their written manifestations they are already mediated thought. This could be the case for prefaces especially: writing a preface, for Hegel, would be an act of abstracting thought that is objective, because of the textuality of the ideas on and in writings, including on and in prefaces, which he interrogates. It follows that his own preface is itself objective since it abstracts his written, completed philosophical work (as "Arbeit") and then instantiates that work as such (as "Werk"). From here it is not much of an imaginative leap to suggest that the negativity of Hegel's preface from 1807 is its own self-reflexivity: the fact that it is a form invoked against itself, *contra* prefacing. In other words, the preface sublates the conventional preface: formally, and in terms of its content. The prefatory antipreface is the contradiction Finocchiaro overlooks: "although the negativity of the procedure in the Phenomenology is obvious from the discussion in the Preface, the negativity of the Preface itself is not."[45] In order to contend, therefore, that the preface overcomes nonphilosophy or other philosophies dialectically and thus philosophically, we must attend to the most obvious textual irony that is apparent from the preface's title (as "Vorrede") coupled with its opening antiprefatory assertion, and which is Hegel's first instance of sublation.

A NEW STYLE OF PREFACE

In the preface to the *Phänomenologie*, Hegel criticizes contemporary prefatorial form as unsuitable for philosophy, because of both its superficial style and its severance from any system. In addressing these two shortcomings by example in 1807, however, Hegel's own preface is as abstruse as his philosophy in general. Afflicted by an extract from it, Goethe comments in a draft letter of November 28, 1812, that "es ist wohl nicht möglich, etwas Monstroseres zu sagen" (FA, 2.7: 129) [it is surely not possible to say something more monstrous]. The passage troubling him seems to suggest that a correct and true conclusion can arise only from a false premise. He accuses Hegel of sophistic word play that annihilates meaningful reality, expressing his regret that Hegel's mind might have been lost in waffle. Appealing to Thomas Johann Seebeck for explanation, he asks whether the confusing sentence is perhaps better understood in context. Goethe's idea that Hegel's obfuscation might be overcome in the context of the philosopher's preface—or indeed, the following work—as a whole was Hegel's intention. But his style is as much a part of his system, and as such, style and substance are philosophically indistinct. In his later aesthetic lectures, Hegel defines style ("Stil") in a broader sense of the word ("weitere Wortbedeutung") as determined by the necessity of the written and conceptual material: a "notwendige Darstellungsweise" (HW, Ä 1, 380) [necessary mode of representation], it must not simply be a subjective whim. But pragmatically, if for Hegel unphilosophically, it makes sense to disentangle style and substance here.

Hegel observes in his preface from 1807 that sophistry is "ein Schlagwort des gemeinen Menschenverstandes gegen die gebildete Vernunft" (HGW, 9: 47) [a slogan by ordinary common sense against educated reason]. He turns the accusation around: it is rather the supporters of common sense, he says, who are guilty of empty rhetoric. Common sense at best reproduces what we already know, through "eine Rhetorik trivialer Wahrheiten" (HGW, 9: 47) [a rhetoric of trivial truths]. He objects not only to the reiteration of accepted philosophical commonplaces but also to the typically succinct and straightforward style in which they are formulated, too often at the cost of tautology. In his preface, Hegel disassociates himself from ordinary, predicative language that fixes the subject, whereby the predicate tends to repeat that which is already in the subject. The speculative judgment and its sentential expression—the "spekulativer Satz"—introduces a tension between a concept and its form (HGW, 9: 43). Philosophy must be read and read again until it is understood: when we first encounter a philosophical proposition, we parse it as such, but philosophy complicates and changes its received meaning; we must correct the meanings we first interpret, return to propositions, and understand them differently. That said, gratuitous linguistic difficulty, which nevertheless has philosophical substance, should be avoided. As "wissenschafftliche[s] Gepränge" (HGW, 9: 36) [scientific ostentation], we might call this latter infelicity of style not rhetorically empty, but instead overblown.

More offensive than trivially underdeveloped or verbose (if profound) words and concepts, though, is an impassioned style. The practitioners of what Hegel calls "natürliches Philosophiren" (HGW, 9: 47) [natural philosophizing] comprise two types of writer, philosophical and literary, who ostensibly immediately reveal the divine but do not undertake actual, real philosophy at all; and they do not write literature, either. Hegel plays on the connotations of "natural philosophizing" to evoke association with Schelling's *Naturphilosophie* that proceeds, via intuition, too quickly toward the Absolute. Here Hegel also means those philosophers governed by religious fervor more generally, who apparently do not strive for insight as much as for edification. Such authors are the German Idealists other than Hegel himself: Jacobi, Fichte, Schelling, and so on, and their schools. Contra Kant, these philosophers all rehabilitated intellectual intuition in cognition in order to know the *thing-in-itself*. For Hegel, such knowledge is possible only after a thoroughgoing process of dialectical logic and sublation, in which one eventually knows the *thing-in-and-for-itself*. Accordingly, true reality is not an immediate unity, but instead emerges from self-reflection in relation to another. Those who participated in natural philosophizing sought to cut short the stages of mediation emphasized in Hegel's method, not least because of their style. They are unable to think abstractly, due to their allegedly bungled mode of written expression.

A further alleged problem of their (non)method is the disorganized imagination Hegel accuses the "natural philosophizers" of having brought onto the book market. His phrasing "zu Markte bringen" (HGW, 9: 47) [to bring to market] perhaps insinuates that they were too quick to tout their wares to an expanding and increasingly commercial publishing sector. In previous decades, genius was the buzzword among bestselling literary authors; and by 1807, impulsive philosophers apparently now laid claim to it too, together with a purported freedom and tolerance of thought. It was philosophers such as Fichte and Schelling who imported the literary aesthetic of genius into their own philosophies, to their peril.[46] (Even if, at the same time, Fichte and Schelling skirmished with other writers' self-declaration of genius: see below.) When literary writers professed genius, Hegel claims, they presented to the public "triviale Prosa" ["trivial prose"] rather than "Poësie" ["poetry"], if they made any sense at all, or "verrückte Reden" (HGW, 9: 47) ["crazed ramblings"], if they did not. Natural philosophizing, then, demonstrates neither the intuitive, visionary "anschauendes" nor the literary, "poëtisches Denken" (HGW, 9: 47) ["poetic thought"] that it asserts for itself. Hegel attacks his literary predecessors as much as his philosophical forebears. And Hegel in this preface sarcastically equates specifically Schelling's school of "natural-philosophical formalism" ("der naturphilosophische Formalismus"), with "eine tiefe Genialität" (HGW, 9: 37) [deep genius].

Chastising allegedly less substantial, literary-philosophical styles was actually quite common among other canonical philosophers around 1800.[47] Schelling himself rebuked works of lamentable, self-styled geniuses in the preface ("Vorbericht") to his *Philosophische Untersuchungen über das Wesen der menschlichen Freiheit und die damit zusammenhängenden Gegenstände* [Philosophical Investigations into the Essence of Human Freedom and Related Subjects] (1809), bemoaning in his interpreters "eine vermeintlich genialischere Sprache" [a language reputed to be of genius], which he—more explicitly than Hegel—historicizes, and blames on the literati.[48] The sentences these followers concocted were characterized by redundancy, and Schelling called for a return to academic toil. Writing in a genius idiom as philosophical prose was, for him, the worst type of composition because it is in practice unintelligible. Thinkers should instead employ comprehensible language, according to Schelling's prefatory polemic.

Hegel's self-severance from rhetorical infelicity on the one hand and the apparently more fundamentally flawed style—implicitly sophistry—of Schelling and Fichte, among others, on the other is of twofold significance for Hegel's prefatorial as well as philosophical arguments. First, it is ironic that despite his pejorative, reductive understanding of rhetorical ability, such skill is actually subsumed within his philosophy, and provides the last words for his preface. We shall return to the rhetorical substrate of Hegel's preface later. For now, it suffices to say that at the end of his preface to the *Phänomenologie*, Hegel conforms to the traditional rhetorical precept of modesty. Beginning with modesty gains our goodwill, disarming our aversion to arrogance, and limits our criticism of a work if we are to judge it according to its intention. Hegel thus concludes a preface in which he has skirmished with the various sorts of styles and philosophical systems of his age by laying claim to individual meekness as a person. But he actually writes that we are all small beings in the world. This generalizing gesture negates as much as it affirms the rhetorical idea of modesty inasmuch as it states that everyone should be modest about what he or she can achieve in history, and so Hegel is no more—or less—insignificant than any other human. What is more, generality is his theoretical concern: however much we skirmish with the details, it is the universal we must grapple with if we are to answer the burning questions of the age. Criticize Hegel not on mere isolated issues, then, but only on the whole account! Not only or perhaps not really a rhetorical convention, the logic of Hegel's modesty as a scientist, or "Wissenschaftler," is also justified within the terms of the original philosophical and historical idea he has started to establish:

> Weil übrigens in einer Zeit, worin die Allgemeinheit des Geistes so sehr erstarkt und die Einzelnheit, wie sich gebührt, um soviel gleichgültiger geworden ist, auch jene an ihrem vollen Umfang und gebildeten Reichthum hält und ihn fodert, der Antheil, der an dem gesamten Werke des Geistes auf die Thätigkeit des Individuums fällt, nur gering seyn kann, so muß dieses, wie die Natur der Wissenschaft schon es mit sich bringt, sich um so mehr vergessen, und zwar werden und thun, was es kann, aber es muß

> ebenso weniger von ihm gefordert werden, wie es selbst weniger von sich erwarten und für sich fordern darf. (HGW, 9: 49)
>
> [Because in an era in which the universality of Spirit has garnered such strength and its particularity has (as is appropriate) become comparatively insignificant, and because that universal perspective lays claim and holds on to the wide-ranging wealth it has cultivated, the share in the total work of Spirit that falls to the activity of the individual can, incidentally, only be very small; and so a particular individual must forget himself all the more, as is the nature of scientific inquiry—of course he should do and become what he can, just as less must be expected of him, as he may demand less for himself.]

The second and greater significance of Hegel's prefatory reflections on style for his preface and thought is that the stylistic problems of most writing around 1800 (ignoring pomposity, on which he does not expand) can be summarized as superficiality. Such superficiality, whether it consists in empty rhetoric or repetitive formalism, is relevant for our understanding of why Hegel resented the preface in general: he declares that as a textual form it is stylistically and structurally superficial. His philosophical method is pitted against a form of reasoning that resembles either an amalgamation of conversational titbits of received information, or historical, empirical details on how a book came to be written, "wie ungefähr auch eine Vorrede ist" (HGW, 9: 36) [as is also the way of a preface]. The preface, for Hegel, typifies an inadequately philosophical style—rather than an absolutely unphilosophical one, perhaps. The problem of the preface might yet be rectifiable.

By first of all thinking and writing on a purely abstract rather than an everyday, conversational, or instructive level, Hegel's philosophical path eventually reaches a concept of knowledge via a thorough process of becoming as it returns to concrete reality. In his view, this method superseded the philosophy of his day, which he considered to be determined by digression, by too much chance or chit-chat: it was, metaphorically, too prefatory. His superior method is preparatory. Hegel describes his style, which is equal to his system or method, as an act of preparation ("Vorbereitung") marked by seriousness and patience. He reasons from the start of that preface, "die Sache ist nicht in ihrem *Zwecke* erschöpft, sondern in ihrer *Ausführung*" (HGW, 9: 10) [the subject is exhausted not by stating its purpose, but by setting it out].

Since a study's topic has to be worked through, the author or reader should spend time with, and lose himself in, philosophical examination. Such an activity surpasses the superficial if the familiar is defamiliarized. For Hegel presumes that the true nature of the familiar is in fact not known to us at all, and thus he delves deep into an individual concept, rather than accepting its meaning and moving onward with it to an associated or a new point, in contrast to a discussion that moves back and forth ("Hin- und Herreden"), and ultimately never moves beyond where it started (HGW, 9: 26–27). He proposes that his alternative, laborious conceptual movement is more flexible and animate—counterintuitively, he tends to call it more *lively* (though it is anything but fast-paced)—than contemporary philosophy that values conceptual fixity, because he gives life to the organic being of the concept. It is this movement, according to Hegel, that defines speculative philosophy, and our preparation for it is his lengthy preface.

In one sense, neither Hegel's style nor system was so new. The Idealist rehabilitation of dialectic on which his method becomes predicated was initiated by Fichte; and an at times garrulous style of German philosophy, if we can characterize Hegel's writing in his preface as such (as Goethe seemed to), was typical of the Romantic era. In his preface to *Clavis Fichtiana seu Leibgerberiana* (1800), Jean Paul mocks Fichte by joking that a clatter of words comes before the philosopher (or reader) can see the truth: "Im Reiche des Wissens kommt—anders als im physischen—der *Schall* immer früher an als das *Licht*" (SW, 1.9: 459) [In the realm of knowledge, unlike in the physical world, *sound* always arrives before *light*]. In Hegel, however, we have a defense of the written noise mocked in Jean Paul's joke, as a necessity: it is needed to express material as the very process of making sense and giving rise to a speculative, dialectical method and thereby truth, or Enlightenment. For Hegel, as for Jean Paul's humor, the words of philosophical prose should not be guided by an intuition, or "Anschauung." They must lead to the latter via writing itself. A contrary, predetermined logical formalism that is not grounded in the act of discussion or dialectic, and is instead superimposed onto it as a ready-made schema, must be wrong from its beginning. Since Fichte and Schelling systematically start with the Absolute, or commonsense and popular philosophers present ideas deductively and didactically, too many thinkers approach philosophical science, or will turn to Hegel's work, with misplaced expectations of immediacy, presuming to understand philosophy straight away. But a premature result would be dizzying, as if we were to stand on our heads: because it would be unmediated by the development of his argument, or his writing.

Like Hegel, Jean Paul was opposed to those whom he called "die kantischen Formschneider": a pun that refers to those men of his time who made figurines (by analogy with engravers and makers of woodcuts), but plays, too, on the fashion for Kantian formalism (SW, 1.11: 8). Jean Paul responded by being unsystematic. In 1796, Kant acknowledged in his essay *Von einem neuerdings erhobenen vornehmen Ton in der Philosophie* [On a Recent Superior Tone in Philosophy] that his own method was objectionable to some, and pejoratively described "als eine Pedanterei unter dem Namen einer *Formgebungsmanufactur*"[49] [as a pedantry by the name of *manufacturing the very production of form*]. But his (non)solution was simply to say that if formalism is disregarded, so too is philosophy: it otherwise becomes (as Hegel criticized Idealism) a discourse "bei der man nicht arbeiten, sondern nur das Orakel in sich selbst anhören und genießen darf"[50] [in which one does not need to work, but must merely listen to and enjoy the oracle inside oneself]. In short, it emerges from genius. Hegel neither seeks recourse to formalism, nor does he reject systematicity. In this respect, then, Hegel's style and system were original enough to present a new challenge, as Goethe's complaint about his style demonstrates; and they were actually an attempt to overcome stylistic problems of contemporary philosophy. The cost was obscurity.

In order to absolve Hegel of intentionally confusing and irreversible obscurity, though, we should turn in more detail to the method and content of his thought. Hegel admits that philosophy is esoteric inasmuch as it is presented to the reader in concepts and as an organic whole, which is only slowly read and understood. But insofar as a philosophy can be understood in the end, it becomes exoteric. If finally Hegel can be said to have written a preface whose content stands in meaningful and comprehensible relation to his time, discipline, and, moreover, the preface as a text type, then surely we can celebrate his stylistic difficulty. Goethe ultimately forgave him, according to the author's letter to Seebeck of January 15, 1813, because his correspondent had contextualized the passage so that, for Goethe, Hegel was "durch den Zusammenhang neutralisiert" (FA, 2.7: 151) [neutralized by the context].

SUBLATION OF CONVENTIONAL PREFATORY CONTENT

Hegel perceived three problems with typical prefatory content, a topic he examines at the beginning, reiterates after the middle, and repeats near the end of his preface to the *Phänomenologie*. To start with, the purpose of a preface as it is conventionally constructed ("nach der Gewohnheit")

(HGW, 9: 9) is contrary to the purpose of philosophy. The preface usually has a threefold function: it summarizes the goal of a book, what led to writing it, and its relationship to existing works in the field. Then the preface becomes reduced to a twofold issue: "eine historische Angabe der Tendenz und des Standpunkts, des allgemeinen Inhalts und der Resultate" [an historical statement concerning the work's main drift and its point of view, its content in general and its results] on the one hand, and "eine Verbindung von hin und her sprechenden Behauptungen und Versicherungen über das Wahre" (HGW, 9: 9) [a string of casual assertions and assurances about truth] on the other. The preface is historicizing and chronicles its composition and context of emergence, as Goethe's prefacing demonstrates so clearly (see chapter 1); and the preface is digressive and declarative, as Jean Paul's prefacing shows so comically (chapter 2). The preface as a kind of conversation or historical instruction, Hegel notes mid-preface, satisfies curiosity rather than insight. By the end of the preface, however, Hegel's definition of prefacing seems to have subtly, but significantly changed.

The shift comes in a humorous, seemingly casual paragraph in which the senses of paratextual subtypes—chief among them, the preface—are carefully adjusted. The passage is worth citing at length:

> Wenn nach einem königlichen Wege zur Wissenschaft gefragt würde, so kann kein bequemerer angegeben werden als der sich auf den gesunden Menschenverstand zu verlassen und, um übrigens auch mit der Zeit und mit der Philosophie fortzuschreiten, Recensionen von philosophischen Schriften, etwa gar die Vorreden und ersten Paragraphen derselben zu lesen, denn diese geben die allgemeine Grundsätze, worauf alles ankommt, und jene neben der historischen Notiz noch die Beurtheilung, die sogar, weil sie Beurtheilung ist, über das Beurtheilte hinaus ist. (HGW, 9: 48)
>
> [Should anyone ask for a royal road to science, there is no more comfortable route to rely on than sound common sense and (incidentally in order to keep abreast of the age and advance with its philosophy) reading reviews of philosophical writings, or prefaces and opening paragraphs to philosophical works. For the latter offer the general principles on which all the rest relies; and the former, along with an historical note also provide an appraisal that, because it is a judgment, goes beyond that which it judges.]

Hegel here mocks the contemporary fashion for reading prefaces and first paragraphs as an easy route into philosophy. But his characterization of prefaces and reviews is now slightly different from his opening description. For prefaces in the above passage, conceptually conflated with first paragraphs, present "die allgemeine Grundsätze" [the general principles]: presumably, like initial paragraphs and introductions, prefaces are part of the work as a whole and, for Hegel, all should become philosophical. Book reviews, meanwhile, recount the historical backstory and provide a second-order criticism. The nature of "eine historische Angabe" [an historical statement] is in this instance not attributed to the preface, and is instead transferred into what is properly outside philosophy: book reviews. This may appear to be a trivial point, since both prefaces and book reviews exhibit the same basic fault of making readers believe that a digest will give them all they need for understanding. IJsseling, however, attributes a significance to the way in which these text types are arranged: she parses prefaces as preferable to book reviews (though she understands the first paragraphs as here referring to those which begin the prefaces, rather than the philosophical works themselves).[51]

Kaufmann alerts us to a posthumously published aphorism that Hegel probably used to compose this section on the relative appropriateness of different textual summaries for philosophy. The earlier line states that prefaces and reviews both give an equally approximate notion of the book.[52] For in his Jena notebooks (1803–1806), we read: "Der gewöhnliche *königliche* Weg in der Philosophie ist, die Vorreden und Recensionen zu lesen, um eine ungefähre Vorstellung von der Sache zu bekommen" (HGW, 5: 500) [The conventional, *royal* path to take in philosophy is to read prefaces and reviews, in order to get an approximate sense of the subject]. Hegel went beyond this idea in his preface, though, and further distinguished between these two forms; he did not incorporate the aphorism wholesale. Furthermore, Hegel's earlier introductory lectures to philosophy, *Introductio in Philosophiam* (1801–1802), include the genre of introductory texts in our group of unphilosophical types of writing: "Diese Vorlesungen, in welchen ich eine Einleitung in die Philosophie vorzutragen versprochen habe, können mit keiner andern Bemerkung anfangen, als daß die Philosophie als Wissenschaft weder einer Einleitung bedarf, noch eine Einleitung verträgt (HGW, 5: 259) [These lectures in which I have promised to present an introduction to philosophy can start with no other remark than the following: that philosophy is a science which neither requires nor tolerates an introduction]. Hegel argues that philosophy is superior, not subordinate or equal, to other disciplines, and therefore does not need to be placed in a fixed relationship to them—as is the fashion in introductions, which contextualize an author's concepts. But of course, this singularity of philosophy needs to be stated and justified preliminarily, if the subsequent philosophical text is to be understood. In the years prior to 1807, then, Hegel was beginning to think through the types of (para)texts that would be appropriate for his *Phänomenologie*, from which only reviews would be excluded in the end, and among which the preface would undergo rehabilitation.

The above passage from the *Phänomenologie* on a supposedly "royal" path into philosophy is no more or less adventitious than any other part of the preface, and to retort that Hegel's sense of prefacing in this paragraph can be understood as utterly conventional is counter to his more general tendency to develop ad hominem arguments. Indeed, at the start of his preface to the *Phänomenologie*, Hegel understands a "Werk" as a philosophical book (HGW, 9: 10); but by the close of this preface, the sense changes to a philosophical "Schrift." "Werk" by this point evokes conceptual activity—a meaning that continues into the introduction (HGW, 9: 49 and 54). So could it be the case that in the course of his prefacing, Hegel similarly defamiliarizes the contemporary, conventional notion of prefacing—culminating in a philosophically readjusted definition? This is indeed a plausible, performative reading of the 1807 preface. For the general principles that characterize prefaces in the above passage are not objectionable, according to Hegel, so long as they are not understood as self-evident truths. Truth, for him, is located in the broad sweep, or self-conscious movement, of history that can be understood through mediation, not least textually: "auch in Büchern nachgeschlagen oder, auf welche Weise es sey untersucht werden" (HGW, 9: 31) [as consulted in books, or as investigated in whatever other way]. For this type of philosophical history, he generally uses the word "(Welt)Geschichte." His use of "historisch," meanwhile, means "empirical fact":[53] the substance of book reviews. Hegel's sense of philosophy as an historical account therefore entails an element of storytelling, or conceptual and coherent narrative prose in which the particular gives rise to the whole, and the whole helps us understand the particular. That is, the parts and their sum stand in dialectical relation to each other. Truth does not lie in Hegel's methodology, or preface, as a given—but rises out of its principles outlined in the preface all the same, once the whole is read and understood in all its concreteness.

Hegel starts and almost finishes his preface with a discussion of prefacing, and in the process the sense of what a preface is has become somewhat, but not entirely, other. Or in Hegelian terms, it is sublated. His preface is thereby founded on figures of a spiral and triplicity: three preface paragraphs, after all, are about prefaces. We return to where we began, but at a higher, more abstract level. In this preface, Hegel describes his philosophical method as "das Werden seiner selbst, der Kreis, der sein Ende als seinen Zweck voraussetzt und zum Anfange hat, und nur durch die Ausführung und sein Ende wirklich ist" (HGW, 9: 18) [its own becoming, the circle that presumes its end as its purpose and its beginning, but which is actual only after having been set out and worked through to its end]. The notorious name for this methodological circularity and triplicity is dialectic. Hegel acknowledges that Kant rediscovered triplicity ("Triplicität") for the modern era: it had been dormant, but on resurrection apparently still lacked its concept, since Kant revived the method through instinct. In Yovel's formulation, within Kant's philosophy triplicity meant that "the third category within each of the four groups making up the table of categories is a synthesis of its two predecessors."[54] In Hegel's historical sketch of philosophy, it was implicitly Fichte who raised this method to its absolute meaning.

According to Hegel, then, Fichte initiated philosophical science, but—as we have by now read frequently—he was too formalist. Indeed, Hegel writes that his general criticism of Fichte's formalism becomes particular in his opposition to this philosopher's allegedly lifeless dialectical schema. Hegel attacks Fichte for employing the mantra *thesis–antithesis–synthesis* repeatedly, applying it to everything in such a fixed way that the organization of scientific thought becomes reduced to a table ("Tabelle") (HGW, 9: 36). The outcome of Fichte's philosophical arguments can therefore be mathematically derived and is predictable, as the method can be a frame for almost any problem, without needing discursive adjustment that would respond to each problem's particularities. Thus Hegel's rejection of a tabular metaphor for philosophy, which can be read as an implicit reference to a prefatory remark of Kant's (as mentioned earlier), is also an attack on Fichtean thinking. For Hegel this trajectory is metaphorically the pursuit of endlessly cataloguing knowledge without examining truths rigorously. Philosophical formalism, in Hegel's logic, is formulaic.

In this respect, Fichte's dialectical recursion is an unproductive circularity. Hegel's preface, by comparison, begins by stating what a preface is: it outlines a work's purpose as well as its historical genesis and context. As we have established above, however, this threefold conventional practice is then reduced to two problems. And by the end of Hegel's preface, the preface is defined as one idea: the dialectical abstraction of philosophy from the concrete, only to return it to the concrete through the following work of philosophy. Recall that prefaces now solely "geben die allgemeine

Grundsätze" (HGW, 9: 48) [give the general principles]. This procedure is the opposite of a reductive textual operation, because it enables Hegel's preface to become all-encompassing: the general principles, of course, include the goal of a book, what led to writing it, and its relationship to existing works in the field—but they need not be written up so matter-of-factly, nor be so upfront. A preface can philosophize about these very aspects of a work, via metaphilosophy, which employs the methodology of philosophy. Hegel's own philosophy, in other words, is the historical high point of its time that proceeds dialectically, and whose relationship to previous writers is also dialectical. It exposes, in Yovel's words, Fichte's "failure to carry his own revolution out."[55] Through dialectic, Hegel's preface has become philosophical (and yet also pragmatic). He problematizes the prevalent practice of a preface often being the only portion of a book that is read, and subverts this norm: the reader of Hegel's work who undoubtedly, he thinks, will read his preface will have to read his whole philosophy also, in order to properly understand the preparatory text. Hegel already gestures toward this strategy at the end of the preface ("Vorerinnerung") to his *Differenz des Fichte'schen und Schelling'schen Systems der Philosophie* [The Difference between Fichte's and Schelling's Systems of Philosophy] (1801). General, prefatorial reflections "[haben] ihre Veranlassung darin, daß mit solchen Formen, als Voraussetzung, Grundsätze u.s.w. der Eingang in die Philosophie noch immer übersponnen und verdekt wird, und es daher in gewissem Grade nöthig ist, sich darauf einzulassen, biß einmal durchaus nur von der Philosophie selbst die Rede ist" (HGW, 4: 8) [are there because these forms, as presumption, principles, and so forth spin a web across, and cover, the entrance into philosophy; thus it is to some extent necessary to engage with them until eventually it is only philosophy proper that becomes our concern].

The present explanation and exposition of Hegel's method clarifies an infamously confusing claim of his preface from 1807, which outraged at least one contemporary reader, Goethe: "Daß ferner ein sogenannter Grundsatz oder Princip der Philosophie, wenn es wahr ist, schon darum auch falsch ist, weil er Grundsatz oder Princip ist" (HGW, 9: 21) [That what we call a philosophical principle, if it is true, is therefore false precisely because it is a principle]. A principle must be substantiated if it is to become true, before which point it is an untruth. But before we can engage in this game, we need to know Hegel's abstract conception of philosophy: what is for him a principle, in principle? In reading only extracts from Hegel and, furthermore, prefatory paragraphs, we might say that Goethe, who was so confused, was initially thrown (or threw himself) in at the deep end.

This sink-or-swim metaphor is Hegel's, and a well-known one at that. In the introduction to his *Encyclopädie der philosophischen Wissenschaften im Grundrisse* [Encyclopaedia of the Philosophical Sciences in Outline Form] (1817, with revised editions in 1827 and 1830), he dismisses Kantian epistemology—justifiably or not—since "die Untersuchung des Erkennens kann nicht anders als *erkennend* geschehen; bei diesem sogenannten Werkzeuge heißt dasselbe untersuchen nichts anderes, als es erkennen" (HGW, 20: 50) [the examination of knowledge cannot be conducted other than *through knowledge*; and to examine what we call this instrument is the same thing as to know it]. For him, it is as absurd as Scholasticus's advice that we should learn to swim before we enter the water, as if to engage in the German pedagogical pursuit of what is today called "Trockenschwimmen" [dry swimming]. Admittedly, this metaphorical comparison is inaccurate: it is logically impossible to know what knowledge is without knowing something; but it is logically possible to know how to swim before entering the water. In Hegelian philosophy, there can be no philosophy, rigorous or otherwise, prior to philosophical inquiry itself: "eine *vorläufige* Explication würde hiemit eine unphilosophische seyn sollen, und könnte nicht mehr seyn, als ein Gewebe von Voraussetzungen, Versicherungen und Raisonnements" (HGW, 20: 50) [a *provisional* explication would be unphilosophical, and would comprise no more than a web of assumptions, assurances, and random arguments]. Hegel begins ontologically; his subject exists in the world, and his preface to the *Phänomenologie* of ten years earlier is here embedded within another preface of his mature philosophy—regardless of whether, more controversially, the *Phänomenologie* as a whole was incorporated into the later *Encyclopädie*. The 1807 preface anticipates Hegel's whole system (and style), of which it is already an abstraction. That is to say, the preface to the *Phänomenologie* comprises the general principles of Hegelian philosophy, and appropriately it sublates itself. In doing so, this preface surpasses his other prefatory, introductory, and initiatory philosophical writings.

A SUPERIOR PREFACE

Hegel's self-framing preface to the *Phänomenologie* is also framed by, and frames, texts outside of the work itself. The first book of his mature system was publicized through a "Selbstanzeige" ("self-advertisement") in three regional periodicals. This text, separate from the work, is not signed; but since it first appeared in the *Bamberger Zeitung* [Bamberg Periodical] under

Hegel's editorship, we can presume that Hegel wrote the advertisement himself (the *Phänomenologie* was also published in Bamberg, as well as Würzburg, by Goebhardt). This advertisement matches the terms of Hegelian philosophy: it states that his 1807 work, as a whole, is preparatory (as its preface is) for science. Further, the preface is presented as fulfilling the three conventional prefatory functions which Hegel's preface begins by dismissing, namely the point of the work at hand and its contribution to the field, its historical precedent, and why the author composed it. Or, in Hegel's words:

> In der Vorrede erklärt sich der Verf. über das, was ihm Bedürfniß der Philosophie auf ihrem itzigen Standpuncte zu seyn scheint; ferner über die Anmaßung und den Unfug der philosophischen Formeln, der gegenwärtig die Philosophie herabwürdigt, und über das, worauf es überhaupt bey ihr und ihrem Studium ankommt. (HGW, 9: 447)
>
> [In the preface the author explains what to him seems to be the desideratum in philosophy at present, and further notes the pretension and nonsense of philosophical formulations that are currently bringing philosophy into disrepute; and he explains what philosophy is about and what is at stake.]

The threefold purpose of prefacing, and apparently of Hegel's preface, is sublated in the course of the preface itself in order that the text of the preface can go beyond such a list. The advertisement, then, re-enforces or prepares the reader with a reminder of the familiar concept of the preface that Hegel's preface proceeds to defamiliarize.

Like his advertisement, Hegel's *Propädeutik* [*Propaedeutics*] summarizes and simplifies his philosophical system. Written from 1808 onward for his school pupils at Nuremberg, it adapted the *Phänomenologie* for a younger audience. Consequently, this later collection of texts—like the advertisement—can be read before his earlier work, but they are hierarchically subordinate to it. That is to say, the sketch selling the work, the reasonably detailed but school-level introduction to it, as well as Hegel's later lectures are all additions external to systematic philosophical exposition: they are neither *works* in any creative, written sense, nor are they conceptual work as philosophy that is properly written out. These supplements, unlike the *Phänomenologie* and its preface, were not intended for attentive criticism in the form in which they were written. The preface to the 1807 text remains the start of Hegel's philosophical system proper, as (meta)philosophical thought and prose.

Hegel sublated the preface once and for all. Just as Jean Paul composed one especially complex and paradigmatic preface in 1796 (published as 1797), so too is Hegel's 1807 preface special among his preparatory texts. Philosophically, he does not need to continue sublating the convention of prefacing. Nor does it logically follow that Hegel must therefore not otherwise preface conventionally. His proclamations of an end of history (formulated implicitly), art (expressed explicitly), or religion (stated implicitly) do not mean that time stands still, artworks are abandoned, or that churches cease after he has systematically written about these topics. Rather, Hegel thinks that his philosophy assumes roles that were previously the privilege of other discourses, and that it thereby appropriates those discourses. Modern art—including literature—continues to contribute to culture what Hegel characterizes as liveliness; but his philosophy emulates such liveliness in a more probing way, since modern society has become so complex that abstract thought is required. And outside of his philosophical habitus, Hegel himself could practice institutional, everyday Christianity, for example, without being contradictory. What matters is that his systematic works form a whole, and that they cohere with, or at least do not contradict, his preface to the *Phänomenologie*.

Hegel's later mature prefaces reiterate claims from his original example. The preface to the second edition of the first volume of *Wissenschaft der Logik* [Science of Logic] in 1832 (first published 1812) repeats what are, to a Hegelian reader, by now familiar assertions. The introduction to this first volume references the preface to the *Phänomenologie* explicitly. Hegel's preface to *Grundlinien der Philosophie des Rechts* [Elements of the Philosophy of Right] (1821) presumes acquaintance with a speculative, dialectical method that was first presented in—again Hegel's 1807 preface. The latter preface then goes on to attack Hegel's contemporaries on account of their overly formalist style and insufficient (that is, intuitive) systematicity. These objections have become commonplaces of Hegel's prefatory practice, a recursion that raises the question: are Hegel's post-1807 introductions and prefaces of parallel or subordinate status to the preface for the *Phänomenologie*?

These prefaces and introductions exclude themselves entirely, as introductions and prefaces, from Hegel's systematic philosophy, by employing the precise terms with which Hegel had characterized the preface as unphilosophical. In the introduction to the first volume of *Wissenschaft der Logik*, we read that the purpose of the introduction ("Einleitung") is to offer reflections and explanations that are incidental judgments and historical (HGW, 21: 27). The preface ("Vorbegriff") following the prefaces and introduction to *Encyclopädie der philosophischen Wissenschaften im Grundrisse* advances the same aim (HGW, 20: 69). And finally, the preface to *Philosophie des Rechts* closes thus:

> Doch es ist Zeit dieses Vorwort zu schließen; als Vorwort kam ihm ohnehin nur zu, äußerlich und subjectiv von dem Standpunkt der Schrift, der es vorangeschickt ist, zu sprechen. Soll philosophisch von einem Inhalte gesprochen werden, so verträgt er nur eine wissenschaftliche, objective Behandlung, wie denn auch dem Verfasser Widerrede anderer Art als eine wissenschaftliche Abhandlung der Sache selbst, nur für ein subjectives Nachwort und beliebige Versicherung gelten und ihm gleichgültig seyn muß. (HGW, 14.1: 17)
>
> [But it is time to close this preface, and in any case as a preface it is here to speak only externally and subjectively about the point of view of the work it precedes. Should we want to speak philosophically about the contents of the work, then that content can only be treated scientifically and objectively, just as objections toward the author other than those that are a scientific investigation into the subject itself must be indifferent to him, and pass as a subjective afterword or arbitrary assertion.]

In these instances, Hegel proposes that his preliminary texts are spaces that are prescientific, and so they are not properly philosophy. His preface to the *Phänomenologie*, on the other hand, is already philosophical. Since Hegel does not claim that his later compositions are inappropriate for philosophy—for they are simply not yet philosophy (in Yovel's terminology, they are truly examples of "*pre*philosophy")—they are neither internally insufficiently elucidated, nor do they contradict his previous philosophical example of the prefatory form, which we can still understand as hierarchically superior. The latter examples explicitly dismiss themselves as only being prefaces or introductions, whereas Hegel's preface from 1807 presents itself as one unapologetically and criticizes the form in general—implicitly excluding his own example. Further, his introduction to *Philosophie des Rechts*, which is substantially philosophical in its arguments, neither refutes nor promotes itself as philosophy. In this regard, the text is as much a part of Hegel's philosophical writing as the introduction to his *Phänomenologie*.

A second edition of the *Phänomenologie* was under contract with Duncker and Humblot from the autumn of 1831. A handwritten, cursory note inside Hegel's copy of the first edition refers to the preface ("re. Vorrede") and plans a change to this preface, to historicize it, or to add a new one: "—auf die damalige Zeit der Abfassung bezüglich—in Vorrede: das abstracte Absolute—herrschte damals" (HGW, 9: 448) [refer to the time during which it was drafted—in the preface: the abstract Absolute dominated back then]. By proposing to somehow update the preface and in doing so chronicle the composition of his early, first part of the system, Hegel suggests that the revised preface to this work would have had renewed interpretative relevance for his oeuvre as a whole. And although he moved in his mature philosophy to more detailed questions than Absolute Spirit, he at no point negates the continuing relevance of his abstract principles outlined in that preface of 1807. His subsequent comments, scattered across later works, instead confirm that earlier systematic fragment.

A serious counterargument for the reading of Hegel presented here, however, deserves our scrutiny. It comes from Hegel himself. In 1829, he reviewed two books in *Jahrbücher für wissenschaftliche Kritik* [Yearbooks for Scientific Criticism]. The first volume under review was *Ueber die Hegel'sche Lehre, oder: absolutes Wissen und moderner Pantheismus* [On Hegel's Teachings, or: Absolute Knowledge and Modern Pantheism], published anonymously; and the second was Karl Ernst Schubarth's and Karl Anton Carganico's *Ueber Philosophie überhaupt und Hegels Encyklopädie der philosophischen Wissenschaften insbesondere* [Concerning Philosophy in General and Hegel's Encyclopedia of the Philosophical Sciences in Particular]. Both works had appeared earlier that year. Hegel's critique ran to three long articles, which were serialized, and his criticism of the latter book's interpretation of his own philosophy is extensive. Schubarth and Carganico are right in summarizing Hegel's philosophy as method, but they are wrong, Hegel writes, in their critique that his method is one that is *presupposed* ("ein nur *Vorausgesetztes*") (HGW, 16: 236). Significantly, Hegel then cites Schubarth and Carganico on himself, and takes them to task for their criticism of the preface and the introduction to *Wissenschaft der Logik* for conveying the general form of its content ("das Allgemeine der Form des Inhalts"), thereby demonstrating that the results of the work precede its scientific investigation. Hegel objects to this misunderstanding of his method, and goes so far as to write:

> In der Logik, die der Verf. citiert, wie in der Encyklopädie, ist es wiederholt gesagt, daß in *Vorreden* und *Einleitungen* d.i. *vor* der Wissenschaft nicht wissenschaftlich, sondern geschichtlich und etwa nur räsonnirend gesprochen werde; es ist wohl noch Niemand eingefallen, in die Vorrede und Einleitung die wissenschaftlichen Grundlagen einer Philosophie zu verlegen, eben so wenig als sie darin zu suchen. Der *Schluß* aber enthält das Resultat; die Prämissen, welche die Grundlage dazu bilden, sind im Vorhergehenden und, im vorliegenden Fall, im ganzen Verlauf der Wissenschaft enthalten. (HGW, 16: 236)
>
> [In the *Logic* to which the author refers, as in the *Encyclopedia*, it is repeatedly stated that in *prefaces* and *introductions*, i.e., *prior* to science we cannot speak scientifically, but rather historically and only in passing judgments; it would occur to nobody to lay the scientific foundations of philosophy in the preface or introduction, just as we would not search for them there. The *conclusion*, by contrast, contains the result; the premises, which form the basis for that, can be found in the preceding sections and, in the present case, in the whole progression of scientific inquiry.]

Since Hegel here refers to his *Logik* and *Encyclopädie*, the preliminary texts to which are (as he reminds us) prior to—that is, outside—systematic philosophy, we might say that this passage does not threaten this chapter's thesis concerning the *Phänomenologie*. Hegel does not assert that his 1807 preface specifically is extra- or rather unphilosophical. But the main source for Hegel's method is of course his preface to the 1807 work. And in the above passage, he generalizes the claim that it would occur to nobody to place or seek the foundation of philosophy in a preface or introduction—a contention that seems to contradict everything we have learned about the preface to the *Phänomenologie*.

On closer reading, however, Hegel's review is quite in keeping with his writing—if not philosophy. We can read it in two ways. On the one hand, we should note that Hegel uses the word "Grundlage"—not "Grundsatz." His preface to the *Phänomenologie* does not appropriate the former term at all; and the preface presents not a set of truths, but abstract generalities which become true in their exposition ("Grundsätze"). Hegel never attempted to outline or fix his philosophy's concrete basis or foundation ("Grundlage") in his 1807 preface, rather his founding, abstract principles. On the other hand, though, we need not read Hegel's review as philosophy at all. It might be interpreted instead as a nonphilosophical, purely rhetorical skirmish. His preface to the *Phänomenologie* philosophizes the preface, but still ostracizes book reviews. To be sure, the review of 1829 has Hegel's philosophy as its central concern, and could not have been written from a more Hegelian standpoint (authored by Hegel himself!). But he concludes his *Philosophie des Rechts* preface, which is external to his philosophical system, with the argument that just as that preface stands apart from systematic philosophy, so too does any counterpoint that seeks to negate him and is not embedded within systematic thought. As a serialized journalistic piece in a contemporary periodical, Hegel's book review hardly constitutes such a thoroughgoing, careful context as he projects his major philosophical works to be. Indeed, at the end of 1828, the journal advertised that Hegel would review five works, but only three reviews appeared the next year. The project was abandoned. For our philosophical interrogation of prefacing, perhaps we can ignore this book review, after all.

Hegel's preface to the *Phänomenologie*, in sum, is a text that is consistent with Hegel's systematic philosophy, since it sublates itself. His system is both his style and substance, mediated by writing and achieved, too, through dialectical movement. Showing a thoroughgoing self-awareness of its textuality, the structure of the preface to the *Phänomenologie* supersedes contemporary prefacing across philosophy at the high point of prefatory self-reflexivity in German writing—around 1800. And Hegel also engages with the literary, Romantic problematization of the preface through his philosophical approach to textual form, or the textual manifestation of his philosophy.

PHILOSOPHICAL AND RHETORICAL PREFACE PARADIGMS

The preface to the *Phänomenologie* is a polemic about the preface as well as philosophy around 1800, and it elevates that polemic to philosophy. The present chapter so far has centered on what and whom Hegel appears to be arguing against, and how he overcomes his opponents philosophically. But whom was he writing *for*; indeed, did he have a reader in mind while prefacing his 1807 work? Aside from his appropriation and subversion of the conventional, rhetorical topos of modesty already mentioned, Hegel does not seem overtly concerned about his reception in his preface—and he addresses no generalized reader. As Thomas Sören Hoffmann rightly quips, he is "in unserem Text wie auch sonst nicht unbedingt ein Meister der *captatio benevolentiae* und Schmeichelei"[56] [in our text and elsewhere not exactly a master of *captatio benevolentiae* and flattery].

John H. Smith has correctly revealed the general rhetorical substrate to Hegel's thinking, reminding us of Hegel's classical education in Stuttgart: in the art of rhetoric.[57] Smith demonstrates that in the 1807 preface, "the parameters pre-established for all discourse by the *ars rhetorica* still hold in a philosophical discourse that would dispense with them."[58] The preface is thus a prediscourse that is "indicative of basic aporias encountered in all antirhetorical speculative philosophy."[59] Smith interprets the conflict between Hegel's traditional education and his effort to wrench himself free of it through philosophy as indicative of "rhetorica contra rhetoricam" as well as, more specifically, "the paradox of the Preface."[60] This core contradiction dovetails with the third preface paradox of the present study, outlined toward the end of the introduction, and formulated as follows:

> Prefacing always retains its textual-rhetorical functions, regardless of whether it attempts to flout them by problematizing prefacing, philosophically or fictionally. Even at its most creative and intellectual, prefacing remains a pragmatic act.

Surprisingly, Smith does not attend to any audience Hegel may have (rhetorically) conceived, or rather, to how Hegel engages with those who may begin reading him. Smith is well versed in ancient rhetorical terms, yet he mentions no classical rhetorical guidelines applicable to the exordium. Instead, Hegel's preface, for Smith, stands in for rhetoric in general: his philosophy, like rhetoric, is purposive and practical (as *technē*), and it draws upon topoi of theories of invention, as well as ancient rules of debate (*ars disputandi*)—though Smith does not consider the specifics of age-old prefatory advice. Hegel's text also evokes rhetorical arguments against genius, emphasizing effort. However, it is worth asking how the preface was intended as a persuasive piece, in order to win appeal and thereby a readership for Hegel's work as a whole. After all, Hegel wrote the *Phänomenologie* in part to make his academic reputation.

Thora Ilin Bayer has proposed that the effect of the *Phänomenologie* matches that of the rhetorical sublime, as schematized by (Pseudo-)Longinus.[61] However, this explanation is inappropriate because it entails the elicitation of awe. An awe-inspiring narrative is an important feature of Hegel's work, but—unlike the sublime—it is crucial that we should in the end understand it. If we initially react to philosophy impulsively or instinctively, we should then reflect on it. As Hegel put it in a jotting among his Jena notebooks (1803–1806): "Der *Effect* am Publicum ist ein absoluter Maaßstab, über den das Subject wohl rasend werden kann. Es hat Alles gethan; aber seiner *Einsicht* steht eben der bewußtlose *Instinct* entgegen" (HGW, 5: 501) [The *effect* on the public is an absolute measure, which can surely turn the subject matter mad: the subject has done everything it could, but its *insight* conflicts with unconscious *instinct*].

Glenn Alexander Magee's version of Hegel melds "rational thought" with "mythopoetic" thinking, but also "wants to raise "mysticism" to the level of *theosophy*, to knowing the wisdom of God."[62] (Kant, by contrast, left God to faith in a pre-Hegelian use of the verb "aufheben" in his second preface to the First Critique, 1787: putting aside knowledge to create a space for belief.)[63] Magee continues: "Mysticism is inadequate because it lets mystery remain. Like Aristotle, Hegel wants to remove wonder."[64] Thus Magee suggests *initiation* as a framework for understanding Hegel's 1807 book (including the preface) that purges "false intellectual standpoints . . . before the reception of the true doctrine."[65] The *Phänomenologie* is "an introduction or propaedeutic to the tripartite system of Logic-Nature-Spirit [. . . it] is the tool by which Hegel puts his readers in the 'frame of mind' necessary to work through the pure determinations of the Idea-in-itself."[66] Magee summarizes those readers from Hegel's time (such as K. J. H. Windischmann) through to today's critics who have all interpreted the *Phänomenologie* as a "Masonic manifesto."[67]

Whether or not Hegel was addressing that specific set, he was also writing philosophy for a much wider audience, publishing the book with a commercial publisher for a general public. Yet Hegel is nevertheless secretive—or at least, far from forthcoming—in his preface. He gives us keys to unlock his thinking that are only obvious as such once we are well acquainted with his writings, similar to Goethe's work as an *open secret*. Hegel was certainly keen for as high a print run (and therefore as high a remuneration from his publisher) as possible, and he was disappointed that this was reduced from 1,000 to 750 copies during negotiations with Goebhardt (HGW, 9: 459). As Stephen Houlgate puts it, the intended readership for the *Phänomenologie* was "ordinary people (and philosophers tied to ordinary beliefs) . . . who although steeped in the certainties of everyday life share in the openness of mind that characterizes true philosophy itself."[68] But this does not mean, as Houlgate thinks, that "those who are prepared to suspend their ordinary certainties can bypass the *Phenomenology* and proceed directly to the *Logic*"[69]—for the preface to the *Phänomenologie* has a generative function.

If the governing idea of Hegel's system is that it should be presuppositionless, then beginning with that conviction implicitly—as a presupposition—surely negates the premise of serious, speculative philosophy. That is to say, the suspension of unscientific presuppositions is the central concern of Hegel's philosophy that requires explication via enactment as it begins, so that the conviction is substantiated in Hegelian terms. His doing so demands our time and effort. The preface to the *Phänomenologie* necessitates that we immerse ourselves in his philosophy as a whole. In Magee's words, it is "hermetic in both form and content."[70] It rewards the attentive reader.

The study of his philosophical science, Hegel says in this preface, "erfodert die Aufmerksamkeit" (HGW, 9: 41) [demands attention]. Let us conclude by delineating two prefatory, rhetorical strategies around 1800 which are as diametrically opposed as they are predicated on the same resource: attention. They are different in their focus. Prefaces either distract readers, or they demand readers' attention. The first method obviously results in gaining the attention of readers, too, so is similar to the second. But its discussions are digressive, its displays witty. The prefaces of Jean Paul or Sterne, for example, are of philosophical import and are remarkably learned, but they also serve as light relief from everyday experience. Jean Paul's and Sterne's prefaces are founded on the aim of achieving readers' goodwill by gently, humorously distracting them—and they appeal to aspects of their readers' lives as well as, in Jean Paul's case, individual feelings in doing so. Hegel, of course, was also concerned with concrete, subjective reality, but the reader must return to it in his work via abstraction and a self-reflection that does not entail authorial intervention. Hegel distracts the reader by demanding his full, rigorous attention to shifting senses of a word (such as "preface") for the benefit of his self-understanding. For Jean Paul, by contrast, it is the preface itself that is continually to be shifted, pre-empted, and postponed.

The rhetorical binary of distraction versus attention enables us to further differentiate between writers and phases of writers. Fritz Rüdiger Sammern-Frankenegg has compared Hegel's and Goethe's notions of attention.[71] Both privilege the concept. But whereas Goethe looks for the general in the particular, Hegel seeks to understand the Absolute in all its particularity. Sammern-Frankenegg's comparison leads to a major functional difference in the mature Goethe's and Hegel's prefacing. As we saw in chapter 1, Goethe wanted to be understood properly, comprehensively—in relation to a unified, if underspecified text, or his entire life and work. Yet the late Goethe's critical prefaces and unfinished work *Dichtung und*

Wahrheit [Poetry and Truth] point toward only sources and events of note, and so they permit (and are part of) ever partial, incremental understanding. They are based on the cliché every little helps, or project and produce a step-by-step, classificatory, cataloguing method. Hegel, however, is more brazen, adopting an all-or-nothing approach. In this sense, he has more in common with the young Goethe of *Werther* or Hölderlin, and the literary avant-garde more generally.

Hegel and the avant-garde are representative of self-declared complexity—too much complexity for a conventional preface—as a possible rhetorical strategy of the modern literary and philosophical preface. This will appeal to some readers and writers, especially those who want to circumvent, or antagonize, scholars they perceive as more pedantic. Nietzsche, for example, comments self-reflexively in his preface to the second edition of *Die fröhliche Wissenschaft* [The Gay Science] (1887; the first edition was published in 1882) that prefaces, however many, are inadequate if he is to be understood. The form cannot reproduce the plurality of an entire reading experience, he notes, and so it is necessarily perspectival: "Diesem Buche thut vielleicht nicht nur Eine Vorrede noth; und zuletzt bliebe immer noch der Zweifel bestehn, ob Jemand, ohne etwas Aehnliches erlebt zu haben, dem *Erlebnisse* dieses Buches durch Vorreden nähergebracht werden kann"[72] [Perhaps this book is in need of more than just one preface, but in the end it remains doubtful whether anyone, without having experienced something similar, can come any closer to the *experiences* of this book through prefaces]. But since Nietzsche's philosophy as a whole promotes perspectivism, the preface would seem as much a part of his project as any other. Nevertheless, both Hegel and Nietzsche demonstrate rhetoric of resistance. With respect to Nietzsche, IJsseling identifies this as the rhetorical technique of *apostrophe*, an appeal to only certain readers and a dismissal of others.[73]

Hegel and the avant-garde thus convey the wider truth that as much as an exordium is an act of willed participation, it is also a means to exclude. Rhetoric rejects as much as it reels in listeners—or readers. Schelling already recognized this function of the preface in *System des transscendenten Idealismus* [System of Transcendental Idealism] (1800); but while he mentions it in closing his preface ("Vorrede"), Hegel enacts the truth formulated by Schelling par excellence:

> Diese kurze Vorrede aber wird hinreichend seyn, in denjenigen, welche mit dem Verfasser auf demselben Puncte stehen, und an der Auflösung derselben Aufgaben mit ihm arbeiten, einiges Interesse

> für dieses Werk zu erwecken, die nach Unterricht und Auskunft Begierigen einzuladen, diejenigen aber, welche weder des ersten sich bewußt sind, noch das andere aufrichtig verlangen, zum voraus davon zurückschrecken, wodurch denn auch alle ihre Zwecke erreicht sind.[74]
>
> [But this short preface will be sufficient to awaken some interest in the work among those who come from the same position as the author and work alongside him on resolving the same problems, and to invite those who are eager for lessons and information into the work; in also frightening away from the start of the work those who are neither aware of its position and these sorts of problems, nor sincerely demand teaching in or knowledge about them, all of the preface's aims are achieved.]

This is a point about prefacing which some authors do not think through. Edward W. Said, for instance, conflates beginnings with intentions as moments of inclusivity, within which a work gets going. But ironically, in the preface to his second edition of *Beginnings* (1984, first edition 1974), he is prescriptive despite promoting congenial perspectivism, drawing a line between his aim and an allegedly presiding authoritarian, orthodox dogma in criticism that he excludes by emphasizing what his work is not:

> [I]f there is some especially urgent claim to be made for [literary] criticism, which is one of the major claims advanced by this book, it is that constant re-experiencing of beginning and beginning-again whose force is neither to give rise to authority nor to promote orthodoxy but to stimulate self-conscious and situated activity, activity with aims non-coercive and communal.[75]

On Said's own definition of *beginning*, his preface cannot begin its book's project.

POST-STRUCTURALIST POSTSCRIPT

Following the high tide of Hegelian philosophy; in the wake of a revolution in German literature, print culture, and Jean Paul's jokes during Romanticism; and after the Age of Goethe, Kierkegaard was a significant prefatorial aftershock—but precisely because the preface to his *Prefaces* (1844) instantiates a satirical insignificance of Hegel's prefacing, and in part invokes

Jean Paul to this end. On the one hand, Kierkegaard's opening preface might seem to begin with hackneyed humor. He contends that the time was due for a preface to take its own path away from a book, because it must otherwise begin, paradoxically, with nothing. As we saw from Coventry's 1751 introduction cited above, Kierkegaard's quip was not new. On the other hand, Kierkegaard is in fact criticizing "the most recent scholarly method," by which he means Hegel's system and contemporary Danish Hegelian philosophy. A preface is pointless, "because when one begins the book with the subject and the system with nothing there is apparently nothing left over to say in a prologue."[76] Regardless of whether this line refers to the introduction and preface(s) of the *Phänomenologie* or perhaps *Wissenschaft der Logik*, Kierkegaard is both wrong and right. Hegel's preface to the former work already makes the abstract, explanatory claim that his method—and so the whole subject and system to which it later gives rise—can be characterized by sheer negativity. His introductions to both mature works then more concretely begin (again) with nothing. Though his later prefaces, therefore, do say something additional, crucial, and specific—methodologically speaking—they state nothing that turns out to be unique (i.e., not much, as a commonsense expression; or the pejorative meaning of nothing as "abstract," in the sense of vague generalities). Kierkegaard pokes textual fun at this philosophical point.

Prefaces in its entirety is not only a response to Hegel, but first and foremost an attack on the Copenhagen Hegelian Johan Ludvig Heiberg, who never directly engaged with this prefatory criticism (which might be in part why its publication fell on deaf ears). According to Lasse Horne Kjældgaard, the Hegelians of mid-nineteenth-century Denmark problematized prefaces and introductions; and it is in response to these that he assumes Kierkegaard conceived *Prefaces*.[77] Kjældgaard's argument is an extension of Jon Stewart's, which contends that this work not only constitutes Kierkegaard's most satirical and polemical writing, but also his most parochial: "Here Kierkegaard is concerned above all, if not exclusively, with his Danish contemporaries rather than any wider or more universal philosophical issue."[78] Stewart's important general differentiation between the German thinker and his Danish adherents notwithstanding, this assertion cannot be entirely correct, for two reasons. First, it rests on Stewart's misunderstanding of Hegel's preface to the *Phänomenologie*. For Stewart states: "Like Hegel, Nicolaus Notabene notes that what seems to be left for the preface is superficialities and trivialities. Thus he seems in agreement with Hegel about the superfluous nature of a preface to a philosophical work."[79] Kierkegaard's preface is indeed a peculiar and petty textual operation, a self-professed *triviality*—"dominated by fashion," prefaces "change like clothing."[80] As Harvie Ferguson writes, "*Prefaces* ironically remains locked in the superficial and banal."[81] But Hegel elevates, through typical Hegelian sublation, the preface to a systematic philosophical interrogation of itself. Hence Hegel rids the preface of its superficiality as a form, only for Kierkegaard to reintroduce it. And second, Kierkegaard elsewhere attacks *Hegel's* philosophy on account of, if not its prefatorial claims, its lack of sufficient prefatory modesty: "If Hegel had written his whole logic and had written in the preface that it was only a thought-experiment, in which at many points he still steered clear of some things, he undoubtedly would have been the greatest thinker who has ever lived. As it is he is comic."[82]

If we were to read Kierkegaard's *Prefaces* intellectually, rather than for enjoyment—the "light reading" for which they were intended—the premises with which we would skirmish would hardly be those of his actual prefacing. While these are the author's pretext for his prefatorial texts, they do not present the core problem of his work. Kierkegaard suggests as much as he closes the book with its "postscript":

> It hardly needs saying that this light reading cannot possibly, that is, without invalidating all experiences and concepts, initiate conflict and quarrelling, because a word in advance [*Forord*] breaks up no quarrel, and the one who strikes back begins the conflict—not with *The Prefaces* [*Forordene*] but with all experiences and concepts.[83]

Prefaces, then, is a place of wordplay and a mockery of domestic, Copenhagen intellectual politics as well as German intellectualism—taking its cue from Jean Paul. It is not a site of serious, systematic philosophy, and it cannot start such philosophy. Indeed, Kierkegaard does not contribute much to the contemplation of prefacing per se, other than to poke fun at it. Consequently, his prefaces are an even lighter distraction for readers than, say, Jean Paul's.

We read a different story in Heidegger's philosophy, which repeats Hegel's preface problem as well as sharing Kierkegaard's humor about the impossibility of the preface (or introduction) as a beginning. Heidegger criticizes the beginning of Hegel's system in both abstract and textual terms. Heidegger and Hegel start from the same page, inasmuch as they both think that the truth is the whole. In Heidegger's 1942–1943 essay *Hegels Begriff der*

Erfahrung [Hegel's Concept of Knowledge] (published in 1950), the post-Hegelian preface problem turns into an introductory issue. Heidegger yokes Hegel to his critique of what he considers to be metaphysics of presence, which posits a self-knowing agent that considers the world real when it is present. We begin instead, thinks Heidegger, less rationally: in a state of greater engagement with the world, albeit less self-aware, which he terms being-with. Experience of the Absolute, in Heidegger's reading of Hegel, is ever present and elevated by thought, such that its conceptual development cannot be summarized, that is reduced, prior to its exposition. Heidegger does not interpret Hegel's "Einleitung" to the *Phänomenologie* as an "introduction" at all, since to call it such is to allegedly, falsely delay a beginning that has already arrived in the philosopher's mind and in our world. Hegel thereby—spuriously, for Heidegger—assumes that the Absolute whose presence he will go on to reveal is not present, when it is. The Absolute in the end at most comes a second time, as a repetition of its original conception; it will appear as a second coming, as *parousia*.

Heidegger then observes that the title "Einleitung" to Hegel's first sixteen paragraphs, which follow his preface, is absent from the original 1807 text, but was added later; "vermutlich aus der Verlegenheit, die sich durch den Zwang eines Verzeichnisses ergab"[84] [probably out of the awkwardness that arises from the pressure of a table of contents]. For Heidegger, this amendment divests the text of its methodological sincerity, because to introduce philosophy is apparently impossible. Just as we are prereflectively preconditioned to being in the world as an entire entity, there can be no prephilosophical discourse within a philosophical work. Philosophy emerges from depiction and interrogation alike, from everyday musing as well as abstract rigor. Thus the philosophical introduction can be legitimate only once it is stated that it is itself a properly philosophical process, as presentation. And finally, Heidegger claims that Hegel composed the comprehensive preface because of the introductory impossibility Heidegger identifies; and the preface, in Heidegger's model, is preparatory.[85]

If we should accept Heidegger's critique of introductions, then we could equally posit, in his terminology, that the preface already belongs to the philosophical presence whose essence unfolds in, and is presumed by, its presentation, or prefacing. Despite the obscurity of his argument, though, one thing is clear in light of our prior discussion of Hegel: Heidegger has displaced Hegel's thematization of prefacing and appropriated it as a critique of introducing. Hegel complained that Fichte, Schelling, and other intuitive philosophers jumped the gun and pre-empted the Absolute in their systems;

and he responded with a long preface and a lengthy, laborious, and lively philosophical road toward the Absolute that requires multiple laps of its course in order to be comprehended. Heidegger now charges Hegel with starting out with his final concept, the Absolute, in hand—precisely what Hegel accuses his Idealist contemporaries of doing—and Heidegger proposes that Hegel disingenuously introduces his Absolute Knowing as not yet present. And just as Hegel quipped that philosophy is not an inventory or contents page, Heidegger criticizes Hegel's *Phänomenologie* as an (impossible, and therefore flawed) introduction.

Throughout his writings, Heidegger's thought centers on, and criticizes, the idea of introducing. His earlier lecture series *Einleitung in die Philosophie* [Introduction to Philosophy] (1928–1929) contended that a philosophical introduction—written from an outsider's, objective, prephilosophical perspective—is impossible. Insofar as we exist as human beings, we always already philosophize: this distinguishes us from animals, and God. We introduce only in the sense that we bring a pre-existing subject of our understanding within the world preconceptually into being: when we discuss a notion before we go on to study it properly, as a concept. The German verb to introduce, "einleiten," would be better substituted by the phrase "in Gang bringen": "to usher something in."[86] (In fact, Kierkegaard had already proposed a similar conception of the introduction: on the same day as his volume of prefaces to unwritten books was published, June 17, 1844, he also published *The Concept of Anxiety: A Simple Psychologically Orienting Deliberation on the Dogmatic Issue of Hereditary Sin*. Here he states that the "task" of the introduction is to "bring out" those presuppositions which will be examined and revised in the work itself; hence the work can be assessed according to them and, turning an Hegelian phrase on its head, "The introduction may be correct, while the deliberation itself concerning the concept of anxiety may be entirely incorrect.")[87] In any case, the reason Hegel's introduction to the *Phänomenologie* remains so objectionable to Heidegger, according to an earlier unpublished manuscript from 1942 ("Erläuterung der 'Einleitung' zu Hegels *Phänomenologie des Geistes*" [Commentary on the "Introduction" to Hegel's *Phenomenology of Spirit*]), is that it attempts to—indeed, must—be "der absolute Einsprung in das Absolute"[88] [the absolute jump into the Absolute]. Yet this interpretation of Hegel's text is tenable only if that absolute jump is made again after reading the work, the second time around; the introduction or preface, for example, are not meant to be pistol shots to the Absolute, but rather its abstract beginnings, which become understandable in its exposition. And Hegel wrote the preface last, once he read and understood his own (introduction to his) system (i.e., the *Phänomenologie*)—so even he could not reach the idea immediately.

Heidegger praises Hegel's preface to the *Phänomenologie*, unlike the introduction. There is "nichts ihresgleichen in der Geschichte des abendländischen Denkens"[89] [nothing like it in the history of Western thought]. He then proceeds to conflate it with introductions before expounding on only the latter:

> "Vorreden" und "Einleitungen" sollen doch, wenn sie überhaupt etwas sollen, in das Werk einführen, für die "Außenstehenden" den Übergang zum Eingang in das Werk darbieten. . . . Eine "Einleitung" in das *philosophische* Denken ist unmöglich; denn hier gibt es *kein* stetiges und unversehentliches Hinübergleiten vom alltäglichen Denken in das denkerische Denken . . . Eine "Einleitung" kann nur hier dazu dienen, den Sprung vorzubereiten . . . Jede Einleitung "in" "die Philosophie" muß sich aber mit den Nicht-darinnen-stehenden doch verständigen und auf *deren* Verständnishorizont sich einlassen. Damit handelt die "Einleitung" stets und notwendig gegen ihre eigene Absicht.[90]
>
> ["Prefaces" and "introductions" should, if they should do anything at all, lead us into the work, offering those who stand outside of it a passage right up to the work's entrance. . . . An "introduction" in *philosophical* thinking is impossible, for here there is *no* smooth way to glide over into thoughtful thinking from everyday thinking without slipping up . . . an "introduction" can here only serve as a way to prepare for the jump . . . each introduction "into" "philosophy" must always acquaint itself with those who do not stand within it and look into the horizon of *their* understanding. In doing so, an "introduction" always and necessarily acts against its own intention.]

Heidegger's objection to conventional, philosophical introductions, despite the inevitability of having to introduce philosophy, is here indebted to Hegel's prefatorial, antiprefatory polemic. However, Heidegger's Hegelian argument is less rhetorically functional inasmuch as it does not preface or introduce any of his published works of his own philosophy as such.

Hegel's prefacing is functionally appropriated in Derrida's "Outwork, Prefacing" to *Dissemination* (1972), although Derrida starts his exposition of the preface problem in an original way. His project of deconstruction is a critique of Western philosophy through to Heidegger, though Heidegger's reappraisal of this heritage was in fact Derrida's impetus. Deconstruction is a criticism of what Derrida characterizes, from Plato onward, as metaphysics of presence. Since a preface is usually written after the completion of a work, yet precedes the work that will be read, there is a tense issue: a preface projects a book into the public sphere that the reader *will* read, but which *has been* written already. The preface is thus an "intention-to-say after the fact."[91] In an intellectual atmosphere that has established the arbitrariness of the sign, the preface cannot be a discrete text type in opposition to others, since its presence is an effect of absence—for example, the absence of a genuinely futural work. Nor is the preface properly derivative: sequentially, it comes before a book, after all. It can exist as a conceptually empty opposition only within a set of textual relations. Consequently, the tense of the preface is the present one: "the *pre* reduces the future to the form of manifest presence."[92] This logic complements Derrida's (and Heidegger's) criticism of Hegel's system more generally, which is in part Hegel's very critique of Fichte and Schelling, among others: "Absolute knowledge is *present* at the zero point of the philosophical exposition. Its teleology has determined the preface as a postface, the last chapter of the *Phenomenology of Spirit* as a foreword, the *Logic* as an Introduction to the *Phenomenology of Spirit*. This point of ontoteleological fusion reduces both precipitation and after-effect to mere appearances or to sublatable negativities."[93]

Derrida offers an extensive reading of Hegel's prefaces and introductions in "Outwork, Prefacing." The introduction to the *Phänomenologie*, for example, is allegedly "more systematic, less historical [and] less circumstantial" than the preface.[94] Timothy Clark notes that Derrida's points about prefaces initially seem similar to Hegel's: "First is the question of method and the insistence that concepts or terms in a philosophical discourse only operate diacritically in a *system*; second, the rejection of any form of simple self-evidence, intuition or immediate perception as the basis for truth of any philosophical argument."[95] However, there is a major difference. Derrida's account of Hegel's prefacing is assimilated into his own philosophy. For Derrida, there are two possible interpretations of the *Phänomenologie* preface. As Clark summarizes: "Firstly, the preface may become an integral part of the necessary progression of the concepts themselves (so losing its merely prefatory character). In effect, as a preface, it would be effaced. Second, it may be considered as falling outside the work itself, becoming a contingent and unnecessary husk to it, of a totally derivative status merely."[96] These are two arguments which we have already encountered in Heidegger and

Kierkegaard respectively. Prefacing is (satirically, or in Derrida's words, "ludicrously") an all or nothing exercise that "already belongs to this exposition of the whole, engages it and is engaged in it, in which case the preface has no specificity and no textual place of its own, being merely a part of philosophical discourse; or else the preface escapes this in some way, in which case it is nothing at all."[97] According to Derrida, then, the *Phänomenologie* preface is an either/or: it is either inside of philosophy, or outside of it. Hegel's text reflects on its impossibility as a philosophical preface and, as such, becomes the "negative of philosophy"—but as such, it cannot be sublated, since Derrida settles on interpreting it as outside of philosophical argument.[98] The 1807 preface is rather a "remainder"; in Clark's words: "The phenomena [*sic*] of the *remainder*, as it is effective in the preface abstracted and *in itself*, is precisely one of rote functioning, without legitimation in the ideal movement of the *aufhebung* [*sic*]."[99] Derrida's move is to overcome Hegel's preface without sublation, and he does so through the idea of a resistance to prefacing that he perceives as reductive in its conventional form. The result is what he calls the "restance."[100] This reads the preface "otherwise than as the excrement of philosophical essentiality," he contends, "not in order to sublate it back into the latter, of course, but in order to learn to take it differently into account."[101]

Derrida's solution entails the affirmation of contradiction. He proposes a dual-logic partly inherited, no doubt, from the Early German Romantics and the doubling of Jean Paul, or in any case a duality equally necessary for irony that is not annulled. Derrida's (non)method, then, is not a Kantian-style dualism but a double-edged logic: "The preface that Hegel *must* write, in order to denounce a preface that is both impossible and inescapable, must be assigned two locations and two sorts of scope. It belongs both to the inside and to the outside of the concept."[102] In other words, the preface is a non-sublatable threshold ("limen").[103] Derrida thereby affirms the preface as existing in its own right, but as a space that is not inherently anything.

Derrida's understanding of the preface is not unique to this text type, but is broadened to the textual frame. In this regard, Genette will follow in Derrida's wake. Derrida's 1972 prefatory discussion mirrors his later reading of the *parergon* in a subchapter of 1978, concerned with aesthetic ornamentation, Kant's *Kritik der Urteilskraft* [Critique of Judgment] (1790), as well as the framing—the *para*meter—of a philosophical work: the "ergon." A frame objectifies, yet is once again determined by absence, or a double lack. First, Derrida contends that we lack a theory of framing, which he provides. Secondly, however, that theory is produced by a gap inasmuch as the external frame adds to the work whatever is internally missing, though it is itself missing the systematic security of the subsequent text, since the frame stands outside philosophy. Framing, then, cannot be achieved through recourse to stable material or conceptual objects: the seeming stability of frames is not stability as such. Their underpinning is undecided; their presence postponement. Derrida concludes: "There is no natural frame. *There is* frame, but the frame *does not exist*."[104]

In arguing for his purportedly new conception of prefacing in 1972—an argument that Derrida repeatedly denies results in a *real* preface insofar as his is no conventional conception—he reiterates, like Heidegger, precisely Hegelian argumentative moves (if not Hegelian arguments as such). He rejects the typical preface, as he understands it, because it represents a form of knowledge that he wishes to counter: a tabular, schematizing, cataloguing mode of inquiry. Derrida writes of his "Outwork, Prefacing," "Hence this is not a preface, at least not if by preface we mean a table, a code, an annotated summary of prominent signifieds, or an index of key words or of proper names."[105] Crucial to this anticonception is a conflation of paratexts; and critical to overcoming his objection and presenting a new kind of preface is their separation. *Dissemination* is professedly more complex—too complex to be reduced to a list of its claims—and thus has license to obfuscate: "To lose one's head, no longer know where one's head is, such is perhaps the effect of dissemination."[106]

Most significantly, a preface is necessitated by its philosophical material in order to counteract formalism and empiricism. While the former was Hegel's chief opponent, the latter occupies an equivalent position within post-Structuralist discourse to pedantry around 1800. Only a preface prevents the scholar from finding holes in individual propositions, Derrida implies, because the preface presents the overarching, irreducible theoretical idea: "A *preface* would retrace and presage here a *general* theory and practice of deconstruction, that strategy without which the possibility of a critique could exist only in fragmentary, empiricist surges that amount in effect to a non-equivocal confirmation of metaphysics."[107] Thus the preface in Hegel's time and today was and is dispensable only in a "prevailing culture [that] still imposes both formalism and empiricism,"[108] and so is an "essential and ludicrous operation."[109] Derrida's prefacing must perform the impossibility of prefacing, within his philosophy's own terms. His functional use of Hegel's prefacing thereby hardly overcomes Hegel at all: it matches it, with a Derridean, post-Romantic twist.

Around the same time as Derrida's *Dissemination*, Foucault was also making a problem out of the preface. A post-Structuralist who departed from intentionalist models of receiving and engaging with the works of others,

Foucault instead used texts in order to examine discursive formations within society. In this method, the individual subject is decentered; the empirical author is understood as discursively functional, affecting adopted positions but not thought to determine historical phenomena with individual, identifiable agency. In this respect, Foucault shares an affinity with Hegel's subordination of the philosopher and—philosophical—historian as personality to critical writing; and he continues the Hegelian project of the *Phänomenologie* of embedding individuals within discursive formations.[110] He can be aligned, too, with Hegel's and Derrida's prefaces, which extend their philosophies into what are usually prosaic and interpersonal textual forms. In fact, Jean-Marie Schaeffer suggests that Hegel's and Derrida's prefaces are remarkable because they are contrary to the philosophical norm of an author situating himself relative to his public and peers as an authorial subject; Foucault could be added to this group that prioritizes method over persona.[111] Foucault's focus is the dispersion, redistribution, and deployment of statements which together form discourse. Appropriately, then, he saw fit to problematize the preface—a text type that seeks to create coherence.

Foucault begins his second, 1972 edition of *History of Madness* by paradoxically denouncing and simultaneously appropriating the preface. Self-aware, the author acknowledges this contradiction in a fictional dialogue, whereby his interlocutor points out that Foucault has prefaced despite the protest he directs at prefatorial tradition. Foucault defends himself on the grounds that his preface is short. But the preface, for Foucault, is otherwise an attempt to exert power over interpretative activity. It is:

> the first act in which the monarchy of the author is established, a declaration of tyranny: my intention should be your precept; you must bend your reading, your analyses, your criticisms to what I was trying to do, and take note of my modesty: when I speak of the limits of my enterprise, I mean to set a boundary for your freedom . . . . My desire is that a book, at least for the person who wrote it, should be nothing other than the sentences of which it is made; that it should not be doubled by that first simulacrum of itself which is a preface, whose intention is to lay down the law for all the simulacra which are to be formed in the future on its basis. . . . In short, my desire is that a book should not create of its own accord that status of text to which teaching and criticism will all too probably reduce it, but that it should have the easy confidence to present itself as discourse.[112]

This passage is a characteristically energetic attack on authors who summarize their work, contextualize its composition, and sketch their development as writers before a text proper, in anticipation that readers will follow suit. Foucault appears to rally against any kind of intentionalist, indeed hermeneutic activity that demands attention, of the type that Goethe and Hegel so desired for themselves. He asserts instead that his own book should remain discontinuous, disruptive: a scattering of statements that might form discourse. His work should not be reduced to, nor made to cohere in, an authoritative, pithy preface. But herein lies a clear, and clearly witty paradox.

In telling us why he does not wish to preface in 1972, Foucault is asserting—as author, and from the privileged position of a preface—how and how not to interpret his work as a whole. By this time, Foucault was notorious, but also already canonical. He was (and wanted to be) studied by critics. In fact, as Raili Poldsaar summarizes, Derrida had attacked Foucault's original, 1961 edition of *History of Madness* in what Foucault considered to be a misreading.[113] As a consequence, he withdrew the preface to the Gallimard edition and wrote the new one under examination here—in an effort to be better understood. Indeed, calling the preface a "first simulacrum" of a book is surely a nod toward Derrida's "Outwork, Prefacing" of the same year. But to correct Derrida and others who had misunderstood him, and still be faithful to his own thinking and writing, was no straightforward task. Foucault had forcefully dismissed the validity of authors' own interpretations of their works in his 1969 essay "What Is an Author?" For him, eighteenth-century novelists such as Ann Radcliffe merely introduced discursive material into circulation, which was then conceptually categorized by the "initiators of discursive practices," who especially came to prominence in the nineteenth century and apparently subordinated their authorial selves—the theorists, such as Karl Marx and Sigmund Freud.[114] Foucault admitted in this essay that theoretical writers (mathematicians, say) appear as individual, empirical personae in their prefaces.[115] However, in addition there are two other selves of the theorist: the one of the work who supposes and concludes, which "anyone could perform provided the same set of axioms, preliminary operations, and an identical set of symbols were used," as well as the self within the existing or emergent theoretical discourse, who interprets.[116] The author function disperses these three personae. To read the *History of Madness* second preface as instructive would be counter to Foucault's 1969 essay. It would be predicated on the very type of question that he suggests we suspend, namely: how does a free subject "accomplish its design by animating the rules of discourse from within?"[117]

The preface is therefore necessarily ironic. If we are to take Foucault at his word, we must bend our reading to Foucault's anti-intentionalist intentions. He has inserted himself into what he perceives to be a conservative interpretative paradigm, one in which he has secured a reputation as subversive. For as soon as we might oblige in reading Foucault's history the way he conceives it, we would read the preface, too, as merely comprising statements of an emergent discourse, from which no abstract authorial principle should be uniformly applied to the rest of the book. In other words, heeding the preface and allowing *History of Madness* "the easy confidence to present itself as discourse" because this is the author's instruction would self-destructively entail not attributing the preface any special significance at all, on account of its textual status as instructions by the author. The preface would become as much text as any other section or sentence of Foucault's, and subject to our own interpretations as readers. Perhaps he thereby attempts to destroy historical-biographical, hermeneutic, or, indeed, Hegelian, systematic, philosophical analyses from the inside: from the preface out, and into the start of the work. But to credit Foucault with such ingenuity, of course, demands that we ultimately do attribute him an intention—that of irony.

Consequently, Foucault is yet another creative thinker and writer in the tradition of contradictory prefacing. Foucault, like Derrida and Heidegger, as well as the young Goethe—and unlike Sterne, Jean Paul, or Kierkegaard—is akin to Hegel in his demand that even if the reader should usually reject the preface, he should pay close attention to the very text type he is rejecting in its individual instantiation at hand, for a full and intricate understanding of a work as a whole. Prefaces by Jean Paul privilege procrastination, repeated recommencement, and momentary curiosity, beginning the entire project of prefacing a book or oeuvre all over again, so that unity is humorously undermined in almost every attempt to establish it (though at times he then renders such fragmentary unity wholesome, through feeling). For the philosophical-literary, Goethean and Hegelian types of author, on the other hand, to preface is not (just) a playful or Sentimental distraction. The latter, Hegelian sort is more demanding still. It is also more fundamentally conceptual. For much of Goethe's prefacing, we recall, is poetically pragmatic rather than poetological; and once it became more content-ful in later life, that poetological content comprised historicizing details rather than abstract ideas.

Conclusion

THIS STUDY HAS read prefaces to German literature and philosophy around 1800 within their shared German, and indeed European, contexts of print and intellectual cultures: from historical, theoretical, rhetorical, and formal perspectives. To write a book at this time meant to think—conceptually and creatively—within the terms of its materiality. It was to be *ambivalent* about the norms of print culture, and to seize the challenge of the book as an object for the world of the mind or the beauty of the soul (to speak in the spirit of that period). It did not mean to conform to or to resist a commonplace idea of the "book," but instead to reflect on and reform what a "book" might mean in an idiosyncratic, inventive, and inductive way. Print culture was a source for metaphors about thinking as well as writing, and thus even for philosophical method in its physical manifestation: on the page. Above all, prefaces around 1800 (and then again in the latter half of the twentieth century) were not to be *tabular*, which would suggest too reductive an understanding of a work. To be sure, at the end of the eighteenth century objectivity was still aspired to. Yet it had to be of a lively—and as such, an individual—sort. These ideas and analogies were employed in anything other than a textbook manner. A focus on prefatory form in the preceding chapters, and an openness to the playful character of the preface, has brought textual irony into the foreground in particular. Prefaces around 1800 were so often *pretexts* for writing in multiple senses. At their most prosaic, they were texts placed before the main work, excusing in formulaic fashion the very practice they enacted. At their most ingenious, prefaces were a ploy for writing itself. And they have prompted the writing of, and so been the pretext for, this book on "Romantic" writing more broadly.

More specifically, over the course of the present book we have attended to three preface paradoxes, which are especially evident from reading Goethe's, Jean Paul's, and Hegel's prefaces. These three authors each wrote one preface that was particularly generative for their wider, paradoxical prefacing in general, and which was interpreted at length here: namely the preface to *Die Leiden des jungen Werthers* [The Sorrows of Young Werther] (1774) and its revisions and alternatives, the preface to a fictive second edition of *Quintus Fixlein* (1797), and the preface to the *Phänomenologie des Geistes* [Phenomenology of Spirit] (1807), respectively.

As for the first paradox, prefaces initiate works by being both immanent and procrastinatory, determined by and deferring the main texts. Thus we can ask: are prefaces (im)pertinent? A foreword could go on forever, as much as it might be omitted (see especially chapter 1, on Goethe). This paradox is summed up in a later aphorism by Johann Jakob Mohr of 1879: "Zu einer nöthigen Vorrede gehört gewöhnlich ein unnöthiges Buch"[1] [It is an unnecessary book that usually belongs to a necessary preface].

Second, an author's own preface is predicated on an act of address to a person external to the work's poetics or thought—but the desired addressee, whether a peculiar or popular readership, is imagined by the writer, and so is integral to his conceptual or creative work. To preface is therefore autopoetic and even, in its exaggerated form, autoerotic (see chapter 2 in particular, on Jean Paul). The irony means that preface writing is as much about and for the authorial self and a writer's own creativity or clarity as it is about and for the readership and a critical reception. This is indicated in the opening definition of Oswald Wiener's preface ("Vorwort") to *Die Verbesserung von Mitteleuropa, Roman* [The Improvement of Central Europe, a Novel] (1969), a work that comprises exclusively paratextual elements: "einfach einwirken auf andere, auf sich selber einwirken, sätze einnehmen wie sonst pillen, sich wohin führen lassen, sich in einen zustand versetzen, lassen, mitteilen wollen; auch wohl sich eine hypothese zurechtlegen"[2] [to have an effect on others, to have an effect on oneself, to swallow sentences like pills, to be led somewhere, to put oneself in somebody else's shoes, to be put in someone else's shoes, to want to convey—or even to concoct a hypothesis].

Third, prefacing always retains its textual-rhetorical functions, regardless of whether it attempts to flout them by problematizing prefacing, philosophically or fictionally. Even at its most creative and intellectual, prefacing remains a pragmatic act. Such pragmatism, in turn, may become paradoxical: ingratiating by not ingratiating—or less paradoxically, by a willingness to forgo the easy applause of the many in favor of the approval of the few (see particularly chapter 3, on Hegel). This contradiction of "rhetorica contra rhetoricam," first explored in the introduction to the present book and then across its main chapters, applies most of all to theoretical prefaces against common sense, formalism, or empiricism (which we can also call positivism); and thus to highbrow, avant-garde, countercultural, autonomous literature. It is relevant for genres which seek to flatter their readership by figuring it as exclusive, and especially able to decode complexity—and to baffle the rest into admiration, or to antagonize them.

Taken together, the examination of these three paradoxes and three canonical authors is significant for both literary and intellectual history, and not just with respect to German letters and thought. Prefaces in the late eighteenth and early nineteenth centuries (and, most of all, those in the German language) were an historical watershed—standing out until the mid-twentieth century. And they were fertile, sowing the seeds for theoretical writers within continental philosophy—and especially of (post-) Structuralism—into the mid-twentieth century.

A written preface, as discussed early on, is distinct from the start of an orally delivered speech. A joke that we encountered in the introduction was that late eighteenth- or early nineteenth-century readers might have either paid attention to only the prefaces of works or otherwise skipped over them, beginning with the main part of the book. But neither of these humorous accusations in an attempt to promote reading of the whole work (instead of an idle reader lazily leafing through it) is unique to the period in the history of the preface that the present study has investigated, nor are they special for the German preface. On the contrary, they are among the most hackneyed examples of prefatory wit and pleading, regardless of national or historical tradition. For instance, Georg Philipp Harsdörffer's prologue to *Frauenzimmer Gesprächspiele* [Ladies' Conversational Games] (1644) quips of the reader: "Du gehst nicht durch die Thür / du steigst zum Fenster ein / Wann du das Buch anfällst / und last die Vorred seyn"[3] [Not through the door you make your entry / No, you climb through the window / stumbling into the book / And so you leave the preface be]. Walter Scott wittily pretends to overcome such disobedience in the last chapter of his novel *Waverley* (1814), which "should have been a prefatory chapter," but "most novel readers" decline to read the preface and others (especially students) "begin with the last chapter of a work"—and so it is prefatorial, after all.[4] Heinrich Zschokke wrote that for *Der Freihof von Aarau* [The Free Court of Aarau] (1822): "Die Vorrede ist der Schlüssel. Wer auf die Ringmauern steigt, wird freilich auch sehen, was im Freihof vorgeht; aber nur das Dach, nicht das Haus; nur die Kappe, nicht das menschliche Antlitz"[5] [The preface is key. Anyone who climbs the border walls will of course also see what is going on at the free court—but will see only the roof, not the house; only a man's cap, not the faces of men]. Perhaps other readers will start a preface, rather than avoid it—but not finish the prefatorial text. Hence Kierkegaard appended to the preface of his early work *From the Papers of One Still Living* (1838) a "postscript" for readers who might be—or, since it follows the preface, have been already—"harmed by reading the preface." He acknowledges that they may jump over the postscript, too, however, and jokingly resigns himself to such a possibility: "if they skipped far enough so that they skipped over the essay as well, it is of no consequence."[6] All of these textual strategies are as historically unspecific as they are singularly significant to the time after Harsdörffer and before Kierkegaard. That is to say, although such quips recur throughout history, over and over again, most instances are on the whole not nearly so complex or creative, nor as important for a work's poetological or philosophical argument as many prefaces around 1800—though they may seem on the face of it, or indeed be said in the prefaces themselves to be, unremarkable, irrelevant, or inappropriate.

Eighteenth- and mid-nineteenth century critics understood this point, and offered their historical explanations. Swift declares in *A Tale of a Tub* (1710 edition) that "*Prefaces, Epistles, Advertisements, Introductions, Prolegomena's, Apparatus's, To-the-Reader's*" could once all fulfil a recipient's curiosity to the extent that whole books remained unread, despite the promise of the preface writer as "the urging and attending Orator, with his last *moving* and *standing* Piece of Rhetorick."[7] But he then notes that Dryden was so very successful in his paratextual instructions that the public subsequently became too wise to the stock topoi and techniques of prefatory persuasion. Thus, in turn, prefaces were ignored. Accordingly: "yawning Readers in our Age, do now a-days twirl over forty or fifty Pages of *Preface* and *Dedication*, (which is the usual *Modern* Stint) as if it were so much *Latin*"—although some, he says, still made a career in criticism or writing by reading nothing else.[8] Swift then professes that he too has what he considers to be the "Modern inclination" to discuss his own writing, and that he "thought best to do it in the Body of the Work."[9] But this decision to "incorporate" the preface, shared by many and discussed in the introduction to the present book, did not mean the disappearance of the preface—and especially not in German letters. Rather, as Eichendorff observes while looking back on the German long eighteenth century and its literary self-reflexivity in *Geschichte der poetischen Literatur Deutschlands* [History of Poetic Literature in Germany] (1857), the preface was dispersed. Eichendorff contends that authors were required to explain and justify their work in this age through "eine beständige Exposition, eine gleichsam durch das Ganze zwischen den Zeilen fortlaufende Vorrede"[10] [a continuous exposition, an ongoing preface, as it were, running on between the lines, through the whole work]. He posits that perpetual prefacing was necessary because the foreign and domestic influences on writing had become so heterogeneous, and their use so subjective. Necessity here is meant only in the sense of a need for understanding; with the autonomy of literature and philosophy, and the specialization of both society and discourses across Europe, prefaces that adhered to general precepts about learning were no longer obligatory. Terms and ideas creatively employed in German literary books of the period were unlikely to be self-evident to readers, and so they required both initial and continual clarification in a mode that was similar to prefacing. The preface was in some way displaced—as Scott jokes in *Waverley*—but it nevertheless somehow remained. For an author, the preface or to preface was no longer obvious, and so prefacing became a part of the author's oeuvre and originality, nowhere more so around the close of the eighteenth century than in German writing.

This study's introduction explored the historical causes of the phenomenon in detail. In essence, once German literature was conceived as an autonomous domain rather than as a branch of general learning; as a popular book market took hold; and once systematic philosophy competed with literature's broad acclaim as well as intellectual independence, the preface became not only a pragmatic, but also a creative and conceptual problem. Hence the preface became complicated as a form, in a broadly *Romantic* tradition of thought in which almost every act of genuine reflection was understood to expose epistemological contradiction. It may seem strange to read Goethe, Jean Paul, and Hegel Romantically—and all three certainly resist the supposed wild subjectivism of Early German Romanticism—but their attention to the book as both a material and conceptual, formal phenomenon, and their struggle with that tension, is nevertheless best described in this way.

After the heyday of particularly German prefacing around 1800—which was, at the same time, the era of its suspect status—and just after Hegel, Heine rehabilitated the prose preface precisely because it can be formally distinguished from his lyric. In 1837, in the second preface to *Buch der Lieder* [Book of Songs], he asserted (amusingly, for any historian of the preface in the long eighteenth century) that prefaces ("Vorworte") in prose were more honest than ones in verse—despite the older accusations that the preface was a text type filled with disingenuous, hackneyed claims. Heine was no doubt aware of his witty inversion, and of his annexing of the preface to a poetological argument that itself has a long history: whether prose or poetry is more trustworthy. Within his work as a whole, and read alongside his other prefaces to this work, Heine's preface from 1837 is ironic—like the prefaces by Goethe, Jean Paul, and Hegel. The preface to the third, 1839 edition is preceded by verse, and the prose paragraph begins: "Das hätte ich alles sehr gut in Prosa sagen können"[11] [I could have put all of that in prose very well]. As Jocelyne Kolb points out, the fact that the above passage is a prose preface to a collection of poems is contradictory: "That contradiction ironizes the statement, but the irony does not come from the fact that Heine is 'lying' in prose while seeming to criticize 'lies' in verse. Rather, it is an irony of the kind one finds in *Buch der Lieder* between different moods and dictions."[12] Terry Pinkard has further suggested that Heine's irony is Hegelian in spirit—Heine was Hegel's pupil, after all.[13]

Be that as it may, prefacing petered out across European fiction as the nineteenth century progressed. It is not true to say that the preface became totally moribund from this time onward, but it undoubtedly became less prevalent, and less self-conscious of its paradoxical potential. Genette observes, citing names such as Austen, Flaubert, Zola, or Proust: "We see the preface, like all other overly obvious paratextual elements, carefully avoided as much as possible by those authors who are most closely associated with classical dignity and/or realistic transparency."[14] The London magazine *Literature* asserted in 1899 that "a few years ago prefaces 'went out'"—in a time during which Realism was the default mode.[15] And Annette Retsch declares of German prefaces (albeit from her small survey—see introduction) that we cannot say that the preface was any longer as "thematized" in the twentieth century as it had been in the past.[16]

However, Hans P. Gabriel notes that Berthold Auerbach and Adalbert Stifter not only prefaced their collections of short stories in the mid-nineteenth century; they did so self-reflexively. He interprets these prefaces, together with preliminary texts by Gottfried Keller, as an inherent impossibility—and yet the noteworthy contradiction, as he says (evoking Derrida's "Outwork, Prefacing" of 1972), is that they were written: as a textual necessity. To pre-inscribe in a preface, as a Realist author, the reality of the subsequent story-worlds in a collection of tales, and at the same time claim that the consequent narratives, being reflections of reality, would have come about regardless of an author's (preface writing) intervention, is paradoxical.[17] But Realist writers did not reflect on this particular irony themselves, if this irony is tenable at all—and the prefatory wit of Auerbach's that Gabriel emphasizes, for example, is rather unremarkable when compared to the more extreme prefatorial creativity less than half a century earlier. It is not so much that prefacing stopped, then, but that whether to preface—and how—ceased to concern and interest authors so much. Even in the invention of a new genre such as the "Dorfgeschichte" [village tale], for instance, prefacing was apparently not the foremost priority. Auerbach's collection *Schwarzwälder Dorfgeschichten* [Village Tales from the Black Forest] appeared as a book series from 1843 through to 1856, but the book of 1843 was in fact unprefaced; the preface was placed instead in the journal *Europa: Chronik einer gebildeten Welt* [Europe: Chronicle of an Educated World], in which Auerbach's first story, "Der Tolpatsch" [The Klutz], had been published the year before.[18] This preface is written as an open letter to J. E. Braun, and begins as an explanation of the preface—a journalistic preface to a journalistic preface—followed by the prefatorial text itself, entitled *Vorreden spart Nachreden*: a pun on prefaces relieving the author of both afterwords (in the plural form of what was by now an antiquated term, "Nachrede") and, if understood as a gerund, either repetition or even a potentially "backbiting" response ("Nachreden"). The following, proper prefatory part was finally printed before the *Dorfgeschichten* in the edition of 1857, once all the stories were complete and could be republished in their entirety. There is no hint here of an inherent prefatory problem, or of any noteworthy formal crisis or special prefatorial creativity, beyond a simple pun that was later omitted.

Around the same time as the preface returned to being prosaic, around 1850, it appears to have become more lexically stable, inasmuch as it was more consistently distinguished terminologically from an introduction. Friedrich Gerstäcker emphasizes the political currency of his narrative in the preface to his first volume of *Pfarre und Schule. Eine Dorfgeschichte* [Parish and School: A Village Tale] of 1849.[19] He does not wish to say much more preliminarily, continuing with the objection: "Ich bin aber kein Freund von langen Vorreden, die Einleitung mag daher den Leser auf den Schauplatz vorbereiten, und das Buch selbst ihm sagen, was er zu erwarten hat"[20] [But I am no friend of long prefaces, and so the introduction will set the scene for the reader, and the book itself will tell him what he may expect]. Stifter's first volume of *Bunte Steine. Ein Festgeschenk* [Colorful Stones: A Gift for a Special Occasion] of 1853 has both a "Vorrede" (also called a "Vorwort," according to the contents page) and an "Einleitung."[21] Its preface presents a conservative attitude after the failed revolution of March 1748, stressing the new values of modest literary ambition rather than grand ideas, and the importance of social order and cohesion, before progressing to the harmless matters ("harmlose Dinge") at hand, the stories set up by the introduction.[22] The introduction, therefore, takes on a similar function to Gerstäcker's, and is an immediate induction to the narratives which follow it rather than a commentary on the work's wider political and poetological significance.

The late twentieth and early twenty-first centuries marked the next major historical moment for the preface as a form, after the late eighteenth and early nineteenth centuries. In 1973, Stanisław Lem published a collection of introductions to fictitious future works.[23] This in part conformed to a tradition that had long been continuing after the period around 1800: Kierkegaard wrote prefaces to unwritten books (inspired by Hegel and Jean Paul, examined in chapters 2 and 3) and for Christmas 1872, just over one hundred years before Lem, Nietzsche presented to Cosima Wagner a handwritten volume solely comprising prefaces to unwritten books.[24] While prefacing as a self-aware and extraordinarily playful practice was the case for Kierkegaard, though, it was not embraced by Nietzsche; and it once again became a frequent ploy in Lem's work, and across postmodern metafiction. Dave Eggers begins his memoir from the year 2000, *A Heartbreaking Work of Staggering Genius*, with what he calls "Rules and Suggestions for the Enjoyment of This Book," the first of which declares: "There is no overwhelming need to read the preface."[25] He then supposes that rather than flicking over the preface, some might turn to it before reading the first page of the book, which outlines the rules: "If you have already read the preface, and wish you had not, we apologize. We should have told you sooner." Eggers's starting suggestion that ignoring the following preface is permissible, even preferable, is as confusing as it is amusing, the first line in the entire text. A twenty-two page preface follows; and to this are appended acknowledgments that take up a further seventeen pages.

It was this later Golden Age of prefacing, the mid-twentieth century onward, which gave rise to Heidegger and Derrida (and following him, Genette and Foucault), who have all problematized the preface and who were explored in the preceding chapters. So, too, has Giorgio Agamben made a problem out of the preface; for him the substantiation of purported truth and, textually, the execution of a whole work is perpetually deferred—like a prologue. In *Infancy and History* (1978), he contends: "Every written work can be regarded as the prologue (or rather, the broken cast) of a work never penned, and destined to remain so, because later works, which in turn will be the prologues or the molds of other absent works, represent only sketches or death masks."[26] Especially Jean Paul's and Hegel's prefaces prompted such late twentieth-century German and French intellectual thought on the preface as a form (although Agamben's philosophy, in Italian, is more Schlegelian). As revealed in chapters 2 and 3, the preface paradoxes of these great German writers are appropriated and recast by later authors, and underpin their common textual and conceptual concerns. The second half of the twentieth century, incidentally, also witnessed the conception of the "preface paradox" of *analytic* philosophy, by D. C. Makinson in 1965.[27] But this was intended only as an intellectual puzzle, and never became a *performance* in print—no analytic philosopher's preface ponders the paradox of the preface—and its ongoing disciplinary discussion bears no relevance to the issues of philosophy's method and mediation through print that primarily preoccupied the European Romantics, and indeed post-Structuralist literary authors and "continental" philosophers, who followed suit.

Those writers who have problematized prefaces as pretexts to writing most playfully—who have rejected the preface as profane for their purpose, yet who have written one all the same—share a common approach, even character. And so the relationship between Goethe, Jean Paul, and Hegel, on the one hand, and the more recent theorists considered here, on the other, is not a mere story of inspiration or influence, or even simply a historical tale. There is a more absolute connection between authors as well: one of attitude. In 1909, Gilbert K. Chesterton wrote of George Bernard Shaw that many knew the author, "as a man who would write a very long preface even to a very short play. . . . He is indeed a very prefatory sort of person."[28] This description could likewise apply to Goethe, Jean Paul, or Hegel, if not more so; or to Derrida, say, and to many others. Hence it is worth pausing for a moment to consider what Chesterton means by a prefatorial individual. In a comical line of reasoning, he states that Shaw is so quick-witted that he is long-winded: he has something worth saying about everything—including, perhaps, the preface when writing a preface. Goethe, Jean Paul, Hegel, and others are indeed encyclopedic and copious in their writings (and verbose, in the cases of Jean Paul and Hegel). However, we could equally well turn Chesterton's formulation around: when writing a lot, we become more inclined to say something about everything—not least the preface when writing a preface. And even more pertinent to self-referencing when prefacing is Chesterton's idea that for a prefatory character, "the philosophy of facts is anterior to the facts themselves."[29] This implies that an author who concerns himself with the preface and its form at any length thinks not just imaginatively, but philosophically as well, in search for conceptual ground. Or such philosophical thought, as we might say, entails as much as it emerges from prefatorial thinking.

Of course, the preface is not the only form that has been plucked from print culture and appropriated for a radical reconception of writing and thought, as was noted in the introduction to this book. Another such form, most similar to the preface and also popular around 1800, was the anecdote. Akin to the preface, the anecdote was fragmentary, seemingly trivial, and yet of fundamental importance to understanding. Like the preface, it flourished in the period's climate against pedantry, and in a craze for historicism. In his treatise on the scourge of pedantry in the eighteenth century, Johann Georg Schlosser supposes that: "Man will, dünkt mich, nicht sowohl Wissenschaften wissen; als nur Anecdoten. . . . Wahrscheinlich wird man bald jeden Gelehrten einen Pedanten nennen, der keine Anecdoten weiß"[30] [It seems to me that one does not so much want to know about the sciences, as know merely anecdotes . . . soon any scholar who does not know an anecdote will be called a pedant]. The sense of the word "anecdote" now extended from meaning a piece of secret, private history to a revelatory episode with broad applicability, accessible to all—and yet an opportunity for uncovering deeper meaning. Over in the English-speaking world, the "Preface" to Maria Edgeworth's *Castle Rackrent* (1800) reads:

> The Prevailing taste of the public for anecdote has been censured and ridiculed by critics who aspire to the character of superior wisdom; but if we consider it in a proper point of view, this taste is an incontestable proof of the good sense and profoundly philosophic temper of the present times. Of the numbers who study, or at least who read history, how few derive any advantage from their labours![31]

Literature around 1800, especially historical fiction, was self-consciously anecdotal in opposition to traditional scholarly works, particularly learned histories. And in the late twentieth century, an intellectual defense of piecemeal, anecdotal analysis in literary historiography emerged in the method of New Historicism—in the same half-century as playful prefacing about prefacing of the type so current around 1800, too, became popular. For Catherine Gallagher and Stephen Greenblatt, "the undisciplined anecdote appealed to those of us who wanted to interrupt the Big Stories."[32] The parallel of the anecdote and the preface, and the possible common cause of their trajectories, is that avant-garde literary, philosophical, and indeed academic thought all draws special attention to the unconventional formal, *written* expression of its ideas as much as to those ideas themselves. In doing so, it declares that its reinvented form overcomes a conventional type of text that it presents as reductive—or as so ridiculous that it is apparently no longer fit for purpose. Such arguments and textual innovations were plentiful in the late eighteenth and early nineteenth centuries, and they have remained productive since. Then, as now, what comprises a book materially enables mind games as much as it gives expression to them.

ACKNOWLEDGMENTS

This book is an abridged and revised version of my DPhil dissertation, defended at the University of Oxford in 2014. The project has been supported at its various stages by the United Kingdom's Arts and Humanities Research Council; Jesus College, Oxford; and the Forschungszentrum für Klassische Deutsche Philosophie [Research Centre for Classical German Philosophy] at the Ruhr University Bochum, Germany. Oliver Lubrich appointed me to the University of Bern, Switzerland, as I neared completion of my doctorate. Henk de Berg and Michael Perraudin supported my subsequent move to Sheffield, and my research here.

There are many people I would like to thank: not least my teacher of German literature early on in my university career, Katrin Kohl; and above all my doctoral supervisor, Kevin Hilliard. To the following I also owe a debt of sincere gratitude: Anne Simon, a supportive reader; my doctoral examiners, Charlie Louth and Angus Nicholls; Nicola Kaminski and Thomas Nehrlich, for rigorous discussion; and the kind and extraordinarily patient reviewers at the North American Goethe Society, especially Jane Brown and Karin Schutjer. I am grateful to Greg Clingham at Bucknell University Press for his guidance, and to Sam Brawand and Michael Durnin for their copy editing. General thanks are due to my colleagues at the Universities of Oxford, Bochum, Bern, and now Sheffield, too, and to my good friend throughout it all—Ellie Browne.

For Novalis, a novel ("Roman") was a life, as a book. Thus he reasons: "Jedes Leben hat ein Motto, einen Titel—einen Verleger—eine Vorrede—Einleitung—Text—*Noten*—etc. oder kann es haben" [every life has a motto, a title—a publisher—a preface—introduction—text—*notes*—etc., or can have them] (Novalis, *Schriften: Die Werke Friedrich von Hardenbergs*, vol. 2, *Das Philosophische Werk I*, ed. Richard Samuel, 2nd ed. [Stuttgart: Kohlhammer, 1965], 599). I have omitted the original preface to this work about prefaces (that in turn reflect on their own form), which reads like a moment of postgraduate provocation: that juvenile exercise of wanting to be examined and pass into the profession, yet to do so as some sort of academic pariah. In a Romantic mood during that rebellious phase, I drafted and then suppressed a fictional preface. So I find Novalis's line quite apt. But—unsurprisingly for the era around 1800—he omits the "dedication" from his catalog of what we now call *paratextual* terms. I want to emphasize that textual convention here. I may not have written a novel, but an academic book is similar not only in assuming a life of its own, or being part of one's life, but also in taking its toll on the lives of others. The present monograph, then, is for my parents and sister, who have borne the brunt: Liz, Graham, and Heather Williams.

NOTES

Introduction

1. Jean Paul, *Sämtliche Werke*, vol. 1.2, *Die Unsichtbare Loge*, ed. Preußische Akademie der Wissenschaften and Eduard Berend (Weimar: Böhlau, 1927), 37. References to Jean Paul's *Sämtliche Werke*, ed. Eduard Berend et al., vols. 1.1–1.17, 2.10.1, and 3.3 ([Weimar: Böhlau, 1927–] hereafter cited SW, by volume and page).

2. Unless otherwise noted, all translations are mine.

3. See Rudolf Wittkower, *Allegory and the Migration of Symbols* (London: Thames and Hudson, 1987), 45–74.

4. Stephen Fennell, *Gleich und Gleich. Die Messianik bei Jean Paul* (Würzburg: Königshausen und Neumann, 1996), 67; Magnus Wieland, *Vexierzüge. Jean Pauls Digressionspoetik* (Hanover: Wehrhahn, 2013), 321.

5. Michael Camille, *Image on the Edge: The Margins of Medieval Art* (London: Reaktion, 1992), 14.

6. Fennell, *Gleich und Gleich*, 66–68.

7. See start of Book 6: "Now will I woo the rustic muse on slender reed." Virgil, *Eclogues. Georgics. Aeneid I–VI*, ed. and trans. H. Rushton Fairclough and G. P. Goold (Cambridge, MA: Harvard University Press, 1999), 60–61.

8. Martin Opitz, *Gesammelte Werke*, vol. 4.1, *Die Werke von Ende 1626 bis 1630*, ed. George Schulz-Behrend (Stuttgart: Anton Hiersemann, 1990), 67.

9. Walther Rehm, *Späte Studien* (Bern and Munich: Francke, 1964), 7–96, see 13 and 15.

10. René Wellek, *A History of Modern Criticism*, vol. 2, *The Romantic Age* (New Haven, CT: Yale University Press, 1955), 100–109, see 101 and 108.

11. René Wellek, "The Concept of Romanticism in Literary History," in *Concepts of Criticism*, ed. Stephen G. Nichols (New Haven, CT: Yale University Press, 1963), 129–198. For discussion on the delineation of German Romanticism(s) in both Anglo-American and German scholarship: Arndt Bohm, "Goethe and the Romantics," in *The Literature of German Romanticism*, ed. Dennis F. Mahoney (Rochester, NY: Camden House, 2004), 35–60; Angus Nicholls, *Goethe's Concept of the Daemonic: After the Ancients* (Rochester, NY: Camden House, 2006), 106–109; Ricarda Schmidt, "From Early to Late Romanticism," in *The Cambridge Companion to German Romanticism*, ed. Nicholas Saul (Cambridge: Cambridge University Press, 2009), 21–39.

12. Peter Küpper, "Author ad Lectorem. Vorreden im 18. Jahrhundert: Ein Forschungsvorschlag," in *Festschrift für Rainer Gruenter*, ed. Bernhard Fabian (Heidelberg:

Winter, 1978), 86–95, see 87; Sven-Aage Jørgensen, "Warum und zu welchem Ende schreibt man eine Vorrede?" *Text und Kontext* 3 (1976): 3–20, see 5, among others.

13. Friedrich von Hagedorn, *Sämmtliche Poetische Werke* (Hamburg: Bohn, 1769), vol. 1, 208.

14. Peter-Henning Haischer, *Historizität und Klassizität. Christoph Martin Wieland und die Werkausgabe im 18. Jahrhundert* (Heidelberg: Winter, 2011), 94.

15. E.T.A. Hoffmann, *Briefwechsel*, vol. 1, *Königsberg bis Leipzig, 1794–1814*, ed. Friedrich Schnapp (Munich: Winkler, 1967), 401.

16. Anne Simon, "Product, Packaging and Purpose: The Recycling of the Reyßbuch (1584–1659)," *Oxford German Studies* 26 (1997): 73–100; Simon, "Publishers' Prefaces: The Sixteenth-Century Reader's Digest?" *German Life and Letters* 49, no. 4 (1996): 387–404.

17. Seán M. Williams, "C. F. Gellert als Vorredner des Genies. Autorschaft um 1750," in *Authorschaft. Reflexionen und Lektüren einer literaturwissenschaftlichen Kategorie*, ed. Matthias Schaffrick and Marcus Willand (Berlin and New York: de Gruyter, 2014), 333–362.

18. Marie-Kristin Hauke, "Die Kunst des Klimperns. Buchhändlerische Werbestrategien und die Kommerzialisierung des Buchmarkts am Ende des 18. Jahrhunderts," *Das achtzehnte Jahrhundert. Zeitschrift der Deutschen Gesellschaft für die Erforschung des achtzehnten Jahrhunderts* 32, no. 2 (2008): 226–239.

19. Steven Tötösy de Zepetnek, *The Social Dimensions of Fiction: On the Rhetoric and Function of Prefacing Novels in the Nineteenth-Century Canadas* (Braunschweig: Vieweg, 1993), 6. For a review of terms in German, French, and English, see also Tötösy de Zepetnek, "Taxonomy of the Preface and Its Rhetoric in English, French, and German," *Neohelicon: Acta comparationis litterarum universarum* 37, no. 1 (2010): 75–90, see 76.

20. Annette Retsch, *Paratext und Textanfang* (Würzburg: Königshausen und Neumann, 2000), 52. In total, Retsch analyzed fifty novels across the eighteenth, nineteenth, and twentieth centuries.

21. Gérard Genette, *Paratexts: Thresholds of Interpretation*, trans. Jane E. Lewin (Cambridge: Cambridge University Press, 1997), 162.

22. Friedrich Gottlieb Klopstock, *Werke und Briefe: Historisch-kritische Ausgabe*, vol. 3.1.1, *Geistliche Lieder*, ed. Laura Bolognesi (Berlin and New York: de Gruyter, 2010).

23. Johann Friedrich Flatt, *Beyträge zur christlichen Dogmatik und Moral und zur Geschichte derselben* (Tübingen: Jakob Friedrich Heerbrandt, 1792); and Carl Philipp Conz, *Abhandlungen für die Geschichte und das Eigenthümliche der späteren Stoischen Philosophie nebst einem Versuche über Christliche, Kantische und Stoische Moral* (Tübingen: Jakob Friedrich Heerbrandt, 1794).

24. Christoph Martin Wieland, *Geheime Geschichte des Philosophen Peregrinus Proteus* (Leipzig: Göschen, 1791), vol. 1, 13.

25. Francis Paul Greene, "Preface, Vorwort, Vorrede: Jean Paul and E.T.A. Hoffmann," *New German Review: A Journal of Germanic Studies* 15–16 (1999): 6–22, see 8.

26. Bruno Markwardt, *Geschichte der deutschen Poetik* (Berlin: de Gruyter, 1964), vol. 4, 491.

27. Bärbel Schwitzgebel, *Noch nicht genug der Vorrede: Zur Vorrede volksprachiger Sammlungen von Exempeln, Fabeln, Sprichwörtern und Schwänken des 16. Jahrhunderts* (Tübingen: Niemeyer, 1996), 2.

28. Ernst Weber, *Die poetologische Selbstreflexion im deutschen Roman des. 18 Jahrhunderts. Zur Theorie und Praxis von "Roman," "Historie," und pragmatischen "Roman"* (Stutt-

gart: Kohlhammer, 1974); Hans Ehrenzeller, *Studien zur Romanvorrede von Grimmelshausen bis Jean Paul* (Bern: Francke, 1955).

29. Hubert Gersch, "Ein Sonderfall im Zeitalter der Vorreden-Poetik des Romans: Grimmelshausens vorwortloser 'Simplicissimus,'" in *Rezeption und Produktion zwischen 1570 und 1730. Festschrift für Günther Weydt zum 65. Geburtstag*, ed. Wolfdietrich Rasch, Hans Geulen, and Klaus Haberkamm (Bern and Munich: Francke, 1972), 267–284. Stefanie Stockhorst offers other examples of prefaceless novels of this earlier period, but in the main she stresses the preface's typical presence, as the primary place of poetic theory: *Reformpoetik. Kodifizierte Genustheorie des Barock und alternative Normenbildung in poetologischen Paratexten* (Tübingen: Niemeyer, 2008), 22.

30. Hermann Riefstahl, "Dichter und Publikum in der ersten Hälfte des 18. Jahrhunderts." DPhil diss., Frankfurt am Main, 1934, 5.

31. Stockhorst, *Reformpoetik*, 23.

32. Johann Gottfried Schnabel, *Der im Irr-Garten der Liebe herum taumelnde Cavalier* (Warnungsstadt: 1738), 2. See also Weber, *Poetologische Selbstreflexion im deutschen Roman*, 38.

33. Johann Arnold Ebert, *Episteln und vermischte Gedichte* (Hamburg: C. E. Bohn, 1789), a4.

34. Ehrenzeller, *Romanvorrede*, 17–18.

35. Deborah N. Losse, *Sampling the Book: Renaissance Prologues and the French "Conteurs"* (Lewisburg, PA: Bucknell University Press, 1994), 79. Clara Gebert suggests that in early seventeenth-century English letters, writers "become satirical," in "prefatory writing": *An Anthology of Elizabethan Dedications and Prefaces*, 2nd ed. (New York: Russell and Russell, 1966), 26.

36. Losse, *Sampling the Book*, 12.

37. Genette, *Paratexts*, 292.

38. Ibid., 229–236, see 235.

39. Weber, *Poetologische Selbstreflexion im deutschen Roman*, 85.

40. Ibid., 93.

41. Christian Ludwig Liscow, *Schriften*, ed. Carl Muchler (Berlin: Himburgische Buchhandlung, 1806), vol. 1, 381.

42. Luise Gottsched, *Die Pietisterey im Fischbein-Rocke, oder die Doctormäßige Frau in einem Lust-Spiele vorgestellet* (Rostock, 1736), 2.

43. Ehrenzeller, *Romanvorrede*, 8.

44. Losse, *Sampling the Book*, 103.

45. Genette, *Paratexts*, 164.

46. Henry Fielding, *Amelia*, ed. Martin C. Battestin (Oxford: Clarendon, 1983), 3. The dedication is also self-consciously short and explicitly notes its own diversion from dedicatory convention, since Fielding is apparently wary of the form's false flattery.

47. Ibid., 15.

48. Ibid., 406.

49. Weber, *Poetologische Selbstreflexion im deutschen Roman*, 20.

50. Ibid., 97.

51. Genette, *Paratexts*, 172.

52. Uwe Wirth, *Die Geburt des Autors aus dem Geist der Herausgeberfiktion. Editoriale Rahmung im Roman um 1800: Wieland, Goethe, Brentano, Jean Paul und E.T.A. Hoffmann*

(Munich: Fink, 2008), 92. See also Hans-Jürgen Ansorge, *Art und Funktion der Vorrede im Roman: Von der Mitte des 18. Jahrhunderts bis zum Ende des 19. Jahrhunderts* (Würzburg: Gugel, 1969), 168; Elvire Steppacher, "Rederpein und Mordgelüst: Neues zur Vorrede des 'Siebenkäs,'" in *Critica Poeticae. Lesarten zur deutschen Literatur*, ed. Andreas Gößling and Stefan Nienhaus (Würzburg: Königshausen und Neumann, 1992), 159–170, see 169.

53. Weber, *Poetologische Selbstreflexion im deutschen Roman*, 20 and 28–30.

54. Ehrenzeller, *Romanvorrede*, 169.

55. Anna Richards, "The Era of Sensibility and the Novel of Self-Fashioning," in *German Literature of the Eighteenth Century: The Enlightenment and Sensibility*, ed. Barbara Becker-Cantarino (Rochester, NY: Camden House, 2005), 223–243, see 225.

56. Johann Gottfied Schnabel, *Insel Felsenburg*, ed. Volker Meid and Ingeborg Springer-Strand (Stuttgart: Reclam, 2006), 13.

57. William Wordsworth and Samuel Taylor Coleridge, *Lyrical Ballads*, rev. ed., ed. R. L. Brett (London: Methuen, 1965), 243.

58. Ibid., 244.

59. Friedrich Schlegel, *Kritische Friedrich-Schlegel-Ausgabe*, vol. 2, *Charakteristiken und Kritiken I (1796–1802)*, ed. Hans Eichner (Paderborn: Schöningh, 1967), 404.

60. August Wilhelm Schlegel and Friedrich Schlegel, "Vorerinnerung," *Athenaeum* 1, no. 1 (1798), iii–iv.

61. Genette, *Paratexts*, 161–293.

62. Ibid., 2.

63. Ibid., 407.

64. Ibid., 293.

65. Frieder von Ammon and Herfried Vögel, eds., *Die Pluralisierung des Paratextes in der Frühen Neuzeit* (Berlin: LIT, 2008).

66. Georg Christoph Lichtenberg, *Schriften und Briefe*, vol. 1, *Südelbücher*, ed. Wolfgang Promies (Munich: Hanser, 1968), 212.

67. Gottlieb Wilhelm Rabener, *Sämmtliche Schriften*, vol. 2, *Satyren* (Leipzig: Dykische Buchhandlung, 1777), 177.

68. Ibid., 176.

69. Ibid., 179.

70. On Rabener's paratexts and autonomy, see also Nadja Reinhard, *Moral und Ironie bei Gottlieb Wilhelm Rabener: Paratext und Palimpsest in den "Satyrischen Schriften"* (Göttingen: Wallstein, 2013).

71. Rabener, *Satyren*, 185.

72. Ibid.

73. Friedrich Justus Riedel, *Sämmtliche Schriften*, vol. 1, *Zehn Satyren, nebst drey Anhängen* (Vienna: Kurzbeck, 1787), 332.

74. Anthony Grafton, *The Footnote: A Curious History* (London: Faber and Faber, 1997), 119–20. For explorations of footnoting in German writing specifically, often with mention of Rabener and Jean Paul: Bernhard Metz and Sabine Zubarik, eds., *Am Rande bemerkt. Anmerkungspraktiken in literarischen Texten* (Berlin: Kulturverlag Kadmos, 2008); Harald Stang, *Einleitung—Fußnote—Kommentar. Fingierte Formen wissenschaftlicher Darstellung als Gestaltungselemente moderner Erzählkunst* (Bielefeld: Aisthesis, 1992), 21–42; and Alexander Košenina, *Der gelehrte Narr. Gelehrtensatire seit der Aufklärung* (Göttingen: Wallstein, 2003), 268–269, among others.

75. Grafton, *Footnote*, 107–108.

76. Peter J. Burgard, *Idioms of Uncertainty: Goethe and the Essay* (University Park: University of Pennsylvania Press, 1992), 35–36.

77. Ibid., 22.

78. Giancarlo Maiorino, *First Pages: A Poetics of Titles* (University Park: Pennsylvania State University Press, 2008), 3; Frank Kermode, *The Sense of an Ending: Studies in the Theory of Fiction*, 2nd ed. (Oxford: Oxford University Press, 2000); A. D. Nuttall, *Openings: Narrative Beginnings from the Epic to the Novel* (Oxford: Clarendon, 1992).

79. See Georg Stanitzek, "Texte, Paratexte, in Medien. Einleitung," in *Paratexte in Literatur, Film, Fernsehen*, ed. Georg Stanitzek and Klaus Kreimeier (Berlin: Akademie, 2004), 3–20. Stanitzek is right to emphasize that Genette, unlike Derrida, employs the paratext to a hermeneutic end. But he takes Genette's structuralist categorization too seriously, understanding it in too systematic a way—albeit a systematic approach that emphasizes a dialogic, not ontological relationship between paratext and work. See also Remigius Bunia, *Faltungen. Fiktion, Erzählen, Medien* (Berlin: Erich Smidt, 2007); Till Dembeck, *Texte rahmen: Grenzregionen literarischer Werke im 18. Jahrhundert (Gottsched, Wieland, Moritz, Jean Paul)* (Berlin and New York: de Gruyter, 2007); and Wirth, *Geburt des Autors*. On Wirth, see too "'Das Vorwort als performative, paratextuelle und parergonale Rahmung," in *Rhetorik. Figuration und Performanz*, ed. Jürgen Fohrmann (Stuttgart: Metzler, 2004), 603–628; and for a theoretical reading of a popular prefatory metaphor of the period around 1800—the antechamber—see Wirth, "Paratext und Text als Übergangszone," in *Raum und Bewegung in der Literatur. Die Literaturwissenschaft und der Spatial Turn*, ed. Wolfgang Hallet and Birgit Neumann (Bielefeld: Transcript Verlag 2009), 167–177.

80. Niklas Luhmann, *Die Kunst der Gesellschaft* (Frankfurt am Main: Suhrkamp, 1995), 393–507; and Niels Werber, *Literatur als System. Zur Ausdifferenzierung literarischer Kommunikation* (Opladen: Westdeutscher Verlag, 1992). See also Hans Esselborn's study on systems theory and Jean Paul's footnotes, another paratextual subcategory: "Niklas Luhmanns Kommunikation mit Jean Paul in Fußnoten. Die Modernität der Beobachtungen und Gedanken des Dichters," *Wirkendes Wort* 63 (2013): 267–296.

81. Marianne Willems, "Wider die Kompensationsthese. Zur Funktion der Genieästhetik der Sturm-und-Drang Bewegung," *Euphorion. Zeitschrift für Literaturgeschichte* 93, no. 2 (1999): 1–40.

82. Nicholas Saul mentions a "drastic decline in the number of book-dedications" around 1800 in Germany: "Aesthetic Humanism (1790–1830)," in *The Cambridge History of German Literature*, ed. Helen Watanabe-O'Kelly (Cambridge: Cambridge University Press, 1997), 202–271, see 210. See also Ulrich Maché, "Author and Patron: On the Function of Dedications in Seventeenth-Century German Literature," in *Literary Culture in the Holy Roman Empire, 1555–1720*, ed. James A. Parente Jr., Richard Erich Schade, and George C. Schoolfield (London and Chapel Hill: University of North Carolina Press, 1991), 195–205. The pattern was similar across the channel: "At no time, and in no community, has the dedication of books been carried to a greater extravagance than it was at the close of the sixteenth, and the beginning of the seventeenth century in England," writes Edmund Gosse, "Elizabethan Dedications of Books," *Harper's Monthly Magazine* 105, no. 626 (1902): 165–172, see 165.

83. Johann Georg Hamann, *Sämtliche Werke*, vol. 2, *Schriften über Philosophie, Philologie, Kritik, 1758–1763*, ed. Josef Nadler (Vienna: Herder, 1949), 59–60.

84. Christian Dietrich Grabbe, *Werke*, vol. 2, *Dramen II, Gedichte, Prosa*, ed. Roy C. Cowen (Darmstadt: Wissenchaftliche Buchgesellschaft, 1977), 491.

85. Horst Jesse, "König Ludwig I. von Bayern und Johann Wolfgang von Goethe," *Goethe-Jahrbuch* 116 (1999): 300–305.

86. Azade Seyhan, *Romanticism and Its Discontents: The Critical Legacy of German Romanticism* (Berkeley: University of California Press, 1992), 136. See also Ernst Behler and Jochen Hörisch, eds., *Die Aktualität der Frühromantik* (Paderborn: Schöningh, 1987); Winfried Menninghaus, *Unendliche Verdopplung. Die frühromantische Grundlegung der Kunsttheorie im Begriff absoluter Selbstreflexion* (Frankfurt am Main: Suhrkamp, 1987); Ernst Behler, *Irony and the Discourse of Modernity* (Seattle: University of Washington Press, 1990).

87. Tilottama Rajan, *The Dark Interpreter: The Discourse of Romanticism* (Ithaca, NY: Cornell University Press, 1980), 15.

88. Alice A. Kuzniar, *Delayed Endings: Nonclosure in Novalis and Hölderlin* (Athens: University of Georgia Press, 1987), 2.

89. Ibid., 5.

90. Burgard, *Idioms of Uncertainty*, 79.

91. The Roman rhetorician Quintilian surveys definitions of Greek and Latin rhetoric in *The Orator's Education*, repeatedly concluding throughout that previous rhetoricians had emphasized persuasion as rhetoric's ultimate function, whereas he privileges speaking well. Quintilian, *The Orator's Education*, ed. and trans. Donald A. Russell (Cambridge, MA: Harvard University Press, 2002), vols. 1 and 4.

92. For a definition of the "exordium" across rhetorical sources, see Heinrich Lausberg, *Handbuch der literarischen Rhetorik. Eine Grundlegung der Literaturwissenschaft* (Munich: M. Hüber, 1960), vol. 1, 150–163.

93. Weber, *Poetologische Selbstreflexion im deutschen Roman*, 38.

94. Ehrenzeller, *Romanvorrede*, 20.

95. Ibid., 30–31.

96. Dirk Niefanger, "*Sfumato*: Traditionsverhalten in Paratexten zwischen 'Barock' und 'Aufklärung.'" *Zeitschrift für Literaturwissenschaft und Linguistik* 25, no. 2 (1995): 94–118, see 118.

97. Peter D. Krause, *Unbestimmte Rhetorik. Friedrich Schlegel und die Redekunst um 1800* (Tübingen: Niemeyer, 2001); Dietmar Till, *Transformationen der Rhetorik: Untersuchungen zum Wandel der Rhetoriktheorie im 17. und 18. Jahrhundert* (Tübingen: Niemeyer, 2004); and Björn Hambsch, *", . . . ganz andre Beredsamkeit": Transformation antiker und moderner Rhetorik bei Johann Gottfried Herder* (Tübingen: Niemeyer, 2004).

98. Antony Ashley Cooper [Third Earl of Shaftesbury], *Characteristics of Men, Manners, Opinions, Times*, ed. Lawrence E. Klein (Cambridge: Cambridge University Press, 1999), 147.

99. Olaf Kramer, *Goethe und die Rhetorik* (Berlin and New York: de Gruyter, 2010).

100. This term was coined by Walter Jens and is discussed at length by Till, *Transformationen der Rhetorik*, 26–32. John H. Smith evokes it specifically in his study of Hegel's rhetoric, and especially Hegel's preface to *Phänomenologie des Geistes* [Phenomenology of Spirit] (1807): *The Spirit and Its Letter: Traces of Rhetoric in Hegel's Philosophy of Bildung* (Ithaca, NY: Cornell University Press, 1988), 4.

101. Kevin Dunn, *Pretexts of Authority: The Rhetoric of Authorship in the Renaissance Preface* (Stanford, CA: Stanford University Press, 1994), x.

102. Aristotle, *The "Art" of Rhetoric*, ed. and trans. John Henry Freese (Cambridge, MA: Harvard University Press, 1926), 434–435 (3.14).

103. Dunn, *Pretexts of Authority*, 1.

104. Quintilian, *Orator's Education*, vol. 2, 206–7 (4.1).

105. Christian Fürchtegott Gellert, *Lustspiele* (Leipzig: Johann Wendler, 1747), 4.

106. Hagedorn, *Sämmtliche Poetische Werke*, vol. 1, xxi.

107. Christian Fürchtegott Gellert, *Gesammelte Schriften. Kritische, kommentierte Ausgabe*, vol. 2, *Geistliche Oden und Lieder*, ed. Heidi John (Berlin and New York: de Gruyter, 1997), 109.

108. Gellert, *Lustspiele*, 4.

109. On the Early Enlightenment's intellectual sparring culture: Martin Gierl, *Pietismus und Aufklärung. Theologische Polemik und die Kommunikationsreform der Wissenschaft am Ende des 17. Jahrhunderts* (Göttingen: Vandenhoeck and Ruprecht, 1997).

110. Christoph Martin Wieland, *Wielands Werke. Historisch-Kritische Ausgabe*, vol. 9.1, *Sokrates mainonemos . . . , Der Neue Amadis . . . , Januar 1770—Mai 1772*, ed. Hans-Peter Nowitzki (Berlin and New York: de Gruyter, 2008), 416.

111. Ibid.

112. Till, *Transformationen der Rhetorik*, 146–181.

113. Gottlieb Wilhelm Rabener, "Der Autor, neuntes Stück," *Belustigungen des Verstandes und des Witzes* (1744): 325–338, see 333.

114. Rabener, "Der Autor, zehntes Stück," *Belustigungen des Verstandes und des Witzes* (1744): 446–461, see 459.

115. Johann Matthias Dreyer, *Schöne Spielwerke beym Wein, Punsch, Bischof und Krambambuli. Trinksprüche oder Gesundheiten und einige Epigramme* (Hamburg and Leipzig, 1763), 2.

116. Stephen Boyd, "Cervantes's Exemplary Prologue," in *A Companion to Cervantes's "Novelas ejemplares,"* ed. Stephen Boyd (Woodbridge, England: Tamesis, 2005), 47–68.

117. Laurence Sterne, *The Florida Edition of the Works of Laurence Sterne*, vol. 1, *The Life and Opinions of Tristram Shandy, Gentleman*, ed. Melvyn New and Joan New (Gainesville: University Presses of Florida, 1978), 235.

118. Johann Georg Heinzmann, *Appell an meine Nation: Über die Pest der deutschen Literatur* (Bern: Heinzmann, 1795), 72.

119. Theodor Gottlieb von Hippel, *Lebensläufe nach aufsteigender Linie nebst Beylagen A, B, C*, vol. 3 (Berlin: Voß, 1781), 234.

120. Heinzmann, *Appell an meine Nation*, 64.

121. Heinrich Bosse, "Gelehrte und Gebildete—die Kinder des 1. Standes," *Das achtzehnte Jahrhundert. Zeitschrift der Deutschen Gesellschaft für die Erforschung des achtzehnten Jahrhunderts* 32, no. 1 (2008): 13–37.

122. Friedrich Schiller, *Werke und Briefe in zwölf Bänden*, vol. 2, *Dramen I: Die Räuber, Fiesko, Kabale und Liebe, Kleine Dramen*, ed. Gerhard Kluge (Frankfurt am Main: Deutscher Klassiker Verlag, 1988), 19 and 177.

123. Alexander Košenina, "Bilder und Gegenbilder des Philologen zwischen Aufklärung und Romantik," *Zeitschrift für deutsche Philologie* 124, no. 2 (2005): 161–179.

124. Schiller, *Dramen I*, 557.

125. Ibid.

126. Friedrich Ast, *Grundlinien der Grammatik, Hermeneutik und Kritik* (Landshut: Jos. Thomann, 1808), 180.

127. Novalis, *Schriften: Die Werke Friedrich von Hardenbergs*, vol. 3, *Das philosophische Werk II*, ed. Richard Samuel, 2nd ed. (Stuttgart: Kohlhammer, 1968), 361.

128. Ibid.

129. Ibid.

130. Clifford Siskin and William Warner, "This Is Enlightenment: An Invitation in the Form of an Argument," in *This Is Enlightenment*, ed. Clifford Siskin and William Warner (Chicago: Chicago University Press, 2010), 2–34, see 7.

131. Ibid., 11.

132. Clifford Siskin and William Warner, "If This Is Enlightenment, Then What Is Romanticism?" *European Romantic Review* 22, no. 3 (2011): 281–291, see 285.

133. Jochen Hörisch, "Des Lesens Überfluss oder: Warum ist Selbstbewusstsein DAS Thema um 1800?," in *Literatur, Wissenschaft und Wissen seit der Epochenschwelle um 1800*, ed. Thomas Klinkert (Berlin and New York: de Gruyter, 2008), 35–52, see 41.

134. Ehrenzeller, *Romanvorrede*, 11.

135. Genette, *Paratexts*, 164.

136. A. K. Gavrilov, "Techniques of Reading in Classical Antiquity," *Classical Quarterly* 47, no. 1 (1997): 56–73, see 69. See also Bernard M. W. Knox, "Silent Reading in Antiquity" (1968), *Greek, Roman and Byzantine Studies* 9, no. 4 (2003): 421–435; and M. F. Burnyeat, "Postscript on Silent Reading," *Classical Quarterly* 47, no. 1 (1997): 74–76.

137. Friedrich Schlegel, *Charakteristiken und Kritiken*, 332.

138. Andrew Piper, *Dreaming in Books: The Making of the Bibliographic Imagination in the Romantic Age* (Chicago: Chicago University Press, 2009), 4.

139. Weber, *Poetologische Selbstreflexion im deutschen Roman*, 40.

140. Edwin Zellweker, *Prolog und Epilog im deutschen Drama. Ein Beitrag zur Geschichte deutscher Dichtung* (Leipzig and Vienna: Franz Deuticke, 1906), 92.

141. Ibid., 93.

142. For others, see Goethe, *Sämtliche Werke. Briefe, Tagebücher und Gespräche*, vol. 1.6, *Der Groß-Cophta/ Der Bürgergeneral/ Pandora /Dramen, 1791–1832*, ed. Dieter Borchmeyer (Frankfurt am Main: Deutscher Klassiker Verlag, 1993), 873–919. References to Goethe's *Sämtliche Werke*, gen. ed. Friedmar Apel et al., 40 vols. (1987–1999) (hereafter cited as FA, by volume and page number).

143. Ehrenzeller, *Romanvorrede*, 14–15. Genette also observes this phenomenon within European prefaces and further specifies apologies about a preface, in a preface, as attempts to excuse the following: prefatory length, dullness, irrelevance, uselessness, presumptuousness, hypocrisy and embellishment (*Paratexts*, 231).

144. Schiller, *Dramen I*, 165.

145. Riedel, *Zehn Satyren*, 4.

146. Ibid., 5.

147. Jacob Fries, *System der Philosophie als evidente Wissenschaft* (Leipzig: Johann Conrad Hinrichs, 1804), xiv.

148. Immanuel Kant, *Gesammelte Schriften*, vol. 4, *Kritik der reinen Vernunft (1. Auflage), Prolegomena . . .*, ed. Königlich Preußische Akademie der Wissenschaften (Berlin: Reimer, 1911), 261.

149. Ibid., 274.

150. Immanuel Kant, *Gesammelte Schriften*, vol. 3, *Kritik der reinen Vernunft (2. Auflage)*, ed. Königlich Preußische Akademie der Wissenschaften (Berlin: Reimer, 1904), 27.

151. Johann Gottlieb Fichte, *Gesamtausgabe*, vol. 2.6, *Nachgelassene Schriften, 1800–1803*, ed. Reinhard Lauth and Hans Gliwitzky (Stuttgart: Frommann, 1983), 135.

152. Birgit Sandkaulen, "Fürwahrhalten ohne Gründe. Eine Provokation philosophischen Denkens," *Deutsche Zeitschrift für Philosophie* 57, no. 2 (2009): 259–272.

153. Carl A. Eschenmayer, *Die Philosophie in ihrem Übergang zur Nichtphilosophie* (Erlangen: Waltersche Buchhandlung, 1803).

Chapter One Goethe

1. Ulrike Landfester, "'(Ist fortzusetzen.)': Goethes Poetik des Paratextes," in *Die Pluralisierung des Paratextes in der Frühen Neuzeit. Theorie, Formen, Funktionen*, ed. Frieder von Ammon and Herfried Vögel (Münster: LIT, 2008), 375–397, see 378–382.

2. Christoph Martin Wieland, *Sämmtliche Werke*, vol. 38, *Das Hexameron von Rosenhain* (Leipzig: Göschen, 1805), 174.

3. See also Georg-Michael Schulz, "Die älteren Brüder Schlegel und ihr *Buch ohne Titel*. Eine Buchgeschichtliche Kuriosität aus dem früheren 18. Jahrhundert," in *Buchkultur und Wissensvermittlung in Mittelalter und früher Neuzeit*, ed. Andreas Gardt, Mireille Schnyder, and Jürgen Wolf (Berlin and New York: de Gruyter, 2011), 41–54.

4. Christoph Martin Wieland, *Wielands Werke*, vol. 12.1, *Historisch-Kritische Ausgabe. Das Urtheil des Midas. Geschichte des Philosophen Danischmende. . . . März 1775–Mai 1776*, ed. Peter-Henning Haischer and Tina Hartmann (Berlin and New York: de Gruyter, 2010), 26.

5. Ibid.

6. Heinrich Wilhelm von Gerstenberg, *Ugolino. Eine Tragödie in fünf Aufzügen* (Hamburg and Bremen: Johann Hinrich Cramer, 1768), 1.

7. Heinrich Leopold Wagner, *Voltaire am Abend vor seiner Apotheose*, ed. Bernhard Seuffert (Heilbronn: Henninger, 1881), 3.

8. Wilhelm August Iffland, *Dramatische Werke*, vol. 4, *Reue versöhnt, Achmet und Zenide, Figaro in Deutschland* (Leipzig: Göschen, 1798), iii–iv.

9. Georg Christoph Lichtenberg, *Schriften und Briefe*, vol. 1, *Sudelbücher*, ed. Wolfgang Promies (Munich: Hanser, 1968), vol. 1, 771.

10. Johann Timotheus Hermes, *Sophiens Reise von Memel nach Sachsen* (Worms: Heinrich Bender, 1776), vol. 1, 7–14, see 12.

11. Anni Carlsson, *Die deutsche Buchkritik* (Stuttgart: Kohlhammer, 1963), 51.

12. Johann Georg Sulzer, *Allgemeine Theorie der Schönen Künste: in einzeln, nach alphabetischer Ordnung der Kunstwörter auf einander folgenden, Artikeln abgehandelt* (Leipzig: Weidmann und Reich, 1771), vol. 2, 632.

13. Ibid.

14. Steffen Martus, *Werkpolitik: Zur Literaturgeschichte kritischer Kommunikation vom 17. bis ins 20. Jahrhundert mit Studien zu Klopstock, Tieck, Goethe und George* (Berlin and New York: de Gruyter, 2007). Matthias Buschmeier correctly criticizes Martus for his historically imprecise discussion of philology in *Poesie und Philologie in der Goethe-Zeit* (Tübingen: Niemeyer, 2008), 47. But Martus's main point is that Goethe himself laid the foundation for future modes of literary study, following Hans-Martin Kruckis,

"Goethe-Philologie als Paradigma neu-philologischer Wissenschaft im 19. Jahrhundert," in *Wissenschaftsgeschichte der Germanistik im 19. Jahrhundert*, ed. Jürgen Fohrmann and Wilhelm Voßkamp (Stuttgart and Weimar: Metzler, 1994), 451–493.

15. On biographical criticism on *Werther*, from publication through to the present day, see Bruce Duncan, *Goethe's "Werther" and the Critics* (Rochester, NY: Camden House, 2005), 107–133.

16. August Wilhelm Iffland, *Die Jäger. Ein ländliches Sittengemälde in fünf Aufzügen* (Berlin: Decker, 1785), 5.

17. Kurt Rothmann, *Johann Wolfgang Goethe. Die Leiden des jungen Werther. Erläuterungen und Dokumente* (Stuttgart: Reclam, 1971), 148.

18. Jürgen Nelles lists various scholars and their terms in "Werthers Herausgeber oder die Rekonstruktion der 'Geschichte des armen Werthers,'" *Berichte des Freien Deutschen Hochstifts* (1996): 1–37, see 3–4.

19. Martin Swales, *Goethe: The Sorrows of Young Werther* (Cambridge: Cambridge University Press, 1987) 79, 82, and 86.

20. Nelles, "Werthers Herausgeber," 7.

21. Erdmann Waniek, "*Werther* lesen und Werther als Leser," *Goethe Yearbook* 1 (1982): 51–92, see 52.

22. On Goethe and consensus more broadly, see Karl Eibl, "Consensus. Eine Denkfigur des 18. Jahrhunderts als Kompositionsprinzip Goethescher Gedichtsammlungen," in *Literarhistorische Begegnungen. Festschrift zum sechszigsten Geburtstag von Bernhard König*, ed. Andreas Kablitz and Ulrich Schulz Buschhaus (Tübingen: Günter Narr, 1993), 29–41.

23. Daniel Defoe, *Robinson Crusoe: An Authoritative Text, Contexts, Criticism*, 2nd ed., ed. Michael Shinagel (New York and London: Norton, 1994), 3.

24. Jean-Jacques Rousseau, *Julie; Or, The New Heloise*, ed. and trans. Philip Steward and Jean Vaché (London and Hanover, NH: University Press of New England, 1997), 4.

25. Pierre Choderlos de Laclos, *Les Liaisons Dangereuses*, trans. Douglas Parmée (Oxford: Oxford University Press, 1995), 7.

26. Swales, *Goethe*, 82; Nelles, "Werthers Herausgeber," 1.

27. Uwe Wirth, *Die Geburt des Autors aus dem Geist der Herausgeberfiktion. Editoriale Rahmung im Roman um 1800: Wieland, Goethe, Brentano, Jean Paul und E.T.A. Hoffmann* (Munich: Fink, 2008), 234–235.

28. Ilse Graham, "Goethes eigener Werther. Eines Künstlers Wahrheit über seine Dichtung," *Jahrbuch der deutschen Schillergesellschaft* 18 (1974): 268–303, see 273–275.

29. Christoph E. Schweitzer, "Who is the Editor in Goethe's *Die Leiden des jungen Werthers*?" *Goethe Yearbook* 12 (2004): 31–40, see 33.

30. Ibid., 34.

31. Deirdre Vincent, *Werther's Goethe and the Game of Literary Creativity* (Toronto: Toronto University Press, 1992), 191.

32. Ibid., 192.

33. Ibid., 186–187.

34. Ibid., 187.

35. Michael Bell, *The Sentiment of Reality: Truth of Feeling in the European Novel* (London: G. Allen and Unwin, 1983), 92.

36. Ingrid Engel, *Werther und die Wertheriaden: Ein Beitrag zur Wirkungsgeschichte* (St. Ingbert: Werner Röhrig, 1986), 88.

37. Karl Philipp Moritz, *Anton Reiser: Ein pyschologischer Roman* (Stuttgart: Reclam, 1972), 294.

38. Nelles, "Werthers Herausgeber," 10.

39. Waniek, "*Werther* lesen," 57; Landfester, "Goethes Poetik des Paratextes," 383.

40. Erich Meuthen, *Selbstüberredung: Rhetorik und Roman im 18. Jahrhundert* (Freiburg: Rombach, 1994), 187.

41. Waniek, "*Werther* lesen," 55.

42. Johann Christoph Gottsched, *Ausgewählte Werke*, vol. 1, *Gedichte und Gedichtübertragungen*, ed. Joachim Birke (Berlin and New York: de Gruyter, 1968), 471.

43. Thomas Wegmann, "Der Dichter als 'Letternkrämer?' Zur Funktion von Paratexten für die Organisation von Aufmerksamkeit und Distinktion im literarischen Feld," *Das achtzehnte Jahrhundert. Zeitschrift der Deutschen Gesellschaft für die Erforschung des achtzehnten Jahrhunderts* 36 (2012): 238–249.

44. Benjamin Bennett, "Goethe's *Werther*: Double Perspective and the Game of Life," *German Quarterly* 53, no. 1 (1980): 64–81, see 76.

45. Ibid., 77.

46. Johann Wolfgang von Goethe, *Die Leiden des jungen Werther. Neue Ausgabe, von dem Dichter selbst eingeleitet* (Leipzig: Weygand, 1825).

47. Hans Rudolf Vaget, "Werther, the Undead," *Goethe Yearbook* 12 (2004): 17–29, see 23.

48. Ibid., 16.

49. Landfester, "Goethes Poetik des Paratextes," 385.

50. Manfred Link, "Goethes Wertheriade: *Briefe aus der Schweiz. Erste Abteilung*," *Doitsu Bungaku* 32 (1964): 107–120.

51. Johann Friedrich Schink, *Empfindsame Reisen durch Italien, die Schweiz und Frankreich. Ein Nachtrag zu den Yorickschen* (Hamburg: Hoffmann, 1794).

52. Kevin Hilliard, "*Römische Elegien* XX: Metapoetic Reflection in Goethe's Classical Poetry," in *Goethe at 250: London Symposium / Goethe mit 250: Londoner Symposium*, ed. T. J. Reed, Martin Swales, and Jeremy Adler (Munich: Iudicium, 2000), 223–232, see 223.

53. Ibid., 224.

54. Olaf Kramer, *Goethe und die Rhetorik* (Berlin and New York: de Gruyter, 2010), 64–65.

55. Quintilian, *The Orator's Education*, ed. and trans. Donald A. Russell (Cambridge, MA: Harvard University Press, 2002), vol. 1, 239 (1.11).

56. Emil Staiger, *Goethe*, vol. 1, *1749–1786* (Zurich: Atlantis, 1952), 479.

57. Friedrich Schiller, *Werke und Briefe in zwölf Bänden*, vol. 12, *Briefe, 1795–1805*, ed. Norbert Oellers (Frankfurt am Main: Deutscher Klassiker Verlag, 2002), 473.

58. Martus, *Werkpolitik*, 656.

59. Holger Dainat, "Goethes *Natur* oder *Was ist ein Autor?*," in *Paratexte in Literatur, Film, Fernsehen*, ed. Klaus Kreimeier, Georg Stanitzek, and Natalie Binczek (Berlin: Akademie Verlag, 2004), 101–116.

60. Karl Viëtor, "Goethe's Gedicht auf Schiller's Schädel," *PMLA* 59 (1944): 142–183, see 183. The discussion was especially animate in the years 1944 and 1945, i.e., volumes 59 and 60.

61. Ibid., 176.

62. Goethe, *Goethe's Werke*, vol. 1, *Vollständige Ausgabe letzter Hand* (Stuttgart: Cotta, 1828), 333.

63. Peter Michelsen, "Goethe's 'Vorspiel auf dem Theater' als Vorspiel zum 'Faust,'" in *Geschichtlichkeit und Gegenwart. Festschrift für Hans Dietrich Irmscher zum 65. Geburtstag*, ed. Hans Esselborn and Werner Keller (Cologne: Böhlau, 1994), 139–158.

64. Oskar Seidlin, "Is the 'Prelude in the Theatre' a Prelude to *Faust*?" *PMLA* 64, no. 3 (1949): 462–470. Jost Schillemeit, "'Das Vorspiel auf dem Theater' zu Goethes 'Faust': Entstehungszusammenhänge und Folgerungen für sein Verständnis," *Euphorion: Zeitschrift für Literaturgeschichte* 80 (1986): 149–166. For an interpretation of the Classicist program through prologues, see Banerjee Nandakishore, "Der Prolog im Drama der deutschen Klassik: Studien zu seiner Poetik" (DPhil diss., Ludwig Maximilian University of Munich, 1970). Note that in scholarship on Weimar Classicism, the extent to which Schiller's opening verses or prologues are representative of the whole subsequent plays is similarly disputed. For a nuanced argument in favor of thematic unity, for instance, see John L. Hibberd, "Das Vorspiel zu Schillers Wilhelm Tell und die 'hervorzubringende Einheit,'" in *Texte, Motive und Gestalten der Goethezeit*, ed. Hibberd and H. B. Nisbet (Tübingen: Niemeyer, 1989), 151–176.

65. Johann Wolfgang von Goethe, *Goethe's Faust*, ed. Calvin Thomas (Boston, MA: D. C. Heath, 1892), vol. 1, 233.

66. Werner Keller, "Der Dichter in der 'Zueignung' und im 'Vorspiel auf dem Theater,'" in *Aufsätze zu Goethes "Faust I,"* ed. Werner Keller (Darmstadt: Wissenschaftliche Buchgesellschaft, 1984), 151–191, see 191.

67. Douglas F. Bub, "The True Prologue to Goethe's *Faust*," *Modern Language Notes* 84, no. 5 (1969): 791–796, see 792. See also Benjamin Bennett, "'Vorspiel auf dem Theater': The Ironic Basis of Goethe's *Faust*," *German Quarterly* 49, no. 4 (1976): 438–455.

68. Johann Wolfgang von Goethe, "Die neue Melusine," *Taschenbuch für Damen* (1817), 1–24, see 1.

69. Andrew Piper, *Dreaming in Books: The Making of the Bibliographic Imagination in the Romantic Age* (Chicago: Chicago University Press, 2009), 24.

70. E.T.A. Hoffmann, *Briefwechsel*, vol. 1, *Königsberg bis Leipzig 1794–1814*, ed. Friedrich Schnapp (Munich: Winkler, 1967), 401.

71. Jeremias Gotthelf, *Uli, der Pächter. Ein Volksbuch* (Berlin: Julius Springer, 1849), unpaginated.

72. Klaus L. Berghahn, "Kritik," in *Goethe-Handbuch in vier Bänden*, vol. 4, *Personen, Sache, Begriffe*, ed. Hans-Dietrich Dahnke and Regine Otto (Stuttgart: Metzler, 1988), 625–629, see 629.

73. Angus Nicholls, "Between Natural and Human Science: Scientific Method in Goethe's *Noten und Abhandlungen zum West-östlichen Divan*," *Publications of the English Goethe Society* 80, no. 1 (2011): 1–18, see 11–12.

74. Buschmeier, *Poesie und Philologie*, 303–321, see 311.

75. Ibid., 305.

76. Ibid.

77. Ulrich Bräker, *Sämtliche Schriften*, vol. 4, *Lebensgeschichte und vermischte Schriften*, ed. Johann Heinrich Füßli (Bern: Haupt, 2000), 363.

78. Wilhelm August Iffland, *Dramatische Werke*, vol. 1, *Ueber meine theatralische Laufbahn* (Leipzig: Göschen, 1798), 1.

79. Hans Ehrenzeller, *Studien zur Romanvorrede von Grimmelshausen bis Jean Paul* (Bern: Francke, 1955), 173–174.

80. Landfester, "Goethes Poetik des Paratextes," 388.

81. Johann Arnold Ebert, *Episteln und vermischte Gedichte* (Hamburg: C. E. Bohn, 1789), a1.

82. Ibid.

83. Ibid., a2.

84. Johann Matthias Dreyer, *Schöne Spielwerke beym Wein, Punsch, Bischof und Krambambuli. Trinksprüche oder Gesundheiten und einige Epigramme* (Hamburg and Leipzig, 1763), 2.

85. Deirdre Vincent, "Text as Image and Self-Image: The Contextualization of Goethe's *Dichtung und Wahrheit* (1810–1813)," *Goethe Yearbook* 10 (2001): 125–153, see 126.

86. Johann Wolfgang von Goethe, *Goethes' Werke*, ed. on behalf of Sophie von Sachsen (Weimar: Böhlau, 1919), vol. 4.22: 390. References to *Goethes' Werke*, ed. on behalf of Sophie von Sachsen, vol. 4.22 and 4.42 in 143 vols. (Weimar: Böhlau, 1919) (hereafter cited WA, by volume and page).

87. Vincent, "Text as Image and Self-Image," 131 and 137–138.

88. Martus, *Werkpolitik*, 447.

89. Goethe, *Goethe's Werke* (Stuttgart and Tübingen: Cotta, 1819), vol. 20, 389 and 391.

90. Christoph Martin Wieland, *Sämmtliche Werke*, vol. 1, *Geschichte des Agathon. Erster Theil* (Leipzig: Göschen, 1794), vi.

91. Martus, *Werkpolitik*, 460. For a study of Wieland in this context, see Peter-Henning Haischer, *Historizität und Klassizität. Christoph Martin Wieland und die Werkausgabe im 18. Jahrhundert* (Heidelberg: Winter, 2011).

92. Landfester, "Goethes Poetik des Paratextes," 375.

93. Andrew Piper, "Rethinking the Print Object: Goethe and the Book of Everything," *PMLA* 121, no. 1 (2006): 124–138, see 127.

Chapter Two Jean Paul

1. Michael North, *"Material Delight and the Joy of Living": Cultural Consumption in the Age of Enlightenment in Germany*, trans. Pamela Selwyn (Aldershot: Ashgate, 2008), 11.

2. Till Dembeck, *Texte rahmen. Grenzregionen literarischer Werke im 18. Jahrhundert (Gottsched, Wieland, Moritz, Jean Paul)* (Berlin and New York: de Gruyter, 2007), 295.

3. Timothy J. Casey, "Digressions for Future Instalments: Some Reflections on Jean Paul's Epic Outlook," *Modern Language Review* 85, no. 4 (1990): 866–878, see 870.

4. Jean Paul, *Werke*, vol. 2.1, *Jugendwerke*, ed. Norbert Miller (Munich: Hanser, 1974–1985), 1032.

5. Heinrich Heine is an early exponent of this view in 1833: *Historisch-kritische Gesamtausgabe der Werke*, vol. 8.1, *Die romantische Schule*, ed. Helga Weidmann (Hamburg: Hoffmann und Campe, 1979), 217–218.

6. Johann Arnold Ebert, *Episteln und vermischte Gedichte* (Hamburg: C. E. Bohn, 1789), a4.

7. Deborah N. Losse, *Sampling the Book: Renaissance Prologues and the French "Conteurs"* (Lewisburg, PA: Bucknell University Press, 1994), 47.

8. Ernst Robert Curtius, *European Literature and the Latin Middle Ages*, trans. Williard R. Trask (London: Routledge and Kegan Paul, 1953), 302–334, see 316.

9. Gottlieb Wilhelm Rabener, "Der Autor," *Belustigungen des Verstandes und des Witzes* (August 1743–May 1744): 499–500.

10. Novalis, *Schriften: Die Werke Friedrich von Hardenbergs*, vol. 2, *Das Philosophische Werk I*, ed. Richard Samuel, 2nd ed. (Stuttgart: Kohlhammer, 1965), 663.

11. William H. Sherman, "On the Threshold: Architecture, Paratext, and Early Print Culture," in *Agent of Change: Print Culture Studies after Elizabeth L. Eisenstein*, ed. Sabrina Alcorn Baron, Eric N. Lindquist, and Eleanor F. Shevlin (Amherst: University of Massachusetts Press, 2007), 67–81, see 71.

12. Ebert, *Episteln und vermischte Gedichte*, a4.

13. Quintilian, *The Orator's Education*, ed. and trans. Donald A. Russell (Cambridge, MA: Harvard University Press, 2001), vol. 2, 183 (4.1).

14. Francis Bacon, *The Works of Francis Bacon*, vol. 4, ed. James Spedding, Robert Leslie Ellis, and Douglas Denon Heath (London: Longmann, 1858), 492. See also: Randall Anderson, "The Rhetoric of the Paratext in Early Printed Books," in *The Cambridge History of the Book in Britain*, ed. John Barnard, D. F. McKenzie, and I. R. Willison, vol. 4, *1557–1695*, ed. John Barnard, D. F. McKenzie, and Maureen Bell (Cambridge: Cambridge University Press, 2002), 636–44.

15. Pindar, *Olympian Odes. Pythian Odes*, ed. and trans. William H. Race (Cambridge, MA: Harvard University Press, 1997), 102–103.

16. Friedrich Schlegel, *Kritische Friedrich-Schlegel-Ausgabe*, vol. 5, *Dichtungen*, ed. Hans Eichner (Paderborn: Schöningh, 1975), 3.

17. Ibid.

18. Sherman, "On the Threshold," 72.

19. Ibid., 77.

20. On religion and the paratexts of Jean Paul and his English predecessors, see Daniel Weidner, "Himmelskarten und Erdkarten. Gott und der Romanerzähler bei Fielding und Jean Paul," in *Autorschaft. Ikonen-Stile-Institutionen*, ed. Christel Meier and Martina Wagner-Egelhaaf (Berlin: Akademie Verlag, 2011), 231–251.

21. References to Hegel, *Gesammelte Werke*, gen. ed. Walter Jaeschke (Hamburg: Felix Meiner, 1968–), in 31 vols. (hereafter cited HGW, by volume and page). In *Phänomenologie des Geistes* [Phenomenology of Spirit] (1807), Hegel writes of "ein Hokuspokus der taschenspielerischen Priester" (HGW, 9: 298) [a hocus pocus of the priests playing card tricks]. Goethe mentions the hocus pocus of the Catholic mass in discussing Schlegel's conversion (FA, 2.6: 321).

22. Bettine Menke, "Ein-Fälle aus Exzerpten. Die *inventio* des Jean Paul," in *Rhetorik als kulturelle Praxis*, ed. Renate Lachmann, Riccardo Nicolosi, and Susanne Strätling (Munich: Fink, 2008), 291–307, see 295–296.

23. The idea that the bookbinder is the preface's addressee alongside the reading public to which a book advertises itself is also formulated in a fragment by Novalis: *Schriften: Die Werke Friedrich von Hardenbergs*, vol. 3, *Das philosophische Werk II*, ed. Richard Samuel, 2nd ed. (Stuttgart: Kohlhammer, 1968), 361.

24. "Billet," in *Grosses vollständiges Universal-Lexicon aller Wissenschafften und Künste, welche bishero durch menschlichen Verstand und Witz erfunden und verbessert worden* (Leipzig and Halle: Zedler, 1733), vol. 3, 1845–1846.

25. Susan J. Leonardi, "Recipes for Reading: Summer Pasta, Lobster à la Riseholme, and Key Lime Pie," *PMLA* 104, no. 3 (1989): 340–347.

26. Jayne Elizabeth Archer, "The 'Quintessence of Wit': Poems and Recipes in Early Modern Women's Writing," in *Reading and Writing Recipe Books, 1550–1800*, ed. Michelle Di Meo and Sara Pennell, 114–134 (Manchester: Manchester University Press, 2013).

27. Johann Gottlieb Fichte, *Gesamtausgabe. Werke*, vol. 1.3, *1794–1796*, ed. Reinhard Lauth and Hans Jacob (Stuttgart: Frommann, 1966), 25.

28. Ibid., 26.

29. E.T.A. Hoffmann, *Sämtliche Werke in sechs Bänden*, vol. 2.1, *Fantasiestücke in Callot's Manier, Werke 1814*, ed. Hartmut Steinecke (Frankfurt am Main: Deutscher Klassiker Verlag, 1993), 11. Francis Paul Greene contends that Jean Paul's preface for Hoffmann is also a self-reflective review inasmuch as it is a self-affirming one; it is a "preemptive strike" against the new writer which initiates "a war of letters, an epistolary conflict which will accompany Hoffmann and his works throughout the history of their reception": "Preface, Vorwort, Vorrede: Jean Paul and E.T.A. Hoffmann," *New German Review: A Journal of Germanic Studies* 15–16 (1999): 6–22, see 11.

30. Gotthold Ephraim Lessing, *Werke und Briefe in zwölf Bänden*, vol. 4, *Werke, 1758–1759*, ed. Gunter E. Grimm (Frankfurt am Main: Deutscher Klassiker Verlag, 1997), 298.

31. Steffen Martus, "Die Entstehung von Tiefsinn im 18. Jahrhundert. Zur Temporalisierung der Poesie in der Verbesserungsästhetik bei Hagedorn, Gellert und Wieland," *Deutsche Vierteljahrsschrift für Literaturwissenschaft und Geistesgeschichte* 74, no. 1 (2000): 27–43.

32. Horace, *Satires. Epistles. The Art of Poetry*, ed. and trans. H. Rushton Fairclough (Cambridge, MA: Harvard University Press, 1926), vol. 5, 294.

33. Anton Ulrich, Herzog von Braunschweig-Wolfenbüttel, *Die römische Octavia* (Braunschweig: Zilliger, 1712), unpaginated.

34. Martus, "Die Entstehung von Tiefsinn," 29.

35. On the decline of "Verbesserungsästhetik" [aesthetics of improvement] in German literature generally around 1800, see Peter-Henning Haischer, *Historizität und Klassizitat. Christoph Martin Wieland und die Werkausgabe im 18. Jahrhundert* (Heidelberg: Winter, 2011), 139–145.

36. Horace, *Art of Poetry*, vol. 5, 389.

37. The question of whether *Don Quixote* inspired, or already advances, Romantic irony is a contentious issue. But critics generally consider the matter through reference to Schlegel's theory of irony, not Jean Paul's. See William Egginton, "Cervantes, Romantic Irony and the Making of Reality," *Modern Language Notes* 117, no. 5 (2002): 1040–1068.

38. Johann Gottfried Herder, *Werke in zehn Bänden*, vol. 8, *Pädagogische und philosophische Schriften. Werke, 1792–1803*, ed. Hans Dietrich Irmscher (Frankfurt am Main: Deutscher Klassiker Verlag, 1998), 759.

39. Friedrich Schlegel, *Kritische Friedrich-Schlegel-Ausgabe*, vol. 2, *Charakteristiken und Kritiken I (1796–1802)*, ed. Hans Eichner (Paderborn: Schöningh, 1967), 204.

40. Ibid., 337.

41. Wendelin Guentner, "The Travel Narrative as Sketch: Préfaces, Avertissements, Avant-propos," in *Beginnings in French Literature*, ed. Freeman G. Henry, 103–117 (New York: Rodopi, 2002).

42. Eric A. Blackall, *The Novels of the German Romantics* (Ithaca, NY: Cornell University Press, 1983), 71.

43. Rüdiger Scholz, *Welt und Form des Romans bei Jean Paul* (Bern: Francke, 1973), 190.

44. Sabine Straub, "'Vorrede zur Vorrede'—Aus Jean Pauls unveröffentlichten Materialien zur Geschichte meiner Vorrede zur zweiten Auflage des Quintus Fixlein (Arbeitsbericht aus der Editorenwerkstatt)," *Jahrbuch der Jean Paul Gesellschaft* 44 (2009): 18–32.

45. Jean Paul, *Werke. Historisch-kritische Ausgabe*, vol. 6.1, *Geschichte meiner Vorrede zur zweiten Auflage des Quintus Fixlein*, ed. Sabine Straub and Barbara Hunfeld (Berlin and Boston: de Gruyter, 2013), 201.

46. Waltraud Wiethölter, "Die krumme Linie: Jean Pauls humoristisches ABC," *Jahrbuch für internationale Germanistik* 18 (1986): 36–56. Fraischdörfer also appears to represent journal editors, since he is equated with "Schütze": Christian Gottfried Schütz cofounded the *Allgemeine Literatur-Zeitung* [General Literary Periodical], and Jean Paul here writes of the "alg. d. Bibliothek" ["gen.[eral] G.[erman] library"]. Further, he laments a readership that now loves journalistic pieces. See Jean Paul, *Werke. Historisch-kritische Ausgabe*, vol 6.1, 196 and 198.

47. Elsabeth Dangel-Pelloquin, "Eheklage als Rührwerk des Erzählens. Jean Paul und Johanne Pauline im Vis-à-Vis," *Jahrbuch der Jean-Paul-Gesellschaft* 34 (1999): 35–55.

48. Novalis, *Das Philosophische Werk I*, 470.

49. Ibid.

50. Peter Michelsen, *Laurence Sterne und der deutsche Roman des achtzehnten Jahrhunderts*, 2nd ed. (Göttingen: Vandenhoeck and Ruprecht, 1972), 311–394.

51. Laurence Sterne, *The Florida Edition of the Works of Laurence Sterne*, vol. 6, *A Sentimental Journey through France and Italy and Continuation of the Bramine's Journal*, ed. Melvyn New and W. G. Day (Gainesville: University Presses of Florida, 2002), 17.

52. Ibid., 12.

53. Ibid., 28.

54. Ibid., 33.

55. Thomas W. Laqueur, *Solitary Sex: A Cultural History of Masturbation* (New York: Zone, 2003), 21.

56. Adrian Daub, *Uncivil Unions: The Metaphysics of Marriage in German Idealism and Romanticism* (Chicago: University of Chicago Press, 2012), 257–263. On Jean Paul's relationship to Fichte in this text, see also Oliver Koch, *Individualität as Fundamentalgefühl. Zur Metaphysik der Person bei Jacobi und Jean Paul* (Hamburg: Felix Meiner, 2013), 175–234.

57. Laurence Sterne, *The Florida Edition of the Works of Laurence Sterne*, vol. 1, *The Life and Opinions of Tristram Shandy, Gentleman*, ed. Melvyn New and Joan New (Gainesville: University Presses of Florida, 1978), 232–233.

58. Michael von Poser, *Der abschweifende Erzähler. Rhetorische Tradition und der deutsche Roman im achtzehnten Jahrhundert* (Bad Homburg: Gehlen, 1969); and Magnus Wieland, who attends to the classical rhetorical heritage of Jean Paul's digressions in general: *Vexierzüge. Jean Pauls Digressionspoetik* (Hanover: Wehrhahn, 2013).

59. Wieland, *Vexierzüge*, understands Jean Paul's digressions as governed by seduction, employing *Geschichte meiner Vorrede* [History of my Preface] as his example: 253–260.

60. Walther Rehm, *Späte Studien* (Bern and Munich: Francke, 1964), 7–96, see 29.

61. Ulrich Profitlich, "Der seelige Leser. Untersuchungen zur Dichtungstheorie Jean Pauls." DPhil diss., University of Bonn, 1964.

62. Walter J. Ong, "The Writer's Audience Is Always a Fiction," *PMLA* 90, no. 1 (1975): 9–21, see 12.

63. Note that Edmund Gosse is of the opposite opinion for writing generally, conceiving of a writer's imagined reader as always a particular person—for which the dedication is the paradigmatic paratext for textuality per se: "There can be no doubt that to compose a dedication is one of the primitive instincts of scribbling man. The most retiring of authors hopes that he may have one reader, and it is strange if he does not determine in his own mind who that reader is to be": "Elizabethan Dedications of Books," *Harper's Monthly Magazine* 105, no. 626 (1902): 165–172, see 165.

64. Ong, "Writer's Audience Is Always a Fiction," 9.

65. Ibid., 11. This process is what Goethe called, in 1795, "eine Art von unsichtbarer Schule" (FA 1:18, 323) [a sort of invisible school].

66. W. Daniel Wilson, "Readers in Texts," *PMLA* 96, no. 5 (1981): 848–863.

67. Hester IJsseling distinguishes between "anticipated" and "actual" readers ("de geanticipeerde lezer" and "de feitelijke lezer"), but she suggests the contrary view to that expressed in this book: that although the anticipated readers may be authors themselves, writers are always external to their writing (*Over voorwoorden. Hegel, Kierkegaard, Nietzsche* [Amsterdam: Boom, 1997], 66).

68. William K. Wimsatt Jr. and Monroe C. Beardsley, "The Intentional Fallacy," in *The Verbal Icon: Studies in the Meaning of Poetry*, ed. William K. Wimsatt Jr. (Lexington: University of Kentucky Press, 1954), 2–18, see 15.

69. Wayne C. Booth, *The Rhetoric of Fiction* (Chicago: Chicago University Press, 1961), 67–77.

70. Alexander Nehamas, "The Postulated Author: Critical Monism as a Regulative Ideal," *Critical Inquiry* 8, no. 1 (1981): 133–149.

71. Wieland, *Vexierzüge*, 74–78.

72. Friedrich Carl von Moser, *Mannigfaltigkeiten* (Zurich: Orell, Gessner und Füßli, 1796), 4.

73. Annina Klappert, *Die Perspektive auf Link und Lücke. Sichtweisen auf Jean Pauls Texte und Hypertexte* (Bielefeld: Aisthesis, 2006).

74. Gérard Genette, *Palimpsests: Literature in the Second Degree*, trans. Channa Newman and Claude Doubinsky (Lincoln: University of Nebraska Press, 1997).

75. Peter Brooks, *Reading for the Plot: Design and Intention in Narrative* (New York: Knopf, 1984), 38.

76. Ibid., 313.

77. Dard Hunter, *Papermaking: The History and Technique of an Ancient Craft* (London: Pleiades, 1947), 347–99. For a brief explanation and illustration of the papermaking process with rags, see Matt Erlin, *Necessary Luxuries: Books, Literature, and the Culture of Consumption in Germany, 1770–1815* (Ithaca, NY: Cornell University Press, 2014), 57–59.

78. Schlegel, *Charakteristiken und Kritiken I*, 290.

79. Heinrich von Kleist, *Kritische Ausgabe sämtlicher Werke*, vol. 2.9, *Sonstige Prosa*, ed. Roland Reuß and Peter Staengle (Frankfurt am Main: Roter Stern, 2007), 30.

80. Schlegel, *Charakteristiken und Kritiken I*, 148 and 404.

81. Ibid., 545.

82. Ibid., 182–183.

83. Hans Jahnke, "Mathematics and Culture: The Case of Novalis," *Science in Context* 4, no. 2 (1991): 279–295, see 282 and 286.

84. Schlegel, *Charakteristiken und Kritiken I*, 404.

85. Novalis, *Das Philosophische Werk I*, 663.

86. Ibid.

87. Novalis, *Schriften: Die Werke Friedrich von Hardenbergs*, vol. 4, *Lebensdokumente; Tagebücher, Briefwechsel, Zeitgenössische Zeugnisse*, ed. Richard Samuel, 2nd ed. (Stuttgart: Kohlhammer, 1975), 255.

88. August Wilhelm von Schlegel, *August Wilhelm von Schlegel's sämmtliche Werke*, vol. 6, *Vorlesungen über dramatische Kunst und Litteratur. 2. Theil.*, ed. Eduard Böcking (Leipzig: Weidemann, 1846), 200.

89. Gary Handwerk, "Romantic Irony," in *The Cambridge History of Literary Criticism*, vol. 5, *Romanticism*, ed. Marshall Brown (Cambridge: Cambridge University Press, 2000), 203–225, see 208.

90. Justus Möser, *Harlekin oder Vertheidigung des Groteske-Komischen*, 2nd ed. (Bremen: Johann Heinrich Cramer, 1777), 6.

91. Paul Fleming, *The Pleasures of Abandonment: Jean Paul and the Life of Humor* (Würzburg: Königshausen und Neumann, 2006), 48.

92. Leif Weatherby, "A Reconsideration of the Romantic Fragment," *The Germanic Review: Literature, Culture, Theory* 92, no. 4 (2017): 407–425, see 422. At the same time, it is clear that Jean Paul is radically more abstract than enlightenment thinkers who embraced the materiality of writing in general for formal, conceptual play—notably Georg Christoph Lichtenberg. On the latter, see Petra McGillen, "Wit, Bookishness, and the Epistemic Impact of Note-taking: Lichtenberg's *Sudelbücher* as Intellectual Tools," *Deutsche Vierteljahrsschrift für Literaturwissenschaft und Geistesgeschichte* 90, no. 4 (2016), 501–528.

93. Ralf Simon, *Die Idee der Prosa. Zur Ästhetikgeschichte von Baumgarten bis Hegel mit einem Schwerpunkt bei Jean Paul* (Munich: Fink, 2013), 248.

94. Ibid., 251.

95. For an alternative view, see Catherine J. Minter, *The Mind-Body Problem in German Literature, 1770–1830: Wezel, Moritz, and Jean Paul* (Oxford: Oxford University Press, 2002), 162: "Jean Paul's early, critical reception of the Enlightenment's materialist anthropological models is supplanted by a new, optimistic anthropology that is ultimately characterized by a thoroughgoing idealist monism."

96. Koch, *Individualität as Fundamentalgefühl*, 271.

97. Ibid., 267.

98. Ibid., 272.

99. Ibid., 235–236.

100. Ibid., 350.

101. "Vorrede," in *Grosses vollständiges Universal-Lexicon aller Wissenschafften und Künste, welche bishero durch menschlichen Verstand und Witz erfunden und verbessert worden* (Leipzig and Halle: Zedler, 1746), vol. 50, 1073–1077, see 1075.

102. See Jean Paul, *Geschichte meiner Vorrede zur zweiten Auflage des Quintus Fixlein* (Bayreuth: Johann Andreas Lübecks Erben, 1797).

103. Dembeck, *Texte rahmen*, 101 and 296; Uwe Wirth, *Die Geburt des Autors aus dem Geist der Herausgeberfiktion. Editoriale Rahmung im Roman um 1800: Wieland, Goethe, Brentano, Jean Paul und E.T.A. Hoffmann* (Munich: Fink, 2008), 423.

104. Hans Ehrenzeller, *Studien zur Romanvorrede von Grimmelshausen bis Jean Paul* (Bern: Francke, 1955), 179.

105. Ibid., 178.

106. Admittedly, Hegel lambasts Jean Paul precisely on this account in his aesthetic lectures: Hegel, *Werke in zwanzig Bändern*, vol. 14, *Vorlesungen über die Ästhetik II*, 2nd ed., ed. Eva Moldenhauer and Karl Markus Michel (Frankfurt am Main: Suhrkamp, 1986), 230. References to Hegel's *Vorlesungen über die Ästhetik I, II, and III*, from *Werke in zwanzig Bändern*, 2nd ed., ed. Eva Moldenhauer and Karl Markus Michel, vols. 13–15 (hereafter cited HW, Ä 1, 2, or 3, and page number).
Jean Paul might, therefore, be included in Hegel's critique of Early German Romantic theory in his *Wissenschaft der Logik* [Science of Logic] (1811, 1831) as "eine und dieselbe langweilige Abwechslung dieses Endlichen und Unendlichen" (HGW, 11: 81) [one and the same, boring alternation between the finite and the infinite].

107. Ehrenzeller, *Romanvorrede*, 182.

108. Ibid., 184.

109. Lucian, *Dialogues 6: How to Write History . . .* , ed. and trans. K. Kilburn (Cambridge, MA: Harvard University Press, 1959), 188–189.

110. Armand D'Angour, *The Greeks and the New: Novelty in Ancient Greek Imagination and Experience* (Cambridge: Cambridge University Press, 2011), 153.

111. Quintilian, *Orator's Education*, vol. 2, 207 (4.1).

112. Ibid., 205 (4.1).

113. Yelena Baraz, *A Written Republic: Cicero's Philosophical Politics* (Princeton, NJ: Princeton University Press, 2012).

114. Hoffmann, *Fantasiestücke in Callot's Manier*, 15–16.

115. E.T.A. Hoffmann, *Briefwechsel*, vol. 1, *Königsberg bis Leipzig, 1794–1814*, ed. Friedrich Schnapp (Munich: Winkler, 1967), 401.

116. Søren Kierkegaard, *Prefaces; Writing Sampler*, ed. and trans. Todd W. Nichol (Princeton, NJ: Princeton University Press, 1997), 4.

117. Ibid., 54. For an overview, see Markus Kleinert, "Apparent and Hidden Relations between Kierkegaard and Jean Paul," in *Kierkegaard and His German Contemporaries*, ed. Jon Stewart (Aldershot: Ashgate, 2008), vol. 3, 155–170.

118. Kierkegaard, *Prefaces*, 5.

119. Ibid., 6.

120. Ibid., 5.

121. Ibid. See Mads Fedder Henriksen, "A Preface to the 'Preface' of *Prefaces*," *Kierkegaardiana* 20 (1999): 7–29.

122. Jacques Derrida, *Dissemination*, trans. Barbara Johnson (Chicago: University of Chicago Press, 1981), 27–28.

123. Ibid., 28.

124. Ibid., 9.

125. Ibid., 7.

126. Ibid., 44–45.

127. Philippe Lacoue-Labarthe and Jean-Luc Nancy, *The Literary Absolute: The Theory of Literature in German Romanticism*, trans. Philip Barnard and Cheryl Lester (Albany: State University of New York Press, 1988), 12 and 49.

128. Derrida, *Dissemination*, 35.

129. Ibid., 57–58.

130. Ibid., 8.

131. Ibid., 27–29, see 27.

132. Ibid., 10.

133. Ibid., 43.

134. Ibid., 27.

135. Ibid., 28, and Gérard Genette, *Paratexts: Thresholds of Interpretation*, trans. Jane E. Lewin (Cambridge: Cambridge University Press, 1997), 213.

136. Derrida, *Dissemination*, 8.

137. Genette, *Paratexts*, 161–162.

138. Derrida, *Dissemination*, 8.

Chapter Three Hegel

1. Klaus Vieweg, *Skepsis und Freiheit—Hegel über den Skeptizismus zwischen Literatur und Philosophie* (Munich: Fink, 2007), 230.

2. Klaus Vieweg, "Die Phänomenologie des Geistes als 'Lebenslauf der Sophie.'" *Hegel-Jahrbuch* 8 (2002): 208–213, see esp. 208; Vieweg, *Skepsis und Freiheit*, 216.

3. Judith Hawley, "*Tristram Shandy*, Learned Wit, and Enlightenment Knowledge," in *The Cambridge Companion to Laurence Sterne*, ed. Thomas Keymer (Cambridge: Cambridge University Press, 2009), 34–48, see 37.

4. Ibid., 38.

5. Laurence Sterne, *The Florida Edition of the Works of Laurence Sterne*, vol. 1, *The Life and Opinions of Tristram Shandy, Gentleman*, ed. Melvyn New and Joan New (Gainesville: University Presses of Florida, 1978), 227.

6. Jacques Derrida, *Dissemination*, trans. Barbara Johnson (Chicago: University of Chicago Press, 1981), 49.

7. Tommaso Pierini, "Consciousness, Time, and System: On the Structure of Hegel's *Phänomenologie des Geistes* in the Light of *Tristram Shandy*," in *Shandean Humour in English and German Literature and Philosophy*, ed. Klaus Vieweg, James Vigus, and Katherine M. Wheeler (Leeds: Legenda, 2013), 78–91.

8. Vieweg, *Skepsis und Freiheit*, 85.

9. Sterne, *Tristram Shandy*, vol. 2, 500.

10. Jeffrey Reid, *Real Words: Language and System in Hegel* (Toronto: University of Toronto Press, 2007), 14.

11. Jochen Schulte-Sasse, "Mediality in Hegel: From Work to Text in the *Phenomenology of Spirit*," in *Idealism without Absolutes: Philosophy and Romantic Culture*, ed. Tilottama Rajan and Arkady Plotnitsky (Albany: State University of New York Press, 2004), 73–91, see esp. 87.

12. Ian Balfour, "Now This: On the Necessity and Impossibility of a Title (Barnett Newman, 1967, with Hegel and Benjamin)," in *Babel. Festschrift für Werner Hamacher*, ed. Aris Fioretos (Weil am Rhein: Urs Engeler, 2008), 22–29, see 24. Balfour refers to Werner Hamacher's *Pleroma: Reading in Hegel*, trans. Nicholas Walker and Simon Jarvis (Stanford, CA: Stanford University Press, 1998), 210.

13. Friedrich Hölderlin, *Sämtliche Werke. Historisch-Kritische Ausgabe*, vol. 11, *Hyperion*, ed. D. E. Sattler and Michael Knaupp (Frankfurt am Main: Roter Stern, 1982), 579.

14. Howard Gaskill, "'So dacht' ich. Nächstens mehr': Translating Hölderlin's *Hyperion*," *Publications of the English Goethe Society* 77, no. 2 (2008): 90–100, see 99–100.

15. Miguel de Cervantes, *Don Quixote*, trans. A. J. Close (Cambridge: Cambridge University Press, 1990), 674–675. The connection is noted by T. M. Knox, "Hegel as Stylist" (1968), *German Life and Letters* 31, no. 1 (2003): 53–57, see 55.

16. Li Sui Gwee, "Night in Novalis, Schelling and Hegel," *Studies in Romanticism* 50, no. 1 (2011): 105–124.

17. Georg Wilhelm Friedrich Hegel, *Briefe von und an Hegel*, vol. 1, *1785–1812*, ed. Johannes Hoffmeister (Hamburg: Felix Meiner, 1969), 162.

18. Heinrich Steffens, *Was ich erlebte* (Breslau: Josef Max und Komp, 1841), vol. 3, 312.

19. Angelica Nuzzo, "'. . . As if truth were a coin!' Lessing and Hegel's Developmental Theory of Truth," *Hegel-Studien* 44 (2009): 131–155.

20. Francis Coventry, *The History of Pompey the Little; Or, The Life and Adventures of a Lap-Dog*, ed. Robert Adams Day (London: Oxford University Press, 1974), 108.

21. Immanuel Kant, *Gesammelte Schriften*, vol. 4, *Kritik der reinen Vernunft (1. Auflage), Prolegomena . . .*, ed. Königlich Preußische Akademie der Wissenschaften (Berlin: Reimer, 1911), 3.

22. Novalis, *Schriften: Die Werke Friedrich von Hardenbergs*, vol. 2, *Das Philosophische Werk I*, ed. Richard Samuel, 2nd ed. (Stuttgart: Kohlhammer, 1965), 663.

23. Friedrich Schlegel, *Kritische Friedrich-Schlegel-Ausgabe*, vol. 2, *Charakteristiken und Kritiken I (1796–1802)*, ed. Hans Eichner (Paderborn: Schöningh, 1967), 179.

24. Jon Stewart, "Hegel's Phenomenology as a Systematic Fragment," in *The Cambridge Companion to Hegel and Nineteenth-Century Philosophy*, ed. Frederick C. Beiser (Cambridge: Cambridge University Press, 2008), 74–93.

25. Rudolf Haym, *Hegel und seine Zeit. Vorlesungen über Entstehung und Entwicklung, Wesen und Werth der Hegel'schen Philosophie* (Berlin: Rudolph Gaertner, 1857), 238.

26. Friedhelm Nicolin, "Zum Titelproblem der Phänomenologie des Geistes," *Hegel-Studien* 4 (1967): 113–123.

27. Haym, *Hegel und seine Zeit*, 215.

28. Werner Marx, *Hegel's Phenomenology of Spirit: A Commentary on the Preface and Introduction*, 2nd ed. (Chicago: Chicago University Press, 1988), 53.

29. Erwin Metzke, *Hegels Vorreden. Mit Kommentar zur Einführung in seine Philosophie* (Heidelberg: Kerle, 1949), 13.

30. Richard Schlacht, "A Commentary on the Preface to Hegel's 'Phenomenology of Spirit,'" *Philosophical Studies* 23, nos. 1–2 (1972): 1–31, see 30.

31. Ibid., 1.

32. Ibid.

33. Hester IJsseling, *Over voorwoorden. Hegel, Kierkegaard, Nietzsche* (Amsterdam: Boom, 1997), 51.

34. Ibid., 53–54.

35. Annette Sell, "Leben in der 'Vorrede' zur 'Phänomenologie des Geistes,'" *Hegel-Jahrbuch* 7 (2001): 41–46, see 41.

36. Ibid., 44.

37. Ardis B. Collins, "The Introductions to the System," in *The Bloomsbury Companion to Hegel*, ed. Allegra de Laurentiis and Jeffrey Edwards (London: Bloomsbury, 2013), 55–70, see 68.

38. Walter Kaufmann, ed. and trans., *Hegel's Preface to His System in a New Translation with Commentary* (New York: Anchor, 1966), 75.

39. Yirmiyahu Yovel, *Hegel's Preface to the Phenomenology of Spirit* (Princeton, NJ: Princeton University Press, 2005), ix.

40. John Sallis, "Hegel's Concept of Presentation: Its Determination in the Preface to the *Phenomenology of Spirit*," *Hegel-Studien* 12 (1977): 129–156, see 131.

41. Ibid., 132–133.

42. M. J. Inwood, *A Hegel Dictionary* (Oxford: Blackwell, 1992), 283–285.

43. Maurice A Finocchiaro, "Dialectic and Argument in Philosophy: A Case Study of Hegel's Phenomenological Preface," *Argumentation* 2, no. 2 (1988): 175–190, see 178.

44. Allen Speight, *Hegel, Literature and the Problem of Agency* (Cambridge: Cambridge University Press, 2001), 3.

45. Finocchiaro, "Dialectic and Argument in Philosophy," 187–188.

46. Jochen Schmidt, *Die Geschichte des Genie-Gedankens in der deutschen Literatur, Philosophie und Politik, 1750–1945*, vol. 1, *Von der Aufklärung bis zum Idealismus* (Heidelberg: Winter, 2004), 381–403.

47. Seán M. Williams, "Kant's Novel Interpretation of History," *Seminar: A Journal of Germanic Studies* 49, no. 2 (2013): 171–190.

48. Friedrich Wilhelm Joseph Schelling, *Ausgewählte Werke*, vol. 4, *Schriften von 1806–1813* (Darmstadt: Wissenschaftliche Buchgesellschaft, 1968), 278.

49. Immanuel Kant, *Gesammelte Schriften*, vol. 8, *Abhandlungen nach 1781*, ed. Königlich Preußische Akademie der Wissenschaften (Berlin: Reimer, 1923), 404.

50. Ibid., 390.

51. IJsseling, *Over voorwoorden*, 48.

52. Kaufmann, *Hegel's Preface*, 107.

53. On Hegel's terminology, see Inwood, *Hegel Dictionary*, 118–120.

54. Yovel, *Hegel's Preface*, 159.

55. Ibid., 161.

56. Thomas Sören Hoffmann, "Hegels phänomenologische Dialektik. Darstellung, Zeitbezug und Wahrheit des erscheinenden Wissens—Thesen zur Vorrede," in *Hegel als Schlüsseldenker der modernen Welt. Beiträge zur Deutung der "Phänomenologie des Geistes" aus Anlaß ihres 200-Jahr-Jubiläums*, ed. Thomas Sören Hoffmann (Hamburg: Felix Meiner, 2009), 31–52, see 33.

57. John H. Smith, *The Spirit and Its Letter: Traces of Rhetoric in Hegel's Philosophy of Bildung* (Ithaca, NY: Cornell University Press, 1988); on prefacing: 1–29.

58. Ibid., 4.

59. Ibid., 2.

60. Ibid., 3 and 4.

61. Thora Ilin Bayer, "Hegelian Rhetoric," *Philosophy and Rhetoric* 42, no. 3 (2009): 203–219.

62. Glenn Alexander Magee, *Hegel and the Hermetic Tradition* (Ithaca, NY: Cornell University Press, 2001), 91.

63. Immanuel Kant, *Gesammelte Schriften*, vol. 3, *Kritik der reinen Vernunft (2. Auflage)*, ed. Königlich Preußische Akademie der Wissenschaften (Berlin: Reimer, 1904), 19.

64. Magee, *Hegel and the Hermetic Tradition*, 137.

65. Ibid., 14.

66. Ibid., 127–128.

67. Ibid., 130–131.

68. Stephen Houlgate, *The Opening of Hegel's Logic: From Being to Infinity* (West Lafayette, IN: Purdue University Press, 2006), 160.

69. Ibid., 146.

70. Magee, *Hegel and the Hermetic Tradition*, 257.

71. Fritz Rüdiger Sammern-Frankenegg, "Zum Begriff der Aufmerksamkeit bei Goethe und Hegel," in *Goethe im Kontext: Kunst und Humanität, Naturwissenschaft und Politik von der Aufklärung bis zur Restauration. Ein Symposium*, ed. Wolfgang Wittkowski (Tübingen: Niemeyer, 1984), 341–354.

72. Friedrich Nietzsche, *Kritische Gesamtausgabe*, vol. 5.2, *Idyllen aus Messina. Die fröhliche Wissenschaft. Nachgelassene Fragmente (1881–1882)*, ed. Giorgio Colli and Mazzino Montinari (Berlin and New York: de Gruyter, 1973), 13.

73. IJsseling, *Over voorwoorden*, 60–98.

74. Friedrich Wilhelm Joseph Schelling, *Historisch-kritische Ausgabe. Reihe I: Werke*, vol. 9.1, *System des transscendenten Idealismus*, ed. Harald Korten and Paul Ziche (Stuttgart: Frommann-Holzboog, 2005), 27–28.

75. Edward W. Said, *Beginnings: Intention and Method*, 2nd ed. (New York: Columbia University Press, 1984), xx.

76. Søren Kierkegaard, *Prefaces; Writing Sampler*, ed. and trans. Todd W. Nichol (Princeton, NJ: Princeton University Press, 1997), 4.

77. Lasse Horne Kjældgaard, "The Age of Miscellaneous Announcements: Paratextualism in Kierkegaard's *Prefaces* and Contemporary Literary Culture," in *Prefaces and Writing Sampler; and Three Discourses on Imagined Occasions. International Kierkegaard Commentary IX*, ed. Robert L. Perkins (Macon, GA: Mercer University Press, 2006), 7–28.

78. Jon Stewart, *Kierkegaard's Relations to Hegel Reconsidered* (Cambridge: Cambridge University Press, 2003), 420. See also George Pattison's summary of Kierkegaard's interpretation of Hegel, which focuses on the later treatise *Concluding Unscientific Postscript to the Philosophical Fragments* (1846): "Hegelianism in Denmark," in *Hegel's Thought in Europe: Currents, Crosscurrents and Undercurrents*, ed. Lisa Herzog (Basingstoke: Palgrave Macmillan, 2013), 93–105.

79. Stewart, *Kierkegaard's Relations to Hegel*, 426.

80. Kierkegaard, *Prefaces*, 3.

81. Harvie Ferguson, "Before the Beginning: Kierkegaard's Literary Hysteria," in *Prefaces and Writing Sampler; and Three Discourses on Imagined Occasions. International Kierkegaard Commentary IX*, ed. Robert L. Perkins (Macon, GA: Mercer University Press, 2006), 41–65, see 55.

82. Søren Kierkegaard, *Journals and Papers*, vol. 2, ed. and trans. Howard V. Hong and Edna H. Hong (Bloomington: Indiana University Press, 1970), 217.

83. Kierkegaard, *Prefaces*, 68. See also 184, which explains the pun on the Danish proverb "Forord bryder ingen Trætte": "a word given in advance prevents later dispute."

84. Martin Heidegger, *Gesamtausgabe*, vol. 1.5, *Holzwege*, ed. Friedrich Wilhelm von Herrmann (Vittorio Klostermann: Frankfurt am Main, 1977), 115–208, see 205.

85. Ibid., 146.

86. Martin Heidegger, *Gesamtausgabe*, vol. 2.27, *Einleitung in die Philosophie*, ed. Otto Saame and Ina Saame-Seidel (Vittorio Klostermann: Frankfurt am Main, 1996), 4.

87. Søren Kierkegaard, *The Concept of Anxiety: A Simple Psychologically Orienting Deliberation on the Dogmatic Issue of Hereditary Sin*, ed. and trans. Reidar Thomte (Princeton, NJ: Princeton University Press, 1981), 24.

88. Martin Heidegger, *Gesamtausgabe*, vol. 3.68, *Hegel*, ed. Ingrid Schlüsser (Vittorio Klostermann: Frankfurt am Main, 1993), 74.

89. Ibid., 73.

90. Ibid., 73–74.

91. Derrida, *Dissemination*, 3.

92. Ibid., 7.

93. Ibid., 20.

94. Ibid., 17.

95. Timothy Clark, "Hegel in Suspense—Derrida/Hegel and the Question of Prefaces," *Philosophy Today* 29, no. 2 (1985): 122–134, see 124.

96. Ibid., 124.

97. Derrida, *Dissemination*, 15.

98. Ibid., 11.

99. Clark, "Hegel in Suspense," 129.

100. Derrida, *Dissemination*, 8.

101. Ibid., 11.

102. Ibid.

103. Ibid., 16.

104. Jacques Derrida, *The Truth in Painting*, trans. Geoff Bennington and Ian McLeod (Chicago: University of Chicago Press, 1987), 37–82, see 81.

105. Derrida, *Dissemination*, 8.

106. Ibid., 20.

107. Ibid., 7.

108. Ibid., 11–12.

109. Ibid., 7.

110. Michael Clifford, "Hegel and Foucault: Toward a History without Man," *Clio* 29, no. 1 (1999): 1–22.

111. Jean-Marie Schaeffer, "Note sur la préface philosophique," *Poetique* 69 (1987): 36–44.

112. Michel Foucault, *History of Madness*, ed. Jean Khalfa, trans. Jonathan Murphy and Jean Khalfa (London: Routledge, 2006), xxxviii.

113. Raili Poldsaar, "Foucault Framing Foucault: The Role of Paratexts in the English Translation of *The Order of Things*," *Neohelicon* 37, no. 1 (2010): 263–273, see 267.

114. Michel Foucault, "What Is an Author?," trans. Donald F. Bouchard and Sherry Simon, in *The Norton Anthology of Theory and Criticism*, ed. Vincent B. Leitch (New York and London: Norton, 2001), 1622–1636, see 1632.

115. Ibid., 1631.

116. Ibid.

117. Ibid., 1635.

Conclusion

1. Johann Jakob Mohr, *Gedanken über Leben und Kunst* (Frankfurt am Main: Mahlau und Waldschmidt, 1879), 6.

2. Oswald Wiener, *Die Verbesserung von Mitteleuropa, Roman* (Hamburg: Rowohlt, 1969), xi.

3. Georg Philipp Harsdörffer, *Frauenzimmer Gesprächspiele*, ed. Irmgard Böttcher (Tübingen: Niemeyer, 1968), vol. 3, 455.

4. Sir Walter Scott, *Waverley*, ed. Peter Garside (Edinburgh: Edinburgh University Press, 2007), 362–363.

5. Heinrich Zschokke, *Novellen und Dichtungen*, 2nd ed. (Aarau: Sauerländer, 1856), vol. 5, 5.

6. Søren Kierkegaard, *Early Polemical Writings*, ed. and trans. Julia Watkin (Princeton, NJ: Princeton University Press, 1990), 60.

7. Jonathan Swift, *A Tale of a Tub and Other Works*, ed. Marcus Walsh (Cambridge: Cambridge University Press, 2010), 85.

8. Ibid.

9. Ibid.

10. Joseph von Eichendorff, *Sämtliche Werke. Historisch-kritische Ausgabe*, vol. 9.3, *Geschichte der poetischen Literatur Deutschlands*, ed. Wolfram Mauser (Stuttgart: Kohlhammer, 1970), 190.

11. Heinrich Heine, *Historisch-kritische Gesamtausgabe der Werke*, vol. 1, *Buch der Lieder*, ed. Pierre Grappin (Hamburg: Hoffmann und Campe, 1975), 564.

12. Jocelyne Kolb, *The Ambiguity of Taste: Freedom and Food in European Romanticism* (Ann Arbor: University of Michigan Press, 1995), 132.

13. Terry Pinkard, "How to Move from Romanticism to Post-Romanticism: Schelling, Hegel, and Heine," *European Romantic Review* 21, no. 3 (2010): 391–407.

14. Gérard Genette, *Paratexts: Thresholds of Interpretation*, trans. by Jane E. Lewin (Cambridge: Cambridge University Press, 1997), 293.

15. "Reappearance of Prefaces," *Literature* 10 (1899): 424–445. Cited in: Eric Leuschner, "Prefacing Fictions: A History of Prefaces to British and American Novels," PhD diss., University of Missouri at Columbia, 2004, 1.

16. Annette Retsch, *Paratext und Textanfang* (Würzburg: Königshausen und Neumann, 2000), 131.

17. Hans P. Gabriel, "Prescribing Reality: The Preface as a Device of Literary Realism in Auerbach, Keller and Stifter," *Colloquia Germanica: Internationale Zeitschrift für Germanistik* 32, no. 4 (1999): 325–344.

18. Madleen Podewski, "*Der Tolpatsch* in Zeitung und Buch: Eine Fallstudie zur Funktionalität von Literatur in medialen Umfeldern," in *Berthold Auerbach. Ein Autor im Kontext des 19. Jahrhunderts*, ed. Christoph Hamann and Michael Scheffel (Trier: Wissenschaftlicher Verlag Trier, 2013), 63–79.

19. Friedrich Gerstäcker, *Pfarre und Schule. Eine Dorfgeschichte. Erster Band* (Leipzig: Georg Wigand, 1849), iii.

20. Ibid., iv.

21. Adalbert Stifter, *Bunte Steine. Ein Festgeschenk. Erster Band* (Pest: Gustav Heckenast, 1853), 1–12 and 13–16.

22. Ibid., 12.

23. Stanisław Lem, *Imaginary Magnitude*, trans. Marc E. Heine (London: Secker and Warburg, 1984), 1.

24. Friedrich Nietzsche, *Kritische Gesamtausgabe*, vol. 3.2, *Nachgelassene Schriften (1870–1873)*, ed. Giorgio Colli and Mazzino Montinari (Berlin and New York: de Gruyter, 1973), 245–286.

25. Dave Eggers, *A Heartbreaking Work of Staggering Genius* (New York: Simon Schuster, 2000), vii.

26. Giorgio Agamben, *Infancy and History: Essays on the Destruction of Experience*, trans. Liz Heron (London and New York: Verso, 1993), 3.

27. D. C. Makinson, "The Paradox of the Preface," *Analysis* 25, no. 6 (1965): 205–207.

28. Gilbert K. Chesterton, *George Bernard Shaw* (New York: John Lane, 1909), 4.

29. Ibid.

30. Johann Georg Schlosser, *Ueber Pedanterie und Pedanten, als eine Warnung für die Gelehrten des XVIII. Jahrhunderts* (Basel: Serini, 1787), 19.

31. Maria Edgeworth, *Castle Rackrent: An Hibernian Tale, Taken from Facts and from the Manners of Irish Squires before the Year 1782* (New York: W. W. Norton, 1965), vii.

32. Catherine Gallagher and Stephen Greenblatt, *Practicing New Historicism* (Chicago: University of Chicago Press, 2000), 51.

BIBLIOGRAPHY

Agamben, Giorgio. *Infancy and History: Essays on the Destruction of Experience*. Translated by Liz Heron. London and New York: Verso, 1993.

Ammon, Frieder von, and Herfried Vögel, eds. *Die Pluralisierung des Paratextes in der Frühen Neuzeit*. Berlin: LIT, 2008.

Anderson, Randall. "The Rhetoric of the Paratext in Early Printed Books." In *The Cambridge History of the Book in Britain*, edited by John Barnard, D. F. McKenzie, and I. R. Willison. Vol. 4, *1557–1695*, edited by John Barnard, D. F. McKenzie, and Maureen Bell, 636–644. Cambridge: Cambridge University Press, 2002.

Ansorge, Hans-Jürgen. *Art und Funktion der Vorrede im Roman: Von der Mitte des 18. Jahrhunderts bis zum Ende des 19. Jahrhunderts*. Würzburg: Gugel, 1969.

Anton Ulrich, Herzog von Braunschweig-Wolfenbüttel. *Die römische Octavia*. Braunschweig: Zilliger, 1712.

Archer, Jayne Elizabeth. "The 'Quintessence of Wit': Poems and Recipes in Early Modern Women's Writing." In *Reading and Writing Recipe Books, 1550–1800*, edited by Michelle Di Meo and Sara Pennell, 114–134. Manchester: Manchester University Press, 2013.

Aristotle. *The "Art" of Rhetoric*. Edited and translated by John Henry Freese. Cambridge, MA: Harvard University Press, 1926.

Ast, Friedrich. *Grundlinien der Grammatik, Hermeneutik und Kritik*. Landshut: Jos. Thomann, 1808.

Bacon, Francis. *The Works of Francis Bacon*. Vol. 4, edited by James Spedding, Robert Leslie Ellis, and Douglas Denon Heath. London: Longmann, 1858.

Balfour, Ian. "Now This: On the Necessity and Impossibility of a Title (Barnett Newman, 1967, with Hegel and Benjamin)." In *Babel. Festschrift für Werner Hamacher*, edited by Aris Fioretos, 22–29. Weil am Rhein: Urs Engeler, 2008.

Baraz, Yelena. *A Written Republic: Cicero's Philosophical Politics*. Princeton, NJ: Princeton University Press, 2012.

Bayer, Thora Ilin. "Hegelian Rhetoric." *Philosophy and Rhetoric* 42, no. 3 (2009): 203–219.

Behler, Ernst. *Irony and the Discourse of Modernity*. Seattle: University of Washington Press, 1990.

Behler, Ernst, and Jochen Hörisch, eds. *Die Aktualität der Frühromantik*. Paderborn: Schöningh, 1987.

Bell, Michael. *The Sentiment of Reality: Truth of Feeling in the European Novel*. London: G. Allen and Unwin, 1983.

Bennett, Benjamin. "Goethe's *Werther*: Double Perspective and the Game of Life." *German Quarterly* 53, no. 1 (1980): 64–81.

———. "'Vorspiel auf dem Theater': The Ironic Basis of Goethe's *Faust*." *German Quarterly* 49, no. 4 (1976): 438–455.

Berghahn, Klaus L. "Kritik." In *Goethe-Handbuch in vier Bänden*, edited by Hans-Dietrich Dahnke and Regine Otto, vol. 4, 625–629. Stuttgart: Metzler, 1988.

"Billet." In *Grosses vollständiges Universal-Lexicon aller Wissenschafften und Künste, welche bishero durch menschlichen Verstand und Witz erfunden und verbessert worden*, vol. 3, 1845–1846. Leipzig and Halle: Zedler, 1733.

Blackall, Eric A. *The Novels of the German Romantics*. Ithaca, NY: Cornell University Press, 1983.

Bohm, Arndt. "Goethe and the Romantics." In *The Literature of German Romanticism*, edited by Dennis F. Mahoney, 35–60. Rochester, NY: Camden House, 2004.

Booth, Wayne C. *The Rhetoric of Fiction*. Chicago: Chicago University Press, 1961.

Bosse, Heinrich. "Gelehrte und Gebildete—die Kinder des 1. Standes." *Das achtzehnte Jahrhundert. Zeitschrift der Deutschen Gesellschaft für die Erforschung des achtzehnten Jahrhunderts* 32, no. 1 (2008): 13–37.

Boyd, Stephen. "Cervantes's Exemplary Prologue." In *A Companion to Cervantes's "Novelas Ejemplares."* edited by Stephen Boyd, 47–68. Woodbridge, UK: Tamesis, 2005.

Bräker, Ulrich. *Sämtliche Schriften*. Vol. 4, *Lebensgeschichte und vermischte Schriften*, edited by Johann Heinrich Füßli. Bern: Haupt, 2000.

Brentano, Clemens. *Sämtliche Werke und Briefe, Historisch-kritische Ausgabe*. Vol. 16, *Prosa 1. Godwi oder das steinerne Bild der Mutter*, edited by Werner Bellmann. Stuttgart: Kohlhammer, 1978.

Brooks, Peter. *Reading for the Plot: Design and Intention in Narrative*. New York: Knopf, 1984.

Bub, Douglas F. "The True Prologue to Goethe's *Faust*." *Modern Language Notes* 84, no. 5 (1969): 791–96.

Bunia, Remigius. *Faltungen. Fiktion, Erzählen, Medien*. Berlin: Erich Smidt, 2007.

Burgard, Peter J. *Idioms of Uncertainty: Goethe and the Essay*. University Park: University of Pennsylvania Press, 1992.

Burnyeat, M. F. "Postscript on Silent Reading." *Classical Quarterly* 47, no. 1 (1997): 74–76.

Buschmeier, Matthias. *Poesie und Philologie in der Goethe-Zeit*. Tübingen: Niemeyer, 2008.

Camille, Michael. *Image on the Edge: The Margins of Medieval Art*. London: Reaktion, 1992.

Carlsson, Anni. *Die deutsche Buchkritik*. Stuttgart: Kohlhammer, 1963.

Casey, Timothy J. "Digressions for Future Instalments: Some Reflections on Jean Paul's Epic Outlook." *Modern Language Review* 85, no. 4 (1990): 866–878.

Cervantes, Miguel de. *Don Quixote*. Translated by A. J. Close. Cambridge: Cambridge University Press, 1990.

Chesterton, Gilbert K. *George Bernard Shaw*. New York: John Lane, 1909.

Choderlos de Laclos, Pierre. *Les Liaisons Dangereuses*. Translated by Douglas Parmée. Oxford: Oxford University Press, 1995.

Clark, Timothy. "Hegel in Suspense—Derrida/Hegel and the Question of Prefaces." *Philosophy Today* 29, no. 2 (1985): 122–134.

Clifford, Michael. "Hegel and Foucault: Toward a History without Man." *Clio* 29, no. 1 (1999): 1–22.

Collins, Ardis B. "The Introductions to the System." In *The Bloomsbury Companion to Hegel*, edited by Allegra de Laurentiis and Jeffrey Edwards, 55–70. London: Bloomsbury, 2013.

Conz, Carl Philipp. *Abhandlungen für die Geschichte und das Eigenthümliche der späteren Stoischen Philosophie nebst einem Versuche über Christliche, Kantische und Stoische Moral.* Tübingen: Jakob Friedrich Heerbrandt, 1794.

Cooper, Antony Ashley [Third Earl of Shaftesbury]. *Characteristics of Men, Manners, Opinions, Times*. Edited by Lawrence E. Klein. Cambridge: Cambridge University Press, 1999.

Coventry, Francis. *The History of Pompey the Little; Or, The Life and Adventures of a Lap-Dog*. Edited by Robert Adams Day. London: Oxford University Press, 1974.

Curtius, Ernst Robert. *European Literature and the Latin Middle Ages*. Translated by Williard R. Trask. London: Routledge and Kegan Paul, 1953.

Dainat, Holger. "Goethes *Natur* oder *Was ist ein Autor?*" In *Paratexte in Literatur, Film, Fernsehen*, edited by Klaus Kreimeier, Georg Stanitzek, and Natalie Binczek, 101–116. Berlin: Akademie Verlag, 2004.

Dangel-Pelloquin, Elsabeth. "Eheklage als Rührwerk des Erzählens. Jean Paul und Johanne Pauline im Vis-à-Vis." *Jahrbuch der Jean-Paul-Gesellschaft* 34 (1999): 35–55.

D'Angour, Armand. *The Greeks and the New: Novelty in Ancient Greek Imagination and Experience*. Cambridge: Cambridge University Press, 2011.

Daub, Adrian. *Uncivil Unions: The Metaphysics of Marriage in German Idealism and Romanticism*. Chicago: University of Chicago Press, 2012.

Defoe, Daniel. *Robinson Crusoe: An Authoritative Text, Contexts, Criticism*. 2nd ed. Edited by Michael Shinagel. New York and London: Norton, 1994.

Dembeck, Till. *Texte rahmen. Grenzregionen literarischer Werke im 18. Jahrhundert (Gottsched, Wieland, Moritz, Jean Paul)*. Berlin and New York: de Gruyter, 2007.

Derrida, Jacques. *Dissemination*. Translated by Barbara Johnson. Chicago: University of Chicago Press, 1981.

———. *The Truth in Painting*. Translated by Geoff Bennington and Ian McLeod. Chicago: University of Chicago Press, 1987.

Dreyer, Johann Matthias. *Schöne Spielwerke beym Wein, Punsch, Bischof und Krambambuli. Trinksprüche oder Gesundheiten und einige Epigramme*. Hamburg and Leipzig, 1763.

Duncan, Bruce. *Goethe's "Werther" and the Critics*. Rochester, NY: Camden House, 2005.

Dunn, Kevin. *Pretexts of Authority: The Rhetoric of Authorship in the Renaissance Preface*. Stanford, CA: Stanford University Press, 1994.

Ebert, Johann Arnold. *Episteln und vermischte Gedichte*. Hamburg: C. E. Bohn, 1789.

Edgeworth, Maria. *Castle Rackrent: An Hibernian Tale, Taken from Facts and from the Manners of Irish Squires before the Year 1782*. New York: W. W. Norton, 1965.

Eggers, Dave. *A Heartbreaking Work of Staggering Genius*. New York: Simon Schuster, 2000.

Egginton, William. "Cervantes, Romantic Irony and the Making of Reality." *Modern Language Notes* 117, no. 5 (2002): 1040–1068.

Ehrenzeller, Hans. *Studien zur Romanvorrede von Grimmelshausen bis Jean Paul*. Bern: Francke, 1955.

Eibl, Karl. "Consensus. Eine Denkfigur des 18. Jahrhunderts als Kompositionsprinzip Goethescher Gedichtsammlungen." In *Literarhistorische Begegnungen. Festschrift zum sechszigsten Geburtstag von Bernhard König*, edited by Andreas Kablitz and Ulrich Schulz Buschhaus, 29–41. Tübingen: Günter Narr, 1993.

Eichendorff, Joseph von. *Sämtliche Werke. Historisch-kritische Ausgabe*. Vol. 9.3, *Geschichte der poetischen Literatur Deutschlands*, edited by Wolfram Mauser. Stuttgart: Kohlhammer, 1970.

Engel, Ingrid. *Werther und die Wertheriaden: Ein Beitrag zur Wirkungsgeschichte*. St. Ingbert: Werner Röhrig, 1986.

Erlin, Matt. *Necessary Luxuries: Books, Literature, and the Culture of Consumption in Germany, 1770–1815*. Ithaca, NY: Cornell University Press, 2014.

Eschenmayer, Carl A. *Die Philosophie in ihrem Übergang zur Nichtphilosophie*. Erlangen: Waltersche Buchhandlung, 1803.

Esselborn, Hans. "Niklas Luhmanns Kommunikation mit Jean Paul in Fußnoten. Die Modernität der Beobachtungen und Gedanken des Dichters." *Wirkendes Wort* 63 (2013): 267–296.

Fennell, Stephen. *Gleich und Gleich. Die Messianik bei Jean Paul*. Würzburg: Königshausen und Neumann, 1996.

Ferguson, Harvie. "Before the Beginning: Kierkegaard's Literary Hysteria." In *Prefaces and Writing Sampler; and Three Discourses on Imagined Occasions. International Kierkegaard Commentary IX*, edited by Robert L. Perkins, 41–65. Macon, GA: Mercer University Press, 2006.

Fichte, Johann Gottlieb. *Gesamtausgabe*. Vol. 1.3, *Werke, 1794–1796*, edited by Reinhard Lauth and Hans Jacob. Stuttgart: Frommann, 1966.

———. *Gesamtausgabe*. Vol. 2.6, *Nachgelassene Schriften, 1800–1803*, edited by Reinhard Lauth and Hans Gliwitzky. Stuttgart: Frommann, 1983.

Fielding, Henry. *Amelia*. Edited by Martin C. Battestin. Oxford: Clarendon, 1983.

———. *The History of Tom Jones: A Foundling*. Edited by Martin C. Battestin and Fredson Bowers. 2 vols. Oxford: Clarendon, 1983.

Finocchiaro, Maurice A. "Dialectic and Argument in Philosophy: A Case Study of Hegel's Phenomenological Preface." *Argumentation* 2, no. 2 (1988): 175–190.

Flatt, Johann Friedrich. *Beyträge zur christlichen Dogmatik und Moral und zur Geschichte derselben*. Tübingen: Jakob Friedrich Heerbrandt, 1792.

Fleming, Paul. *The Pleasures of Abandonment: Jean Paul and the Life of Humor*. Würzburg: Königshausen und Neumann, 2006.

Foucault, Michel. *History of Madness*. Edited by Jean Khalfa. Translated by Jonathan Murphy and Jean Khalfa. London: Routledge, 2006.

———. "What Is an Author?" Translated by Donald F. Bouchard and Sherry Simon. In *The Norton Anthology of Theory and Criticism*, edited by Vincent B. Leitch, 1622–1636. New York and London: Norton, 2001.

Fries, Jacob. *System der Philosophie als evidente Wissenschaft*. Leipzig: Johann Conrad Hinrichs, 1804.

Gabriel, Hans P. "Prescribing Reality: The Preface as a Device of Literary Realism in Auerbach, Keller and Stifter." *Colloquia Germanica: Internationale Zeitschrift für Germanistik* 32, no. 4 (1999): 325–344.

Gallagher, Catherine, and Stephen Greenblatt. *Practicing New Historicism*. Chicago: University of Chicago Press, 2000.

Gaskill, Howard. "'So dacht' ich. Nächstens mehr': Translating Hölderlin's *Hyperion*." *Publications of the English Goethe Society* 77, no. 2 (2008): 90–100.

Gavrilov, A. K. "Techniques of Reading in Classical Antiquity." *Classical Quarterly* 47, no. 1 (1997): 56–73.

Gebert, Clara. *An Anthology of Elizabethan Dedications and Prefaces*. 2nd ed. New York: Russell and Russell, 1966.

Gellert, Christian Fürchtegott. *Gesammelte Schriften. Kritische, kommentierte Ausgabe*. Vol. 2, *Geistliche Oden und Lieder*, edited by Heidi John. Berlin and New York: de Gruyter, 1997.

———. *Gesammelte Schriften*. Vol. 4, *Roman und Briefsteller*, edited by Bernd Witte. Berlin and New York: de Gruyter, 1988.

———. *Lustspiele*. Leipzig: Johann Wendler, 1747.

Genette, Gérard. *Palimpsests: Literature in the Second Degree*. Translated by Channa Newman and Claude Doubinsky. Lincoln: University of Nebraska Press, 1997.

———. *Paratexts: Thresholds of Interpretation*. Translated by Jane E. Lewin. Cambridge: Cambridge University Press, 1997.

Gersch, Hubert. "Ein Sonderfall im Zeitalter der Vorreden-Poetik des Romans: Grimmelshausens vorwortloser 'Simplicissimus.'" In *Rezeption und Produktion zwischen 1570 und 1730. Festschrift für Günther Weydt zum 65. Geburtstag*, edited by Wolfdietrich Rasch, Hans Geulen, and Klaus Haberkamm, 267–284. Bern and Munich: Francke, 1972.

Gerstäcker, Friedrich. *Pfarre und Schule. Eine Dorfgeschichte. Erster Band*. Leipzig: Georg Wigand, 1849.

Gerstenberg, Heinrich Wilhelm von. *Ugolino. Eine Tragödie in fünf Aufzügen*. Hamburg and Bremen: Johann Hinrich Cramer, 1768.

Gierl, Martin. *Pietismus und Aufklärung. Theologische Polemik und die Kommunikationsreform der Wissenschaft am Ende des 17. Jahrhunderts*. Göttingen: Vandenhoeck and Ruprecht, 1997.

Goethe, Johann Wolfgang von. *Goethe's Faust*, vol. 1. Edited by Calvin Thomas. Boston, MA: D. C. Heath, 1892.

———. [WA]. *Goethes' Werke*. Edited on behalf of Sophie von Sachsen. 143 vols. Weimar: Böhlau, 1919.

———. *Goethe's Werke*. Vol. 1. *Vollständige Ausgabe letzter Hand*. Stuttgart: Cotta, 1828.

———. *Goethes' Werke*. Vol. 4.22, *Briefe, Januar 1811–April 1812*, edited on behalf of Sophie von Sachsen. Weimar: Böhlau, 1901.

———. *Goethes' Werke*. Vol. 4.42, *Briefe, Januar–Juli 1827*, edited on behalf of Sophie von Sachsen. Weimar: Böhlau, 1907.

———. *Goethe's Werke*. Vol. 20. Stuttgart and Tübingen: Cotta, 1819.

———. *Die Leiden des jungen Werther. Neue Ausgabe, von dem Dichter selbst eingeleitet*. Leipzig: Weygand, 1825.

———. "Die neue Melusine." *Taschenbuch für Damen* (1817): 1–24.

———. [FA]. *Sämtliche Werke*. General editor Friedmar Apel et al. 40 vols. Frankfurt am Main: Deutscher Klassiker Verlag, 1987–2013.

———. *Sämtliche Werke. Briefe, Tagebücher und Gespräche*. Vol. 1.1, *Gedichte, 1756–1799*, edited by Karl Eibl. Frankfurt am Main. Deutscher Klassiker Verlag, 1987.

———. *Sämtliche Werke*. Vol. 1.2, *Gedichte, 1800–1832*, edited by Karl Eibl. Frankfurt am Main: Deutscher Klassiker Verlag, 1988.

———. *Sämtliche Werke*. Vol. 1.3.1 and 1.3.2, *West-östlicher Divan*, edited by Hendrik Birus. Frankfurt am Main: Deutscher Klassiker Verlag, 1994.

———. *Sämtliche Werke*. Vol. 1.4, *Götz von Berlichingen / Clavigo / Stella / Dramen, 1765–1775*, edited by Dieter Borchmeyer. Frankfurt am Main: Deutscher Klassiker Verlag, 1985.

———. *Sämtliche Werke*. Vol. 1.5, *Iphigenie auf Tauris / Egmont / Torquato Tasso / Dramen, 1776–1790*, edited by Dieter Borchmeyer. Frankfurt am Main: Deutscher Klassiker Verlag, 1988.

———. *Sämtliche Werke*. Vol. 1.6, *Der Groß-Cophta / Der Bürgergeneral / Pandora /Dramen, 1791–1832*, edited by Dieter Borchmeyer. Frankfurt am Main: Deutscher Klassiker Verlag, 1993.

———. *Sämtliche Werke*. Vol. 1.7.1 and 1.7.2, *Faust*, edited by Albrecht Schöne. Frankfurt am Main: Deutscher Klassiker Verlag, 1994.

———. *Sämtliche Werke*. Vol. 1.8, *Werther / Wahlverwandtschaften*, edited by Waltraud Wiethölter. Frankfurt am Main: Deutscher Klassiker Verlag, 1994.

———. *Sämtliche Werke*. Vol. 1.9, *Wilhelm Meisters Lehrjahre*, edited by Wilhelm Voßkamp and Herbert Jaumann. Frankfurt am Main: Deutscher Klassiker Verlag, 1992.

———. *Sämtliche Werke*. Vol. 1.10, *Wanderjahre*, edited by Gerhard Neumann. Frankfurt am Main: Deutscher Klassiker Verlag, 1989.

———. *Sämtliche Werke*. Vol. 1.12, *Übersetzungen II/ Bearbeitungen*, edited by Hans-Georg Dewitz. Frankfurt am Main: Deutscher Klassiker Verlag, 1999.

———. *Sämtliche Werke*. Vol. 1.14, *Dichtung und Wahrheit*, edited by Klaus-Detlef Müller. Frankfurt am Main: Deutscher Klassiker Verlag, 1986.

———. *Sämtliche Werke*. Vol. 1.18, *Ästhetische Schriften I (1771–1805)*, edited by Friedmar Apel. Frankfurt am Main: Deutscher Klassiker Verlag, 1998.

———. *Sämtliche Werke*. Vol. 1.19, *Ästhetische Schriften II (1806–1815)*, edited by Friedmar Apel. Frankfurt am Main: Deutscher Klassiker Verlag, 1998.

———. *Sämtliche Werke*. Vol. 1.20, *Ästhetische Schriften III (1816–1820)*, edited by Hendrik Birus. Frankfurt am Main: Deutscher Klassiker Verlag, 1999.

———. *Sämtliche Werke*. Vol. 1.21, *Ästhetische Schriften IV (1821–1824)*, edited by Stefan Greif and Andrea Ruhlig. Frankfurt am Main: Deutscher Klassiker Verlag, 1998.

———. *Sämtliche Werke*. Vol. 1.22, *Ästhetische Schriften V (1824–1832).*, edited by Anne Bohnenkamp. Frankfurt am Main: Deutscher Klassiker Verlag, 1999.

———. *Sämtliche Werke*. Vol. 1.23.1 and 1.23.2, *Farbenlehre/ Schriften zur Farbenlehre, 1790–1807*, edited by Manfred Wenzel. Frankfurt am Main: Deutscher Klassiker Verlag, 1991.

———. *Sämtliche Werke*. Vol. 1.24, *Schriften zur Morphologie*, edited by Dorothea Kuhn. Frankfurt am Main: Deutscher Klassiker Verlag, 1987.

———. *Sämtliche Werke*. Vol. 1.25, *Schriften zur Allgemeinen Naturlehre, Physik und zur Farbenlehre nach 1810*, edited by Wolf von Engelhardt and Manfred Wenzel. Frankfurt am Main: Deutscher Klassiker Verlag: 1989.

———. *Sämtliche Werke*. Vol. 2.4, *Briefe, Tagebücher und Gespräche mit Schiller, 1794–1799*, edited by Volker C. Dörr and Norbert Oellers. Frankfurt am Main: Deutscher Klassiker Verlag, 1998.

———. *Sämtliche Werke*. Vol. 2.6, *Napoleonische Zeit. Teil 1: Von Schillers Tod bis 1811*, edited by Rose Unterberger. Frankfurt am Main: Deutscher Klassiker Verlag, 1993.

———. *Sämtliche Werke*. Vol. 2.7, *Napoleonische Zeit. Teil II: Von 1812 bis zu Christianes Tod*, edited by Rose Unterberger. Frankfurt am Main: Deutscher Klassiker Verlag, 1994.

Gosse, Edmund. "Elizabethan Dedications of Books." *Harper's Monthly Magazine* 105, no. 626 (1902): 165–172.

Gotthelf, Jeremias. *Uli, der Pächter. Ein Volksbuch*. Berlin: Julius Springer, 1849.

Gottsched, Johann Christoph. *Ausgewählte Werke*. Vol. 1, *Gedichte und Gedichtübertragungen*, edited by Joachim Birke. Berlin and New York: de Gruyter, 1968.

Gottsched, Luise. *Die Pietisterey im Fischbein-Rocke, oder die Doctormäßige Frau in einem Lust-Spiele vorgestellet*. Rostock, 1736.

Grabbe, Christian Dietrich. *Werke*. Vol. 2, *Dramen II, Gedichte, Prosa*, edited by Roy C. Cowen. Darmstadt: Wissenchaftliche Buchgesellschaft, 1977.

Grafton, Anthony. *The Footnote: A Curious History*. London: Faber and Faber, 1997.

Graham, Ilse. "Goethes eigener Werther. Eines Künstlers Wahrheit über seine Dichtung." *Jahrbuch der deutschen Schillergesellschaft* 18 (1974): 268–303.

Greene, Francis Paul. "Preface, Vorwort, Vorrede: Jean Paul and E.T.A. Hoffmann." *New German Review: A Journal of Germanic Studies* 15–16 (1999): 6–22.

Guentner, Wendelin. "The Travel Narrative as Sketch: Préfaces, Avertissements, Avant-propos." In *Beginnings in French Literature*, edited by Freeman G. Henry, 103–117. New York: Rodopi, 2002.

Gwee, Li Sui. "Night in Novalis, Schelling and Hegel." *Studies in Romanticism* 50, no. 1 (2011): 105–124.

Hagedorn, Friedrich von. *Sämmtliche Poetische Werke*. Vol. 1. Hamburg: Bohn, 1769.

Haischer, Peter-Henning. *Historizität und Klassizität. Christoph Martin Wieland und die Werkausgabe im 18. Jahrhundert*. Heidelberg: Winter, 2011.

Hamacher, Werner. *Pleroma: Reading in Hegel*. Translated by Nicholas Walker and Simon Jarvis. Stanford, CA: Stanford University Press, 1998.

Hamann, Johann Georg. *Sämtliche Werke*. Vol. 2, *Schriften über Philosophie, Philologie, Kritik, 1758–1763*, edited by Josef Nadler. Vienna: Herder, 1949.

Hambsch, Björn. *", . . . ganz andre Beredsamkeit": Transformation antiker und moderner Rhetorik bei Johann Gottfried Herder*. Tübingen: Niemeyer, 2004.

Handwerk, Gary. "Romantic Irony." In *The Cambridge History of Literary Criticism*, vol. 5, *Romanticism*, edited by Marshall Brown, 203–225. Cambridge: Cambridge University Press, 2000.

Harsdörffer, Georg Philipp. *Frauenzimmer Gesprächspiele*. Vol. 3, edited by Irmgard Böttcher. Tübingen: Niemeyer, 1968.

Hauke, Marie-Kristin. "Die Kunst des Klimperns. Buchhändlerische Werbestrategien und die Kommerzialisierung des Buchmarkts am Ende des 18. Jahrhunderts." *Das achtzehnte*

Jahrhundert. Zeitschrift der Deutschen Gesellschaft für die Erforschung des achtzehnten Jahrhunderts 32, no. 2 (2008): 226–239.

Hawley, Judith. "*Tristram Shandy*, Learned Wit, and Enlightenment Knowledge." In *The Cambridge Companion to Laurence Sterne*, edited by Thomas Keymer, 34–48. Cambridge: Cambridge University Press, 2009.

Haym, Rudolf. *Hegel und seine Zeit. Vorlesungen über Entstehung und Entwicklung, Wesen und Werth der Hegel'schen Philosophie*. Berlin: Rudolph Gaertner, 1857.

Hegel, Georg Wilhelm Friedrich. *Briefe von und an Hegel*. Vol. 1, *1785–1812*, edited by Johannes Hoffmeister. Hamburg: Felix Meiner, 1969.

———. [HGW]. *Gesammelte Werke*. General editor Walter Jaeschke. 31 vols. Hamburg: Felix Meiner, 1968–.

———. *Gesammelte Werke. Erste Abteilung*. Vol. 4, *Jenaer kritische Schriften*, edited by Hartmut Buchner and Otto Pöggeler. Hamburg: Felix Meiner, 1968.

———. *Gesammelte Werke*. Vol. 5, *Schriften und Entwürfe (1799–1808)*, edited by Manfred Baum and Kurt Rainer Meist. Hamburg: Felix Meiner, 1998.

———. *Gesammelte Werke*. Vol. 9, *Phänomenologie des Geistes*, edited by Wolfgang Bonsiepen and Reinhard Heede. Hamburg: Felix Meiner, 1980.

———. *Gesammelte Werke*. Vol. 11, *Wissenschaft der Logik. Erster Band. Die objektive Logik (1812/13)*, edited by Friedrich Hogemann and Walter Jaeschke. Hamburg: Felix Meiner, 1978.

———. *Gesammelte Werke*. Vol. 12, *Wissenschaft der Logik. Zweiter Band. Die subjektive Logik (1816)*, edited by Friedrich Hogemann and Walter Jaeschke. Hamburg: Felix Meiner, 1981.

———. *Gesammelte Werke*. Vol. 13, *Enzyklopädie der philosophischen Wissenschaften im Grundrisse (1817)*, edited by Wolfgang Bonsiepen and Klaus Grotsch. Hamburg: Felix Meiner, 2001.

———. *Gesammelte Werke*. Vol. 14.1, *Naturrecht und Staatswissenschaft im Grundrisse. Grundlinien der Philosophie des Rechts*, edited by Klaus Grotsch and Elisabeth Weisser-Lohmann. Hamburg: Felix Meiner, 2009.

———. *Gesammelte Werke*. Vol. 16, *Schriften und Entwürfe II (1826–1831)*, edited by Friedrich Hogemann and Christoph Jamme. Hamburg: Felix Meiner, 2001.

———. *Gesammelte Werke*. Vol. 19, *Enzyklopädie der philosophischen Wissenschaften im Grundrisse (1827)*, edited by Wolfgang Bonsiepen and Hans-Christian Lucas. Hamburg: Felix Meiner, 1989.

———. *Gesammelte Werke*. Vol. 20, *Enzyklopädie der philosophischen Wissenschaften im Grundrisse (1830)*, edited by Wolfgang Bonsiepen and Hans-Christian Lucas. Hamburg: Felix Meiner, 1992.

———. *Gesammelte Werke*. Vol. 21, *Wissenschaft der Logik. Erster Teil. Die objective Logik. Erster Band. Die Lehre vom Sein (1832)*, edited by Friedrich Hogemann and Walter Jaeschke, Hamburg: Felix Meiner, 1985.

———. [HW]. *Werke in zwanzig Bändern*. 2nd ed. Edited by Eva Moldenhauer and Karl Markus Michel. 21 vols.: vol. 13, *Vorlesungen über die Ästhetik I* (Ä 1); vol. 14, *Vorlesungen über die Ästhetik II* (Ä 2); vol. 15, *Vorlesungen über die Ästhetik III* (Ä 3). Frankfurt am Main: Suhrkamp, 1986.

Heidegger, Martin. *Gesamtausgabe*. Vol. 1.5, *Holzwege*, edited by Friedrich Wilhelm von Herrmann. Frankfurt am Main: Vittorio Klostermann, 1977.

———. *Gesamtausgabe*. Vol. 2.27, *Einleitung in die Philosophie*, edited by Otto Saame and Ina Saame-Seidel. Frankfurt am Main: Vittorio Klostermann, 1996.

———. *Gesamtausgabe*. Vol. 3.68, *Hegel*, edited by Ingrid Schlüsser. Frankfurt am Main: Vittorio Klostermann, 1993.

Heine, Heinrich. *Historisch-kritische Gesamtausgabe der Werke*. Vol. 1, *Buch der Lieder*, edited by Pierre Grappin. Hamburg: Hoffmann und Campe, 1975.

———. *Historisch-kritische Gesamtausgabe der Werke*. Vol. 8.1, *Die romantische Schule*, edited by Helga Weidmann. Hamburg: Hoffmann und Campe, 1979.

Heinzmann, Johann Georg. *Appell an meine Nation: Über die Pest der deutschen Literatur*. Bern: Heinzmann, 1795.

Henriksen, Mads Fedder. "A Preface to the 'Preface' of *Prefaces*." *Kierkegaardiana* 20 (1999): 7–29.

Herder, Johann Gottfried. *Werke in zehn Bänden*. Vol. 8, *Pädagogische und philosophische Schriften. Werke, 1792–1803*, edited by Hans Dietrich Irmscher. Frankfurt am Main: Deutscher Klassiker Verlag, 1998.

Hermes, Johann Timotheus. *Sophiens Reise von Memel nach Sachsen*. 6 vols. Worms: Heinrich Bender, 1776.

Hibberd, John L. "Das Vorspiel zu Schillers Wilhelm Tell und die 'hervorzubringende Einheit.'" In *Texte, Motive und Gestalten der Goethezeit*, edited by John L. Hibberd and H. B. Nisbet, 151–176. Tübingen: Niemeyer, 1989.

Hilliard, Kevin. "*Römische Elegien* XX: Metapoetic Reflection in Goethe's Classical Poetry." In *Goethe at 250: London Symposium / Goethe mit 250: Londoner Symposium*, edited by T. J. Reed, Martin Swales, and Jeremy Adler, 223–232. Munich: Iudicium, 2000.

Hippel, Theodor Gottlieb von. *Lebensläufe nach aufsteigender Linie nebst Beylagen A, B, C*. Vol. 3. Berlin: Voß, 1781.

Hoffmann, E.T.A. *Briefwechsel*. Vol. 1, *Königsberg bis Leipzig, 1794–1814*, edited by Friedrich Schnapp. Munich: Winkler, 1967.

———. *Sämtliche Werke in sechs Bänden*. Vol. 2.1, *Fantasiestücke in Callot's Manier, Werke 1814*, edited by Hartmut Steinecke. Frankfurt am Main: Deutscher Klassiker Verlag, 1993.

Hoffmann, Thomas Sören. "Hegels phänomenologische Dialektik. Darstellung, Zeitbezug und Wahrheit des erscheinenden Wissens—Thesen zur Vorrede." In *Hegel als Schlüsseldenker der modernen Welt. Beiträge zur Deutung der "Phänomenologie des Geistes" aus Anlaß ihres 200-Jahr-Jubiläums*, edited by Thomas Sören Hoffmann, 31–52. Hamburg: Felix Meiner, 2009.

Hölderlin, Friedrich. *Sämtliche Werke. Historisch-Kritische Ausgabe*. Vol. 11, *Hyperion*, edited by D. E. Sattler and Michael Knaupp. Frankfurt am Main: Roter Stern, 1982.

Horace. *Satires. Epistles. The Art of Poetry*. Edited and translated by H. Rushton Fairclough. Cambridge, MA: Harvard University Press, 1926.

Hörisch, Jochen. "Des Lesens Überfluss oder: Warum ist Selbstbewusstsein DAS Thema um 1800?" In *Literatur, Wissenschaft und Wissen seit der Epochenschwelle um 1800*, edited by Thomas Klinkert, 32–52. Berlin and New York: de Gruyter, 2008.

Houlgate, Stephen. *The Opening of Hegel's Logic: From Being to Infinity*. West Lafayette, IN: Purdue University Press, 2006.

Hunter, Dard. *Papermaking: The History and Technique of an Ancient Craft*. London: Pleiades, 1947.

Iffland, August Wilhelm. *Dramatische Werke*. Vol. 1, *Ueber meine theatralische Laufbahn*. Leipzig: Göschen, 1798.

———. *Die Jäger. Ein ländliches Sittengemälde in fünf Aufzügen*. Berlin: Decker, 1785.

———. *Werke*. Vol. 3, *Die Jäger, Bewußtseyn, Der Spieler*. Leipzig: Göschen, 1798.

———. *Werke*. Vol. 4, *Reue versöhnt, Achmet und Zenide, Figaro in Deutschland*. Leipzig: Göschen, 1798.

IJsseling, Hester. *Over voorwoorden. Hegel, Kierkegaard, Nietzsche*. Amsterdam: Boom, 1997.

Inwood, M. J. *A Hegel Dictionary*. Oxford: Blackwell, 1992.

Jahnke, Hans. "Mathematics and Culture: The Case of Novalis." *Science in Context* 4, no. 2 (1991): 279–295.

Jean Paul. *Geschichte meiner Vorrede zur zweiten Auflage des Quintus Fixlein*. Bayreuth: Johann Andreas Lübecks Erben, 1797.

———. [SW]. *Sämtliche Werke*. Edited by Eduard Berend et al. Vols. 1.1–1.17, 2.10.1, and 3.3. Weimar: Böhlau, 1927–.

———. *Sämtliche Werke. Historisch-kritische Ausgabe*. Vol. 1.1, *Satirische Jugendwerke*. Edited by Preußische Akademie der Wissenschaften and Eduard Berend. Weimar: Böhlau, 1927.

———. *Sämtliche Werke*. Vol. 1.2, *Die Unsichtbare Loge*, edited by Preußische Akademie der Wissenschaften and Eduard Berend. Weimar: Böhlau, 1927.

———. *Sämtliche Werke*. Vol. 1.3, *Hesperus 1–2*, edited by Preußische Akademie der Wissenschaften and Eduard Berend. Weimar: Böhlau, 1929.

———. *Sämtliche Werke*. Vol. 1.4, *Hesperus 3–4*, edited by Preußische Akademie der Wissenschaften and Eduard Berend. Weimar: Böhlau, 1929.

———. *Sämtliche Werke*. Vol. 1.5, *Quintus Fixlein, Biographische Belustigungen, Der Jubelsenior*, edited by Preußische Akademie der Wissenschaften and Eduard Berend. Weimar: Böhlau, 1930.

———. *Sämtliche Werke*. Vol. 1.6, *Blumen-, Frucht- und Dornenstücke (Siebenkäs)*, edited by Preußische Akademie der Wissenschaften and Eduard Berend et al. Weimar: Böhlau, 1928.

———. *Sämtliche Werke*. Vol. 1.8, *Titan 1–2*, edited by Preußische Akademie der Wissenschaften and Eduard Berend. Weimar: Böhlau, 1933.

———. *Sämtliche Werke*. Vol. 1.9, *Titan 3–4*, edited by Preußische Akademie der Wissenschaften and Eduard Berend. Weimar: Böhlau, 1933.

———. *Sämtliche Werke*. Vol. 1.11, *Vorschule der Ästhetik*, edited by Preußische Akademie der Wissenschaften and Eduard Berend. Weimar: Böhlau, 1935.

———. *Sämtliche Werke*. Vol. 1.12, *Freiheits-Büchlein, Levana, Ergänzblatt zur Levana*, edited by Preußische Akademie der Wissenschaften and Eduard Berend. Weimar: Böhlau, 1937.

———. *Sämtliche Werke*. Vol. 1.13, *Des Feldpredigers Schmelzle, Reise nach Flätz, Dr. Katzenbergers Badereise, Leben Fibels*, edited by Preußische Akademie der Wissenschaften and Eduard Berend. Weimar: Böhlau, 1935.

———. *Sämtliche Werke*. Vol. 1.14, *Politische Schriften*, edited by Preußische Akademie der Wissenschaften and Eduard Berend. Weimar: Böhlau, 1939.

———. *Sämtliche Werke*. Vol. 1. 15, *Der Komet*, edited by Preußische Akademie der Wissenschaften and Eduard Berend. Weimar: Böhlau, 1937.

———. *Sämtliche Werke*. Vol. 1.16, *Museum, Über die deutschen Doppelwörter, Kleine Bücherschau*, edited by Preußische Akademie der Wissenschaften and Eduard Berend. Weimar: Böhlau, 1938.

———. *Sämtliche Werke*. Vol. 1.17, *Herbst-Blumine*, edited by Preußische Akademie der Wissenschaften and Eduard Berend. Weimar: Böhlau, 1942.

———. *Sämtliche Werke, Zweite Abteilung: Nachlaß*. Vol. 2.10.1, *Satiren und Ironien Bände 14 bis 18 (1789—ca. 1794)*, edited by Birgit Sick. Stuttgart: Metzler, 2010.

———. *Sämtliche Werke, Dritte Abteilung: Briefe*. Vol. 3.3, *1797–1800*, edited by Eduard Berend. Berlin: Akadamie Verlag, 1959.

———. *Werke*. Vol. 2.1, *Jugendwerke*, edited by Norbert Miller. Munich: Hanser, 1974.

———. *Werke. Historisch-kritische Ausgabe*. Vol. 6.1, *Geschichte meiner Vorrede zur zweiten Auflage des Quintus Fixlein*, edited by Sabine Straub and Barbara Hunfeld. Berlin and Boston: de Gruyter, 2013.

Jesse, Horst. "König Ludwig I. von Bayern und Johann Wolfgang von Goethe." *Goethe-Jahrbuch* 116 (1999): 300–305.

Jørgensen, Sven-Aage. "Warum und zu welchem Ende schreibt man eine Vorrede?" *Text und Kontext* 3 (1976): 3–20.

Kant, Immanuel. *Gesammelte Schriften*. Vol. 3, *Kritik der reinen Vernunft (2. Auflage)*, edited by Königlich Preußische Akademie der Wissenschaften. Berlin: Reimer, 1904.

———. *Gesammelte Schriften*. Vol. 4, *Kritik der reinen Vernunft (1. Auflage), Prolegomena . . .*, edited by Königlich Preußische Akademie der Wissenschaften. Berlin: Reimer, 1911.

———. *Gesammelte Schriften*. Vol. 8, *Abhandlungen nach 1781*, edited by Königlich Preußische Akademie der Wissenschaften. Berlin: Reimer, 1923.

Kaufmann, Walter, ed. and trans. *Hegel's Preface to His System in a New Translation with Commentary*. New York: Anchor, 1966.

Keller, Werner. "Der Dichter in der 'Zueignung' und im 'Vorspiel auf dem Theater.'" In *Aufsätze zu Goethes "Faust I,"* edited by Werner Keller, 151–191. Darmstadt: Wissenschaftliche Buchgesellschaft, 1984.

Kermode, Frank. *The Sense of an Ending: Studies in the Theory of Fiction*. 2nd ed. Oxford: Oxford University Press, 2000.

Kierkegaard, Søren. *The Concept of Anxiety: A Simple Psychologically Orienting Deliberation on the Dogmatic Issue of Hereditary Sin*. Edited and translated by Reidar Thomte. Princeton, NJ: Princeton University Press, 1981.

———. *Early Polemical Writings*. Edited and translated by Julia Watkin. Princeton, NJ: Princeton University Press, 1990.

———. *Journals and Papers*. Vol. 2. Edited and translated by Howard V. Hong and Edna H. Hong. Bloomington: Indiana University Press, 1970.

———. *Prefaces; Writing Sampler*. Edited and translated by Todd W. Nichol. Princeton, NJ: Princeton University Press, 1997.

Kjældgaard, Lasse Horne. "The Age of Miscellaneous Announcements: Paratextualism in Kierkegaard's *Prefaces* and Contemporary Literary Culture." In *Prefaces and Writing Sampler; and Three Discourses on Imagined Occasions. International Kierkegaard Commentary IX*, edited by Robert L. Perkins, 7–28. Macon, GA: Mercer University Press, 2006.

Klappert, Annina. *Die Perspektive auf Link und Lücke. Sichtweisen auf Jean Pauls Texte und Hypertexte*. Bielefeld: Aisthesis, 2006.

Kleinert, Markus. "Apparent and Hidden Relations between Kierkegaard and Jean Paul." In *Kierkegaard and His German Contemporaries*, edited by Jon Stewart, vol. 3, 155–170. Aldershot: Ashgate, 2008.

Kleist, Heinrich von. *Kritische Ausgabe sämtlicher Werke*. Vol. 2.9, *Sonstige Prosa*, edited by Roland Reuß and Peter Staengle. Frankfurt am Main: Roter Stern, 2007.

Klopstock, Friedrich Gottlieb. *Werke und Briefe: Historisch-kritische Ausgabe*. Vol. 3.1.1, *Geistliche Lieder*, edited by Laura Bolognesi. Berlin and New York: de Gruyter, 2010.

Knox, Bernard M. W. "Silent Reading in Antiquity" (1968). *Greek, Roman and Byzantine Studies* 9, no. 4 (2003): 421–435.

Knox, T. M. "Hegel as Stylist." *German Life and Letters* 31, no. 1 (1977): 53–57.

Koch, Oliver. *Individualität as Fundamentalgefühl. Zur Metaphysik der Person bei Jacobi und Jean Paul*. Hamburg: Felix Meiner, 2013.

Kolb, Jocelyne. *The Ambiguity of Taste: Freedom and Food in European Romanticism*. Ann Arbor: University of Michigan Press, 1995.

Košenina, Alexander. "Bilder und Gegenbilder des Philologen zwischen Aufklärung und Romantik." *Zeitschrift für deutsche Philologie* 124, no. 2 (2005): 161–179.

———. *Der gelehrte Narr. Gelehrtensatire seit der Aufklärung*. Göttingen: Wallstein, 2003.

Kramer, Olaf. *Goethe und die Rhetorik*. Berlin and New York: de Gruyter, 2010.

Krause, Peter D. *Unbestimmte Rhetorik. Friedrich Schlegel und die Redekunst um 1800*. Tübingen: Niemeyer, 2001.

Kruckis, Hans-Martin. "Goethe-Philologie als Paradigma neu-philologischer Wissenschaft im 19. Jahrhundert." In *Wissenschaftsgeschichte der Germanistik im 19. Jahrhundert*, edited by Jürgen Fohrmann and Wilhelm Voßkamp, 451–493. Stuttgart and Weimar: Metzler, 1994.

Küpper, Peter. "Author ad Lectorem. Vorreden im 18. Jahrhundert: Ein Forschungsvorschlag." In *Festschrift für Rainer Gruenter*, edited by Bernhard Fabian, 86–95. Heidelberg: Winter, 1978.

Kuzniar, Alice A. *Delayed Endings: Nonclosure in Novalis and Hölderlin*. Athens: University of Georgia Press, 1987.

Lacoue-Labarthe, Philippe, and Jean-Luc Nancy. *The Literary Absolute: The Theory of Literature in German Romanticism*. Translated by Philip Barnard and Cheryl Lester. Albany: State University of New York Press, 1988.

Landfester, Ulrike. "'(Ist fortzusetzen.)': Goethes Poetik des Paratextes." In *Die Pluralisierung des Paratextes in der Frühen Neuzeit. Theorie, Formen, Funktionen*, edited by Frieder von Ammon and Herfried Vögel, 375–397. Münster: LIT, 2008.

Laqueur, Thomas W. *Solitary Sex: A Cultural History of Masturbation*. New York: Zone, 2003.

Lausberg, Heinrich. *Handbuch der literarischen Rhetorik. Eine Grundlegung der Literaturwissenschaft*. Munich: M. Hüber, 1960.

Lem, Stanisław. *Imaginary Magnitude*. Translated by Marc E. Heine. London: Secker and Warburg, 1984.

Lenz, Jakob Michael Reinhold. *Werke in einem Band*. 2nd ed. Edited by Helmut Richter and Rosalinde Gotha. Berlin and Weimar: Aufbau, 1975.

Leonardi, Susan J. "Recipes for Reading: Summer Pasta, Lobster à la Riseholme, and Key Lime Pie." *PMLA* 104, no. 3 (1989): 340–347.

Lessing, Gotthold Ephraim. *Werke und Briefe in zwölf Bänden*. Vol. 4, *Werke, 1758–1759*, edited by Gunter E. Grimm. Frankfurt am Main: Deutscher Klassiker Verlag, 1997.

Leuschner, Eric. "Prefacing Fictions: A History of Prefaces to British and American Novels." PhD diss., University of Missouri at Columbia, 2004.

Lichtenberg, Georg Christoph. *Schriften und Briefe*. Vol. 1, *Südelbücher*, edited by Wolfgang Promies. Munich: Hanser, 1968.

Link, Manfred. "Goethes Wertheriade: *Briefe aus der Schweiz. Erste Abteilung*." *Doitsu Bungaku* 32 (1964): 107–120.

Liscow, Christian Ludwig. *Schriften*. Vol. 1. Edited by Carl Müchler. Berlin: Himburgische Buchhandlung, 1806.

Losse, Deborah N. *Sampling the Book: Renaissance Prologues and the French "Conteurs."* Lewisburg, PA: Bucknell University Press, 1994.

Lucian. *Dialogues 6: How to Write History*. . . . Edited and translated by K. Kilburn. Cambridge, MA: Harvard University Press, 1959.

Luhmann, Niklas. *Die Kunst der Gesellschaft*. Frankfurt am Main: Suhrkamp, 1995.

Maché, Ulrich. "Author and Patron: On the Function of Dedications in Seventeenth-Century German Literature." In *Literary Culture in the Holy Roman Empire, 1555–1720*, edited by James A. Parente Jr., Richard Erich Schade, and George C. Schoolfield, 195–205. London and Chapel Hill: University of North Carolina Press, 1991.

Magee, Glenn Alexander. *Hegel and the Hermetic Tradition*. Ithaca, NY: Cornell University Press, 2001.

Maiorino, Giancarlo. *First Pages: A Poetics of Titles*. University Park: Pennsylvania State University Press, 2008.

Makinson, D. C. "The Paradox of the Preface." *Analysis* 25, no. 6 (1965): 205–207.

Markwardt, Bruno. *Geschichte der deutschen Poetik*. 5 vols. Berlin: de Gruyter, 1964.

Martus, Steffen. "Die Entstehung von Tiefsinn im 18. Jahrhundert. Zur Temporalisierung der Poesie in der Verbesserungsästhetik bei Hagedorn, Gellert und Wieland." *Deutsche Vierteljahrsschrift für Literaturwissenschaft und Geistesgeschichte* 74, no. 1 (2000): 27–43.

———. *Werkpolitik: Zur Literaturgeschichte kritischer Kommunikation vom 17. bis ins 20. Jahrhundert mit Studien zu Klopstock, Tieck, Goethe und George*. Berlin and New York: de Gruyter, 2007.

Marx, Werner. *Hegel's Phenomenology of Spirit: A Commentary on the Preface and Introduction*. 2nd ed. Chicago: Chicago University Press, 1988.

McGillen, Petra. "Wit, Bookishness, and the Epistemic Impact of Note-taking: Lichtenberg's *Sudelbücher* as Intellectual Tools." *Deutsche Vierteljahrsschrift für Literaturwissenschaft und Geistesgeschichte* 90, no. 4 (2016): 501–528.

Menke, Bettine. "Ein-Fälle aus Exzerpten. Die *inventio* des Jean Paul." In *Rhetorik als kulturelle Praxis*, edited by Renate Lachmann, Riccardo Nicolosi, and Susanne Strätling, 291–307. Munich: Fink, 2008.

Menninghaus, Winfried. *Unendliche Verdopplung. Die frühromantische Grundlegung der Kunsttheorie im Begriff absoluter Selbstreflexion*. Frankfurt am Main: Suhrkamp, 1987.

Metz, Bernhard, and Sabine Zubarik, eds. *Am Rande bemerkt. Anmerkungspraktiken in literarischen Texten*. Berlin: Kulturverlag Kadmos, 2008.

Metzke, Erwin. *Hegels Vorreden. Mit Kommentar zur Einführung in seine Philosophie.* Heidelberg: Kerle, 1949.

Meuthen, Erich. *Selbstüberredung: Rhetorik und Roman im 18. Jahrhundert.* Freiburg: Rombach, 1994.

Michelsen, Peter. "Goethe's 'Vorspiel auf dem Theater' als Vorspiel zum 'Faust.'" In *Geschichtlichkeit und Gegenwart. Festschrift für Hans Dietrich Irmscher zum 65. Geburtstag*, edited by Hans Esselborn and Werner Keller, 139–158. Cologne: Böhlau, 1994.

———. *Laurence Sterne und der deutsche Roman des achtzehnten Jahrhunderts.* 2nd ed. Göttingen: Vandenhoeck and Ruprecht, 1972.

Minter, Catherine J. *The Mind-Body Problem in German Literature, 1770–1830: Wezel, Moritz, and Jean Paul.* Oxford: Oxford University Press, 2002.

Mohr, Johann Jakob. *Gedanken über Leben und Kunst.* Frankfurt am Main: Mahlau und Waldschmidt, 1879.

Moritz, Karl Philipp. *Anton Reiser: Ein pyschologischer Roman.* Stuttgart: Reclam, 1972.

Moser, Friedrich Carl von. *Mannigfaltigkeiten.* Zurich: Orell, Gessner und Füßli, 1796.

Möser, Justus. *Harlekin oder Vertheidigung des Groteske-Komischen.* 2nd ed. Bremen: Johann Heinrich Cramer, 1777.

Nandakishore, Banerjee. "Der Prolog im Drama der deutschen Klassik: Studien zu seiner Poetik." DPhil diss., Ludwig Maximilian University of Munich, 1970.

Nehamas, Alexander. "The Postulated Author: Critical Monism as a Regulative Ideal." *Critical Inquiry* 8, no. 1 (1981): 133–149.

Nelles, Jürgen. "Werthers Herausgeber oder die Rekonstruktion der 'Geschichte des armen Werthers.'" *Berichte des Freien Deutschen Hochstifts* (1996): 1–37.

Nicholls, Angus. "Between Natural and Human Science: Scientific Method in Goethe's *Noten und Abhandlungen zum West-östlichen Divan.*" *Publications of the English Goethe Society* 80, no. 1 (2011): 1–18.

———. *Goethe's Concept of the Daemonic: After the Ancients.* Rochester, NY: Camden House, 2006.

———. "Goethe, Romanticism and the Anglo-American Critical Tradition." *Romanticism on the Net* 28 (2002). https://www.erudit.org/fr/revues/ron/2002-n28-ron560/007207ar/ (accessed March 31, 2018).

Nicolin, Friedhelm. "Zum Titelproblem der Phänomenologie des Geistes." *Hegel-Studien* 4 (1967): 113–123.

Niefanger, Dirk. "*Sfumato*: Traditionsverhalten in Paratexten zwischen 'Barock' und 'Aufklärung.'" *Zeitschrift für Literaturwissenschaft und Linguistik* 25, no. 2 (1995): 94–118.

Nietzsche, Friedrich. *Kritische Gesamtausgabe.* Vol. 3.2, *Nachgelassene Schriften (1870–1873)*, edited by Giorgio Colli and Mazzino Montinari. Berlin and New York: de Gruyter, 1973.

———. *Kritische Gesamtausgabe.* Vol. 5.2, *Idyllen aus Messina. Die fröhliche Wissenschaft. Nachgelassene Fragmente (1881–1882)*, edited by Giorgio Colli and Mazzino Montinari. Berlin and New York: de Gruyter, 1973.

North, Michael. *"Material Delight and the Joy of Living": Cultural Consumption in the Age of Enlightenment in Germany.* Translated by Pamela Selwyn. Aldershot: Ashgate, 2008.

Novalis. *Schriften: Die Werke Friedrich von Hardenbergs*. Vol. 2, *Das Philosophische Werk I*, edited by Richard Samuel. 2nd ed. Stuttgart: Kohlhammer, 1965.

———. *Schriften*. Vol. 3, *Das Philosophische Werk II*, edited by Richard Samuel. 2nd ed. Stuttgart: Kohlhammer, 1968.

———. *Schriften*. Vol. 4, *Lebensdokumente; Tagebücher, Briefwechsel, Zeitgenössische Zeugnisse*, edited by Richard Samuel. 2nd ed. Stuttgart: Kohlhammer, 1975.

Nuttall, A. D. *Openings: Narrative Beginnings from the Epic to the Novel*. Oxford: Clarendon, 1992.

Nuzzo, Angelica. "'. . . As if truth were a coin!' Lessing and Hegel's Developmental Theory of Truth." *Hegel-Studien* 44 (2009): 131–155.

Ong, Walter J. "The Writer's Audience Is Always a Fiction." *PMLA* 90, no. 1 (1975): 9–21.

Opitz, Martin. *Gesammelte Werke*. Vol. 4.1, *Die Werke von Ende 1626 bis 1630*, edited by George Schulz-Behrend. Stuttgart: Anton Hiersemann, 1968–1990.

Pattison, George. "Hegelianism in Denmark." In *Hegel's Thought in Europe: Currents, Cross-currents and Undercurrents*, edited by Lisa Herzog, 93–105. Basingstoke: Palgrave Macmillan, 2013.

Pierini, Tommaso. "Consciousness, Time, and System: On the Structure of Hegel's *Phänomenologie des Geistes* in the Light of *Tristram Shandy*." In *Shandean Humour in English and German Literature and Philosophy*, edited by Klaus Vieweg, James Vigus, and Katherine M. Wheeler, 78–91. Leeds: Legenda, 2013.

Pindar. *Olympian Odes. Pythian Odes*. Edited and translated by William H. Race. Cambridge, MA: Harvard University Press, 1997.

Pinkard, Terry. "How to Move from Romanticism to Post-Romanticism: Schelling, Hegel, and Heine." *European Romantic Review* 21, no. 3 (2010): 391–407.

Piper, Andrew. *Dreaming in Books: The Making of the Bibliographic Imagination in the Romantic Age*. Chicago: Chicago University Press, 2009.

———. "Rethinking the Print Object: Goethe and the Book of Everything." *PMLA* 121, no. 1 (2006): 124–138.

Podewski, Madleen. "*Der Tolpatsch* in Zeitung und Buch: Eine Fallstudie zur Funktionalität von Literatur in medialen Umfeldern." In *Berthold Auerbach. Ein Autor im Kontext des 19. Jahrhunderts*, edited by Christoph Hamann and Michael Scheffel, 63–79. Trier: Wissenschaftlicher Verlag Trier, 2013.

Poldsaar, Raili. "Foucault Framing Foucault: The Role of Paratexts in the English Translation of *The Order of Things*." *Neohelicon* 37, no. 1 (2010): 263–273.

Poser, Michael von. *Der abschweifende Erzähler: Rhetorische Tradition und der deutsche Roman im achtzehnten Jahrhundert*. Bad Homburg: Gehlen, 1969.

Profitlich, Ulrich. "Der seelige Leser. Untersuchungen zur Dichtungstheorie Jean Pauls." DPhil diss., University of Bonn, 1964.

Quintilian. *The Orator's Education*. Vols. 1 and 4. Edited and translated by Donald A. Russell. 5 vols. Cambridge, MA: Harvard University Press, 2002.

Rabener, Gottlieb Wilhelm. "Der Autor, neuntes Stück." *Belustigungen des Verstandes und des Witzes* (1744): 325–338.

———. "Der Autor, zehntes Stück." *Belustigungen des Verstandes und des Witzes* (1744): 446–461.

———. *Sämmtliche Schriften*. Vol. 2, *Satyren*. Leipzig: Dykische Buchhandlung, 1777.

Rajan, Tilottama. *The Dark Interpreter: The Discourse of Romanticism*. Ithaca, NY: Cornell University Press, 1980.

"Reappearance of Prefaces." *Literature* 10 (1899): 424–425.

Rehm, Walther. *Späte Studien*. Bern and Munich: Francke, 1964.

Reid, Jeffrey. *Real Words: Language and System in Hegel*. Toronto: University of Toronto Press, 2007.

Reinhard, Nadja. *Moral und Ironie bei Gottlieb Wilhelm Rabener: Paratext und Palimpsest in den "Satyrischen Schriften."* Göttingen: Wallstein, 2013.

Retsch, Annette. *Paratext und Textanfang*. Würzburg: Königshausen und Neumann, 2000.

Richards, Anna. "The Era of Sensibility and the Novel of Self-Fashioning." In *German Literature of the Eighteenth Century: The Enlightenment and Sensibility*, edited by Barbara Becker-Cantarino, 223–243. Rochester, NY: Camden House, 2005.

Riedel, Friedrich Justus. *Sämmtliche Schriften*. Vol. 1, *Zehn Satyren, nebst drey Anhängen*. Vienna: Kurzbeck, 1787.

Riefstahl, Hermann, "Dichter und Publikum in der ersten Hälfte des 18. Jahrhunderts." DPhil diss., Frankfurt am Main, 1934.

Rothmann, Kurt. *Johann Wolfgang Goethe. Die Leiden des jungen Werther. Erläuterungen und Dokumente*. Stuttgart: Reclam, 1971.

Rousseau, Jean-Jacques. *Julie; Or, The New Heloise*. Edited and translated by Philip Steward and Jean Vaché. London and Hanover, NH: University Press of New England, 1997.

Said, Edward W. *Beginnings: Intention and Method*. 2nd ed. New York: Columbia University Press, 1984.

Sallis, John. "Hegel's Concept of Presentation: Its Determination in the Preface to the *Phenomenology of Spirit*." *Hegel-Studien* 12 (1977): 129–156.

Sammern-Frankenegg, Fritz Rüdiger. "Zum Begriff der Aufmerksamkeit bei Goethe und Hegel." In *Goethe im Kontext: Kunst und Humanität, Naturwissenschaft und Politik von der Aufklärung bis zur Restauration. Ein Symposium*, edited by Wolfgang Wittkowski, 341–354. Tübingen: Niemeyer, 1984.

Sandkaulen, Birgit. "Fürwahrhalten ohne Gründe. Eine Provokation philosophischen Denkens." *Deutsche Zeitschrift für Philosophie* 57, no. 2 (2009): 259–272.

Saul, Nicholas. "Aesthetic Humanism (1790–1830)." In *The Cambridge History of German Literature*, edited by Helen Watanabe-O'Kelly, 202–271. Cambridge: Cambridge University Press, 1997.

Schaeffer, Jean-Marie. "Note sur la préface philosophique." *Poetique* 69 (1987): 36–44.

Schelling, Friedrich Wilhelm Joseph. *Ausgewählte Werke*. Vol. 4, *Schriften von 1806–1813*. Darmstadt: Wissenschaftliche Buchgesellschaft, 1968.

———. *Historisch-kritische Ausgabe. Reihe I: Werke*. Vol. 9.1, *System des transscendenten Idealismus*, edited by Harald Korten and Paul Ziche. Stuttgart: Frommann-Holzboog, 2005.

Schillemeit, Jost. "'Das Vorspiel auf dem Theater' zu Goethes 'Faust': Entstehungszusammenhänge und Folgerungen für sein Verständnis." *Euphorion: Zeitschrift für Literaturgeschichte* 80 (1986): 149–166.

Schiller, Friedrich. *Werke und Briefe in zwölf Bänden*. Vol. 2, *Dramen I: Die Räuber, Fiesko, Kabale und Liebe, Kleine Dramen*, edited by Gerhard Kluge. Frankfurt am Main: Deutscher Klassiker Verlag, 1988.

———. *Werke und Briefe*. Vol. 12, *Briefe, 1795–1805*, edited by Norbert Oellers. Frankfurt am Main: Deutscher Klassiker Verlag, 2002.

Schink, Johann Friedrich. *Empfindsame Reisen durch Italien, die Schweiz und Frankreich. Ein Nachtrag zu den Yorickschen*. Hamburg: Hoffmann, 1794.

Schlacht, Richard. "A Commentary on the Preface to Hegel's 'Phenomenology of Spirit.'" *Philosophical Studies* 23, nos. 1–2 (1972): 1–31.

Schlegel, August Wilhelm von. *August Wilhelm von Schlegel's sämmtliche Werke*. Vol. 6, *Vorlesungen über dramatische Kunst und Litteratur. 2. Theil*, edited by Eduard Böcking. Leipzig: Weidemann, 1846.

Schlegel, August Wilhelm, and Friedrich Schlegel. "Vorerinnerung." *Athenaeum* 1, no. 1 (1798): iii–iv.

Schlegel, Friedrich. *Kritische Friedrich-Schlegel-Ausgabe*. Vol. 2, *Charakteristiken und Kritiken I (1796–1802)*, edited by Hans Eichner. Paderborn: Schöningh, 1967.

———. *Kritische Ausgabe*. Vol. 5, *Dichtungen*, edited by Hans Eichner. Paderborn: Schöningh, 1975.

Schlosser, Johann Georg. *Ueber Pedanterie und Pedanten, als eine Warnung für die Gelehrten des XVIII. Jahrhunderts*. Basel: Serini, 1787.

Schmidt, Jochen. *Die Geschichte des Genie-Gedankens in der deutschen Literatur, Philosophie und Politik, 1750–1945*. Vol. 1, *Von der Aufklärung bis zum Idealismus*. 3rd ed. Heidelberg: Winter, 2004.

Schmidt, Ricarda. "From Early to Late Romanticism." In *The Cambridge Companion to German Romanticism*, edited by Nicholas Saul, 21–39. Cambridge: Cambridge University Press, 2009.

Schnabel, Johann Gottfried. *Der im Irr-Garten der Liebe herum taumelnde Cavalier*. "Warnungsstadt," 1738.

———. *Insel Felsenburg*. Edited by Volker Meid and Ingeborg Springer-Strand. Stuttgart: Reclam, 2006.

Scholz, Rüdiger. *Welt und Form des Romans bei Jean Paul*. Bern: Francke, 1973.

Schulte-Sasse, Jochen. "Mediality in Hegel: From Work to Text in the *Phenomenology of Spirit*." In *Idealism without Absolutes: Philosophy and Romantic Culture*, edited by Tilottama Rajan and Arkady Plotnitsky, 73–91. Albany: State University of New York Press, 2004.

Schulz, Georg-Michael. "Die älteren Brüder Schlegel und ihr *Buch ohne Titel*. Eine Buchgeschichtliche Kuriosität aus dem früheren 18. Jahrhundert." In *Buchkultur und Wissensvermittlung in Mittelalter und früher Neuzeit*, edited by Andreas Gardt, Mireille Schnyder, and Jürgen Wolf, 41–54. Berlin and New York: de Gruyter, 2011.

Schweitzer, Christoph E. "Who is the Editor in Goethe's *Die Leiden des jungen Werthers*?" *Goethe Yearbook* 12 (2004): 31–40.

Schwitzgebel, Bärbel. *Noch nicht genug der Vorrede: Zur Vorrede volksprachiger Sammlungen von Exempeln, Fabeln, Sprichwörtern und Schwänken des 16. Jahrhunderts*. Tübingen: Niemeyer, 1996.

Scott, Sir Walter. *Waverley*. Edited by Peter Garside. Edinburgh: Edinburgh University Press, 2007.

Seidlin, Oskar. "Is the 'Prelude in the Theatre' a Prelude to *Faust*?" *PMLA* 64, no. 3 (1949): 462–470.

Sell, Annette. "Leben in der 'Vorrede' zur 'Phänomenologie des Geistes.'" *Hegel-Jahrbuch* 7 (2001), 41–46.

Seyhan, Azade. *Romanticism and Its Discontents: The Critical Legacy of German Romanticism*. Berkeley: University of California Press, 1992.

Sherman, William H. "On the Threshold: Architecture, Paratext, and Early Print Culture." In *Agent of Change: Print Culture Studies after Elizabeth L. Eisenstein*, edited by Sabrina Alcorn Baron, Eric N. Lindquist, and Eleanor F. Shevlin, 67–81. Amherst: University of Massachusetts Press, 2007.

Simon, Anne. "Product, Packaging and Purpose: The Recycling of the Reyßbuch (1584–1659)." *Oxford German Studies* 26 (1997): 73–100.

———. "Publishers' Prefaces: The Sixteenth-Century Reader's Digest?" *German Life and Letters* 49, no. 4 (1996): 387–404.

Simon, Ralf. *Die Idee der Prosa. Zur Ästhetikgeschichte von Baumgarten bis Hegel mit einem Schwerpunkt bei Jean Paul*. Munich: Fink, 2013.

Siskin, Clifford, and William Warner. "If This Is Enlightenment, Then What Is Romanticism?" *European Romantic Review* 22, no. 3 (2011): 281–291.

———. "This Is Enlightenment: An Invitation in the Form of an Argument." In *This Is Enlightenment*, edited by Clifford Siskin and William Warner, 2–34. Chicago: Chicago University Press, 2010.

Smith, John H. *The Spirit and Its Letter: Traces of Rhetoric in Hegel's Philosophy of Bildung*. Ithaca, NY: Cornell University Press, 1988.

Speight, Allen. *Hegel, Literature and the Problem of Agency*. Cambridge: Cambridge University Press, 2001.

Staiger, Emil. *Goethe*. Vol. 1, *1749–1786*. Zurich: Atlantis, 1952.

Stang, Harald. *Einleitung—Fußnote—Kommentar. Fingierte Formen wissenschaftlicher Darstellung als Gestaltungselemente moderner Erzählkunst*. Bielefeld: Aisthesis, 1992.

Stanitzek, Georg. "Texte, Paratexte, in Medien. Einleitung." In *Paratexte in Literatur, Film, Fernsehen*, edited by Georg Stanitzek and Klaus Kreimeier, 3–20. Berlin, Akademie, 2004.

Steffens, Heinrich. *Was ich erlebte*. Vol. 3. Breslau: Josef Max und Komp, 1841.

Steppacher, Elvire. "Rederpein und Mordgelüst: Neues zur Vorrede des 'Siebenkäs.'" In *Critica Poeticae. Lesarten zur deutschen Literatur*, edited by Andreas Gößling and Stefan Nienhaus, 159–170. Würzburg: Königshausen und Neumann, 1992.

Sterne, Laurence. *The Florida Edition of the Works of Laurence Sterne*. Vols. 1–2, *The Life and Opinions of Tristram Shandy, Gentleman*, edited by Melvyn New and Joan New. Gainesville: University Presses of Florida, 1978.

———. *The Florida Edition of the Works of Laurence Sterne*. Vol. 6, *A Sentimental Journey through France and Italy and Continuation of the Bramine's Journal*. Edited by Melvyn New and W. G. Day. Gainesville: University Presses of Florida, 2002.

Stewart, Jon. "Hegel's Phenomenology as a Systematic Fragment." In *The Cambridge Companion to Hegel and Nineteenth-Century Philosophy*, edited by Frederick C. Beiser, 74–93. Cambridge: Cambridge University Press, 2008.

———. *Kierkegaard's Relations to Hegel Reconsidered*. Cambridge: Cambridge University Press, 2003.

Stifter, Adalbert. *Bunte Steine. Ein Festgeschenk. Erster Band*. Pest: Gustav Heckenast, 1853.

Stockhorst, Stefanie. *Reformpoetik. Kodifizierte Genustheorie des Barock und alternative Normenbildung in poetologischen Paratexten*. Tübingen: Niemeyer, 2008.

Straub, Sabine. "'Vorrede zur Vorrede'—Aus Jean Pauls unveröffentlichten Materialien zur Geschichte meiner Vorrede zur zweiten Auflage des Quintus Fixlein (Arbeitsbericht aus der Editorenwerkstatt)." *Jahrbuch der Jean Paul Gesellschaft* 44 (2009): 18–32.

Sulzer, Johann Georg. *Allgemeine Theorie der Schönen Künste: in einzeln, nach alphabetischer Ordnung der Kunstwörter auf einander folgenden, Artikeln abgehandelt*. Vol. 2. Leipzig: Weidmann und Reich, 1774.

Swales, Martin. *Goethe: The Sorrows of Young Werther*. Cambridge: Cambridge University Press, 1987.

Swift, Jonathan. *A Tale of a Tub and Other Works*. Edited by Marcus Walsh. Cambridge: Cambridge University Press, 2010.

Till, Dietmar. *Transformationen der Rhetorik: Untersuchungen zum Wandel der Rhetoriktheorie im 17. und 18. Jahrhundert*. Tübingen: Niemeyer, 2004.

Tötösy de Zepetnek, Steven. *The Social Dimensions of Fiction: On the Rhetoric and Function of Prefacing Novels in the Nineteenth-Century Canadas*. Braunschweig: Vieweg, 1993.

———. "Taxonomy of the Preface and Its Rhetoric in English, French, and German." *Neohelicon: Acta comparationis litterarum universarum* 37, no. 1 (2010): 75–90.

Vaget, Hans Rudolf. "Werther, the Undead." *Goethe Yearbook* 12 (2004): 17–29.

Viëtor, Karl. "Goethe's Gedicht auf Schiller's Schädel." *PMLA* 59, no. 1 (1944): 142–183.

Vieweg, Klaus. "Die Phänomenologie des Geistes als 'Lebenslauf der Sophie.'" *Hegel-Jahrbuch* 8 (2002): 208–213.

———. *Skepsis und Freiheit—Hegel über den Skeptizismus zwischen Literatur und Philosophie*. Munich: Fink, 2007.

Vincent, Deirdre. "Text as Image and Self-Image: The Contextualization of Goethe's *Dichtung und Wahrheit* (1810–1813)." *Goethe Yearbook* 10 (2001): 125–153.

———. *Werther's Goethe and the Game of Literary Creativity*. Toronto: Toronto University Press, 1992.

Virgil. *Eclogues. Georgics. Aeneid I–VI*. Edited and translated by H. Rushton Fairclough and G. P. Goold. Cambridge, MA: Harvard University Press, 1999.

"Vorrede." *Grosses vollständiges Universal-Lexicon aller Wissenschafften und Künste, welche bishero durch menschlichen Verstand und Witz erfunden und verbessert worden*, vol. 50, 1073–1077 (Leipzig and Halle: Zedler, 1746).

Wagner, Heinrich Leopold. *Voltaire am Abend vor seiner Apotheose*. Edited by Bernhard Seuffert. Heilbronn: Henninger, 1881.

Waniek, Erdmann. "*Werther* lesen und Werther als Leser." *Goethe Yearbook* 1 (1982): 51–92.

Weatherby, Leif. "A Reconsideration of the Romantic Fragment." *The Germanic Review: Literature, Culture, Theory* 92, no. 4 (2017): 407–425.

Weber, Ernst. *Die poetologische Selbstreflexion im deutschen Roman des. 18 Jahrhunderts. Zur Theorie und Praxis von "Roman," "Historie," und pragmatischen "Roman."* Stuttgart: Kohlhammer, 1974.

Wegmann, Thomas, "Der Dichter als 'Letternkrämer?' Zur Funktion von Paratexten für die Organisation von Aufmerksamkeit und Distinktion im literarischen Feld." *Das achtzehnte Jahrhundert. Zeitschrift der Deutschen Gesellschaft für die Erforschung des achtzehnten Jahrhunderts* 36 (2012): 238–249.

Weidner, Daniel. "Himmelskarten und Erdkarten. Gott und der Romanerzähler bei Fielding und Jean Paul." In *Autorschaft. Ikonen-Stile-Institutionen*, edited by Christel Meier and Martina Wagner-Egelhaaf, 231–251. Berlin: Akademie Verlag, 2011.

Wellek, René. "The Concept of Romanticism in Literary History." In *Concepts of Criticism*, edited by Stephen G. Nichols, 128–198. New Haven, CT: Yale University Press, 1963.

———. *A History of Modern Criticism*. Vol. 2, *The Romantic Age*. New Haven, CT: Yale University Press, 1955.

Werber, Niels. *Literatur als System. Zur Ausdifferenzierung literarischer Kommunikation*. Opladen: Westdeutscher Verlag, 1992.

Wieland, Christoph Martin. *Geheime Geschichte des Philosophen Peregrinus Proteus*. Vol. 1. Leipzig: Göschen, 1791.

———. *Sämmtliche Werke*. Vol. 1, *Geschichte des Agathon. Erster Theil*. Leipzig: Göschen 1794.

———. *Sämmtliche Werke*. Vol. 11, *Poetische Werke*. Leipzig: Göschen, 1839.

———. *Sämmtliche Werke*. Vol. 25, *Vermischte Schriften*. Leipzig: Göschen, 1839.

———. *Sämmtliche Werke*. Vol. 26, *Vermischte Schriften*. Leipzig: Göschen, 1839.

———. *Sämmtliche Werke*. Vol. 38, *Das Hexameron von Rosenhain*. Leipzig: Göschen, 1805.

———. *Wielands Werke. Historisch-Kritische Ausgabe*. Vol. 7.1, *Der Sieg der Natur über die Schwärmerey, oder die Abentheuer des Don Sylvio von Rosalva / Comische Erzählungen*, edited by Nikolas Immer. Berlin and New York: de Gruyter, 2009.

———. *Wielands Werke. Historisch-Kritische Ausgabe*. Vol. 9.1, *Sokrates mainonemos . . . , Der Neue Amadis . . . , Januar 1770–Mai 1772*, edited by Hans-Peter Nowitzki. Berlin and New York: de Gruyter, 2008.

———. *Wielands Werke*. Vol. 12.1, *Das Urtheil des Midas. Geschichte des Philosophen Danischmende. . . . März 1775–Mai 1776*, edited by Peter-Henning Haischer and Tina Hartmann. Berlin and New York: de Gruyter, 2010.

———. *Wielands Werke*. Vol. 13.1, *Rosamund . . . Beiträge zum "Teutschen Merkur" . . . Juni 1776–Januar 1778*, edited by Peter-Henning Haischer and Tina Hartmann. Berlin and New York: de Gruyter, 2011.

———. *Wielands Werke*. Vol. 14.1, *Pandora . . . Februar 1778–Januar 1780*, edited by Peter-Henning Haischer, Hans-Peter Nowitzki, and Tina Hartmann. Berlin and New York: de Gruyter, 2012.

Wieland, Magnus. *Vexierzüge. Jean Pauls Digressionspoetik*. Hanover: Wehrhahn, 2013.

Wiener, Oswald. *Die Verbesserung von Mitteleuropa, Roman*. Hamburg: Rowohlt, 1969.

Wiethölter, Waltraud. "Die krumme Linie: Jean Pauls humoristisches ABC." *Jahrbuch für internationale Germanistik* 18 (1986): 36–56.

Willems, Marianne. "Wider die Kompensationsthese. Zur Funktion der Genieästhetik der Sturm-und-Drang Bewegung." *Euphorion. Zeitschrift für Literaturgeschichte* 93, no. 2 (1999): 1–40.

Williams, Seán M. "C. F. Gellert als Vorredner des Genies. Autorschaft um 1750." In *Authorschaft. Reflexionen und Lektüren einer literaturwissenschaftlichen Kategorie*, edited by Matthias Schaffrick and Marcus Willand, 333–362. Berlin and New York: de Gruyter, 2014.

———."Kant's Novel Interpretation of History." *Seminar: A Journal of Germanic Studies* 49, no. 2 (2013): 171–190.

Wilson, W. Daniel. "Readers in Texts." *PMLA* 96, no. 5 (1981): 848–863.

Wimsatt, William K., Jr., and Monroe C. Beardsley. "The Intentional Fallacy." In *The Verbal Icon: Studies in the Meaning of Poetry*, edited by William K. Wimsatt Jr., 2–18. Lexington: University of Kentucky Press, 1954.

Wirth, Uwe. *Die Geburt des Autors aus dem Geist der Herausgeberfiktion. Editoriale Rahmung im Roman um 1800: Wieland, Goethe, Brentano, Jean Paul und E.T.A. Hoffmann*. Munich: Fink, 2008.

———."Paratext und Text als Übergangszone." In *Raum und Bewegung in der Literatur. Die Literaturwissenschaft und der Spatial Turn*, edited by Wolfgang Hallet and Birgit Neumann, 167–177. Bielefeld: Transcript Verlag 2009.

———. "Das Vorwort als performative, paratextuelle und parergonale Rahmung." In *Rhetorik. Figuration und Performanz*, edited by Jürgen Fohrmann, 603–628. Stuttgart: Metzler, 2004.

Wittkower, Rudolf. *Allegory and the Migration of Symbols*. London: Thames and Hudson, 1987.

Wordsworth, William, and Samuel Taylor Coleridge. *Lyrical Ballads*. Revised ed. Edited by R. L. Brett. London: Methuen, 1965.

Yovel, Yirmiyahu. *Hegel's Preface to the Phenomenology of Spirit*. Princeton, NJ: Princeton University Press, 2005.

Zellweker, Edwin. *Prolog und Epilog im deutschen Drama. Ein Beitrag zur Geschichte deutscher Dichtung*. Leipzig and Vienna: Franz Deuticke, 1906.

Zschokke, Heinrich. *Novellen und Dichtungen*. Vol. 5. 2nd ed. Aarau: Sauerländer, 1856.

INDEX

ABOUT THE AUTHOR

SEÁN M. WILLIAMS is lecturer in German and European cultural history in the School of Languages and Cultures at the University of Sheffield, UK, following an appointment as vice-chancellor's fellow. He was previously lecturer ("wissenschaftlicher Assistent") in German and comparative literature at the University of Bern, Switzerland. He has published on German literature, philosophy, and culture around 1800, in comparative contexts.